The Almanac of Scottish Politics

The Almanac of Scottish Politics

Gerry Hassan
and Peter Lynch

First published in Great Britain 2001
Politico's Publishing
8 Artillery Row
Westminster
London
SW1P 1RZ

Tel 020 7931 0090
Fax 020 7828 8111
Email publishing@politicos.co.uk
Website http://www.politicos.co.uk/publishing

First published in hardback 2001

A catalogue record of this book is available from the British Library.

ISBN 1 902301 53 6

Printed and bound in Great Britain by Creative Print and Design.

CONTENTS

In memory of Donald Dewar 1937–2000, First Minister of Scotland who died on 11 October 2000. And with thanks and love to Rosie Ilett and Christine Warkentin, Hilary and Brooklyn.

INTRODUCTION

This is the first edition of a new reference book on Scottish politics. Today, the world of Scottish politics is fast-moving and ever-changing, so we felt that there was a gap in the market for a book such as this. The establishment of a Scottish Parliament has changed the focus of Scottish politics from Westminster back to Scotland, and introduced a new, larger Scottish political class of MSPs, MPs, MEPs and councillors – a world of complex, multi-layered politics and governance, just as likely to confuse as clarify.

A recent Institute for Public Policy Research report commented that a Scottish voter now has the staggering total of eighteen representatives: a constituency MSP, seven regional list MSPs, a Westminster MP and eight Scottish MEPs elected by the list plus a local councillor. It could be argued that the voter was spoilt for choice, but how is anyone, from the public to the politicians, to make sense of this complex system? In this book, with the exception of their local councillor, the voter will be able to get detailed biographies of each of the people who claim to represent them.

The title of this book, *The Almanac of Scottish Politics*, states both the subject of this book, Scottish politics, and its intention to be a comprehensive almanac – a single resource book which contains most of the facts people would realistically want to find on Scottish politics. It is not so long ago that many political commentators disputed the extent to which a distinct Scottish politics existed. If we go back to the very different and seemingly far off world of the 1950s, British politics were seen by Robert McKenzie, in his classic *British Political Parties*, as an increasingly homogenised politics of two parties, where even the Liberals were squeezed out. In the 1970s, Peter Pulzer commented that in Britain: 'class is the basis of party politics; all else is embellishment and detail'. Today, the patterns and dynamics of British and Scottish politics are now much more complex and less open to caricature.

James Kellas talked of 'the Scottish political system' in his classic book of the same name, but other political scientists saw Scottish politics as merely a sub-set of the British political system, an extension of Westminster practices and traditions exemplified whenever George Robertson or Alex Salmond were interviewed for BBC *Reporting Scotland* or *Scotland Today* on the Green at Westminster. This has all been radically changed by the establishment of a Scottish Parliament with a new political environment and institutions, with the hope that these develop a distinct political culture, values and policy, evolving into a Scottish political system, which is not merely a sub-set of Westminster.

This book is divided into sixteen sections which attempt to give the reader the maximum amount of information on Scottish politics in one volume. The main section of the book chronicles the changing patterns of electoral behaviour in Scotland's constituencies. In each Scottish parliamentary seat we have tried to give a sense of place through a variety of local information and references. We have looked at political trends over past elections and tried to interpret what may happen in the future.

Each constituency profile is by its nature impressionistic, but we believe that together they paint a picture of the shifting sands of Scottish politics. This has two main purposes. First, it portrays the changing historic fortunes of the parties. We have included every election result in Scotland at a parliamentary level back to 1945, and at points, gone back to the inter-war period, and the elections of 1918 and 1922, where we think appropriate. Thus, the book charts the arrival of Labour in the 1920s and in particular, its breakthrough in the 1922 'Red Clydeside' election, the emergence of the SNP from the mid-1960s onwards, and its twin peaks in the 1974 elections, as well as Scotland's growing disenchantment with the Conservatives in the 1980s and 1990s.

Second, this book illustrates the political geography of Scotland. It charts the shifting geographic patterns of politics over time, and particularly the post-war period: Labour's increasing dominance in the West of Scotland and across most of the Central Belt, and the decline of the Scottish Tories, first in urban, then rural Scotland. Trends can be traced like the increasing hold of Labour in Glasgow from the mid-1950s, when Labour won eight seats to the Conservatives' seven, to the situation today, where at Westminster level, Labour hold all ten seats and all ten First Past the Post Seats in the Scottish Parliament. The story is a complex one: the decline of the Scottish Conservatives; changing voting patterns in terms of class, religion and national identity and the decline of Glasgow's middle-class population. The constituency profiles also reflect the increasingly regional nature of party competition in Scotland: the weakness of Labour in the rural parts of Grampian and large parts of the Highlands and Islands, and the largely rural support for the Liberal Democrats and SNP in the same areas.

The constituency section is merely one part, albeit the most substantial part, of a sixteen-section book and we hope readers will find useful facts, figures and commentary in other sections. These range from: details of every parliamentary by-election fought since 1945; local government, Scottish Parliament, Westminster and European election results; holders of government office at Westminster and the Scottish Executive; biographies of prominent Scottish political figures this century and an extensive chronology of post-war Scottish politics.

This project has been inspired by many trailblazers in the world of political reference books to whom we owe a debt of gratitude. First and foremost by a sizeable distance is the definitive political reference book of UK constituencies, Robert Waller and Bryon Criddle's *The Almanac of British Politics*, which provided us with inspiration for the constituency section of our book. David Butler's *British Political Facts* was the second reference point. Our book attempts to combine elements from both of these works. However, we could also not leave unmentioned the influence of Richard Parry's *Scottish Political Facts*, a book written thirteen years ago in that dark, long and seemingly never-ending period of Scottish politics, when the majority of Scots voted one way, and we got a government of a different political persuasion. All of these books were sources of inspiration and offered signposts and suggestions to us.

Many events happened during the researching, writing and production of this book, some expected, some surprising and others tragic and unforeseen. The resignation of Alex Salmond as SNP leader produced a leadership contest and opposition spokesperson reshuffle. However, the tragic death of Donald Dewar on 11 October 2000 changed the perspective of everything in this book. On the political level, it meant a hastily arranged Labour leadership contest, a substantial Scottish Executive ministerial reshuffle and the establishment of a new administration. More importantly, it meant the closing of a period of Scottish politics and the opening of a new one. And as Donald Dewar's legacy begins to shift from contemporary politics to the historical arena, it will become easier to measure this one man's unique contribution to Scottish life and politics, with all its undoubted qualities and its limitations as well.

We, the authors, feel saddened by Donald's loss, but also aware that something profound happened in Scotland's reaction to his death, that enhanced Scottish society and underlined the profound shift of the last few years. This book is dedicated to the memory of Donald Dewar, his determination to bring decency and honesty to public life, the genuineness he brought to his work and passions, shorn of artifice and spin, and acknowledges that whatever happens in future years, he helped to create and shape the terrain we set out and describe in this book.

The Almanac of Scottish Politics is an ambitious and, we hope, entertaining and illuminating guide to the world of Scottish politics at this crucial point in our political history. We welcome readers' comments on it for future editions, either in the form of corrections, additional facts and commentary, or suggestions for future sections. We hope that this book will become like Scottish politics – something organic and constantly changing, reflecting the times it reports and chronicles. We hope we have done some small justice to the strange world of Scottish politics, with all its paradoxes, contradictions and its uniqueness, and we hope you enjoy using *The Almanac of Scottish Politics* as much as we enjoyed putting it together.

Gerry Hassan
gerry.hassan@virgin.net

Peter Lynch
p.a.lynch@stir.ac.uk

ACKNOWLEDGEMENTS

The research and production of a book such as this involves the contribution and assistance of so many people that it is impossible to mention them all without doing those excluded a disservice. It also includes the assistance of people whose contributions should be acknowledged but for whom it would be politically disadvantageous to be mentioned.

Suffice to say in this abbreviated list, we would like to thank John Curtice, Stephen Low, Joe McGinley, Lynne Macmillan and Richard Parry for help and assistance, and Nicola Jeffress and Steven Birrell of the Department of Politics at the University of Stirling for helping with material and inputting data. Numerous Electoral Registration Departments across the length and breadth of Scotland gave time and resources to the most detailed enquiries, but in particular, Glasgow and Edinburgh should be thanked for explaining the details of how seats have moved over the years in their respective cities. The Labour Party, SNP, Conservative and Liberal Democrats headquarters and press departments were always available to check pieces of information for us, as were the numerous MPs, researchers and constituency offices, who provided a wealth of information. We would also like to thank Chris Eynon of System Three, Simon Braunholtz of MORI and Martin Boon of ICM for giving us access to their opinion poll data. A special mention has to go to the Scottish Parliament Information Centre, which made a lot of data available to us and who did so with humour and patience, considering the number of enquiries they deal with from the general public and politicians. To all of you and everyone who contributed, a big thanks.

We are also grateful to the support and encouragement we received from everyone at Politico's Publishing with whom it has been a pleasure to work. A particular thanks to Iain Dale, for originally commissioning this project, and to John Berry, for overseeing it to its conclusion and publication.

Finally, as is often the case with projects and research with which Gerry Hassan is involved, this book was ably assisted by Rosie Ilett, who proofed this collection and to whom this book is also dedicated with love and gratitude. Peter Lynch would also like to dedicate this book to Christine Warkentin as well as Hilary and Brooklyn.

Section One

A GUIDE TO PARLIAMENTARY CONSTITUENCIES, MPs AND MSPs

On the following pages are profiles of Scottish Parliamentary constituencies, arranged in alphabetical order. Each profile contains full details of the results of the 1999 Scottish Parliament Elections and the 1997 UK general election and the results of previous post-war elections in the same constiuency and its predecessors. Also given is an outline of the political history of the constituency, the social background and detailed profiles of its MP and MSP.

KEY:

Change for the 1999 Scottish Parliament election refers to comparison with the 1997 UK general election result.

Change for the 1997 UK general election refers to comparison with the 1992 UK genral election result or notional result if there have been boundary changes.

1974O and *1974F* in the constituency election results refer to the February and October UK general elections in 1974. The letter *B* refers to a by-election.

ABERDEEN CENTRAL

Predecessor Constituencies: created anew from Aberdeen North and Aberdeen South (1945–92) for the 1997 general election.

1999

Electorate: 52,715
Turnout: 26,495 (50.26%)

Candidate	Party	Votes	Votes%	Change%
Lewis Macdonald	Labour	10,305	38.89	-10.93
Richard Lochhead	SNP	7,609	28.72	+12.53
Eleanor Anderson	Liberal Democrat	4,403	16.62	+3.38
Tom Mason	Conservative	3,655	13.80	-5.70
Andrew Cumbers	SSP	523	1.97	—

Labour majority: 2,696 (10.17%)
Swing: 11.73% Labour to SNP

1997

Electorate: 54,257
Turnout: 35,616 (65.64%)

Candidate	Party	Votes	Votes%	Change%
Frank Doran	Labour	17,745	49.82	+6.74
Jillian Wisely	Conservative	6,944	19.50	-9.29
Brian Topping	SNP	5,767	16.19	-1.38
John Brown	Liberal Democrat	4,714	13.24	+2.69
James Farquharson	Referendum	446	1.25	—

Labour majority: 10,801 (30.32%)
Swing: 8.02% Conservative to Labour

Aberdeen is Scotland's third city after Glasgow and Edinburgh and the economic and social hub of Grampian and the North-East. Its politics have since the mid-1970s and the discovery of North Sea Oil been shaped by the resulting economic boom in jobs, house prices and growth in population. This has, of course, meant good times and bad times for the city dependent on the level of oil prices, but what is interesting is that for all the potency of the 'It's Scotland's Oil' message, the SNP has until recently never made any headway in the city.

The strength of the North East economy is such that although Aberdeen Central has the highest level of unemployment benefit claimants of the three Aberdeen seats, it is still only 5.8 per cent among men. This is a buoyant economy far removed from some constituencies in the central belt.

Whilst Aberdeen North had been a safe Labour seat for many years, South had been mostly Conservative in recent years with occasional Labour victories such as Donald Dewar's from 1966 until 1970 and Frank Doran's from 1987 until 1992. The new Central seat contained mostly Labour council wards, and this fact has been demonstrated by subsequent election results. Labour did extremely well here in 1997, with a crushing lead over all other parties. The new MP was Frank Doran, who had previously held the Aberdeen South seat at Westminster from 1987 to 1992. Doran was unexpectedly defeated by the Tories in 1992 – it was their only gain in Scotland – and re-emerged to fight the new seat, rather than contest a substantially remodelled Aberdeen South which could remain with the Conservatives. The wisdom of this decision was evident from the different results in Aberdeen Central and South at the Scottish election: Labour won Central with a reduced majority, but lost South to the Liberal Democrats. Doran therefore occupies the safest of the Aberdeen seats for Labour, especially when the narrowness of the Aberdeen North result of 1999 is taken into account.

Though support for the SNP increased at the 1999 election with a real increase in votes of 1,842 (+12.53 per cent), this seat should remain safely Labour given a turnout of UK general election proportions. In 1997 Frank Doran won with nearly 50 per cent of the vote and, though the Labour majority of 2,696 in 1999 makes this seat appear a marginal, it should not be considered one for the Westminster election and Labour should hold on convincingly.

MP Frank Doran was born in 1949. He was educated at Leith Academy, Edinburgh and is a law graduate of Dundee University, where he became active in local Labour politics alongside George Galloway and Willie McKelvey with whom he was implicated in financial impropriety involving the Dundee Labour Clubs after the 1987 election. The issue was the subject of a Channel Four programme and Tayside Police investigations. Doran was a solicitor before his election to Aberdeen South in 1987 and, after the Tories retook that seat in 1992, he became co-ordinator of the National Trade Union Political Fund Ballot Campaign until his re-election to Westminster in 1997. Doran was Parliamentary Private Secretary to Ian McCartney at the Department of Trade and Industry in 1997 to 1998 and is currently Parliamentary Private Secretary to the same Minister at the Cabinet Office. Doran is partner of Joan Ruddock, MP for Lewisham Deptford and previously Chair of CND, and he worked as her secretary from 1992 to 1997 in addition to his duties with the National Trade Union Ballot Fund.

MSP Lewis Macdonald was born in Stornoway in 1957, but grew up in the North East as a son of the manse. He was educated at Inverurie Academy and is a graduate of Aberdeen University with a MA (Hons) in History and a PhD in African Studies. He joined the Labour Party in 1980 and has been a member of the party's Scottish Executive Committee from 1997 onwards. He was employed as a researcher for MP Frank Doran from 1987 until 1992 and 1997 until 1999, was a lecturer in history at the University of Aberdeen from 1992 until 1993 and worked as a Shadow Cabinet Advisor for Tom Clarke MP from 1993 until 1997. He previously contested the Moray constituency at the 1997 Westminster election. He sat on the Audit and Education Committees of the Scottish Parliament from 1999 until October 2000 and played a very vocal role in each committee. He is also a member of Cross Party Groups on Gaelic, Crofting, Oil and Gas, Strategic Rail Services, Media and Agriculture and Horticulture. He is Convenor of the Holyrood Progress Group overseeing the construction of the new Parliament building.

ABERDEEN NORTH

Predecessor Constituencies: none.

1999

Electorate: 54,553
Turnout: 27,821 (51%)

Candidate	Party	Votes	Votes%	Change%
Elaine Thomson	Labour	10,340	37.17	-10.70
Brian Adam	SNP	9,942	35.74	+13.93
James Donaldson	Liberal Democrat	4,767	17.13	+3.02
Iain Haughie	Conservative	2,772	9.96	-5.04

Labour majority: 398 (1.43%)
Swing: 12.31% Labour to SNP

1997

Electorate: 54,302
Turnout: 38,415 (70.74%)

Candidate	Party	Votes	Votes%	Change%
Malcolm Savidge	Labour	18,389	47.87	+12.78
Brian Adam	SNP	8,379	21.81	-0.65
James Gifford	Conservative	5,763	15.00	-3.63
Mike Rumbles	Liberal Democrat	5,421	14.11	-9.71
Alisdair MacKenzie	Referendum	463	1.21	—

Labour majority: 10,010 (26.06%)
Swing: 6.72% SNP to Labour

1945–92

	Lab%	Con%	SNP%	Lib%	Other%	Turnout%
1992	47.0	17.1	24.0	11.9	—	66.5
1987	54.7	14.3	13.2	17.8	—	70.0
1983	47.0	18.1	9.3	24.7	0.9	65.0
1979	59.3	17.0	12.9	10.8	—	69.7
1974O	50.9	11.3	29.7	8.1	—	69.7
1974F	47.7	16.7	23.3	12.3	—	75.5
1970	62.0	22.0	8.4	6.4	1.2	69.9

	Lab%	Con%	SNP%	Lib%	Other%	Turnout%
1966	67.5	20.6	–	10.2	1.7	72.1
1964	68.9	31.1	–	–	–	74.8
1959	64.5	29.7	5.8	–	–	76.7
1955	67.0	33.0	–	–	–	74.6
1951	64.7	35.3	–	–	–	82.9
1950	60.5	30.0	–	6.8	2.7	82.9
1945	69.6	25.1	5.3	–	–	67.2

Aberdeen North was a rock-solid safe Labour seat before the substantial changes that came with the boundary revisions of the mid-1990s. Before then the predominance of council schemes in the seat often provided Labour with over 50 per cent of the vote and it was easily able to withstand the SNP challenges of the 1970s. Labour first won Aberdeen North in 1918 and William Wedgwood Benn, Tony Benn's father, won the seat in a 1928 by-election for Labour, holding it until 1931 and serving in the 1929–31 government as Secretary of State for India. The SNP came second in October 1974, but Labour's majority was 9,621, so the Nationalist challenge in this seat was a very distant one. In addition, the SDP-Liberal Alliance challenge of 1983 was significant, but its second place was still 9,144 votes behind Labour. This was how safe Aberdeen North was for Labour.

However, the situation changed with the boundary revisions that came into effect in 1997. At the 1997 general election, the restructured Aberdeen North seat had lost safe Labour wards to Aberdeen Central while retaining the core Labour council estates of Mastrick and Northfield and also seen the addition of around 20,000 voters from the northern suburbs which were previously in Gordon constituency: Bridge of Don and Dyce for example. Thus part of Labour's core electorate had been replaced with Conservatives and Liberal Democrats and this had substantial implications for party support in Aberdeen North. All these changes had come about because of the population boom in the North East, with changes to all of the North East seats.

The constituency also saw the retirement of Bob Hughes, who had held the seat from 1970 until the 1997 election. The new Labour candidate was Malcolm Savidge, who held the seat comfortably in 1997 in spite of the boundary changes. Indeed, Labour's vote increased in 1997 as that of its competitors declined. There was no Conservative or Liberal Democrat growth in the constituency in spite of the transfer of Gordon voters. Indeed, at the 1999 election it was the SNP which emerged as the main challenger to Labour: in direct contradiction of the assumptions about the impact of the Gordon transfer.

The Nationalists ran Labour desperately close in 1999, in what should have been a safe Labour seat. Labour held on with just 398 votes in 1999, a far cry from the

10,010 majority of 1997. The SNP benefited from fielding Brian Adam, a candidate who had fought the constituency before, in 1997, and was a well-known local councillor. In addition, the SNP clearly benefited from its successful and extensive campaigning at the North East Scotland European Parliamentary by-election in November 1998, following the death of Allan Macartney. The electoral information the SNP gained in the constituency in 1998 was extremely useful come 1999, a fact ably demonstrated in Dundee West (see below): another unlikely Labour-SNP marginal given previous electoral trends. Labour should hold the constituency at the UK general election, but remains susceptible to an SNP challenge on a reduced turnout. However, this challenge might come at a future Scottish election rather than a Westminster contest.

MP Malcolm Savidge was born in Redhill in 1946 and educated at Wallingham Grammar School, Aberdeen University and College. He was a maths teacher in Peterhead and Aberdeen from 1972 until 1997 as well as a district councillor in Aberdeen from 1980 until 1996. He was Finance Convenor, Policy Vice-Convenor and deputy leader of Aberdeen District Council from 1994 until 1996. In Parliament, he sits on the Environmental Audit Committee.

MSP Elaine Thomson was born in Inverness in 1957. She was educated at Aberdeen High School for girls and graduated from Aberdeen University with a BSc in Pure Science and worked in computing in the oil and gas industry and was employed by a small IT consultancy, Absoft Ltd, in Aberdeen from 1995 until the 1999 election. She originally joined the Labour Party in 1982 and was a co-opted member of Aberdeen Council's Women's and Equal Opportunities Committee from 1988 until 1995. In the Parliament, she is Deputy Convenor of the Finance Committee as well as a member of the Enterprise and Lifelong Learning Committee. She sits on the Cross Party Groups for Animal Welfare, Information, Knowledge and Enlightenment, Older People, Age and Aging, Strategic Rail Services, Media, and Women. She is also Convenor of the Oil and Gas group.

ABERDEEN SOUTH

Predecessor Constituencies: Aberdeen South (1945–92) and Kincardine and Deeside (1983–92).

1999

Electorate: 60,579
Turnout: 34,690 (57.26%)

Candidate	Party	Votes	Votes%	Change%
Nicol Stephen	Liberal Democrat	11,300	32.57	+4.94
Mike Elrick	Labour	9,540	27.50	-7.77
Nanette Milne	Conservative	6,993	20.16	-6.21
Irene McGugan	SNP	6,651	19.17	+9.41
Scott Sutherland	SWP	206	0.59	–

Liberal Democrat majority: 1,760 (5.07%)
Swing: 6.36% Labour to Liberal Democrat

1997

Electorate: 60,490
Turnout: 44,062 (72.84%)

Candidate	Party	Votes	Votes%	Change%
Anne Begg	Labour	15,541	35.27	+11.37
Nicol Stephen	Liberal Democrat	12,176	27.63	+0.98
Raymond Robertson	Conservative	11,621	26.37	-10.99
Jim Towers	SNP	4,299	9.76	-2.33
Richard Wharton	Referendum	425	0.96	–

Labour majority: 3,365 (7.64%)
Swing: 11.18% Conservative to Labour

1945–92

	Lab%	Con%	SNP%	Lib%	Other%	Turnout%
1992	34.8	48.5	15.1	11.6	–	69.8
1987	37.7	34.8	6.6	20.9	–	67.2
1983	29.9	38.9	5.0	26.2	–	68.7
1979	39.2	40.7	8.5	11.6	–	78.6

	Lab%	Con%	SNP%	Lib%	Other%	Turnout%
1974O	34.8	35.3	20.6	9.6	–	76.3
1974F	33.2	39.6	13.5	13.7	–	82.1
1970	45.3	45.4	5.3	6.0	–	77.2
1966	46.0	42.5	–	11.5	–	81.3
1964	43.9	51.7	4.4	–	–	81.0
1959	36.6	53.8	–	9.6	–	81.6
1955	42.3	57.7	–	–	–	80.2
1951	41.3	58.7	–	–	–	82.7
1950	35.5	53.7	–	10.8	–	84.9
1946B	45.2	54.8	–	–	–	65.6
1945	42.3	46.8	–	10.9	–	71.9

The Aberdeen South constituency has existed for decades, but was substantially altered by the 1990s boundary changes. The seat lost wards to the new Aberdeen Central constituency and gained wards from the Conservative-Liberal Democrat marginal seat of Kincardine and Deeside, which became Aberdeenshire West and Kincardine. The River Dee runs through the heart of this constituency, which includes such affluent communities as Cults and Peterculter which have a tradition of strong Liberal Democrat support.

Historically, Aberdeen South was Conservative and the party won convincingly from 1918 to 1966, when Donald Dewar held the seat for Labour for a brief interlude. Conservative tenure was restored from 1970 until 1987, though there was often a degree of marginality about the result. Interestingly, this was never a seat in which the SNP nor the Liberal-SDP Alliance or Liberals did well. The SNP's best vote was a mere 20.5 per cent in October 1974. The Alliance's best vote was third place with 26.2 per cent in 1983, though that figure was substantially improved upon in 1997 and 1999 with the boundary changes. Indeed, the Conservative-Labour marginal has now become that rare thing – a Labour-Liberal Democrat marginal.

The seat also witnessed a very strange shift in personal political fortunes in the early 1980s. The sitting Tory MP from 1970 to 1983, Iain Sproat, abandoned the constituency to fight Roxburgh and Berwickshire in the Borders. Sproat had only held the Aberdeen South seat by a whisker in 1979, he expected to lose to Labour and this was the motive behind his decision to contest the new seat which was a more likely bet for the Tories. However, not only did Sproat fail to win in the Borders, where Archy Kirkwood won with just over 50 per cent of the vote, but Sproat's Conservative successor in Aberdeen South, Gerry Malone, won the seat comfortably in 1983 with a majority of 3,581.

The seat has changed hands at each of the last four elections. It was won in 1987 by Frank Doran for Labour with a 1,198 majority over the Conservatives, but he only held it for one term, losing the seat to the Conservatives Raymond Robertson with a majority of 1,517 in 1992. This was the only seat in the whole of the UK which the Conservatives gained from Labour in the 1992 election (although interestingly they won back neighbouring Kincardine and Deeside which they had lost in a 1991 by-election to the Lib Dems). It was then rewon by Anne Begg for Labour in the 1997 landslide with a majority of 3,365 over the Liberal Democrats with the Conservatives reduced to third place, and then won by Nicol Stephen for the Lib Dems in the Scottish Parliament elections with a 1,760 majority over Labour. Due to such changes, its future partisan status is uncertain, though a tough contest between Labour and Liberal Democrats should be expected, unless there are signs of a significant Conservative recovery. The Tories hope to prosper from the performance of the Labour-Liberal Democrat coalition in the Scottish Executive, and the fact that these two parties must fight tooth and nail at the Westminster election when they are in government together in Edinburgh.

The SNP has also increased its support in the seat at the last two elections, and its ability to chip away Labour voters may have an important impact on the result. Given a good performance of 1999 proportions, the SNP could push the Tories into fourth place and also take enough votes from Labour to hand victory to the Liberal Democrats. However, the sitting MP, Anne Begg, has a good profile in the constituency and should retain the seat for Labour, especially as her former challenger, Nicol Stephen, is now an MSP. The former Conservative MP for the seat, Raymond Robertson, has abandoned the seat and was selected to fight the Eastwood constituency at the next UK general election: clear recognition of the fact that the Conservatives are no longer in contention in the seat.

MP Anne Begg was born in Forfar in 1955. She was educated at Brechin High School, Aberdeen University and Aberdeen College and was an English teacher before her election, teaching in Kirriemuir and Arbroath to the south of Aberdeen. She has used a wheelchair for many years and has had a high profile as one of Westminster's few disabled MPs. She was elected for the first time in 1997 and has been a member of the Scottish Affairs Committee in the Commons from 1997 onwards, in addition to serving on Labour's National Executive Committee from 1998 until 1999.

MSP Nicol Stephen was born in Aberdeen in 1963. He was educated at Robert Gordon's College, Aberdeen, studied law at Aberdeen and Edinburgh Universities and was a practising solicitor for C. and P. H. Chalmers, Milne and MacKinnon and then Touche Ross before his initial election in 1991 and was Director of Glassbox Ltd from 1992 until the 1999 Scottish election. He was a regional councillor in Grampian from 1986 until 1992 and a founder and director of Grampian Enterprise. He was Liberal Democrat MP for Kincardine and Deeside from 1991 to 1992, a seat he also contested at the 1987 and 1992 elections, making it a marginal constituency. His current seat, Aberdeen South, includes part of the old Kincardine and Deeside seat, which ran into the southern suburbs of Aberdeen itself. He stood in Aberdeen South in 1997, coming second, before winning in 1999. His victory in 1999 was aided by the fact that he had previously represented parts of the constituency and was also the candidate here in 1997 and came a good second to Labour. He was Deputy Minister for Enterprise and Lifelong Learning in the Scottish Executive from 1999 until the October 2000 reshuffle when he became Deputy Minister for Education, Europe and External Affairs.

ABERDEENSHIRE WEST AND KINCARDINE

Predecessor Constituencies: Angus North and Mearns (1950–70) and Kincardine and Deeside (1983–92).

1999

Electorate: 60,702
Turnout: 35,736 (58.87%)

Candidate	Party	Votes	Votes%	Change%
Mike Rumbles	Liberal Democrat	12,838	35.92	−5.16
Ben Wallace	Conservative	10,549	29.52	−5.40
Maureen Watt	SNP	7,699	21.54	+8.48
Gordon Guthrie	Labour	4,650	13.01	+3.93

Liberal Democrat majority: 2,289 (6.4%)
Swing: 0.12% Conservative to Liberal Democrat

1997

Electorate: 59,123
Turnout: 43,189 (73.05%)

Candidate	Party	Votes	Votes%	Change%
Robert Smith	Liberal Democrat	17,742	41.08	+6.41
George Kynoch	Conservative	15,080	34.92	−10.23
Joy Mowatt	SNP	5,639	13.06	+0.59
Qaisra Khan	Labour	3,923	9.08	+2.27
Steve Ball	Referendum	805	1.86	−

Liberal Democrat majority: 2,662 (6.16%)
Swing: 8.32% Conservative to Liberal Democrat

Kincardine and Deeside 1983–1992

	Lab%	Con%	SNP%	Lib%	Other%	Turnout%
1992	9.1	43.7	11.3	35.1	0.7	78.7
1991B	7.7	30.6	11.1	49.0	1.6	67.0
1987	15.9	40.6	6.4	36.3	0.6	75.3
1983	15.2	47.7	7.7	29.4	−	71.5

Aberdeen and Kincardineshire, Kincardine and Western (1945); Angus North and Mearns (1950–70)

	Lab%	Con%	SNP%	Lib%	Other%	Turnout%
1979	19.3	57.5	23.2	–	–	73.8
1974O	12.3	43.6	34.2	9.9	–	72.3
1974F	12.8	48.8	23.3	15.1	–	78.6
1970	18.4	53.1	16.9	11.6	–	74.7
1966	20.2	50.4	–	29.4	–	76.2
1964	16.6	49.3	–	34.1	–	77.0
1959	32.6	67.4	–	–	–	71.3
1955	31.0	69.0	–	–	–	72.3
1951	35.9	64.1	–	–	–	76.3
1950	27.7	51.5	–	20.8	–	81.4
1945	–	51.5	–	48.5	–	68.7

Montrose District of Burghs (1945)

	Lab%	Con%	SNP%	Lib%	Other%	Turnout%
1945	41.8	58.2	–	–	–	72.3

Aberdeenshire West and Kincardine contains the towns of Portlethen and Stonehaven, which are effectively commuter towns for Aberdeen, as well as the Royal Deeside rural towns of Aboyne, Ballater, Banchory and Braemar. This seat contains the Royal Family's Scottish residency, Balmoral, as well as the Mearns, an area of fishing and farming communities immortalised in Lewis Grassic Gibbon's legendary trilogy 'A Scots Quair'. The seat has as well as royal connections, a long tradition of association with the military: the Lib Dem MSP Mike Rumbles is an ex-army officer, as was Ben Wallace, his Conservative opponent in 1999, while the seat has been in the past represented by as colourful and controversial figures as Colonel 'Mad Mitch' Miller, Conservative MP for the area from 1970 until February 1974, and better known as the 'hero of Aden'. Economically, this is a wealthy constituency, with a male unemployment rate of only 2.3 per cent in June 2000: the lowest in Scotland. It is also the healthiest constituency in Scotland with 15 per cent of the population living in poverty. Politically, this constituency had a long Liberal tradition which was submerged when the National Liberal and Unionists (Conservatives) contested the seat in the absence of the Liberal themselves. The seat saw a long series of Liberal-Conservative two-way contests from 1923 to 1945, before Labour began contesting the seat from 1950 onwards and the Liberals faded away.

When the Liberals began contesting the seat again in the 1960s the depth of their support showed: going from zero in 1959 to 34.1 per cent in 1964. Though the party slipped back in the seat after 1964, coinciding with the temporary rise of the SNP in the constituency, the Liberal-SDP Alliance re-emerged in 1983 and was a serious challenger to the Tories – indeed the sole challenger – from then until the present day. Indeed, neither Labour nor the SNP have performed well in this constituency, though the SNP did well in October 1974, when the party came second just 2,551 votes behind the Tories, with the Liberals in last place on 2,700 votes (with Malcolm Bruce as candidate). The SNP surge was temporary and from then on the Liberals were able to rebuild support. Labour has also struggled in the constituency, both historically and recently. The party's best result in the post-war period was in 1951, and Labour has usually been in third or last place in this seat recently.

The seat was held by the centrist and popular Conservative, Alick Buchanan-Smith, from 1964. The Lib Dems had cut Alick Buchanan Smith's majority in 1987 to 2,063 and Nicol Stephen won the subsequent by-election in November 1991 with a majority of 7,824 over the Conservatives. This Lib Dem victory reduced the Conservatives to third party status in Scottish seats and ignited the constitutional question in the run-up to the 1992 election. This was to prove another false dawn for home rulers, as the Tories were re-elected at a UK level in 1992 and George Kynoch won back the seat with a 4,495 majority over the Lib Dems. The Liberal Democrats then won the seat back again in 1997 with Sir Robert Smith, with a relatively narrow majority of 2,662, and then retained it at the Scottish election with Mike Rumbles in 1999 with a majority of 2,289, in both cases over the Conservatives. However, this seat remains a marginal between the Tories and the Liberal Democrats, and is prone to a Tory revival.

The Tory vote has fallen in this seat, but not melted away as it has done in some former seats in Scotland. The Conservatives have some council seats in the constituency and are close behind the Liberal Democrats in some wards. The seat was a key target for the Tories in 1999, with a prominent candidate, Ben Wallace. The latter is now a list MSP for Scotland North East but wants to serve at Westminster and has sought the nomination for a number of Westminster constituencies without success. But the narrowness of the result in both 1997 and 1999 must give the Conservatives hope. They have selected West Lothian councillor Tom Kerr to fight the seat at the UK general election. The other parties are not serious competitors in the seat, though the rise of the SNP at the 1999 election may have implications for the actual result. Given the affluence of Aberdeenshire West and Kincardine and the fact that the Conservatives have retained a significant local base, this seat must be a potential target for them in future UK and Scottish elections.

MP Sir Robert Smith was born in 1958 and is the third baronet. He was educated at Merchant Taylors' School in London and Aberdeen University. The first baronet, his grandfather, was Sir William Smith, MP for Central Aberdeenshire and

Kincardine from 1924 to 1945, while he is also distantly related to Alick Buchanan-Smith, Tory MP for Kincardine and Deeside from 1964 to 1991.

He was an estate manager and landowner in Inverurie before his election. He stood for the Liberal-SDP Alliance in Aberdeen North in 1987 and was Liberal Democrat education spokesperson in Scotland from 1995 until 1997. He sat on Aberdeenshire Council from 1995 until 1997 and was Vice-Chair of Grampian Police Board. He is part of the Liberal Democrat Transport team at Westminster and sits on the Scottish Affairs and Catering Committees in the Commons.

MSP Mike Rumbles was born in South Shields in 1956. He was educated at St James' School, Hebburn, Durham University and the University of Wales and was an officer with the army for 15 years before becoming a team leader in Business Management at Aberdeen College from 1995 until 1999. He was Liberal Democrat spokesperson for Rural Affairs and Political Standards until November 2000, before becoming Spokesperson for Rural Development. He is Convenor of the Parliament's Standards Committee, which gave him a high profile at the time of the 'Lobbygate' affair in 1999. He is also a member of the Parliament's Rural Development Committee.

AIRDRIE AND SHOTTS

Predecessor Constituencies: Coatbridge (1945), Coatbridge and Airdrie (1950–82) and Monklands East (1983–92).

1999

Electorate: 58,481
Turnout: 31,213 (56.79%)

Candidate	Party	Votes	Votes%	Change%
Karen Whitefield	Labour	18,338	55.21	-6.61
Gil Paterson	SNP	9,353	28.16	+3.76
Patrick Ross-Taylor	Conservative	3,177	9.57	+0.68
David Miller	Liberal Democrat	2,345	7.06	+2.89

Labour majority: 8,985 (29.05%)
Swing: 5.19% Labour to SNP

1997

Electorate: 57,673
Turnout: 41,181 (71.4%)

Candidate	Party	Votes	Votes%	Change%
Helen Liddell	Labour	25,460	61.82	-0.68
Keith Robertson	SNP	10,048	24.40	+6.28
Nicholas Brook	Conservative	3,660	8.89	-5.99
Richard Wolseley	Liberal Democrat	1,719	4.17	-0.34
Crawford Semple	Referendum	294	0.71	—

Labour majority: 15,412 (37.42%)
Swing: 3.48% Labour to SNP

1945–92

	Lab%	Con%	SNP%	Lib%	Other%	Turnout%
1994B	49.8	2.3	44.9	2.6	0.4	70.0
1992	61.3	16.0	18.0	4.6	—	75.0
1987	61.0	16.9	12.9	9.3	—	74.8
1983	51.2	23.9	8.9	16.0	—	73.0
1982B	55.1	26.2	10.5	8.2	—	56.3
1979	60.9	27.5	11.6	—	—	75.3

	Lab%	Con%	SNP%	Lib%	Other%	Turnout%
1974O	51.6	17.2	27.9	3.3	–	77.8
1974F	54.1	28.6	17.3	–	–	77.8
1970	58.9	35.1	6.0	–	–	76.5
1966	64.2	35.8	–	–	–	77.2
1964	62.1	37.9	–	–	–	81.2
1959	50.9	49.1	–	–	–	84.0
1955	55.8	44.2	–	–	–	79.4
1951	57.4	42.6	–	–	–	85.5
1950	56.6	40.2	–	–	3.2	86.1
1945	61.1	38.9	–	–	–	76.0

Airdrie and Shotts was previously the Monklands East constituency held by Labour leader John Smith until his death in 1994. The political manoeuvring and allegations of corruption in the local authority, Monklands District Council, gave the constituency and Labour a level of notoriety across the UK at the time of the by-election. The Monklands name vanished with local government reorganisation in 1995 and the boundary changes which provided the constituency with a new name. The seat contains the town of Airdrie, the main population centre, as well as the smaller towns and villages of Bonkle, Cleland, Dykehead, Greengairs, Harthill, Newmains, Salsburgh and Shotts (joint home of the reigning world pipeband champions!).

The constituency is very strongly working class. Its rate of unemployment is 8.0 per cent amongst men. At the 1991 census, this constituency had the joint highest level of council housing in Scotland at 62.5 per cent (along with Motherwell and Wishaw), though the intervening years of council house sales may have altered this fact. Labour held this seat from 1922 until 1999, with one solitary Tory victory in the exceptional circumstances of 1931 and a near miss for the Tories in 1959. The SNP's best result here – by-elections aside – was in October 1974, but the party was still 8,341 votes behind Labour, with Labour winning over half of the vote. The seat has also shown considerable antipathy towards the Liberals. There is next to no Liberal Democrat support in the constituency currently or historically. Indeed, the party's best result was in the electoral high point of the Liberal–SDP Alliance in 1983. Even then, the Alliance still came third behind Labour and the Conservatives.

Politically, the seat is safely Labour and will remain so at the next general election. However, there have been SNP incursions in recent years. The SNP is currently a distant second in the constituency, despite nearly overcoming Labour in the by-election in 1994 when Labour retained the seat with a majority of just 1,640. The SNP candidate Kay Ullrich fought an intense campaign against Labour, which was badly damaged by allegations of corruption involving Monklands District

Council. The council's Labour leadership, known as the 'Coatbrig Mafia', was accused of favouring relatives of councillors in job applications as well as providing more finance and services for the Coatbridge part of the constituency (large Catholic population) as against the Airdrie part (large Protestant population). Labour rejected any need for an independent inquiry into the corruption issue, until Helen Liddell was forced to support one during the by-election campaign: a considerable U-turn. She did so even though the neighbouring MP, Labour's Tom Clarke, opposed any inquiry. However, despite the scandal and Labour's mishandling of the issue, it clung on to the seat in 1994.

That result was as close as the SNP got. At the following general election the Nationalists slipped back; though the party has managed to build upon its by-election performance to increase its percentage of the vote between the 1997 general and 1999 Scottish elections, it is nowhere near to challenging Labour in the constituency. Indeed, despite a percentage increase in votes for the SNP between 1997 and 1999, the party actually had 695 fewer votes at the Scottish election compared to Westminster. The SNP's lack of organisation in the constituency and weakness at local elections will help to ensure Labour retains this seat comfortably for the fore-seeable future.

MP Helen Liddell was born in Coatbridge in 1950 and educated at St Patrick's High School, Coatbridge and Strathclyde University. She was a researcher with the STUC from 1971 until 1976, worked briefly as economics correspondent for BBC Scotland from 1976 until 1977 and served as Scottish Labour General Secretary from 1977 until 1988. As General Secretary, she was responsible for the infamous 1978 Liddell memorandum which discouraged Labour co-operation with other parties in the 1979 devolution referendum. It stated 'the Labour Party is the only party which believes in devolution for its own sake.' And she went on at a press conference: 'We will not be soiling our hands by joining any umbrella Yes group.' She then worked for Bob Maxwell as Director of Personnel and Public Affairs at Mirror Group in Glasgow from 1988 until 1992 and then subsequently as Chief Executive of a business venture programme. At this time she also published a novel *Elite*, which she perhaps wishes to forget. The novel was a rip-roaring read about Ann Clarke, who wanted 'power – in politics and in bed'. Clarke, Deputy Prime Minister, was (according to the publisher's blurb) 'a ruthless, politically ambitious, beautiful and brilliant woman . . . a modern Joan of Arc wrapped in the tartan flag of the Scottish Labour Party'. Obviously this was a purely fictional character.

Liddell was elected in 1994 having previously only stood once as a candidate in East Fife in October 1974, and has had a variety of junior Ministerial posts in the government from the 1997 election until the run-in to the 2001 election. She was Economic Secretary to the Treasury from 1997 until 1998, Minister of State at the Scottish Office from 1998 until 1999, Minister for Transport briefly in 1999 and then moved to the post of Minister for Energy and Competitiveness at the Department of

Trade and Industry, which she held from 1999 to 2001. A confirmed Nat-basher in her time as General Secretary and as Scottish Office Minister, she was passed over for the post of Scottish Secretary after the devolved elections of 1999 – much to the disappointment of the SNP and relief of many within Labour. However, Liddell finally became Secretary of State for Scotland in January 2001 in the unexpected circumstances after Peter Mandleson's resignation and John Reid's move to Northern Ireland. She is the first woman to occupy the post and may well become one of its shortest incumbents, when if the Northern Ireland peace process continues, the three territorial ministeries may well be amalgamated at some point after the UK election.

MSP Karen Whitefield was born in Bellshill in 1970. She was educated locally at Dykehead Primary and Calderhead High School, Shotts and graduated from Glasgow Caledonian University with a degree in Public Administration, then worked briefly as a civil servant with the Benefits Agency. From 1992 to 1999, she was personal assistant to Rachel Squire, the Dunfermline West MP. She held a number of offices in her local Labour Party and became a CLP representative on the National Policy Forum in 1998. She was a member of the Social Inclusion Committee and Audit Committee in the Scottish Parliament from May 1999 to December 2000 and now sits on the Social Justice and Justice II Committees. Whitefield also sits on the Cross Party Groups for Animal Welfare, Drug Misuse, Palliative Care and Strategic Rail Services. In the June 1999 debate on MSPs' allowances, Whitefield was criticised for the quality of her contribution which led to the 'shoal of Karens' debate in the media about the quality of Labour women representation; many observers felt male chauvinism was not far removed from this debate, especially given the calibre of some of the male MPs at Westminster.

ANGUS

Predecessor Constituencies: Forfarshire (1945), Angus South (1950–79) and Angus East (1983–92).

1999

Electorate: 59,891
Turnout: 34,536 (57.66%)

Candidate	Party	Votes	Votes%	Change%
Andrew Welsh	SNP	16,055	46.49	-1.78
Ron Harris	Conservative	7,154	20.71	-3.90
Ian McFatridge	Labour	6,914	20.02	+4.39
Dick Speirs	Liberal Democrat	4,413	12.78	-7.66

SNP majority: 8,901 (25.78%)
Swing: 1.06% Conservative to SNP

1997

Electorate: 59,708
Turnout: 43,076 (72.14%)

Candidate	Party	Votes	Votes%	Change%
Andrew Welsh	SNP	20,792	48.27	+9.11
Sebastian Leslie	Conservative	10,603	24.61	-13.48
Catherine Taylor	Labour	6,733	15.63	+2.69
Dick Speirs	Liberal Democrat	4,065	9.44	+0.65
Brian Taylor	Referendum	883	2.05	–

SNP majority: 10,189 (23.66%)
Swing: 11.30% Conservative to SNP

1945–1992

	Lab%	Con%	SNP%	Lib%	Other%	Turnout%
1992	12.6	38.1	40.1	8.2	0.9	75.0
1987	10.8	39.0	42.4	7.8	–	75.5
1983	8.0	44.1	36.0	11.4	0.5	73.5
1979	10.1	43.6	41.5	4.8	–	79.9
1974O	10.5	39.2	43.8	6.5	–	74.5
1974F	13.8	49.5	36.7	–	–	79.8

	Lab%	Con%	SNP%	Lib%	Other%	Turnout%
1970	20.8	56.1	23.1	–	–	73.9
1966	29.6	70.4	–	–	–	71.2
1964	22.6	58.2	–	19.2	–	75.6
1959	19.0	57.1	–	23.9	–	75.9
1955	27.3	72.7	–	–	–	73.6
1951	29.1	70.9	–	–	–	76.6
1950	25.6	53.9	–	20.5	–	82.0
1945	31.1	51.6	–	17.3	–	68.9

Geographically, the seat takes in the coastal towns of Arbroath and Montrose, which are the main population centres, and also includes Carnoustie and Monifieth, which are effectively suburbs of Dundee. From 1924 until 1974, this constituency was safely Conservative, with the party usually winning well over 50% of the vote. It mostly competed with Labour as the Liberals seldom contested this seat, though neither party has been able to mount any challenge since the emergence of the SNP. Curiously, the SNP first contested the seat only in 1970, coming second, before winning the seat at the October election in 1974. Angus has gradually become a safe SNP seat in recent years, though at certain elections its marginal nature has been clearly apparent. For instance, in 1992, the SNP just held on by 473 votes over the resurgent Conservatives. Yet, by 1997, the SNP had a 10,189 majority and the seat appeared very safe by the Scottish election of 1999.

Despite the retirement of the sitting MP, Andrew Welsh, to concentrate on his role as an MSP, this seat should remain safely SNP as the Conservatives slumped badly here in recent elections. The SNP has controlled the local council in Angus since 1984, the only local authority it has held consistently. Despite a few losses in 1999, the Nationalists won 21 of the 29 wards, with victories in all major towns. The SNP's council success and its ability to win parliamentary representation in Angus since 1987 have gone hand in hand. Indeed, apart from 1992, Angus appears a very unusual phenomenon – a safe SNP seat.

Of course, the ability of the SNP to retain the seat at a Westminster election without Andrew Welsh will be the real evidence that this is safe SNP territory, but seems likely given the Conservative decline. Whilst the Tories held this seat under Jock Bruce-Gardyne from 1964 until October 1974 and then Peter Fraser from 1979 until 1987, the SNP challenge was consistent from 1974 onwards. Indeed, the Nationalists, worst result since then was 36 per cent in 1983 and second place. This result was a radically better performance than the Tories' worst result of 20.71 per cent in 1999. Indeed, the last two elections make it appear that the Conservatives can no longer compete in this seat and that they could face future competition from Labour for second place.

The current MP/MSP, Andrew Welsh, had originally won the seat in October 1974, only to lose it in 1979. He contested the seat unsuccessfully in 1983, but afterwards adopted a new approach to the constituency. Welsh was elected as a councillor in 1984, when the SNP took control of Angus District Council. He became Provost of the Council and developed a political profile that assisted him in winning the seat in 1987 from the Conservatives' Peter Fraser. Though the Conservatives came close to retaking the seat in 1992, the constituency appears a safe prospect for the Nationalists at the next UK election.

MP/MSP Andrew Welsh was born in Glasgow in 1944 educated at Govan High School, Glasgow and graduated from Glasgow University in Modern History and Politics and is a qualified teacher with a diploma in education from the same university. Before his election he was a teacher and also a Senior Lecturer in Business Studies and Public Administration. He was first elected as an MP for Angus South in October 1974 until 1979 and then again from 1987 onwards for Angus East, which became Angus from 1997. Before re-entering Westminster he was a councillor on Angus District and became Provost of the Council from 1984 until 1987. He has held a variety of posts within the SNP Executive as well as operating as Chief Whip in the parliamentary party at Westminster. At Westminster he was a member of the Select Committee on Members Interests from 1990 until 1992 and of the Scottish Affairs Committee from 1992 onwards as well as a member of the Chairmen's Panel from 1997 on. Within the Scottish Parliament he is Convenor of the Audit Committee as well as a member of the Scottish Parliamentary Corporate Body.

ARGYLL AND BUTE

Predecessor Constituencies: Argyll (1945–79).

1999

Electorate: 49,609
Turnout: 32,177 (64.86%)

Candidate	Party	Votes	Votes%	Change%
George Lyon	Liberal Democrat	11,226	34.89	−5.31
Duncan Hamilton	SNP	9,169	28.50	+5.33
Hugh Raven	Labour	6,470	20.11	+4.44
David Petrie	Conservative	5,312	16.51	−2.54

Liberal Democrat majority: 2,057 (6.39%)
Swing: 5.32% Liberal Democrat to SNP

1997

Electorate: 49,451
Turnout: 35,720 (72.23%)

Candidate	Party	Votes	Votes%	Change%
Rae Michie	Liberal Democrat	14,359	40.20	+5.29
Neil MacCormick	SNP	8,278	23.17	−0.64
Ralph Leishman	Conservative	6,774	18.96	−8.76
Ali Syed	Labour	5,596	15.67	+2.12
Michael Stewart	Referendum	713	2.00	−

Liberal Democrat majority: 6,081 (17.03%)
Swing: 2.97% SNP to Liberal Democrat

1945–92

	Lab%	Con%	SNP%	Lib%	Other%	Turnout%
1992	13.6	27.7	23.8	34.9	−	76.2
1987	12.1	33.5	17.1	37.3	−	75.4
1983	9.3	38.6	24.6	27.5	−	72.8
1979	16.0	36.8	31.8	15.4	−	76.1
1974O	13.6	36.7	49.7	−	−	72.0
1974F	12.6	38.4	49.0	−	−	77.0
1970	25.3	44.8	29.9	−	−	74.0

	Lab%	Con%	SNP%	Lib%	Other%	Turnout%
1966	30.1	43.2	–	26.7	–	72.3
1964	28.9	47.2	–	23.9	–	70.3
1959	25.9	58.4	–	15.7	–	71.0
1958B	25.7	46.8	–	27.5	–	67.1
1955	32.4	67.6	–	–	–	66.6
1951	31.9	68.1	–	–	–	67.1
1950	31.8	66.5	–	–	1.7	75.1
1945	31.9	56.5	–	11.6	–	63.7

Argyll and Bute is a geographically challenging constituency running from Oban to Campbeltown, including the islands of Islay and Jura amongst others, as well as Bute and Dunoon. The seat is not blessed with good transport links, which must be rather trying for the local MP and MSP, with male unemployment running at 6.0 per cent in June 2000.

Argyll and Bute has swapped political hands in the past but has been Liberal Democrat since 1987: with the party holding both Westminster and Scottish seats. The seat was comfortably Conservative from 1924 until 1974, when the intervention of the SNP proved successful at both elections in 1974 – significantly the Liberals failed to contest the constituency on either occasion and the SNP was able to win with 49–50 per cent of the vote at each election. Even then the seat was quite marginal, though the SNP's 3,913 majority in a three-party contest in October 1974 is much better than the Liberal Democrats' 2,057 majority in a four -party contest in 1999.

When the Liberals fought the seat again in 1979, the SNP lost and the Conservatives regained the seat with a vote very similar to that with which it lost in 1974. Since then, SNP support has fluctuated and the Conservative vote has declined, with the Liberal Democrats the main beneficiary. The SNP is now the main challenger to the Liberal Democrats in the constituency and the Nationalists will hope to capitalise on the retirement of the incumbent MP, Ray Michie, at the forthcoming Westminster election. Personality does count in this constituency as well as party, evident from the fact that the local authority contains a considerable number of Independent councillors: 21 out of a total of 36.

Also, support for the Conservatives in the constituency has fundamentally declined in recent years. Though this was a seat the party once held with impressive majorities, recent elections have demonstrated the Tories' decline in the seat and across Scotland. Given that the Conservatives held this seat before the 1987 election, it is somewhat incredible that it found itself coming third in 1997 and then last in 1999. Recent electoral contests in the seat used to be Conservative-SNP, then Conservative-Liberal, but now appear to involve the Liberal Democrats and the SNP.

The Tories therefore seem to have been consigned to the history books in terms of competing in this constituency.

The Liberal Democrats selected Michie's replacement in May 2000, Paul Coleshill, a local councillor for the Roseneath, Clyder and Kilcreggan ward and Convenor of the Policy and Resources Committee of Argyll and Bute Council. However, he resigned as candidate in the early part of the summer of 2000 and computer analyst Alan Reid was selected. Of course, the SNP must also field a new candidate in the constituency. Their last two candidates in the seat have moved on to other elected office. Neil McCormick, whose brother was the MP from 1974 until 1979, was the SNP candidate in 1997, but is now an MEP. Duncan Hamilton, the candidate in 1999, is now a list MSP for the Highlands and Islands, though likely to contest the seat at future Scottish elections. The SNP candidate is Agnes Samuel, head of Glasgow Opportunities, and secretary to the SNP parliamentary group from 1974 until 1979. This is a key seat for the SNP if they are to make progress in winning more Westminster seats and conquering their weaknesses shown in both 1997 and 1999, when SNP support was evident across Scotland but the party unable to win in the first-past-the-post constituencies. However, the Liberal Democrats have both organisational strength and popular support in the constituency and may well hold on.

MP Ray Michie was born in 1934, educated at Aberdeen High School for Girls, Lansdowne House School, Edinburgh, and the Edinburgh School for Speech Therapy and worked as a speech therapist for Argyll and Clyde Health Board before her election in 1987. She was a Liberal Democrat spokesperson on a variety of policy areas and chair of the Scottish Liberal Democrats from 1992 until 1993. At Westminster she has been a member of the Scottish Affairs Committee from 1992 until 1993 and currently serves on the Chairmen's Panel.

MSP George Lyon was born in Rothesay in 1956 and was educated at Rothesay Academy. He is a farmer with a family-owned farm and became National Farmers' Union of Scotland President in 1997. He was the recipient of a Nuffield Scholarship to New Zealand in 1987 and is a former member of Argyll and Islands Enterprise company. He serves as the Liberal Democrat spokesperson on Enterprise and Lifelong Learning and sits on the Parliament's Enterprise and Lifelong Learning and Public Petitions Committees and is a member of the Cross Party Groups on Crofting and Renewable Energy. He is Joint Convenor of the Cross Party Group on Agriculture and Horticulture. He is also a high-profile Liberal Democrat, as leader of the parliamentary group in the absence of Jim Wallace in the Scottish Executive. He developed a strong media profile in 1999 and 2000, prominently defending the performance of the coalition administration across a host of issues.

AYR

Predecessor Constituencies: Ayr District of Burghs (1945).

Scottish Parliament By-election 16 March 2000

Electorate: 56,715
Turnout: 31,900 (56.25%)

Candidate	Party	Votes	Votes%	Change%
John Scott	Conservative	12,580	39.44	+1.43
Jim Mather	SNP	9,236	28.95	+9.48
Rita Miller	Labour	7,054	22.11	-15.97
James Stewart	SSP	1,345	4.22	+4.22
Stuart Ritchie	Liberal Democrat	800	2.51	- 1.93
Gavin Corbett	Greens	460	1.44	—
William Botcherby	Radio Vet	186	0.58	—
Alistair McConnachie	UK Independence	113	0.35	—
Robert Graham	Pro-Life	111	0.35	—
Kevin Dillon	Independent	15	0.05	—

Conservative majority: 3,344 (10.49%)
Swing: 4.02% Conservative to SNP

1999

Electorate 56,338
Turnout 37,454 (66.48%)

Candidate	Party	Votes	Votes%	Change%
Ian Welsh	Labour	14,263	38.08	-10.36
Phil Gallie	Conservative	14,238	38.01	+4.19
Roger Mullin	SNP	7,291	19.47	+6.90
Elaine Morris	Liberal Democrat	1,662	4.44	-0.29

Labour majority: 25 (0.07%)
Swing: 7.27% Labour to Conservative

1997

Electorate: 55,829
Turnout: 44,756 (80.17%)

Candidate	Party	Votes	Votes%	Change%
Sandra Osborne	Labour	21,679	48.44	+5.81
Phil Gallie	Conservative	15,136	33.82	− 4.63
Ian Blackford	SNP	5,625	12.57	+1.41
Clare Hamblen	Liberal Democrat	2,116	4.73	−2.74
John Enos	Referendum	200	0.45	−

Labour majority: 6,543 (14.62%)
Swing: 5.22% Conservative to Labour

1945–92

	Lab%	Con%	SNP%	Lib%	Other%	Turnout%
1992	40.6	40.8	10.9	7.5	0.2	83.1
1987	39.1	39.4	6.7	14.8	−	80.0
1983	26.8	42.8	4.9	25.6	−	76.6
1979	36.9	43.3	9.2	10.6	−	79.8
1974O	34.6	42.4	16.9	6.3	−	79.4
1974F	38.6	50.4	11.0	−	−	83.1
1970	42.1	52.7	5.2	−	−	81.6
1966	49.4	50.6	−	−	−	85.3
1964	47.8	52.2	−	−	−	83.0
1959	45.3	54.7	−	−	−	79.1
1955	40.9	59.1	−	−	−	77.1
1951	41.7	58.3	−	−	−	86.5
1950	41.4	58.6	−	−	−	84.7
1945	49.2	50.8	−	−	−	71.5

Ayr encompasses some of the most exclusive residential areas to be found in Scotland, including Troon and Prestwick – golfing country with a 'Costa Geriatrica' reputation. Troon still managed in 1999 to elect three out of four Conservative councillors with a 68 per cent vote in Troon South. Ayr itself is a Labour town with expensive neighbourhoods sitting beside run-down council estates with high unemployment. The recent boundary changes took Conservative areas such as Alloway, Forehill and Holmston out of the seat and gave Labour an advantage.

Ayr had a long, rich Conservative lineage until recently. In 1918, it was won for the Conservatives by Sir George Younger with a majority over the Liberals of

4,155. The only threats to Conservative hegemony came at the high mark of Labour's appeal: their majority fell to 728 in 1945 and 484 in 1966. Ayr's second George Younger (grandson of the first) represented the seat from 1964, holding it with a majority of 3,219 in October 1974 over Labour and 2,768 in 1979. At this point, one would not have given Younger much chance of holding out during the Thatcher-Major years with such a wafer-thin majority, but he did; in 1983 Younger increased the Conservative majority to 7,987 over Labour, before seeing it fall to 182 in 1987.

Younger retired in 1992 and surprisingly Phil Gallie held the seat by 85 votes over Labour. The 1997 boundary redistribution removed some of the most Tory wards and gave Labour a notional majority of 1,895. In 1997, in a notional Labour seat, Sandra Osborne increased Labour's vote by 3,000, while the Conservative vote fell by over 2,000 resulting in a Labour majority of 6,543.

In the Scottish Parliament elections, Labour's Ian Welsh just managed to hold on with a majority of 25, making Ayr the most marginal seat in Scotland, as Labour's vote fell by over 7,000 and the Conservatives' by under 1,000. Six months into the Parliament, Welsh resigned, disenchanted with the life of a Labour backbencher. The March 2000 contest was the first by-election of the new Parliament and the Conservatives' John Scott was elected with a majority of 3,344, as the SNP's Jim Mather finished second, pushing Labour into third. This was a watershed result: the first Scottish by-election victory by the Conservatives since Edinburgh North in 1973 and their first gain since Glasgow Pollok in 1967. Ayr was a significant result, ending the Conservatives' pariah status and giving them their first constituency MSP in the new Parliament.

MP Sandra Osborne was born in 1956 in Paisley and was elected MP for Ayr in 1997, the first time Labour has ever held the seat, after her husband, Alistair Osborne, had come within 85 votes of winning it in 1992 (and was only prevented from standing again by a women-only shortlist). Educated at Campshill High School, Paisley, Anniesland College, Jordanhill College and Strathclyde University, Osborne went on to be a community worker in Glasgow from 1976 to 1980 and a Women's Aid worker in Kilmarnock from 1983 to 1987.

On her election to the Commons, she became a member of the Select Committee on Information and the Scottish Affairs Select Committee from 1998 until 1999. In the reshuffle of Scottish ministers after the establishment of the Scottish Parliament, Osborne became Parliamentary Private Secretary to Brian Wilson shifting in January 2001 to work for George Foulkes. Whether she can be more than a one-term Labour MP and an aberration in the long, and until recently uninter-rupted, Tory history of this seat remains to be seen.

MSP John Scott was born in 1951 in Irvine and elected Conservative MSP for Ayr in March 2000 in the first ever by-election of the Scottish Parliament. Scott thus had the honour of becoming the first Conservative MSP elected by the old fashioned constituency method (all the others being list MSPs). He was educated at George Watson's College, Edinburgh and Edinburgh University where he gained a BSc in Civil Engineering.

After leaving university, Scott became part of the family farming business, W. Scott and Son, went on to set up a fertiliser selling agency and was a founding director of Ayrshire Country Lamb. In 1999 he set up Ayrshire Farmers' Market. From 1994 until 1996 he was President of the National Farmers' Union of Scotland, Ayrshire and Convenor of the NFU Farming Committee from 1993 until 1999. In the Scottish election of 1999 Scott stood in Carrick, Cumnock and Doon Valley where he polled respectably, increasing the Conservative vote by 3.0 per cent. Since his election, he has become a member of the Public Petitions Committee and the Cross Party Group on Agriculture and Horticulture.

BANFF AND BUCHAN

Predecessor Constituencies: Aberdeen and Kincardineshire Eastern (1945) and Aberdeenshire East (1950–79).

1999

Electorate: 57,639
Turnout: 31,734 (55.06%)

Candidate	Party	Votes	Votes%	Change%
Alex Salmond	SNP	16,695	52.61	-3.16
David Davidson	Conservative	5,403	17.03	-6.77
Maitland Mackie	Liberal Democrat	5,315	16.75	+10.78
Megan Harris	Labour	4,321	13.62	+1.81

SNP Majority: 11,292 (35.58%)
Swing: 1.80% Conservative to SNP

1997

Electorate: 58,493
Turnout: 40,178 (68.69%)

Candidate	Party	Votes	Votes%	Change%
Alex Salmond	SNP	22,409	55.77	+4.94
William Frain–Bell	Conservative	9,564	23.80	-10.92
Megan Harris	Labour	4,747	11.81	+3.22
Neil Fletcher	Liberal Democrat	2,398	5.97	+0.11
Alan Buchan	Referendum	1,060	2.64	–

SNP majority: 12,845 (31.97%)
Swing: 7.93% Conservative to SNP

1945–92

	Lab%	Con%	SNP%	Lib%	Other%	Turnout%
1992	8.2	38.6	47.5	5.6	–	71.2
1987	7.5	38.7	44.2	9.6	–	70.8
1983	7.8	39.7	37.4	15.0	–	67.0
1979	15.8	42.8	41.4	–	–	72.4
1974O	9.4	35.5	48.5	6.6	–	70.5
1974F	6.7	35.0	50.8	7.5	–	76.5

	Lab%	Con%	SNP%	Lib%	Other%	Turnout%
1970	18.0	40.9	29.8	11.3	–	68.8
1966	22.1	41.4	8.9	27.6	–	68.2
1964	22.4	48.0	6.3	23.3	–	70.1
1959	36.6	63.4	–	–	–	67.1
1958B	27.1	48.6	–	24.3	–	65.9
1955	31.5	68.5	–	–	–	59.8
1951	31.9	68.1	–	–	–	70.0
1950	34.0	66.0	–	–	–	75.6
1945	45.1	54.9	–	–	–	65.7

Banff and Buchan contains the fishing towns of Fraserburgh and Peterhead, the coastal towns of Banff and Macduff and a number of inland towns and villages. The constituency is highly rural with a strong farming community and a substantial interest in fishing, indeed the biggest fishing port in Britain, as well as the oil industry. Local employers also include RAF Buchan and Peterhead high security prison.

Over the years, this constituency has progressed from being safely Conservative to a marginal seat between the Tories and SNP to a safe SNP seat in which the Conservatives appear a spent force. From February 1924 to 1974, the seat was safely Conservative in spite of challenges from Labour then the Liberal Democrats. In 1974, the SNP succeeded in winning the seat with over 50 per cent of the vote as the Labour and Liberal votes collapsed. When the Labour vote increased in 1979, the SNP lost the seat back to the Tories. The Tories retained the seat narrowly in 1983 over former SNP MP Douglas Henderson before Salmond emerged to recover the seat in 1987.

The Tories have been in decline in the seat since Bob Boothby's demise in 1958. Tory support then was in the high 60 per cent range. Since then it fell to the 40 per cent range and then lower to its current level of 17 per cent at the Scottish election of 1999. In this seat, Conservative support has never been lower. The other two parties have not performed well in the constituency in recent years either and this is testament to the SNP's success. Labour's best result was in 1945 when it won 45.1 per cent of the vote. The Liberals' best result came in 1966 finishing second with 28 per cent. Even in good Liberal years such as 1983, the party came third with only 15 per cent, though the party gained 17 per cent in 1999.

The seat is both small town and rural. Fishing towns such as Fraserburgh (the Broch) and Peterhead (the Blue Toun) are strongly SNP, evident in both national and local elections. In 1999, the SNP won almost all of the council seats in these towns, a number of which were uncontested. The SNP also won council seats across the constituency from Aberchirder to Banff to Mintlaw. The Nationalists picked up a total of 23 wards on Aberdeenshire Council: almost all from Banff and Buchan itself.

SNP support in the constituency has therefore become entrenched and widespread. This situation has resulted from historic factors such as the strong SNP presence in the seat since the 1960s, the improvements in local party organisation and the excellent performance of the local MP/MSP Alex Salmond.

Both within the constituency and across Scotland, Salmond has built an impressive political profile which helped to turn Banff and Buchan into a safe SNP seat. Alex Salmond was originally meant to be retiring from Westminster to concentrate on the Scottish Parliament, and in 2000, the SNP selected a new candidate, Stewart Stevenson, a close confidante of Alex Salmond, a former IT director with the Bank of Scotland and previously a candidate in Linlithgow in the 1999 Scottish Parliament elections. However, after Salmond's surprising resignation as SNP leader in July 2000, he reconsidered his position and with the agreement of the local party, became the SNP's candidate for the forthcoming Westminster elections, while Stevenson became the candidate for the more distant Scottish Parliament elections.

The strong level of SNP support in this constituency, as well as Salmond's renewed candidature, along with the long-term decline of the Conservatives, who as recently as 1992 polled 39% here, but won a mere 17% in 1999, make this a certain SNP hold in the UK election, and probably well into the future.

MP/MSP Alex Salmond was born in Linlithgow in 1954. He was educated at Linlithgow Academy and graduated in Economics and History at St Andrews University and worked as an economist for the Scottish Office and the Royal Bank of Scotland before his election in 1987. He won Banff and Buchan at the first time of asking in 1987 and was already recognised as a high flier within the SNP. His elevation to SNP leader in 1990 was not unexpected, though his resignation in 2000 was. He was first elected to the SNP National Executive in 1981, was Vice-Chair for Publicity from 1985 until 1987 and deputy leader from 1987 until 1990. His rise within the SNP was nothing short of phenomenal. Salmond was a leading figure in the left-wing '79 Group formed after the 1979 electoral disaster to develop a more radical agenda appealing to Central Belt Labour voters. When the party leadership proscribed the group in 1982, seven of its leading members were expelled, including Salmond, their sentence later reduced to suspension. Within five years of courting political oblivion he was elected an MP and three years after that he became party leader.

His tactical and media skills were a boon to the SNP throughout his tenure as SNP leader, and provided the party with a strong political profile across Scotland and in the UK media too. Such attributes, alongside a strong organisation, progessively turned Banff and Buchan into a safe seat. He also brought about a long-term gradualist ascendancy within the SNP during his leadership, which did so much to infuriate fundamentalist critics such as Jim Sillars and Margo MacDonald and is one reason behind the feud between Salmond and Sillars which is partly political and partly personal.

His partnership with Mike Russell, who was SNP Chief Executive before becoming an MSP, was the key to professionalising SNP campaigning and fundraising and put the party on a much firmer footing as the 1990s progressed. In the long run up to the Scottish Parliament elections, Salmond initially outmanoeuvred the Labour Party and by the summer of 1998 had stolen the initiative with the SNP nine points ahead of Labour in the polls. They then faced a concerted Labour fightback and onslaught, followed by significant SNP mistakes, such as Salmond's comments on the war in Kosovo being 'an unpardonable folly' and the 'A Penny for Scotland' campaign: both attempts to win back ground from Labour. The SNP's performance in the 1999 elections was disappointing compared to the expectations raised in 1998, but it was the highest SNP vote for twenty-five years.

Despite standing down as party leader, he could well play a key role in the SNP. He eschewed any immediate frontbench role within the SNP after standing down as party leader in September 2000. At such a young age, however, this formidable politician is anything but ready for retirement. Notably, he topped the elections to the SNP's NEC following his retirement as party leader.

In his post-leader role, Salmond re-considered his options and decided to stand for Westminster at the next UK election. This will provide Salmond with an ideal role, considering the breadth of his Westminster skills and experience, while giving the SNP the advantage of having a senior figure at Westminster who will be able to maintain a high Nationalist profile in London in the post-devolution environment.

CAITHNESS, SUTHERLAND AND EASTER ROSS

Predecessor Constituencies: Caithness and Sutherland (1945–92).

1999

Electorate: 41,581
Turnout: 26,029 (62.6%)

Candidate	Party	Votes	Votes%	Change%
Jamie Stone	Liberal Democrat	10,691	41.07	+5.48
James Hendry	Labour	6,300	24.20	-5.64
Jean Urquhart	SNP	6,035	23.19	+0.19
Richard Jenkins	Conservative	2,167	8.33	-2.26
James Campbell	Independent	554	2.13	–
Ewen Stewart	Independent	282	1.08	–

Liberal Democrat majority: 4,391 (16.87%)
Swing: 4.56% Labour to Liberal Democrat

1997

Electorate: 41,566
Turnout: 29,172 (70.18%)

Candidate	Party	Votes	Votes%	Change%
Robert Maclennan	Liberal Democrat	10,381	35.59	-8.82
James Hendry	Labour	8,122	27.84	+12.21
Euan Harper	SNP	6,710	23.00	+4.63
Tom Miers	Conservative	3,148	10.79	-10.79
Carolyn Ryder	Referendum	369	1.26	–
John Martin	Green	230	0.79	–
Martin Carr	UK Independence	212	0.73	–

Liberal Democrat majority: 2,259 (7.75%)
Swing: 10.52% Liberal Democrat to Labour

	Lab%	Con%	SNP%	Lib%	Other%	Turnout%
1992	15.7	21.0	18.2	45.1	–	71.9
1987	14.9	16.7	10.3	53.6	4.4	73.6
1983	14.3	22.7	11.0	52.0	–	75.5
1979	41.5	30.5	28.0	–	–	78.4
1974O	35.3	18.8	23.9	22.0	–	78.1
1974F	36.2	21.5	16.1	26.2	–	83.0
1970	36.7	22.4	15.5	25.4	–	83.1
1966	39.1	22.0	–	38.9	–	79.2
1964	30.3	20.8	–	36.1	12.8	80.1
1959	34.6	65.4	–	–	–	69.6
1955	29.0	56.5	–	14.5	–	69.5
1951	34.1	49.3	–	16.6	–	73.5
1950	29.7	35.8	–	34.5	–	76.5
1945	33.4	33.5	–	33.1	–	64.0

A vast seat geographically and one that has swapped political hands at Westminster in a unique fashion. Its main towns are Wick, Thurso, John O'Groats, Invergordon and Tain and the seat enjoys a large, sparsely populated interior and north-western coast of sea lochs and mountains. This seat has a long Liberal tradition – being won by the party from 1918 to 1945 and was held by Sir Archibald Sinclair from 1922 to 1945, leader of the Liberals from 1935 to 1945. In one of the most sensational results in 1945, the Conservative Eric Gandar-Dower won the seat by six votes over Labour with Sinclair in third place, 55 votes behind. David Robertson won it for the Conservatives in 1950 by the wider margin of 269 votes over Sinclair and held the seat in 1951 and 1955, before being returned as an Independent Conservative in 1959. In 1964, the seat was won by the Liberal George Mackie, who was then defeated in 1966 by Robert Maclennan who won the seat in Wilson's Labour landslide with a majority of only 64 votes over the Liberals. Unlike many of Labour's gains in that year, he held the seat in 1970 and retained it in the two 1974 elections, winning in October with a 2,560 majority over the SNP.

In 1979, Maclennan as a Labour candidate had a majority of 2,539 over the Conservatives. In 1983, under the Social Democratic banner he transformed this into a 6,843 Liberal-SDP majority over the Conservatives. This was a result of epic proportions, both locally and nationally. There had been no Liberal candidate in 1979, and Labour's vote was cut by over 6,000 and nearly 27 per cent; it was also achieved against a backdrop of Social Democratic failure at a parliamentary level with only five defectors from Labour retaining their seats, including David Owen and Roy Jenkins.

The SDP with Charles Kennedy gaining Ross, Cromarty and Skye had half of their parliamentary representation based in Scotland. Maclennan has since held the seat through the various transformations of the centre parties in the 1980s, winning in 1997 by the narrow margin of 2,259 over Labour.

It says a lot for Maclennan as a local MP that his electors have continued to support him regardless of his party affiliation over the years, though his Liberal Democrat affiliation has rubbed off on the Scottish electoral situation in the area as Jamie Stone won the constituency for the party in 1999. Though the Liberal Democrat vote declined in 1997, the party will likely emerge victorious at the Westminster election. This area has had a strong Liberal vote since the 1945 election, which faded in the 1970s, but has recovered with Maclennan's involvement.

The SNP has never performed particularly well in this seat. Its opposition to the Dounreay nuclear facility is one reason, but strong historical support for the Liberal Democrats and Labour are more important factors. The SNP has never challenged in this constituency. Ironically, its best result was in 1979 when the SNP peaked in Caithness just as the party's support plummeted across Scotland after the high of October 1974: a very bizarre statistic indeed. Significantly, the 1979 result was achieved when the Liberals failed to contest the seat and their vote benefited the Nationalists as well as the other two parties. Labour was a more convincing challenger in this constituency, especially as the seat was Labour before Maclennan's defection. The party did well in 1997 to come within a couple of thousand votes of the Liberal Democrats. However, this was the party's best result for years and was not replicated at the 1999 Scottish election, even though that was still a comparatively good result for Labour.

Any successful challenge to the Liberal Democrats in this seat must await Bob Maclennan's retirement at the forthcoming election. Jamie Stone's convincing victory in 1999 – his vote rose whilst Labour's fell – suggests that the seat is safely Liberal Democrat rather than merely relying on Maclennan's personal vote. Given Maclennan's retirement from Westminster, this must be Labour's best chance of success in the seat for some time, but the Liberal Democrats should hold on, especially given the Labour Government's unpopularity in rural areas on issues such as agriculture and fuel duty.

MP Robert Maclennan was born in 1936 in Glasgow and educated at Glasgow Academy, Balliol, Oxford and Trinity, Cambridge as well as Columbia University. He was a barrister before his election in 1966. Back in the 1960s, as a Labour MP, he was a right-winger in the Gaitskellite mould; he was Parliamentary Private Secretary to George Thomson from 1967 until 1970 and Parliamentary Under-Secretary at the Department of Prices and Consumer Protection from 1974 until 1979. He defected to the SDP in 1981 and later became leader of the SDP in 1987 when it merged with the Liberals. He led the pro-merger wing of the SDP in the opposite direction of David Owen's anti-mergerites and later became President of the Liberal Democrats from 1994 until 1998. He has been Liberal Democrat Spokesman on Culture and Media and Constitutional Affairs since 1994. With the latter responsibility, in the run-up to the 1997 election, Maclennan was responsible for leading the Liberal discussions with Labour's Robin Cook on constitutional reform which led after the election to the historic establishment of a Cabinet Committee including Labour and the Lib Dems which discussed such matters. He was a member of the Public Accounts Committee in the Commons from 1979 until 1999 and, following retirement, a position in the House of Lords beckons.

MSP Jamie Stone was born in Edinburgh in 1954. He was educated at Tain Royal Academy and Gordonstoun, gained an MA in History and Geology from St Andrews University and had a varied career in the oil industry, cheese-making and freelance journalism. For example, he was an English teacher in Catania in Italy from 1977 to 1978, a fish gutter in the Faroes in 1978, a stores clerk for Wimpey from 1979 to 1981 and Director of Highland Fine Cheeses Ltd from 1986 until 1994, amongst other things (including time as a lavatory attendant!). He was also Director of the Highland Festival. He was a councillor on Ross and Cromarty District from 1986 until 1992 and subsequently a member of the Highland Council from 1998 onwards. In the Scottish Parliament, he served on the Education and Local Government Committees from May 1999 to December 2000, before joining the Rural Development Committee and is the Liberal Democrat Spokesperson for the Highlands and Islands and Fishing. He is a member of the Cross Party Group on Crofting and the Holyrood Progress Committee.

CARRICK, CUMNOCK AND DOON VALLEY

Predecessor Constituencies: Ayrshire South (1945–79).

1999

Electorate: 65,580
Turnout: 41,095 (62.66%)

Candidate	Party	Votes	Votes%	Change%
Cathy Jamieson	Labour	19,667	47.86	-11.93
Adam Ingram	SNP	10,864	26.44	+9.78
John Scott	Conservative	8,123	19.77	+2.82
David Hannay	Liberal Democrat	2,441	5.94	+0.63

Labour majority: 8,803 (21.42%)
Swing: 10.86% Labour to SNP

1997

Electorate: 65,593
Turnout: 49,171 (74.96%)

Candidate	Party	Votes	Votes%	Change%
George Foulkes	Labour	29,398	59.79	+5.74
Alasdair Marshall	Conservative	8,336	16.95	-8.71
Christine Hamilton	SNP	8,190	16.66	+1.57
Derek Young	Liberal Democrat	2,613	5.31	+0.11
John Higgins	Referendum	634	1.29	–

Labour majority: 21,062 (42.84%)
Swing: 7.23% Conservative to Labour

1945–92

	Lab%	Con%	SNP%	Lib%	Other%	Turnout%
1992	59.1	20.0	16.2	4.7	–	77.0
1987	60.1	20.7	9.6	9.6	–	75.8
1983	51.5	24.1	6.5	17.9	–	74.2
1979	35.2	25.4	8.0	–	31.4	78.9
1974O	56.2	18.6	19.8	5.4	–	77.4

	Lab%	Con%	SNP%	Lib%	Other%	Turnout%
1974F	57.2	26.4	16.4	–	–	79.4
1970	61.8	30.2	8.0	–	–	76.9
1970B	54.0	25.6	20.4	–	–	76.3
1966	67.2	32.8	–	–	–	75.1
1964	66.7	33.3	–	–	–	77.6
1959	63.7	36.3	–	–	–	80.9
1955	61.6	38.4	–	–	–	76.8
1951	60.5	39.5	–	–	–	82.9
1950	60.2	39.8	–	–	–	85.4
1946B	63.6	36.4	–	–	–	69.0
1945	61.3	38.7	–	–	–	75.0

The awkward sounding Carrick, Cumnock and Doon Valley is the remnants of the old Ayrshire South constituency. Carrick sits south of Ayr and ranges from towns on the outskirts of Ayr like Alloway, to coastal resorts like Girvan, both Conservative voting areas, to the more populous Labour areas of Cumnock and Doon Valley, old South Ayrshire mining areas.

Labour has a long tradition here, winning the seat in 1918 and holding it continuously through the inter-war years and since, with the exception of the aberration of 1931. Emrys Hughes was Labour MP from 1946 until 1970, driving his vote up to 67.2 per cent in 1966. In 1970 a by-election was called in which the Labour candidate was a young Jim Sillars, who fought the campaign on a hard anti-nationalist platform. Along with the Gorbals by-election the previous year, Sillars victory with 54 per cent to the SNP's 20.4 per cent was seen as the end of the SNP post-Hamilton surge.

Great things were expected from Sillars in the Scottish Labour Party where his energy and intelligence were widely recognised and Sillars' clearly expected great things to come to him. In October 1974, his majority over the SNP was 14,478, the safest Labour seat in Scotland. By this point however he had become a passionate devolutionist and he left Labour over its foot-dragging on devolution and set up his own Scottish Labour Party with one other MP in 1976. This one-man band of a party was briefly, in the heady days of the 1970s, a shooting star in Scottish politics, mesmerising media and politicians alike, and quickly burning out.

By 1979, Sillars faced the task of holding Ayrshire South against Labour's George Foulkes. Sillars polled a respectable 31.4 per cent, attracting nearly two-thirds of his previous Labour vote, and saw the Labour vote fall by a massive 21 per cent, but he lost by the small margin of 1,521 votes. Sillars' political trajectory is well-documented, and as Carrick, Cumnock and Doon Valley from 1983 onwards it quietly returned to the Labour fold giving Foulkes majorities over the Conservatives of 11,370 in 1983 and 16,802 in 1987.

Labour's majority fell slightly in 1992 to 16,666 with boundary changes taking another 2,000 off that. In 1997, Foulkes put nearly 1,500 on Labour's vote, the Conservatives lost 5,000 and the SNP remained static and finished in third place just over 100 votes behind; Labour's majority was 21,062. The Scottish Parliament elections showed Labour's strength as it lost 10,000 votes without facing any threat, while the SNP increased their support by 2,500 securing a decent but distant second place 8,803 behind Labour. Carrick, Cumnock and Doon Valley is the kind of seat Labour can count on to win, having failed to hold it only once and having succeeded in retaining it in difficult circumstances in 1979. No seismic political trends should be looked for here.

MP George Foulkes was born in 1942 in Oswestry, was elected for South Ayrshire in 1979, narrowly beating Jim Sillars, and has held Carrick, Cumnock and Doon Valley since 1983. He previously and unsuccessfully stood in Edinburgh West in 1970 and Edinburgh Pentlands in October 1974. Educated at Keith Grammar School, Haberdashers Askes, Hampstead, and Edinburgh University, he went on to be President of the National Union of Students Scotland from 1964 until 1966.

Foulkes was Director of the European League for Economic Co-operation from 1967 until 1968, Scottish Organiser of the European Movement from 1968 to 1969 and Director of Age Concern Scotland from 1973 until 1979. Elected to Edinburgh Corporation from 1970 until 1974 and Lothian Region from 1974 until 1979, he was Chair of the Lothian Region Education Committee from 1974 to 1979 and was also a member of COSLA's Education Committee from 1975 to 1979. He was Spokesman on European and Community Affairs from 1983 until 1985, Spokesman on Foreign Affairs from 1985 until 1992, Defence Spokesman from 1992 to 1993 and Spokesman on Overseas Development from 1994 until 1997. In office, Foulkes became Parliamentary Under-Secretary of State at the Department of International Development from 1997 to January 2001. Foulkes has been a consistent devolutionist post-1979 and was Chair of the Labour Campaign for a Scottish Assembly from 1982 until 1997 and author after Labour's defeat in 1983 of the 'Foulkes Memorandum'. It argued that the Tories had no mandate and it was 'no longer enough to put the head down and wait for the return of a Labour Government' and that instead Labour had to consider the heresy of working with the SNP and Liberal-SDP Alliance to get a Parliament. Donald Dewar dismissed such ideas, but after the 1987 election defeat, Labour joined the cross-party Convention.

He has been a passionate supporter of the first-past-the-post electoral system and became chair of the Labour Campaign for Electoral Success which was set up in early 1991 and included Labour local government leaders, Pat Lally and Eric Milligan. Their aim was to reverse the 1990 Scottish Conference decision to support an alternative to FPTP for the Scottish Parliament, but they were heavily defeated at the 1991 conference. He eventually accepted the additional member system as a compromise, while continuing to oppose electoral reform at Westminster. With John

Reid's shift to the Northern Ireland Office in January 2001, Foulkes became Deputy Minister to Helen Liddell in the Scotland Office.

MSP Cathy Jamieson was born in 1956 in Kilmarnock and educated at James Hamilton Academy, Kilmarnock, Glasgow Art School where she obtained a BA Hons in Fine Art at Goldsmiths College, London, where she gained a Higher Diploma in Art; Glasgow University and Glasgow Caledonian University where she gained her CQSW in Social Work.

Jamieson is a qualified art therapist and was a social worker with Strathclyde Regional Council from 1980 until 1986, a Community Intermediate Treatment Worker from 1986 until 1992 and Principal Officer of 'Who Cares? Scotland' from 1992 until 1999, an advocacy organisation for young people in care. In the Scottish Parliament, she was Deputy Convenor of the European Committee and a member of the Transport and Environment Committee from May 1999 to December 2000, before joining the Rural Development Committee. Jamieson is also a member of the Cross Party Group on Animal Welfare, of which she is Vice-Convenor. She is also a member of the groups on Children, Citizenship, Income, Economy and Society, both of which she is Convenor of, Drug Misuse, Epilepsy, Information, Knowledge and Enlightenment, Older People, Rail Services, Media, Tobacco Control, Women, Sports, Renewable Energy, Refugees and Asylum Seekers, of which she is Vice-Convenor.

A member of the Edinburgh Inquiry into Abuse in residential care homes, Jamieson is on the left of the party and an active member of the hard left Campaign for Socialism group which grew out of grass roots opposition to Blair's rewriting of Clause Four in 1994. She was elected to the NEC as a member of the left wing Grassroots Alliance from 1998 to 1999.

Following the death of Donald Dewar, First Minister, and Henry McLeish's election as Labour leader and First Minister, Cathy Jamieson put herself forward as a candidate for Deputy Labour leader. As the Campaign for Socialism candidate she would normally have stood little chance of winning, given the minority support this group can muster in the Labour Group of MSPs. However, none of the Labour establishment figures or modernisers was prepared or could stand for the post, so Jamieson found herself in the unexpected position of being elected Deputy Leader of the party. How she carves out a niche for herself in the post will be interesting to see, as will be the extent to which she can promote her own socialist values and beliefs, versus the need to compromise and follow Labour's collective line.

CLYDEBANK AND MILNGAVIE

Predecessor Constituencies: Dunbartonshire Central (1974–9).

1999

Electorate: 52,461
Turnout: 33,337 (63.55%)

Candidate	Party	Votes	Votes%	Change%
Des McNulty	Labour	15,105	45.31	-9.91
Jim Yuill	SNP	10,395	31.18	+10.04
Rod Ackland	Liberal Democrat	4,149	12.45	+2.00
Dorothy Luckhurst	Conservative	3,688	11.06	-1.44

Labour majority: 4,710 (14.13%)
Swing: 9.97% Labour to SNP

1997

Electorate: 52,092
Turnout: 39,086 (75.03%)

Candidate	Party	Votes	Votes%	Change%
Tony Worthington	Labour	21,583	55.22	+4.96
Jim Yuill	SNP	8,263	21.14	+2.68
Nancy Morgan	Conservative	4,885	12.50	-8.95
Keith Moody	Liberal Democrat	4,086	10.45	+0.92
Iain Sanderson	Referendum	269	0.69	–

Labour majority: 13,320 (34.08%)
Swing: 1.14% SNP to Labour

1974–92

	Lab%	Con%	SNP%	Lib%	Other%	Turnout%
1992	53.3	18.1	19.6	8.7	0.3	78.0
1987	56.9	15.7	12.5	14.9	–	78.9
1983	44.8	20.3	9.2	24.8	0.8	75.9
1979	51.9	21.6	15.3	7.8	3.4	80.0
1974O	40.2	17.2	29.1	4.8	8.7	79.8
1974F	40.4	24.0	14.5	6.4	14.7	83.1

Clydebank and Milngavie contains two distinct communities with little in common but geographical proximity. The former is working class, with a high concentration of council houses and above average unemployment, the latter is middle class, upwardly mobile, with a high degree of owner occupation, spiralling property prices and near to negligible unemployment.

The predecessor constituency Dunbartonshire Central was created in 1974 and enjoyed celebrity status as Jimmy Reid, popular tribune of the Upper Clyde Shipworkers' work-in, stood there for the Communists in February 1974 winning an impressive 5,928 votes (14.6 pert cent) – the highest Communist vote in a UK election since 1959. Reid's star faded in the October 1974 election, while the SNP cut Labour's majority to 4,385.

Tony Worthington became Labour MP for the seat in 1987, increasing his majority over the Conservatives to 16,304. In the following election, the SNP re-established themselves in second place – 12,435 votes behind Labour. In 1997, boundary changes reduced Labour's notional majority to 11,420 over the Conservatives, with the SNP in third place. Worthington increased Labour's vote by 1,500, while the SNP moved back into second place adding 1,000 votes to their support. As the Conservatives fell back into third place losing 3,500 votes, Worthington was returned with a 13,220 majority over the SNP.

The SNP polled respectably in the Scottish Parliament elections reducing Labour's majority to 4,710. Des McNulty, Labour candidate, was comfortably elected, but saw the Labour vote fall by 6,000 on a lower turnout, while the SNP increased their support by 2,132. The Conservatives, a notional second in 1992, fell to a humiliating fourth, losing another 1,000 votes. Clydebank and Milngavie in its short history has never shown a capacity to shock – bar Jimmy Reid's unique appeal – but this is the sort of seat the SNP need to mount a serious challenge in if they are ever to get anywhere.

MP Tony Worthington was born in 1941 in Hertfordshire and was elected for Clydebank and Milngavie in 1987. He was educated at City School, Lincoln, London School of Economics, York University and Glasgow University. Worthington worked at HM Borstal, Dover, from 1962 until 1966 and Monkwearmouth College of Further Education, Sutherland from 1967 to 1971. He was elected to Strathclyde Regional Council from 1974 until 1987, and was Convenor of the Finance Committee from 1986 to 1987.

Upon his election to Westminster, Worthington was Chair of the Labour Campaign for Criminal Justice from 1987 to 1989 and Spokesman on Scotland from 1989 until 1992, Overseas Development from 1992 to 1993, Foreign Affairs from 1993 to 1994 and Northern Ireland from 1995 to 1997. Upon Labour's election in 1997, he became Under-Secretary at the Northern Ireland Office where he lasted just over one year, being sacked in Blair's first government reshuffle in 1998.

MSP Des McNulty was born in Stockport in 1952 and educated at St Bede's

College, Manchester, the University of York and University of Glasgow. He worked for twenty-one years at Glasgow Caledonian University, as a lecturer in Sociology from 1978 until 1990, senior lecturer from 1990 to 1991, Assistant Head of Social Sciences from 1991 until 1997 and as Strategic Planning Officer from 1997 until 1999. McNulty was elected to Strathclyde Regional Council from 1990 until 1996 and Glasgow City Council 1995 until 1999 where he was Secretary to the Labour Group and Vice-Chair of the Policy and Resources Committee.

He has taken a leading role in a range of organisations, as Chair of Glasgow Healthy City Partnership from 1995 until 1999 and Chair of Glasgow 1999 Festival of Architecture and Design. It came as a shock to McNulty then that upon his election to the Scottish Parliament, his obvious talents were not met with the call of ministerial office or a convenership. Instead, he has to make do with being a member of the Scottish Parliamentary Corporate Body, the Standards Committee and Rural Affairs Committee, the latter two of which he came off in December 2000. He has been a member of the Transport and Environment Committee from May 1999 and became a member of the Enterprise and Lifelong Learning Committee at the end of 2000. He is also a member of the Cross Party Groups on Care, Epilepsy, Information, Knowledge and Enlightenment, and Tobacco Control.

CLYDESDALE

Predecessor Constituencies: Lanark (1945–79).

1999

Electorate: 64,262
Turnout: 38,947 (60.61%)

Candidate	Party	Votes	Votes%	Change%
Karen Gillon	Labour	16,755	43.02	– 9.52
Ann Winning	SNP	12,875	33.06	+10.93
Charles Cormack	Conservative	5,814	14.93	–1.36
Sandra Grieve	Liberal Democrat	3,503	8.99	+0.63

Labour majority: 3,880 (9.96%)
Swing: 10.22% Labour to SNP

1997

Electorate: 63,428
Turnout: 45,412 (71.60%)

Candidate	Party	Votes	Votes%	Change%
Jimmy Hood	Labour	23,859	52.54	+7.95
Andrew Doig	SNP	10,050	22.13	–0.95
Mark Izatt	Conservative	7,396	16.29	–7.09
Sandra Grieve	Liberal Democrat	3,796	8.36	+0.12
Kenneth Smith	BNP	311	0.68	–0.03

Labour majority: 13,809 (30.41%)
Swing: 4.45% SNP to Labour

1945–92

	Lab%	Con%	SNP%	Lib%	Other%	Turnout%
1992	44.6	23.4	23.1	8.2	0.7	77.6
1987	45.3	23.5	14.8	16.4	–	78.1
1983	38.8	28.2	11.4	21.5	–	76.4
1979	43.2	30.9	18.8	7.1	–	81.8
1974O	37.6	23.2	35.8	3.4	–	82.2
1974F	41.7	36.5	21.8	–	–	84.1
1970	45.0	41.4	11.7	–	1.9	78.9

	Lab%	Con%	SNP%	Lib%	Other%	Turnout%
1966	51.7	38.2	10.1	–	–	83.7
1964	54.8	45.2	–	–	–	86.0
1959	50.5	49.5	–	–	–	87.2
1955	48.9	51.1	–	–	–	85.9
1951	47.8	52.2	–	–	–	87.0
1950	49.1	50.9	–	–	–	84.7
1945	52.8	47.2	–	–	–	74.8

Clydesdale sits in a position south of Glasgow and Edinburgh midway between the connurbations, but within its northern end is more drawn into the Greater Glasgow economy. It contains small towns which used to be part of Lanarkshire's mining industry such as Coalburn, Douglas and Lesmahagow in the west, while further east is Biggar. This is Labour territory, but the SNP is increasingly strong on South Lanarkshire Council; Tom McAlpine has been returned in Biggar for some time, winning 59 per cent of the vote in the 1999 elections.

Previously known as Lanark, the seat was held by the Conservatives for most of the inter-war era – Labour winning it in 1923 and 1929. Walter Elliot held the seat from 1919 until 1923 and went on to be Secretary of State for Scotland; Lord Dunglass (Alec Douglas Home) was MP from 1931 until 1945 during which time he was Parliamentary Private Secretary to Neville Chamberlain from 1937 until 1940. Labour's Tom Steele defeated Dunglass in 1945, who won it back for the Conservatives in 1950 by 685 votes.

Labour's Judith Hart took the seat from Conservative P. F. Maitland narrowly in 1959 with 50.5 per cent to 49.5 per cent. In October 1974, she held on against the SNP's Tom McAlpine by 698 votes before increasing her majority to 5,139 over the Conservatives in 1979, driving the SNP into a distant third place. In 1983 the seat was renamed Clydesdale and Judith Hart won it with a majority of 4,866 over the Conservatives. Jimmy Hood was then elected for the seat for the first time in 1987, doubling Labour's majority over the Conservatives to 10,502. This fell slightly to 10,187 in 1992, but increased significantly in 1997 to 13,809, with Hood increasing Labour's vote to 52.5 per cent – its highest level since 1964 – while the SNP re-established themselves in a far-off second place.

The 1999 elections saw Clydesdale become less of a safe Labour seat. Karen Gillon presided over Labour's vote falling by 7,000 on a turnout 11 per cent down, while the SNP in their new role as challengers put on over 2,500 votes and 11 per cent, reducing Labour's majority to 3,880. Clydesdale should remain Labour in the forthcoming UK and Scottish elections, but it is the sort of seat in which the SNP has to put a serious challenge if it is to broaden its support.

MP Jimmy Hood was born in 1948 in Lesmahagow and elected MP for

Clydesdale in 1983. Educated at Lesmahagow High School and Nottingham University, he was a mining engineer in Lanarkshire and Nottingham and NUM official from 1973 until 1987, and was elected as a Labour councillor on Newark and Sherwood District Council from 1979 until 1987. Hood is a former Chair and Vice-Chair of the Scottish Group of Labour MPs and was Chair of the Miners Group of MPs from 1990 until 1992. He has been Chair of the European Legislation Committee from 1992 onward.

Hood led the Nottingham striking miners during the 1984–5 strike, a minority in that county, and was regarded as a Scargillite loyalist fighting a difficult corner. Seen by some as a typical Labour Jimmy, he suffered a heart attack in 1998 from which he fully recovered.

MSP Karen Gillon was born in Edinburgh in 1967 and educated at Jedburgh Grammar School and Birmingham University. She worked as a youth worker at the Terminal One Youth Centre, Blantyre, from 1991 to 1994 and as a Community Education Worker for North Lanarkshire Council from 1994 to 1997, before becoming Personal Assistant to Helen Liddell, MP for Airdrie and Shotts, from 1997 until 1999.

She was Deputy Convenor of the Education, Culture and Sport Committee from 1999 until 2000 and a member of the Standards Committee of the Scottish Parliament and became Convenor of the Education, Culture and Sport Committee in January 2001. Gillon is also a member of the Cross Party Groups on Borders Rail, Epilepsy, Older People, Sport, and Agriculture and Horticulture. In the early days of the Parliament, adverse media comment was made on the quality of some of the Labour women MSPs, including Gillon – nicknamed 'a shoal of Karens' by male journalists. Others felt this was misogynist, belittling the contribution of Labour women. Gillon has been unfairly judged by commentators who underestimate the working class people living in Lanarkshire. She has grown in confidence and ability in the first year-and-a-half of Parliament, and in particular, made a valuable contribution to the 'Lobbygate' hearings of the Standards Committee.

COATBRIDGE AND CHRYSTON

Predecessor Constituencies: Monklands West (1983–92).

1999

Electorate: 52,178
Turnout: 30,198 (57.87%)

Candidate	Party	Votes	Votes%	Change%
Elaine Smith	Labour	17,923	59.35	−8.97
Peter Kearney	SNP	7,519	24.90	+7.88
Gordon Lind	Conservative	2,867	9.49	+0.94
Jane Hook	Liberal Democrat	1,889	6.26	+0.81

Labour majority: 10,404 (34.45%)
Swing: 8.42% Labour to SNP

1997

Electorate: 52,024
Turnout: 37,612 (72.03%)

Candidate	Party	Votes	Votes%	Change%
Tom Clarke	Labour	25,697	68.32	+6.54
Brian Nugent	SNP	6,402	17.02	+0.25
Andrew Wauchope	Conservative	3,216	8.55	−6.97
Morag Daly	Liberal Democrat	2,048	5.45	−0.49
Bernard Bowsley	Referendum	249	0.66	−

Labour majority: 19,295 (51.3%)
Swing: 3.15% SNP to Labour

1983–92

	Lab%	Con%	SNP%	Lib%	Other%	Turnout%
1992	61.3	15.9	16.6	6.2	−	77.5
1987	62.3	15.7	10.8	11.2	−	77.2
1983	54.2	22.0	6.5	17.3	−	75.6

Coatbridge and Chryston is safely Labour, with a strong working-class and council house component to its population: at the 1991 census 56.0 per cent of housing was rented from the council. Male unemployment was running at 7.1 per cent in June 2000. This seat was created in 1983 with Monklands East, but has its origins in the Coatbridge and Airdrie constituency of 1950 to 1982 (see Airdrie and Shotts for results). Tom Clarke, the current MP, first won Coatbridge and Airdrie relatively easily in a 1982 by-election, and the pattern of party competition (ie: Labour dominance) has continued into Monklands East and now Coatbridge and Chryston. Indeed, this seat and its predecessors have always returned Labour MPs. Even in October 1974, the SNP's best performance in Coatbridge and Airdrie with 27.9 per cent, the Nationalists were still 10,658 votes behind Labour which held the seat with over 50 per cent of the vote. Similarly, the Liberal-SDP Alliance's best result in 1983 was only 17.3 per cent and third place.

The SNP has improved its position in the seat in recent elections, consolidating its second place position and improving its share of the vote, but its challenge is an extremely distant one in a seat in which the Labour vote could be weighed rather than counted. Indeed, Labour's performance in 1997 was its best in the post-war period, gaining a whopping 68.32 per cent of the vote. The boundary changes that created this seat gave Labour a notional majority of 18,000 and 61.3 per cent of the vote in 1997: it exceeded both at the actual election, which demonstrated just how well Labour did here.

Even in Coatbridge and Airdrie in 1974, the SNP challenge did not reach 30 per cent, whilst Labour's worst performance in this seat in recent times was the 51.6 per cent gained in October 1974. Just as in Airdrie and Shotts, Labour in this seat was tainted by the Monklands council corruption scandals, though sitting MP Tom Clarke rejected charges of wrong-doing within Monklands council at the Airdrie and Shotts by-election, in 1994 calling them a 'McCarthyite smear' which looked rather odd given Helen Liddell's denunciation of the same council and calls for an inquiry into council nepotism. In the short term this presented problems, but over the longer term the issue faded away. Indeed Labour's convincing majorities make these problems appear as if they never occurred. The party remains strong here at local and national elections and well capable of seeing off any challenger and dominating the seat.

MP Tom Clarke was born in 1941 in Coatbridge. He was educated at Columba High School, Coatbridge, the Scottish College of Commerce and worked for the Scottish Council for Educational Technology in film before his election. He was a councillor for many years, on Coatbridge Town Council from 1964 until 1974 and then on Monklands District Council from 1974 to 1982. He was Provost of the Council and also President of COSLA from 1978 until 1980. He was first elected at the Coatbridge and Airdrie by-election in 1982 and was Shadow Scottish Secretary from 1992 to 1993 and Shadow Minister for Disabled People from 1995 to 1997. As a backbench MP he steered through the private members bill, the Disabled Persons (Services Consultation and Representation) Act 1986, which was widely seen as a significant advance in disability rights.

As Shadow Scottish Secretary following in Donald Dewar's footsteps, he was given a difficult task of holding the Scottish Labour Party together after the unexpected election defeat in 1992. In the post-election environment some felt Labour had been too enthusiastically involved in the Scottish Constitutional Convention, while those in 'Scotland United' pushed for Labour to go further. Clarke, holding the middle position, had criticism directed at him from both sides. He was Minister of State in the Department of Culture from 1997 to 1998, responsible for film and tourism, but since then his career prospects have plummeted with no signs of recovery.

MSP Elaine Smith was born in Coatbridge in 1963. She was educated at St Patrick's School, Coatbridge, Glasgow College where she obtained a degree in social sciences and St Andrew's Teacher Training Centre where she became a qualified teacher, and has subsequently specialised in modern studies and economics. She also gained a diploma in public sector management and worked in local government, the teaching profession and as a manager for a Scottish Office pilot project in primary health care. She is a member of the Equal Opportunities Committee in the Scottish Parliament and sits on the Cross Party Group for Children and Women.

CUMBERNAULD AND KILSYTH

Predecessor Constituencies: created anew at the 1983 election, mostly from Dunbartonshire East.

1999

Electorate: 49,395
Turnout: 30,612 (61.97%)

Candidate	Party	Votes	Votes%	Change%
Cathie Craigie	Labour	15,182	49.58	-9.10
Andrew Wilson	SNP	10,923	35.68	+7.88
Hugh O'Donnell	Liberal Democrat	2,029	6.63	+2.83
Robin Slack	Conservative	1,362	4.45	-2.33
Kenny McEwan	SSP	1,116	3.65	+2.69

Labour majority: 4,259 (13.9%)
Swing: 8.49% Labour to SNP

1997

Electorate: 48,032
Turnout: 36,024 (75%)

Candidate	Party	Votes	Votes%	Change%
Rosemary McKenna	Labour	21,141	58.69	+4.67
Colin Barrie	SNP	10,013	27.80	-1.15
Ian Sewell	Conservative	2,441	6.78	-4.49
John Biggam	Liberal Democrat	1,368	3.80	-1.96
Jan Kara	Pro-Life	609	1.69	—
Kenny McEwan	SSA	345	0.96	—
Pamela Cook	Referendum	107	0.30	—

Labour majority: 11,128 (30.89%)
Swing: 2.91% SNP to Labour

1983–92

	Lab%	Con%	SNP%	Lib%	Other%	Turnout%
1992	54.0	11.3	28.9	5.8	—	79.1
1987	60.0	9.1	19.6	11.4	—	78.5
1983	49.2	13.6	17.4	19.8	—	76.5

This constituency contains the new town of Cumbernauld as well as smaller towns such as Croy and Kilsyth. Despite the apparent closeness of the 1999 Scottish election result, this seat is safely Labour. The SNP's success in 1999 was purely in percentage terms. Indeed, in numerical terms the Nationalists have achieved around 10,000 votes in the seat at each of the last three elections. The SNP was therefore much more effective than Labour at turning out its vote in 1999 – hence Labour's 'Operation Turnout' strategy at the forthcoming UK election – but the SNP's overall support in the seat has reached a plateau which is insufficient to deliver victory.

The Nationalists have enjoyed historic support in this constituency, which is evident in a clutch of good council election results in Cumbernauld in particular. Indeed, the SNP controlled Cumbernauld and Kilsyth District Council from 1974 until 1982 and also gained success there in the later 1980s. Had this constituency been around in the 1970s, it would have been an SNP gain. Indeed, the Nationalists' Margaret Ewing (then Bain) was able to win Dunbartonshire East back in 1974 because of the presence of Cumbernauld in the constituency. In those days, this seat was classic SNP territory, with young, confident, upwardly mobile voters in skilled occupations, who were SNP supporters in the mid-1970s. However, this particular segment of the electorate appears to have drifted away from the Nationalists since that period leaving them with very disappointing results in this area in the 1980s.

Also, despite the SNP's former local successes in the constituency, the Nationalists have not performed as well in the town following local government reorganisation in 1995 and support for the party has slipped back to make success a much more distant prospect. Labour has comfortably held the seat at every general election since the establishment of the constituency. Apart from the SNP, no other party has a significant vote in the constituency and it can be expected that support for the Nationalists will increase at the next general election but still leave Labour with a healthy majority. For example, even at a bad election in 1999, Labour was able to triumph with close to 50 per cent of the vote and a majority of 4,259. This situation is likely to continue.

MP Rosemary McKenna was born in 1941 in Kilmacolm. She was educated at St Augustine's Secondary School, Glasgow and St Andrew's College, Bearsden and worked as a primary school teacher before her election in 1997. She was a councillor in the constituency for many years, from 1984 until 1996, and also leader from 1984 to 1988, Provost from 1988 until 1992 and COSLA President from 1994 until 1996. She was also a board member of Scottish Enterprise from 1993 until 1996, Chair of Scotland Europa from 1994 until 1996 and a representative on the Committee of the Regions from 1993 until 1997. At Westminster, she was a member of a variety of committees including Scottish Affairs from 1997 to 1998, European Scrutiny from 1998 to 1999 and Statutory Instruments from 1997 to 1999. She is currently Parliamentary Private Secretary to the Ministers of State at the Foreign Office. She was also a founding member of Scottish Labour Forum, the Blairite organisation which was responsible for defeating leading left-wingers on Scottish Labour's Executive in 1997. She was Chair of Labour's selection panel process for the Scottish Parliament, which was criticised for excluding left-wingers and elements of the nationalist wing. Labour's candidates were quickly dubbed 'Rosemary's babies', and McKenna faced criticism for the inclusion of her own daughter on the list, even though she had not taken part in the process.

MSP Cathie Craigie was born in Stirling in 1954 and was educated at Kilsyth Academy. She was a councillor in Cumbernauld from 1984 until 1996 and became leader of the council from 1994 to 1996, as well as chairing the Equal Opportunities, Planning, Housing, Policy and Resources Committees. She subsequently served on North Lanarkshire Council from 1995 until 1999 and became chair of Environmental Services and acted as one of the council's representatives on COSLA. In the Scottish Parliament, she sat on the Audit and Social Inclusion Committees from May 1999 to December 2000, before becoming a member of the Social Justice Committee. She is also a member of the Cross Party Groups for Animal Welfare, Drug Misuse, Epilepsy, Older People, Age and Aging, and Palliative Care.

CUNNINGHAME NORTH

Predecessor Constituencies: Ayrshire North and Bute (1945–79).

1999

Electorate: 55,867
Turnout: 33,491 (59.95%)

Candidate	Party	Votes	Votes%	Change%
Allan Wilson	Labour	14,369	42.90	-7.40
Kay Ullrich	SNP	9,573	28.58	+10.14
Mike Johnston	Conservative	6,649	19.85	-3.61
Calum Irving	Liberal Democrat	2,900	8.66	+3.14

Labour majority: 4,796 (14.32%)
Swing: 8.77% Labour to SNP

1997

Electorate: 55,526
Turnout: 41,129 (74.07%)

Candidate	Party	Votes	Votes%	Change%
Brian Wilson	Labour	20,686	50.30	+9.33
Margaret Mitchell	Conservative	9,647	23.46	-10.66
Kim Nicholl	SNP	7,584	18.44	+0.21
Karen Freel	Liberal Democrat	2,271	5.52	-1.16
Louise McDaid	Socialist Labour	501	1.22	–
Ian Winton	Referendum	440	1.07	–

Labour majority: 11,039 (26.84%)
Swing: 10.00% Conservative to Labour

1945–92

	Lab%	Con%	SNP%	Lib%	Other%	Turnout%
1992	41.0	34.1	18.2	6.7	–	78.2
1987	44.4	34.0	9.5	12.1	–	78.2
1983	34.6	38.7	8.6	18.1	–	75.7
1979	34.4	45.7	13.9	6.0	–	75.9
1974O	28.9	38.9	25.9	6.3	–	71.3
1974F	27.8	45.7	16.3	10.2	–	77.0

	Lab%	Con%	SNP%	Lib%	Other%	Turnout%
1970	35.4	53.6	11.0	–	–	73.6
1966	40.7	48.6	–	10.7	–	76.0
1964	36.1	49.8	–	14.1	–	74.6
1959	37.6	62.4	–	–	–	73.4
1955	35.5	64.5	–	–	–	71.5
1951	35.8	64.2	–	–	–	77.3
1950	35.7	64.3	–	–	–	79.1
1945	47.0	53.0	–	–	–	68.5

Cunninghame North combines a mixture of seaside resorts and islands in the Firth of Clyde, one of the most picturesque parts of Scotland. The seaside towns, including Largs, Ardrossan and Saltcoats, were once some of the primary destinations of the Glasgow working class on holiday. Largs has managed to reinvent itself enough to prosper; others, such as Ardrossan and Saltcoats, are in economic decline and face uncertain futures. The islands of Arran and Great and Little Cumbrae are in the seat, the former, with its main town Brodick, a prosperous tourist location. Further inland, old mining towns such as Beith, Dalry and Kilbirnie are to be found. Cunninghame North was not changed in the 1997 boundary redistribution, having been created in the previous 1983 round from Ayrshire North and Bute. To this day, Cunninghame North still has deep pockets of Conservative voting, and was until recently, as Ayrshire North and Bute, a safe Tory seat. It elected Conservatives for the whole inter-war period from 1918 onwards. In 1945, Charles MacAndrew's majority over Labour was cut to 2,443, but thereafter expanded dramatically. The legendary Fitzroy Maclean was MP for the area from 1959 until February 1974. He had previously been commander of the British military mission working with Tito's Communist partisans in Yugoslavia during the Second World War.

John Corrie became MP from February 1974 onward and won the seat in its first incarnation as Cunninghame North in 1983 with a majority of 1,639 over Labour. The year of 1987 was Scottish Labour's year of advance as it won several middle-class Conservative seats such as Glasgow Hillhead, Edinburgh South and Strathkelvin and Bearsden. Brian Wilson, Labour's candidate, seized the seat with a majority of 4,422 over the Conservatives, increasing Labour's vote by 5,000, as the Conservatives' fell by 1,000. The 1992 election was a year of relative Tory success in Scotland and Wilson saw his majority fall to 2,939 and Labour's vote by 1,500. Wilson was re-elected in 1997 with a sizeable 11,039 lead over the Conservatives, increasing his vote by 3,000, while the Conservatives' declined by 4,000. Two years later in the Scottish Parliament elections Labour's vote fell by 6,000 as the SNP's Kay Ullrich increased her vote by 2,000 and by 10% to establish the SNP in second place. The Conservatives continued their recent marked decline, losing another 3,000 votes, and slipped into third place in a seat they held until 1987.

Cunninghame North is a new type of Labour seat in Scotland, rather than a New Labour seat. It is a product of the party's ability to win middle-class and working-class support in the 1980s, long before UK Labour learnt how to do it. Labour's hold on this seat may be challenged at some point in the future, but will depend on the changing fortunes of the opposition parties. The Conservatives have fallen from 39 per cent in 1983 to under 20 per cent in 1999, with the SNP rising from 9 per cent to 29 per cent over the same period. Whether they can mount a serious challenge in the years to come remains to be seen.

MP Brian Wilson was born in 1948 in Dunoon and elected Labour MP for Cunninghame North from 1987. Educated at Dunoon Grammar School, Dundee University and the University College, Cardiff, Wilson was the founding editor and publisher of the *West Highland Free Press* which has gained near-mythological status in certain circles, managing to survive commercially, while pursuing an anti-landlord, radical line. He had previously stood for Labour unsuccessfully in three Highlands seats, in Ross and Cromarty in October 1974, Inverness in 1979 and the Western Isles in 1983. Wilson was frontbench spokesman on Scottish Affairs from 1988 until 1992, on Transport from 1992 to 1994, on Trade and Industry from 1994 to 1995 and again on Transport between 1995 and 1996. He was Minister of State for Scotland from 1997 to 1998, was at the Department of Trade and Industry from 1998 to 1999, and back as Minister of State for Scotland from 1999 to the beginning of 2001. Wilson was passionate in his anti-devolution views in the 1970s and his loathing for the SNP and Scottish nationalism. He was an active supporter of 'Labour Says No' in the 1979 referendum, and many feel his conversion to devolution was skin-deep and not genuine. However, his near-hatred of the SNP has if anything increased. He was responsible for the immortal phrase 'nationalist shibbeloth' in relation to Calton Hill, site of the Royal High School, which was once to house the Parliament. Wilson has been part of many TV scraps, more often than not putting the boot into the SNP, rather than the Tories. One of his most recent was in February 2000 on the BBC *Newsnight Scotland* opt-out, when Wilson blew up at an item on the role of Westminster MPs, alleging that a separate Scottish Six news would lead to the break-up of Britain. When John Reid shifted from the Scotland Office to Northern Ireland in January 2001 after Mandleson's second resignation, Brian Wilson was Downing Street's first choice for the post of Secretary of State for Scotland. However, Wilson's move northwards was blocked by Henry McLeish and he was instead appointed Minister of State at the Foreign Office.

MSP Allan Wilson was born in 1954 in Glasgow and educated at Spiers School, Beith. A Trainee Officer for the NUPE from 1972 until 1975, an Area Officer from 1975 until 1993 and a Senior Regional Officer with UNISON from 1993 to 1994, he became Head of Higher Education (Scotland) with UNISON from 1994 until 1999. He has also been a member of the Independent Review of Pay and Conditions in

Higher Education Institutions in Scotland. Previously Brian Wilson's election agent, upon his election to the Scottish Parliament he became a member of the European Committee and the Enterprise and Lifelong Learning Committee from 1999 to 2000. He was also a member of the Cross Party Group on Sport. In Henry McLeish's ministerial reshuffle, Wilson was given the post of Deputy Minister for Sport and Culture, with responsibility for arts, culture, sports, the built heritage, architecture, Historic Scotland and lottery funding. This was widely seen as a politically astute appointment, reinforcing Labour's links with its traditional trade union support.

CUNNINGHAME SOUTH

Predecessor Constituencies: Ayrshire Central (1950–79).

1999

Electorate: 50,443
Turnout: 28,277 (56.06%)

Candidate	Party	Votes	Votes%	Change%
Irene Oldfather	Labour	14,936	52.82	-9.91
Michael Russell	SNP	8,395	29.69	+8.91
Murray Tosh	Conservative	3,229	11.42	+1.34
Stuart Ritchie	Liberal Democrat	1,717	6.07	+1.54

Labour majority: 6,541 (23.13%)
Swing: 9.41% Labour to SNP

1997

Electorate: 49,543
Turnout: 35,444 (71.54%)

Candidate	Party	Votes	Votes%	Change%
Brian Donohoe	Labour	22,233	62.73	+9.80
Margaret Burgess	SNP	7,364	20.78	-3.44
Pamela Paterson	Conservative	3,571	10.08	-6.24
Erlend Watson	Liberal Democrat	1,604	4.53	-1.65
Krishna Edwin	Socialist Labour	494	1.39	–
Allan Martlew	Referendum	178	0.50	–

Labour majority: 14,869 (41.95%)
Swing: 6.62% SNP to Labour

1950–92

	Lab%	Con%	SNP%	Lib%	Other%	Turnout%
1992	52.9	16.3	24.2	6.2	0.3	75.9
1987	60.8	16.3	11.0	11.8	–	74.9
1983	54.1	21.2	6.9	17.8	–	73.3
1979	51.2	29.3	10.4	9.1	–	79.8
1974O	45.1	24.8	24.5	5.6	–	79.3
1974F	49.0	35.9	15.1	–	–	82.0

	Lab%	Con%	SNP%	Lib%	Other%	Turnout%
1970	52.4	41.8	5.1	–	0.7	80.7
1966	57.7	42.3	–	–	–	82.1
1964	56.4	43.6	–	–	–	84.2
1959	52.0	48.0	–	–	–	86.7
1955	49.8	50.2	–	–	–	83.3
1951	52.1	47.9	–	–	–	86.3
1950	49.0	43.8	–	7.2	–	85.6

Cunninghame South is situated on the Firth of Clyde. Its principal town is Irvine – one of Scotland's five post-war New Towns. The other main centres, Kilwinning and Stevenson, are working-class towns, which, like Irvine, have a solid Labour vote and little truck with other parties, whether the SNP, Lib Dems or Tories.

As Ayrshire Central, the seat was a wafer-thin marginal. Archie Manuel won it for Labour in 1950 when it was first created, by 1,962 votes, and in 1951 by 1,693 votes over the Conservatives. The Tories took the seat at their Scottish high point of 1955 with Douglas Nairn winning 50.2 per cent of the vote; Manuel rewon it for Labour in 1959 and held it until 1970 when David Lambie was returned. Even at the SNP's zenith of October 1974, Lambie enjoyed a 9,555 majority over the Conservatives with the SNP just behind them; by 1987, the last time Lambie stood, his majority had rocketed to 16,633 over the Conservatives.

In 1992 Brian Donohoe was returned as the Labour MP with his majority cut to 10,680 as the SNP's Ricky Bell more than doubled the SNP vote putting on 5,000 votes and rising from fourth to second. There was no such excitement in 1997 as Donohoe increased Labour's vote by 2,500, while the SNP's vote fell by the same amount resulting in a Labour majority of 14,869. In 1999, Irene Oldfather saw Labour's support decline by over 7,000, while Mike Russell for the SNP increased his support by 1,000 to leave Labour with a 6,541 majority. Cunninghame South is the sort of seat Scottish Labour depends on for steadfast support, which should continue for the foreseeable future.

MP Brian Donohoe was born in 1948 in Kilmarnock and first elected MP for Cunninghame South in 1992. Educated at Irvine Royal Academy and Kilmarnock Technical College, he worked at Ailsa Shipbuilding in Troon as an apprenticeship fitter-turner from 1965 until 1970, was a contract draughtsman at ICI from 1977 to 1981 and was a NALGO full-time union official from 1981 until 1992. He was previously Convenor of the Scottish Political and Education Committee of TASS from 1973 until 1979, Secretary of Irvine and District Trades Council from 1973 to 1978 and Chair of North Ayrshire and Arran Local Health Council in 1977.

Donohoe was a member of the Transport Select Committee from 1993 until 1997 and is seen as a party loyalist and active constituency MP who works hard for constituents and has a resulting high profile in the local press. Donohoe and Oldfather have a very amicable understanding for dealing with constituency enquiries, Donohoe dealing directly with constituency enquiries on devolved matters that come to him.

MSP Irene Oldfather was born in Glasgow in 1954 and educated at Irvine Royal Academy, the University of Strathclyde and University of Arizona. She was a Dumbarton Council on Alcohol researcher from 1976 until 1977, a University of Arizona lecturer from 1977 to 1978, a Glasgow City Council researcher from 1980 to 1990, a Paisley University lecturer from 1996 until 1998, a freelance journalist on European issues from 1994 until 1998 and political researcher to Alex Smith MEP from 1990 until 1997.

Elected to North Ayrshire Council from 1995 until 1999, she was Vice-Chair of the Education Committee and Chair of the COSLA Task Group on EMU, Vice-Chair of the West of Scotland European Consortium and a member of the European Committee of the Regions. Oldfather is a member of the European Committee and was a member of the Health and Community Care Committee of the Parliament until the end of 2000. She is also a member of the Cross Party Groups on Animal Welfare and Tobacco Control, of which she is Vice-Convenor.

DUMBARTON

Predecessor Constituencies: Dunbartonshire (1945) and Dunbartonshire West (1950–79).

1999

Electorate: 56,090
Turnout: 34,699 (61.86%)

Candidate	Party	Votes	Votes%	Change%
Jackie Baillie	Labour	15,181	43.75	-5.86
Lloyd Quinan	SNP	10,423	30.04	+6.81
Donald Reece	Conservative	5,060	14.58	-3.07
Paul Coleshill	Liberal Democrat	4,035	11.63	+4.01

Labour majority: 4,758 (13.71%)
Swing: 6.33% Labour to SNP

1997

Electorate: 56,229
Turnout: 41,264 (73.39%)

Candidate	Party	Votes	Votes%	Change%
John McFall	Labour	20,470	49.61	+5.97
Bill Mackechnie	SNP	9,587	23.23	+4.81
Peter Ramsay	Conservative	7,283	17.65	-12.10
Alan Reid	Liberal Democrat	3,144	7.62	-0.14
Les Robertson	SSA	283	0.69	—
George Dempster	Referendum	255	0.62	—
Derek Lancaster	UK Independence	242	0.59	—

Labour majority: 10,883 (26.38%)
Swing: 0.58% SNP to Labour

1945–92

	Lab%	Con%	SNP%	Lib%	Other%	Turnout%
1992	43.6	29.7	18.4	7.8	0.4	77.1
1987	43.0	31.7	12.1	13.2	—	78.2
1983	36.7	31.8	8.7	22.8	—	75.0
1979	48.4	33.7	17.9	—	—	80.2

	Lab%	Con%	SNP%	Lib%	Other%	Turnout%
1974O	38.1	23.2	33.7	5.0	–	78.3
1974F	39.6	33.2	27.2	–	–	79.6
1970	50.9	37.1	12.0	–	–	78.0
1966	52.3	33.1	14.6	–	–	81.9
1964	50.8	37.2	12.0	–	–	82.1
1959	52.5	47.5	–	–	–	83.7
1955	52.3	47.7	–	–	–	84.8
1951	51.3	45.4	–	3.3	–	86.6
1950B	50.4	49.6	–	–	–	83.4
1950	49.3	47.8	–	–	2.9	85.5
1945	50.7	49.3	–	–	–	71.7

Dumbarton is situated on the north side of the Clyde positioned in between the rural landscapes of Argyll and Bute and the urban and suburban mix of Clydebank and Milngavie. Dumbarton is the largest town in the constituency; other communities include Helensburgh, one of the most prosperous towns in all of Scotland, and the Vale of Leven, which includes the small towns of Alexandria and Renton. This last area was one of the legendary 'Little Moscows' of the 1920s and 1930s where Communists working in co-operation with Labour ran the local council; other 'Little Moscows' included West Fife and the Rhondda Valley.

Dumbarton was first won by Labour in 1923 and has leaned to Labour ever since, but not always by convincing margins. In 1945, the Labour candidate Adam McKinlay defeated the Conservatives by a slender 747 votes. As Dunbartonshire West, Labour held the seat in 1950 by 613, which narrowed in a 1950 by-election caused by McKinlay's death to a mere 293 which saw Tom Steele elected, who remained MP until 1970. Iain Campbell succeeded Steele as Labour MP in 1970 and in October 1974 his majority was reduced to 1,814 over the SNP, before increasing to 6,457 over the Conservatives in 1979. In 1983, a strong challenge from the Conservative Iain Lawson cut Labour's majority to 2,115. Even in 1987, Scottish Labour's moment of glory, while John McFall increased his majority over the Conservatives to 5,222, the swing to Labour was well below the national average. However, McFall marginally increased his majority over the Conservatives in 1992 to 6,129. Up until 1997, the Conservatives had polled respectably in Dumbarton, unusual for a Labour seat they had not won in post-war times; all through the Tory years post-1979 they polled at least 30% with only a slight decline. This all changed in 1997, as McFall increased Labour's majority to 10,883 and the SNP moved into second place for the first time since 1974. The Conservative vote fell by nearly 6,000 and they dropped to third place.

The Scottish Parliament election produced a Labour majority over the SNP of 4,758. Labour's vote declined by 5,000 on a reduced turnout, while Lloyd Quinan increased his vote by 1,000, and the Conservatives lost another 2,000 votes. Dumbarton has never been an entirely safe or typical Labour seat, but in the shift of opposition politics from Tory to SNP, Labour has increased its hold on the seat. Twenty years ago, the Tories polled 34 per cent here, today they get 15 per cent; in 1983, the SNP got 9 per cent and now they poll 30 per cent, but Labour should be able to hold on easily in future UK and Scottish elections.

MP John McFall was born in 1944 in Glasgow and has been Labour MP for Dumbarton since 1987. Educated at St Patrick's Secondary, Dumbarton, Paisley College of Technology, Strathclyde University and the Open University, he was previously a chemistry teacher and assistant head in Glasgow at Belarmine Secondary. After his arrival at the House of Commons, McFall became a member of the Defence Select Committee from 1990 until 1992 and the Commons Information Committee from 1990 until 1997, as well as being a Labour Whip from 1989 to 1991 and Labour spokesperson in 1992. After the 1997 election, he became a Scottish Whip from 1997 to 1998 and then Parliamentary Under-Secretary of State for Northern Ireland from 1998. A pragmatic centre-left politician, McFall has shown the ability to combine old Labour sensibilities with an awareness of new Labour priorities; he has in his past, like most of the party, been much more left-wing than he is now. McFall was at one time a CND supporter and advocate of unilateralism, and took a particular interest in the presence of Faslane nuclear base in his constituency.

MSP Jackie Baillie was born in 1964 in Hong Kong and was educated at St Anne's School, Windermere and Glasgow University where she is currently studying for a post-graduate degree in local economic development. Baillie worked in Ruchill Unemployed Workers' Centre from 1986 to 1987, before becoming Co-ordinator of Gorbals Unemployed Workers' Centre from 1987 until 1990. She then became Resource Centre Manager with Strathkelvin District Council from 1990 until 1996 and Community Development Manager, East Dunbartonshire Council, 1996 until 1999.

Baillie was Chair of the Scottish Labour Party from 1997 to 1998 and has been a member of the Scottish Labour National Executive. In the 1999 elections, she was campaign spokesperson on Social Inclusion, and after the elections was appointed as Deputy Minister for Social Inclusion, Equality and the Voluntary Sector. She was widely seen as having an impressive first year as Wendy Alexander's Deputy and was tipped by many commentators for higher things, so it was no surprise that Henry McLeish promoted her to the renamed post of Minister for Social Justice in his ministerial reshuffle upon becoming First Minister in October 2000. Baillie will be covering the areas Alexander and she previously held under the Communities portfolio with the exception of local government which was moved to Finance. Baillie's responsibilities include social inclusion, housing, equality issues and the voluntary sector. She will have to deal with forthcoming controversies such as the housing stock transfer of council houses, which alienates many of Labour's traditional supporters, and the issue of extending the right to buy to housing associations of tenants.

DUMFRIES

Predecessor Constituencies: Dumfriesshire (1945–70).

1999

Electorate: 63,162
Turnout: 38,482 (60.93%)

Candidate	Party	Votes	Votes%	Change%
Elaine Murray	Labour	14,101	36.64	-10.87
David Mundell	Conservative	10,447	27.15	-0.89
Stephen Norris	SNP	7,625	19.81	+7.74
Neil Wallace	Liberal Democrat	6,309	16.39	+5.31

Labour majority: 3,654 (9.49%)
Swing: 4.99% Labour to Conservative

1997

Electorate: 62,759
Turnout: 49,527 (78.92%)

Candidate	Party	Votes	Votes%	Change%
Russell Brown	Labour	23,528	47.51	+17.91
Struan Stevenson	Conservative	13,885	28.04	-15.06
Robert Higgins	SNP	5,977	12.07	-2.72
Neil Wallace	Liberal Democrat	5,487	11.08	-0.60
David Parker	Referendum	533	1.08	–
Liz Hunter	NLP	117	0.24	–

Labour majority: 9,643 (19.47%)
Swing: 16.49% Conservative to Labour

1945–92

	Lab%	Con%	SNP%	Lib%	Other%	Turnout%
1992	30.0	43.1	14.3	11.8	0.9	80.0
1987	25.2	41.8	14.2	18.0	0.8	75.6
1983	20.8	44.5	10.8	23.9	–	73.0
1979	27.3	45.2	13.2	14.3	–	78.1
1974O	26.5	38.8	26.4	8.3	–	76.7
1974F	25.9	44.1	18.6	11.4	–	80.4

	Lab%	Con%	SNP%	Lib%	Other%	Turnout%
1970	33.5	53.1	13.4	–	–	76.2
1966	35.9	45.6	12.6	5.9	–	80.2
1964	39.1	48.7	12.2	–	–	81.6
1963B	38.5	40.9	9.7	10.9	–	71.6
1959	41.6	58.4	–	–	–	77.4
1955	38.7	61.3	–	–	–	73.7
1951	38.7	61.3	–	–	–	80.2
1950	40.7	59.3	–	–	–	78.6
1945	16.9	47.4	–	16.9	–	72.2

Dumfries is situated between Galloway and Upper Nithsdale to the west with the two Borders seats to its east and Carlisle and England to the south. The largest town in the seat is Dumfries itself but there are also smaller towns such as Annan and Annandale and many noteworthy towns such as Ecclefechan, birthplace of historian Thomas Carlyle, Gretna Green, site of many elicit and runaway marriages, and Lockerbie, known worldwide for Pan Am flight 103 which was blown up above the town in December 1988, killing local residents as well as those on board.

The seat has had a long and proud Conservative history. Major Murray won it comfortably in 1918 and Niall Macpherson easily held it for the National Liberals in 1945 with a 4,077 majority over Labour. He remained MP until 1963 when David Anderson held the seat for the Conservatives in a by-election with 40.9 per cent to Labour's 38.5 per cent. In the subsequent general election in 1964 Hector Munro was elected and remained MP until 1997. Even in October 1974, Munro held Dumfries without much difficulty gaining a 5,828 majority over Labour with the SNP just behind them. In 1979 Munro increased his majority to 9,004 over Labour and held the seat with slightly reduced majorities in 1983 and 1987. In 1992, the last time Munro stood and was elected, he retained the seat with a 6,415 lead, while Labour's Peter Rennie increased Labour's vote by 4.8 per cent, achieving a swing to Labour against the Scottish trend.

At the 1997 election Munro made way for Struan Stevenson, defending the second safest Conservative seat in Scotland (Eastwood being the safest), with a notional majority now of 6,766 over Labour. Stevenson presided over a collapse in the Conservative vote of over 7,000 votes (a decline of 15 per cent) as Labour's Russell Brown increased his vote by an impressive 9,000 and 18 per cent: this represented a swing to Labour of 16.5 per cent, over twice the Scottish average, and resulted in Labour achieving a majority of 9,643 over the Conservatives.

The 1997 result was an exceptional one for Labour; Russell's majority was the largest Labour won in any of the Conservative seats it gained in Scotland. It was to prove no aberration, as Labour held the seat in 1999 with its vote falling 9,000 back to its 1992 levels and the Tory vote falling back a further 3,000. This represented a significant 5 per cent swing from Labour to Conservatives and a Labour majority of 3,654. Unless the Conservatives remain permanently in the doldrums in Scotland, there must be hope for them in Dumfries. One would imagine that with Labour in power at Westminster and Holyrood, the Conservatives at some point have a chance of retaking Dumfries and Labour's hold will prove to be temporary. That has been said before about ex-Conservative seats in Scotland, but in this case it should be true.

MP Russell Brown was born in Arran in 1951 and won Dumfries for Labour in 1997. Educated at Annan Academy, he worked as a production supervisor in ICI Explosives, Dumfries, from 1974 to 1992 and as a plant operative in ICI Films from 1992 to 1997. He was elected to Dumfries and Galloway Regional Council from 1986 to 1996 and was Chair of Dumfries and Galloway Public Protection Committee from 1990 to 1994, and also served on Annandale and Eskdale District Council from 1988 until 1996. In 1995 he was elected to Dumfries and Galloway Council and sat on it until 1999. Elected to the House of Commons in 1997, he was one of the few of that year's intake in Blair's PLP to come from a genuine working-class background.

MSP Elaine Murray was born in 1954 in Hitchin, Hertfordshire, and educated at Edinburgh University and Cambridge University with a PhD in Physical Chemistry. She worked as a Research Fellow at the Cavendish Laboratory from 1979 until 1981, before becoming a Research Fellow at the Royal Free Hospital, London, from 1981 until 1984, then Senior Research Officer, Institute of Food Research, Reading, from 1984 to 1987, Assistant to Alex Smith MEP from 1990 to 1993 and Assistant Lecturer with the Open University in 1992.

Murray was elected to Strathclyde Regional Council from 1994 until 1996 and South Ayrshire Council from 1995 until 1999 and was Convenor of the Educational Services Committee and Chair of the Women's Advisory Committee. She was also COSLA Spokesperson on Cultural Issues from 1996 to 1999. She was a member of the Enterprise and Lifelong Learning Committee and Rural Affairs Committee of the Parliament from 1999 to December 2000 and is now a member of the Rural Development Committee. Murray is also a member of the Cross Party Groups on Animal Welfare, Borders Rail, Children, Drug Misuse, Information, Knowledge and Enlightenment, Older People, Media, Agriculture and Horticulture, of which she is Joint Convenor, and Renewable Energy.

DUNDEE EAST

Predecessor Constituencies: none.

1999

Electorate: 57,222
Turnout: 31,663 (55.33%)

Candidate	Party	Votes	Votes%	Change%
John McAllion	Labour	13,703	43.28	-7.84
Shona Robison	SNP	10,849	34.26	+7.72
Iain Mitchell	Conservative	4,428	13.98	-1.80
Raymond Lawrie	Liberal Democrat	2,153	6.80	+2.66
Harvey Duke	SSP	530	1.67	+1.33

Labour majority: 2,854 (9.02%)
Swing: 7.78% Labour to SNP

1997

Electorate: 58,388
Turnout: 40,528 (69.41%)

Candidate	Party	Votes	Votes%	Change%
John McAllion	Labour	20,718	51.12	+6.67
Shona Robison	SNP	10,757	26.54	-5.54
Bruce Mackie	Conservative	6,397	15.78	-2.26
Gurudeo Saluja	Liberal Democrat	1,677	4.14	-0.17
Edward Galloway	Referendum	601	1.48	—
Harvey Duke	SSA	232	0.57	—
Elizabeth MacKenzie	NLP	146	0.36	—

Labour majority: 9,961 (24.58%)
Swing: 6.16% SNP to Labour

1950–92

	Lab%	Con%	SNP%	Lib%	Other%	Turnout%
1992	44.1	17.8	33.4	4.1	0.7	72.1
1987	42.3	12.9	40.2	4.6	—	75.9
1983	33.0	15.5	43.8	7.7	—	73.7
1979	36.0	18.2	41.0	4.6	—	77.7

	Lab%	Con%	SNP%	Lib%	Other%	Turnout%
1974O	32.7	16.8	47.7	2.8	–	73.4
1974F	33.7	26.4	39.5	–	0.4	81.1
1973B	32.7	25.2	30.2	8.3	3.6	70.0
1970	48.3	42.4	8.9	–	0.4	76.1
1966	56.3	43.7	–	–	–	78.8
1964	54.8	45.2	–	–	–	80.0
1959	54.3	45.7	–	–	–	82.6
1955	54.3	45.7	–	–	–	82.3
1952B	56.3	35.6	7.4	–	0.7	71.5
1951	53.8	46.2	–	–	–	87.2
1950	53.4	44.4	–	–	2.2	88.6

Dundee has a long tradition of radicalism and causing upsets which challenge political orthodoxies. Dundee was the first Scottish city to elect a Labour representative when Alexander Wilkie won in 1906 and sat for the city until 1922. At this point, Dundee, a two-member seat was known as 'Juteopolis' due to the dominance of the jute and textile industries in the city's employment. The city was called 'a woman's town' because of the high rate of women working in the industries, while men were known as 'kettle boilers': a dynamic which has influenced gender relations, if not politics in the city since.

The character of Edwin Scrymgeour contributed much to the city's politics in the early 20th century. He set up the Scottish Prohibition Party in 1904 and his mixture of ILP-style socialism, temperance and independence allowed him to attract Labour, Liberal and Conservative votes. In 1922, Scrymgeour was elected to Parliament, along with Edmund Dene Morel, the anti-war campaigner, decisively defeating Winston Churchill, who had been Liberal MP for the city since 1908 and served in the Asquith and Lloyd George governments. T. E. Lawrence commented to Churchill on his defeat, 'What bloody shits the Dundeans (sic) must be', to which he replied, given the life 'the Dundee folk have to live', they have 'many excuses'. Scrymgeour was MP from 1922-31, falling in the National Government landslide of that year; Thomas Johnston, later to be Secretary of State for Scotland from 1941-45, was also briefly a Dundee MP from winning a by-election in 1924 until 1929.

Dundee remained a two member seat until 1950. Dundee East returned Thomas Cook as its first Labour MP from 1950-52, who had previously been MP for Dundee from 1945-50. He was followed by George Thomson from 1952 to 1973, who went off to become a European Commissioner, then was anointed Lord Thomson and defected to the SDP.

Dundee East contains the eastern parts of the city out to the coastal town and

Dundee suburb of Broughty Ferry. The Ferry is the most prominent middle-class area in a constituency which is strongly working class, with large council schemes in Douglas, Fintry and Whitfield. Male unemployment was running at 11.2 per cent in June 2000, which was the sixth highest in Scotland. Since the 1970s this seat has been a Labour-SNP marginal and the SNP has done well in the city ever since. Former SNP leader Gordon Wilson nearly unseated Labour at a by-election in 1973 reduced Labour's majority to 1,141 and went on to win the seat in February 1974 with a majority of 2,966 over Labour and 6,983 in October 1974, succeeding in holding it against the anti-SNP swing in 1979 with a majority of 2,519. This latter result was partly a product of the controversy caused by the Labour candidate, Jimmy Reid, who had in the previous year defected from the Communists, and whose selection as Labour candidate had resulted in opposition on the NEC from Shirley Williams and others. Wilson held on to the seat until he was narrowly defeated by the present incumbent, John McAllion. Wilson's 1983 majority of 5,016 was overturned in 1987 to provide McAllion with a narrow 1,015 lead, which Labour built on in subsequent elections to turn a marginal into a safe Labour seat at the 1992 and 1997 elections. The 1999 result was much closer and gave the appearance of turning Dundee East back into a Labour-SNP marginal, though it was in the special circumstances of a Scottish rather than a Westminster election.

McAllion is retiring from Westminster at the next general election to concentrate on his role within the Scottish Parliament, which might encourage the SNP. The Nationalists' candidate at the last two elections, Shona Robison, is now a list MSP for the North East, so will not contest the seat at Westminster. Her replacement as candidate is Stewart Hosie, the SNP National Secretary, who contested Kirkcaldy at the Scottish election. Clearly the SNP has work to do in Dundee East to recover support. Its performance in 1997 was its worst in the seat since 1970, as a result of the Labour landslide, and the 1999 result was only slightly better than the result from 1992 in terms of votes, though much better in percentage terms. The 1999 election left the Nationalists only 2,854 votes behind Labour, but that was largely attributable to a low turnout amongst Labour voters. Moreover, the SNP's numerical vote was around 8,000 less than the amount Gordon Wilson lost with in 1987, votes which the Nationalists have not recovered.

However, the SNP also did well in Dundee at the 1999 local council elections, at which they polled more than Labour in Dundee and deprived Labour of control of the council. The Nationalists were also extremely close to overturning Labour in a number of wards in the city. The SNP's performance was especially good in heavily working-class areas, retaining Whitfield comfortably and losing in Douglas by only 17 votes. Of course, the great irony about Dundee East is that it has to some extent- been eclipsed by Dundee West as an SNP prospect. Dundee East was always an SNP target, West was never a target. But the Scottish election of 1999 made West a very tight marginal, whilst Labour held East with a reasonable majority given the seat's history. Both Dundee seats are now high on the SNP's list of Westminster targets, with East's SNP tradition making it the more likely Nationalist gain though Labour should hold on if its national support remains high at the Westminster election. Labour has selected local councillor Iain Luke to contest the seat at Westminster.

MP/MSP John McAllion was born in Glasgow in 1948 and educated at St Augustine's Secondary School, Glasgow, St Andrews University and Dundee College of Education. He was a teacher from 1973 until 1982 in Dundee, at St Saviour's High and Balgowan School, and worked as a research assistant for Bob McTaggart from 1982 until 1986. He was elected to Tayside Regional Council in 1984 and rose rapidly to become council leader in 1986. This position gave him the political profile in Dundee to win the seat from the SNP in 1987. He has a reputation as a maverick of sorts within Labour, and a member of its nationalist tendency. He was a member of 'Scotland United' and resigned as one of Labour's Scottish Affairs spokespersons in 1996 following Tony Blair's decision to hold a pre-legislative referendum on Scottish devolution commenting: 'This decision has been imposed on the Scottish party without consultation.'

In the run-up to the Scottish Parliament elections, as the most prominent member of the Campaign for Socialism he was widely seen as the leader of Labour's left and as a potential left-wing Deputy Leader of the Labour Group as opposed to the leadership candidate, Henry McLeish. The position did not materialise, partly because party managers must have been unsure about whether they could stop him. McAllion was Labour Spokesperson on the New Deal and Youth during the election campaign for the Scottish Parliament, and was one of only two spokespeople not offered a ministerial post after the election, the other being his fellow left-winger and Dundee MSP Kate MacLean. Instead, he was given the Convenorship of the Petitions Committee, a relatively junior post for someone who until the previous year had been a prominent player in Scottish Labour's Westminster team.

He has had a difficult first year and a half in the Parliament – marginalised, excluded and unsure of what role to play, particularly given the lack of formal factions in the Labour Group. At Westminster he was a member of the Select Committee on Energy in 1992 and the Scottish Affairs Committee from 1997 to 1998. Within the Scottish Parliament he is Convenor of the Public Petitions Committee and was a member of the Social Inclusion, Housing and Voluntary Sector Committee from May 1999 to December 2000, when he became a member of the Health and Community Care Committee. He sits on the Cross Party Groups for Strategic Rail Services, Men's Violence Against Women, Renewable Energy and Sports.

After the death of Donald Dewar in October 2000 and the election of Henry McLeish as Labour leader and First Minister, McAllion had been thought likely to stand against McLeish for the full electoral college contest in December 2000. However, this did not happen, partly because of a wish by Labour to unite around

McLeish and because McAllion must have calculated that it would have proved counter-productive to stand, resulting in a derisory vote that would have marginalised even more the Labour left.

DUNDEE WEST

Predecessor Constituencies: none.

1999

Electorate: 55,725
Turnout: 29,082 (52.19%)

Candidate	Party	Votes	Votes%	Change%
Kate MacLean	Labour	10,925	37.57	-16.22
Calum Cashley	SNP	10,804	37.15	+13.92
Gordon Buchan	Conservative	3,345	11.50	-1.65
Elizabeth Dick	Liberal Democrat	2,998	10.31	+2.65
James McFarlane	SSP	1,010	3.47	+2.37

Labour majority: 121 (0.42%)
Swing: 15.07% Labour to SNP

1997

Electorate: 57,346
Turnout: 38,807 (67.67%)

Candidate	Party	Votes	Votes%	Change%
Ernie Ross	Labour	20,875	53.79	+6.13
John Dorward	SNP	9,016	23.23	-1.32
Neil Powrie	Conservative	5,105	13.15	-5.69
Elizabeth Dick	Liberal Democrat	2,972	7.66	+0.16
Mary Ward	SSA	428	1.10	—
John MacMillan	Referendum	411	1.06	—

Labour majority: 11,859 (30.56%)
Swing: 3.73% SNP to Labour

1950–92

	Lab%	Con%	SNP%	Lib%	Other%	Turnout%
1992	49.0	18.5	23.6	7.5	1.4	69.8
1987	53.3	18.0	15.3	12.7	0.7	75.5
1983	43.5	21.7	17.1	17.1	0.6	74.4
1979	47.2	25.8	26.4	—	0.6	78.4
1974O	41.0	18.5	35.1	4.6	0.8	74.3

	Lab%	Con%	SNP%	Lib%	Other%	Turnout%
1974F	43.1	30.5	25.1	–	1.3	81.2
1970	51.5	38.2	8.7	–	1.6	76.3
1966	53.8	36.9	–	6.9	2.4	79.9
1964	53.4	44.2	–	–	2.4	81.5
1963B	50.6	39.4	7.4	–	2.6	71.6
1959	49.6	48.3	–	–	2.1	82.9
1955	50.5	46.9	–	–	2.6	82.7
1951	51.6	–	–	45.7	2.7	86.8
1950	53.5	44.6	–	1.9	–	88.1

Dundee West contains the western part of Dundee. It includes middle-class areas such as Riverside, Roseangle, Gowrie Park and the West End around the University of Dundee and Duncan of Jordanstone College campus, as well as working-class areas such as Ardler, Charleston, Lochee, St Mary's and Menzieshill. When Dundee was once known as 'Juteopolis' at the turn of the century, it was at the centre of the global economy in the jute and textile industries. One of the main concentrations of industry and employment was in the close-knit community of Lochee, and a whole infrastructure of houses, social facilities and networks grew up around it which shape such areas to this day. When the jute industries declined in the immediate post-war period, Dundee was at the forefront of attracting American multi-nationals such as Timex and NCR, the former seeing several bitter labour disputes, including a 1988 dispute between trade unions after the AEEU had agreed a no-strike agreement which fell through and cost the city thousands of potential jobs. Eventually Timex pulled out, but NCR remain, and Dundee has reinvented itself, not only as a 'City of Discovery', but an international city of bio-chemistry.

Traditionally, this has been a solidly Labour seat, until the 1999 Scottish election that is. It was represented by John Strachey, the ex-Marxist thinker who by the 1950s was one of the leading social democratic revisionists in the Labour Party and represented Dundee from 1945 to 1950 and Dundee West from 1950 to 1963, followed by Peter Doig from 1963 to 1979, a loyal and faceless Labour right-winger.

Labour has seldom faced an electoral challenge here, barring the SNP's 35% in October 1974 which placed them 2,802 votes behind Labour. Sitting MP Ernie Ross built up a comfortable majority here since first contesting the seat in 1979, and that majority was extremely healthy in 1997 despite the slow growth of support for the SNP in the constituency. Labour has won this seat at every election since the Second World War, often with impressive majorities and over half of the vote and there were few occasions in which other parties challenged Labour's hegemony on this side of Dundee.

However, this situation changed dramatically in 1999 when the SNP came within

121 votes of unseating Labour. This seat was never a Labour–SNP marginal pre-1999 and this result was certainly unexpected. Though the SNP had diligently worked the constituency, it was the marked drop in the Labour vote which turned it into a marginal. The SNP was extremely effective in identifying and turning out its vote, a clear legacy of the 1998 North East of Scotland European Parliamentary by-election, and the party's local organisational capacity was at its best against a complacent Labour Party. The Labour majority of 121 was its second lowest in Scotland – and the vote went to a recount on election night. Had the seat fallen to the SNP it would have been one of the shock results of the election and an ironic one as the Nationalists failed to win any of their target seats from Labour, barring Inverness East, Nairn and Lochaber, and came closest in a non-target seat.

The SNP's recent success was also evident at the local elections in Dundee in 1999, and it won a number of wards in Dundee West for the first time. It also succeeded in winning the Logie seat from Labour in a council by-election in 2000. Of course, whether these council results can be repeated at the general election is another matter. A low turnout, especially amongst Labour voters, was partly responsible for the 1999 result. Indeed, numerical support for the SNP did not markedly increase between 1997 and 1999, despite the dramatic percentage increase. However, the SNP has finally arrived in Dundee West, and its council success in the city is an illustration of its popularity. The seat may not be marginal at the general election, but the SNP will target resources at the seat in order to emulate its success in Dundee East. They have selected former Glasgow Labour councillor, and ex-Mohammed Sarwar advisor, Gordon Archer, to contest the seat.

MP Ernie Ross was born in 1942 in Dundee and educated at St John's Secondary School, Dundee. He worked as an engineer with Timex before his election. He gained a reputation as a left-winger due to his uncompromising hard left politics in the early 1980s. He was a pro-Soviet supporter of 'world peace', an advocate of the most militant kind of 'class politics' associated with Tony Benn and Arthur Scargill and pro-Stalinist and 'tankie' in the internal battles of the Communist Party: aligning himself with the Morning Star hard-liners against the Eurocommunists. He was a supporter of the Bennite campaign to develop internal party democracy in the early 1980s and with Willie McKelvey, then MP for Kilmarnock, he drew up in 1981 proposals to get Labour MPs to support the party manifesto and party policy and then drew up what was seen as a 'loyalty oath' binding MPs to conference decisions. In the hothouse atmosphere of the early 1980s, such proposals were seen as an attack on parliamentary democracy and Western civilisation as we know it.

Surprisingly, he was never concerned about the effect on his electorate of appearing pro-Arab in Dundee. He was affectionately known as 'Afghan Ernie' in Dundee Labour circles following a photo of him posing in front of a Soviet tank in Afghanistan the Soviet invasion of which he defended as defeating feudalism and spreading progressive ideas around the world. He was a senior member of Scottish

Labour's selection panel for approving prospective candidates for the Scottish Parliament. As a once rebellious left-winger, his role brought dismay and criticism from the left-wing MPs who were excluded – Dennis Canavan, Michael Connarty and Ian Davidson. He has never gained any ministerial position, sitting through many long years of opposition, but has been a member of the Standards, Education and Employment and Foreign Affairs Committees in the Commons. He was suspended from the latter committee following the leaking of a sensitive report to Robin Cook at the Foreign Office. He currently sits on the Standing Orders and Court of References Committees.

MSP Kate MacLean was born in Dundee in 1958 and educated at Craigie High School, Dundee. She was elected to Dundee District Council in 1988 and served as chief whip of the Labour group in 1990. She became leader of Dundee Council from 1992 onwards, before and after the reorganisation of the council to become a single-tier authority in 1995. She also served as Vice-President of COSLA from 1996 to 1999. In the election campaign for the Scottish Parliament, MacLean was appointed Spokesperson on Equalities, and was one of only two Labour spokespeople not given ministerial responsibilities, the other being her fellow left-winger John McAllion. Instead, she became Convenor of the Equal Opportunities Committee and was also a member of the Justice and Home Affairs Committee until December 2000. She is a member of the Cross Party Groups on Animal Welfare, Drug Misuse and Women. MacLean's greatest claim to fame in the first year and a half of the Parliament was when she admitted to *The Big Issue* that she had smoked cannabis: something which in pre-Ann Widdecombe days caused a brief sensation in the press.

DUNFERMLINE EAST

Predecessor Constituencies: none.

1999

Electorate: 52,087
Turnout: 29,659 (56.94%)

Candidate	Party	Votes	Votes%	Change%
Helen Eadie	Labour	16,576	55.89	-10.92
David McCarthy	SNP	7,877	26.56	+11.01
Carrie Ruxton	Conservative	2,931	9.88	-0.11
Fred Lawson	Liberal Democrat	2,275	7.67	+1.75

Labour majority: 8,699 (29.33%)
Swing: 10.96% Labour to SNP

1997

Electorate: 52,072
Turnout: 36,583 (70.25%)

Candidate	Party	Votes	Votes%	Change%
Gordon Brown	Labour	24,441	66.81	+3.95
John Ramage	SNP	5,690	15.55	+0.81
Ian Mitchell	Conservative	3,656	9.99	-6.30
Jim Tolson	Liberal Democrat	2,164	5.92	-0.19
Thomas Dunsmore	Referendum	632	1.73	—

Labour majority: 18,751 (51.26%)
Swing: 1.57% SNP to Labour

1983–92

	Lab%	Con%	SNP%	Lib%	Other%	Turnout%
1992	62.4	16.5	15.1	6.0	—	75.6
1987	64.8	14.8	10.0	10.5	—	76.5
1983	51.5	18.8	7.2	20.1	2.4	72.0

Safely Labour, as a result of the social make-up of the constituency, its electoral history and the popularity of the current MP, Gordon Brown, Dunfermline East is a large, working-class constituency, with a substantial element of council housing. The constituency as it is currently composed is slightly misleading in its title of Dunfermline East, neither containing the town of Dunfermline (that is in West), nor being the successor seat to the old post-war seat of the town. Instead, the predecessors of this 1983 created seat can be found in the Fife West and Fife Central seats which were dominated until their latter days by the economics and politics of coal mining, which meant in Fife, a certain kind of left-wing politics (see Fife Central for results). Known for its 'little Moscows' such as Lumphinnans, with street names such as Gagarin Way, and a long Communist tradition, through electing Willie Gallacher as its MP from 1935 to 1950, this seat has proven a Labour heartland ever since. The Communist legacy still makes its presence felt though, with a Scottish Communist councillor in Ballingry and Lochore and a Democratic Left councillor in Cowdenbeath Central: whose votes should have been weighed rather than counted at the 1999 local elections. Despite such popularity, none of the far left parties contested the seat at the Scottish elections though Tommy Sheridan's SSP would be wise to remedy this failing at future elections given the far left history of the seat.

Many of the towns in the constituency are former mining towns, with a legacy of high unemployment, such as Cowdenbeath, Ballingry, Lochore and Kelty. The constituency also includes more middle-class commuter towns on the Fife coast such as Aberdour, Dalgety Bay and Inverkeithing which appear like fish out of water compared to the rest of the constituency. Notably, the constituency also stretches westwards to Rosyth, which includes the docks and naval base, and northwards to the Ian Rankin mecca of Cardenden.

Electorally, there is no challenger to Labour. Pre-1983, when this seat was divided between Dunfermline and Fife Central the SNP was a possible challenger, but the boundary changes which created Dunfermline East did not involve the New Town of Glenrothes in which the SNP had considerable support. Dunfermline East therefore remains dominated by Labour with no prospect of change. For example, even in a bad year for Labour such as 1999, it still polled 56 per cent. Its best result in the post-war period was in 1997, which saw Brown home with a stunning 66.81 per cent. Easily retaining this seat will not be difficult for Labour; achieving a respectable second place such as the SNP won in the 1999 Scottish elections is the limit of any of the opposition parties aspirations here.

MP Gordon Brown was born in 1951 in Govan, Glasgow. A son of the manse, he was educated at Kirkcaldy High School and Edinburgh University, with an MA in 1972 and a PhD, awarded in 1982, dealing with Labour in the inter-war years: much of which fed into his later biography of James Maxton. He was also Rector of Edinburgh University from 1972 to 1975 and subsequently a lecturer at Edinburgh and Glasgow College from 1975 to 1980. He was editor and contributor to *The Red Paper on Scotland* in 1975 – a book shaped by the politics of the Upper Clyde Shipworkers' work-in and Allende's Chile, which tried from a socialist perspective to understand the appeal and rationale of nationalism. Now its message is more in keeping with the longest suicide note in history of the 1983 general election than with the New Labour gospel of the post-1997 government. After lecturing for a period Brown then worked as a journalist and editor for STV until his election in 1983. He held a number of frontbench posts within the Labour Party at Westminster, including Shadow Chief Secretary to the Treasury from 1987 to 1989 and Shadow spokesperson on Trade and Industry from 1989 to 1992. He was Shadow Chancellor from 1992 until 1997 and Chancellor of the Exchequer since 1997. He has proven central to the performance of the Labour Government in all areas, not merely the economy, and had a key behind-the-scenes role at the Scottish election in 1999 and in the workings of the Scottish Executive. He is immensely popular within the Labour Party at large, winning the most votes at the Shadow Cabinet elections four times during the opposition years, in 1988, 1989, 1991 and 1992. However, as Shadow Chancellor, he was responsible for vetting all of his colleagues spending commitments and his popularity nose-dived in the latter years of opposition; he fell to 14th in the 1996 Shadow Cabinet elections.

Brown sees himself as the self-appointed conscience of the Labour movement. He is someone who knows the history of the party and movement, and under-stands its sense of itself, its idealism and romanticised view of its past. Indeed, he personifies the compromises Labour has to make to win power between a socialist idealism and a sense of realism and economic orthodoxy. He has a close, but prob-lematic relationship with Tony Blair: when both were rising stars under Neil Kinnock and John Smith, their relationship was a harmonious one, with Brown, the senior of the two. However, Smith's unexpected death, and the manoeuvring in the weeks after that led to Tony Blair emerging as the moderniser's candidate, has left a damaged and over-sensitive relationship. Brown's tempestuous relation-ship with Blair has continued in office, and has often been fuelled by advisers and courtiers on both sides, rather than the two directly. Brown also has an estranged relationship with Robin Cook, with each of the two seeing himself as keeper of the party's soul.

The death of First Minister Donald Dewar in October 2000 and the resulting succession revealed all kinds of tensions and fault lines in Scottish Labour, one of which was Gordon Brown's role in the party. In a difficult situation, Brown tried to persuade the Scottish party into anointing Henry McLeish as leader without any contest or debate: a role that drew comparisons with the way Blair emerged as the modernisers' candidate to Brown's cost in 1994. Browns attempt to assist McLeish backfired and was widely seen as insensitive, Jack McConnell stood for the leader-ship, forcing a contest, and although defeated, he polled better than anyone expected. After the contest, Brown advocated that Wendy Alexander, a Brown ally, should become Deputy Leader without any contest, a move that was prevented by Cathy Jamieson standing for the post and winning it without any competition. Brown's role in the Scottish party following Dewar's death left questions about his judgement and in particular his view of how devolution should develop.

Brown is author of numerous books and publications including *The Politics of Devolution and Nationalism* (1980), *Scotland: The Real Divide* (with Robin Cook) and *Where There is Greed* (1989) and *Values, Visions and Voices: An Anthology of Socialism* (1995). He is already the subject of two biographies, one a hagiographic account by Brownite supporter and journalist Paul Routledge, Brown hopes as Chancellor to play a central role in winning Labour's second term under Blair and has not given up hopes that one day he will be Prime Minister. He became the main Co-ordinator of Labour's election campaign for the 2001 UK election, a role he was originally meant to share with Peter Mandleson, but which he now holds on his own after Mandleson's resignation. Whether this prefigures a more influential role for 'Prime Minister' Brown to 'President' Blair in the much talked about Labour second term remains to be seen.

MSP Helen Eadie was born in Stenhousemuir in 1947 and educated at Larbert High School, Falkirk Technical College and London School of Economics. Her father-in-law, Alex Eadie, was formerly MP for Midlothian and Minister for Energy. She held a number of jobs including administrator for the General and Municipal Boiler's Workers Union (GMB) in Glasgow, Equal Opportunities Officer for the same union in London, and political researcher for Harry Ewing (MP for Falkirk East until 1992) and her father-in-law, Alex Eadie, in Midlothian. She also had a strong local government background as a councillor in Fife from 1986 until 1999, posts held including Chair of the Equal Opportunities Committee, Deputy Leader, COSLA representative on the Channel Tunnel initiative and member of the bureau of the Conference of Peripheral and Maritime Regions. She joined the Labour Party in the 1960s and held a number of local party posts in London and Fife. For example, she was an executive member of Greater London Labour Party and later chair of the women's section of Dunfermline East CLP. She also contested the Roxburgh and Berwickshire constituency at the 1997 Westminster election. Within the Scottish Parliament, she is a member of the Public Petitions and Transport and Environment Committee the last of which she served upon until the end of 2000, when she became a member of the European Committee. She also serves on the Cross Party Groups for Borders Rail, Information, Knowledge and Enlightenment, Oil and Gas, and Women. She is also Convenor of the Strategic Rail Services group.

DUNFERMLINE WEST

Predecessor Constituencies: Dunfermline District of Burghs (1945–70) and Dunfermline (1974–9).

1999

Electorate: 53,112
Turnout: 30,671 (57.75%)

Candidate	Party	Votes	Votes%	Change%
Scott Barrie	Labour	13,560	44.21	-8.87
Douglas Chapman	SNP	8,539	27.84	+8.67
Elizabeth Harris	Liberal Democrat	5,591	18.23	+4.61
James Mackie	Conservative	2,981	9.72	-2.92

Labour majority: 5,021 (16.37%)
Swing: 8.77% Labour to SNP

1997

Electorate: 52,467
Turnout: 36,434 (69.44%)

Candidate	Party	Votes	Votes%	Change%
Rachel Squire	Labour	19,338	53.08	+11.56
John Lloyd	SNP	6,984	19.17	-0.66
Elizabeth Harris	Liberal Democrat	4,963	13.62	-1.99
Kevin Newton	Conservative	4,606	12.64	-10.39
James Bain	Referendum	543	1.49	—

Labour majority: 12,354 (33.91%)
Swing: 6.11% SNP to Labour

1945–92

	Lab%	Con%	SNP%	Lib%	Other%	Turnout%
1992	42.0	22.8	19.4	15.7	—	76.4
1987	47.1	23.1	8.7	21.1	—	76.9
1983	36.0	29.2	7.8	26.2	0.9	73.5
1979	44.3	30.1	14.3	11.3	—	79.3
1974O	40.1	23.0	28.6	8.3	—	75.9
1974F	39.3	30.3	17.8	12.6	—	81.1

	Lab%	Con%	SNP%	Lib%	Other%	Turnout%
1970	57.1	32.0	9.7	–	1.2	74.1
1966	58.4	26.6	15.0	–	–	76.3
1964	61.6	38.4	–	–	–	77.2
1959	61.4	38.6	–	–	–	80.1
1955	61.0	39.0	–	–	–	77.6
1951	61.1	38.9	–	–	–	85.5
1950	61.2	38.8	–	–	–	83.9
1945	64.7	35.3	–	–	–	73.0

This constituency takes in Dunfermline itself and the towns and villages of West Fife such as Culross, Kincardine and Saline. It is safely Labour, despite the relative closeness of the result in 1999. Given the working-class nature of the constituency, with a coalmining history in West Fife, this is nothing if not safe Labour territory. Surprisingly, the seat is not one with substantial council housing. At the 1991 census, 62.7 per cent of homes were owner-occupied, whilst only 29.7 per cent were owned by the local authority: and yet Labour still triumphed comfortably. Indeed, Labour's vote in 1997 was its highest in the seat since 1970.

Despite Labour's historic electoral strength in the area, Dunfermline itself is politically mixed at local elections with all other paries capable of winning some council seats, though ending up dwarfed within Fife Council. The few challenges to Labour came from the SNP in October 1974 when Labour still had a majority of 5,291 and the Tories in 1983 when the Labour majority was as low as 2,474, due almost entirely to the emergence of the Liberal-SPD Alliance at that election. The latter party came a disappointing third on 26.2 per cent of the vote and has never mounted much of a challenge in the seat, though it picks up a decent enough vote in the constituency.

The Conservatives have traditionally done well in this constituency, but their vote slid heavily at recent elections in 1997 and 1999, so gone are the days when they could look to lead the pack of also-rans to Labour. However, despite this development, no real challenger has emerged and none appears likely. The SNP has increased its support in the constituency to come second at the last two elections, but that is all it can hope for at the next general election. At least its increased vote in 1999 was based on gaining over 1,500 new voters, rather than a simple percentage increase based on a lower turnout amongst Labour voters. Consolidation and further growth will be the SNP's goal at the next general election. Besides Labour, none of the parties has any considerable strength evident at local elections, so they lack a base to build from in order to mount a more convincing electoral challenge.

MP Rachel Squire was born in Carshalton in 1954. She was educated at Godolphin and Latymer Girls School, studied anthropology at Durham University followed by social work at Birmingham University. She was a social worker in Birmingham from 1975 until 1981 and then worked as an officer for the trade union NUPE from 1981 to 1992. She was elected in 1992 following the retirement of Dick Douglas who had held the seat since 1979 but defected to the SNP over Labour's weak opposition to the poll tax whilst he was still an MP. Squire then gained or more accurately regained the seat for Labour and has held it ever since. She was a member of the Procedure Committee in the Commons from 1992 until 1997, as well as European Legislation from 1994 until 1997 and Modernisation of the House of Commons from 1997 to 1999. She was a Parliamentary Private Secretary to Stephen Byers at Education and Employment from 1997 to 1998, and then to schools standards minister Estelle Morris from 1998 onwards.

MSP Scott Barrie was born in St Andrews in 1962 and was a former councillor on Dunfermline District Council. He was elected to the council in 1988 and served as the vice-chair of the Leisure and Recreation Committee. He joined Labour in 1979 and was a former chair of his local CLP. He is a social worker by profession, having worked for Fife Region and then Fife Council where he was a manager in the Children and Families department. He was educated at Auchmuty High School, Glenrothes and is a graduate of Edinburgh University and also obtained a CQSW from Stirling University. In the Scottish Parliament he is a member of both the Audit and Justice and Home Affairs Committee, the latter of which he was a member until December 2000, when he became a member of the Justice II Committee. He is a member of the Cross Party Groups on Children, Drug Misuse, Strategic Rail Services, and Sport.

EAST KILBRIDE

Predecessor Constituencies: created anew in 1974.

1999

Electorate: 66,111
Turnout: 41,313 (62.49%)

Candidate	Party	Votes	Votes%	Change%
Andy Kerr	Labour	19,987	48.38	-8.15
Linda Fabiani	SNP	13,488	32.65	+11.75
Craig Stevenson	Conservative	4,465	10.81	-1.21
Ewan Hawthorn	Liberal Democrat	3,373	8.16	+0.93

Labour majority: 6,499 (15.73%)
Swing: 9.95% Labour to SNP

1997

Electorate: 65,229
Turnout: 48,796 (74.81%)

Candidate	Party	Votes	Votes%	Change%
Adam Ingram	Labour	27,584	56.53	+9.16
George Gebbie	SNP	10,200	20.90	-2.70
Clifford Herbertson	Conservative	5,863	12.02	-6.62
Kate Philbrick	Liberal Democrat	3,527	7.23	-3.16
John Deighan	Pro-Life	1,170	2.40	-
Julie Gray	Referendum	306	0.63	-
Ewan Gilmour	NLP	146	0.30	-

Labour majority: 17,384 (35.63%)
Swing: 5.93% SNP to Labour

1974–92

	Lab%	Con%	SNP%	Lib%	Other%	Turnout%
1992	46.9	19.1	23.5	10.5	-	80.0
1987	49.0	14.7	12.6	23.7	-	79.2
1983	37.1	24.3	10.1	27.9	0.5	76.9
1979	53.9	29.4	15.6	-	1.1	79.7
1974O	41.9	16.3	36.7	5.1	-	79.1
1974F	43.9	28.9	25.9	-	1.3	82.0

A safe Labour seat since its creation in 1974. As a New Town, just to the south of Glasgow, this is a constituency in which the SNP would have been expected to make some progress – similar to Cumbernauld, Glenrothes and Livingston – but the party's impact has been limited to the 1974 elections. In October 1974 the SNP got within 2,704 votes of Labour, but this excellent result in a new constituency was never repeated by the Nationalists as their appeal faded in the town. In 1983 and 1987 it was the Liberal Democrats who took second place to Labour, before the SNP reasserted itself in the constituency in 1992. But neither party came close to upsetting Labour, which has maintained a very healthy majority down the years: a situation which looks set to continue.

The safeness of the seat must be of some disappointment to the Nationalists. New Towns proved important territory for them in the 1960s and 1970s as they were one of the areas in which they could look to make gains in straight fights with Labour. However, with the exception of council success in Cumbernauld, a few near misses in the New Towns has not translated into electoral success here, largely due to poor organisation. The 1999 result would have given them encouragement though, as the party increased its number of voters by 3,288 and substantially improved upon its share of the vote from 1997. Labour, meantime, saw its voters and share of the vote decline dramatically between the two elections, though still gained 48.38 per cent in 1999, which was better than in 1992, 1983 and in each of the 1974 general elections.

Economically, the constituency has a strong service and manufacturing base as well as considerable levels of employment in public services: notably Centre One, the main tax office in Scotland, in addition to the Overseas Development Administration. The seat also had a considerable proportion of owner-occupied housing in 1991, which at 62.8 per cent has probably grown considerably in the intervening years, and yet not damaged Labour's prospects in the constituency.

MP Adam Ingram was born in Glasgow in 1947 and became MP for this seat in 1987. Ingram was educated at Cranhill Senior Secondary School and is a graduate of the Open University and worked in computers with the South of Scotland Electricity Board and then for the trade union, NALGO, as an official from 1977 until 1987. He was a district councillor in East Kilbride from 1980 until 1997 and council leader from 1984 to 1987. He was Parliamentary Private Secretary to Neil Kinnock from 1988 to 1992, opposition spokesperson on Social Security from 1993 to 1995 and on Science and Technology from 1995 to 1997. Within the post-1997 Labour Government he became Minister of State at the Northern Ireland Office.

MSP Andy Kerr was born in East Kilbride in 1962. He is a graduate of Glasgow College (now Glasgow Caledonian University), with a BA (Hons) in Social Sciences. He was a full-time officer with the National Union of Students before beginning a career in local government. He was a Research and Development Officer with Strathkelvin District Council from 1987 until 1990, Managing Director of Achieving Quality from 1990 to 1993 and Strategy and Development Manager within the Land

Services Department of Glasgow City Council from 1993 until 1999. He was a Secretary of East Kilbride CLP from 1989 until his election and acted as Adam Ingram's election agent and campaign co-ordinator. He was interviewed for the post of Scottish Labour General Secretary after Jack McConnell left and was seen as the favoured choice of the 'Blairites' against the 'Brownite' Alex Rowley who in 1998 was appointed and sacked within a year. He is Convenor of the Scottish Parliament's Committee on Transport and the Environment and was also a member of the Procedures Committee from May 1999 to December 2000. He sits on the Cross Party Group for Older People, Age and Aging. Kerr was Jack McConnell's campaign manager in his bid for the Labour leadership following Donald Dewar's death in October 2000. McConnell's campaign, which the party hierarchy tried to stop, was well organised, took Henry McLeish by surprise and defined the agenda. It also tapped into widespread unease and resentment about the top-down nature of the Executive under Dewar, resulting in McConnell losing to McLeish by the narrow margin of 44:36. Part of this was down to Kerr's organisational abilities and he is undoubtably someone to watch in future years.

EAST LOTHIAN

Predecessor Constituencies: Berwickshire and Haddington (1945) and Berwickshire and East Lothian (1950–79).

1999

Electorate: 58,579
Turnout 35,582 (60.74%)

Candidate	Party	Votes	Votes%	Change%
John Home Robertson	Labour	19,220	54.02	+1.34
Calum Miller	SNP	8,274	23.25	+7.54
Christine Richard	Conservative	5,941	16.70	-3.24
Judy Hayman	Liberal Democrat	2,147	6.03	-4.50

Labour majority: 10,946 (30.77%)
Swing: 3.10% Labour to SNP

1997

Electorate: 57,441
Turnout: 43,432 (75.61%)

Candidate	Party	Votes	Votes%	Change%
John Home Robertson	Labour	22,881	52.68	+7.22
Murdo Fraser	Conservative	8,660	19.94	-10.24
David McCarthy	SNP	6,825	15.71	+2.43
Alison MacAskill	Liberal Democrat	4,575	10.53	-0.55
Norman Nash	Referendum	491	1.13	—

Labour majority: 14,221 (32.74%)
Swing: 8.73% Conservative to Labour

1945–92

	Lab%	Con%	SNP%	Lib%	Other%	Turnout%
1992	46.5	28.2	14.2	11.2	—	82.4
1987	48.0	28.3	7.3	15.5	0.9	78.7
1983	43.9	30.8	4.4	20.9	—	76.2
1979	43.5	40.2	6.5	9.8	—	82.9
1978B	47.4	40.2	8.8	3.6	—	71.2
1974O	43.3	37.6	13.2	5.9	—	83.0

	Lab%	Con%	SNP%	Lib%	Other%	Turnout%
1974F	42.3	43.5	14.2	–	–	85.8
1970	45.6	44.2	10.2	–	–	83.8
1966	51.9	48.1	–	–	–	86.1
1964	49.3	50.7	–	–	–	85.0
1959	46.6	53.4	–	–	–	83.2
1955	46.7	53.3	–	–	–	80.3
1951	47.2	52.8	–	–	–	83.8
1950	40.8	36.8	–	22.4	–	82.8
1945	54.5	45.5	–	–	–	70.3

East Lothian sits to the east of Edinburgh in the Firth of Forth. It combines very affluent, picturesque communities such as the market town of Haddington and the seaside resorts of Dunbar and North Berwick, with the working-class towns of Prestonpans and Tranent. As Berwickshire and Haddington, and Berwickshire and East Lothian, this has been a real maverick seat in the past. It elected Conservatives and National Liberals for most of the inter-war period, but went Labour with a majority of 68 in 1923. John Robertson won it back for Labour with a majority of 3,157 over the Conservatives in 1945, but the Conservatives' William Anstruther-Gray won it in 1951 with a majority of 2,358 and held it until Labour's landslide year of 1966 when a young Labour candidate, John Mackintosh, regained it for Labour.

In February 1974 as the UK swung to Labour and returned a Labour Government, Mackintosh lost his seat to the Conservative Michael Ancram, but won it back in October 1974 with a majority of 2,740. John Mackintosh's premature death in 1978 was a major shock and loss to Scottish Labour and the unexpected by-election could have caused major problems. However, John Home Robertson held the seat easily with a small but significant swing from the Conservatives to Labour, with the SNP in a distant third place seeing their vote reduced.

Boundary changes in 1983 saw the creation of East Lothian and the addition of the Labour area of Musselburgh and in that year's general election, Home Robertson increased his majority to 6,241, rising to 10,105 in 1987 over the Conservatives. The movement of Musselburgh back to Edinburgh East reduced Labour's notional 1992 majority to 7,099, but this was no problem in Labour's year of triumph as Home Robertson romped home with a 14,221 majority, while the Conservative vote fell by over 5,000. In the subsequent Scottish Parliament elections, Home Robertson was one of the few candidates who saw Labour's share of the vote go up, while the SNP added nearly 1,500 to finish in a distant second place 10,946 behind Labour. East Lothian's days as an unpredictable constituency seem long behind it, and unless there is a major upset Labour look safe here for quite some time.

MP/MSP John Home Robertson was born in 1948 in Edinburgh, elected MP for Berwick and East Lothian from 1978 until 1983 and for East Lothian from 1983, being elected MSP in 1999. He was educated at Ampleforth College and West of Scotland Agriculture College, and was a farmer before being elected to Berwickshire District Council from 1974 to 1978. Robertson was a member of the Scottish Affairs Select Committee from 1979 to 1983, Chair of the Scottish Labour Group of MPs 1982 to 1983; he was an Opposition Scottish Whip from 1983 to 1984, Opposition Front Bench Spokesman on Agriculture from 1984 to 1987 and on Scottish Affairs from 1987 to 1988; from 1990 to 1997 he was a member of the Defence Select Committee.

In 1997, he became Parliamentary Private Secretary to Jack Cunningham, Minister of Agriculture, Fisheries and Food and in 1998 shifted with Cunningham when he became Minister for the Cabinet Office from 1998 to 1999. Robertson worked on David Steel's successful 1965 by-election campaign in Roxburgh, Selkirk and Peebles, before joining the Labour Party in 1970. He has for long been identified in the Labour Party as a home rule supporter, and was one of only four Labour MPs who supported Gordon Wilson's idea of a cross-party Convention in 1980. He was one of six Labour MPs to stand for the Scottish Parliament and all were elected – all in their existing Westminster seats. In the Scottish elections, he was campaign spokesperson on agriculture, fisheries and rural affairs and after the elections was appointed Deputy Minister for Rural Affairs. Robertson has never shone as a parliamentary performer and did not as a minister. He was unceremoniously sacked in Henry McLeish's first ministerial reshuffle upon becoming First Minister in October 2000 – one of only two Labour casualties in the reshuffle. Robertson became a member of the European Committee in January 2001.

EASTWOOD

Predecessor Constituencies: Renfrewshire East (1945–79).

1999

Electorate: 67,248

Turnout: 45,396 (67.51%)

Candidate	Party	Votes	Votes%	Change%
Ken Macintosh	Labour	16,970	37.38	-2.37
John Young	Conservative	14,845	32.70	-0.86
Rachel Findlay	SNP	8,760	19.30	+6.23
Anna McCurley	Liberal Democrat	4,472	9.85	-1.85
Manar Tayan	Independent	349	0.77	–

Labour majority: 2,125 (5.08%)

Swing: 0.75% Labour to Conservative

1997

Electorate: 66,697

Turnout: 52,235 (78.32%)

Candidate	Party	Votes	Votes%	Change%
Jim Murphy	Labour	20,766	39.75	+15.61
Paul Cullen	Conservative	17,530	33.56	-13.07
Douglas Yates	SNP	6,826	13.07	+ 0.55
Christopher Mason	Liberal Democrat	6,110	11.70	- 4.74
David Miller	Referendum	497	0.95	–
Manar Tayan	Pro-Life	393	0.75	–
Douglas McPherson	UK Independence	113	0.22	–

Labour majority: 3,236 (6.19%)

Swing: 14.34% Conservative to Labour

1945–92

	Lab%	Con%	SNP%	Lib%	Other%	Turnout%
1992	24.1	46.8	12.4	16.5	0.3	81.0
1987	25.1	39.5	8.2	27.2	–	79.6
1983	20.1	46.6	5.8	27.6	–	76.2
1979	24.4	49.9	7.7	18.0	–	80.6

	Lab%	Con%	SNP%	Lib%	Other%	Turnout%
1974O	20.8	41.4	23.2	14.6	–	77.7
1974F	20.1	50.6	10.4	18.9	–	82.9
1970	28.1	52.0	6.7	12.6	–	76.2
1966	33.1	53.1	–	13.8	–	79.9
1964	31.1	52.6	–	16.3	–	82.6
1959	28.8	58.7	–	12.5	–	82.9
1955	31.7	68.3	–	–	–	78.1
1951	34.2	65.8	–	–	–	81.7
1950	34.6	65.4	–	–	–	78.9
1945	46.4	53.6	–	–	–	67.2

Eastwood sits south of Glasgow and is to all intents and purposes part of the Greater Glasgow conurbation. This is one of the most affluent and middle-class parts of the West of Scotland and of Scotland overall. Its main communities – Newton Mearns, Giffnock and Busby, are middle-class areas with high degrees of Tory support. The ex-mining town of Barrhead is the most working-class area in the seat, which is predominantly Labour. Eastwood is not surprisingly the second most healthy constituency in the whole of Scotland, with only West Aberdeenshire and Kincardine ranked above it. 15 per cent of its population live in poverty and in June 2000 it had 3.5 per cent male unemployment, the ninth lowest in Scotland and the lowest in the West.

As Eastwood and previously Renfrewshire East, this was once safe Conservative territory, and is now temporarily under the claim of New Labour. Strangely, in the intense competition between Labour, Conservatives and Liberals in the inter-war era, Labour briefly held the seat in 1922 and 1923, but this was an aberration in its history until now. Guy Lloyd won the seat for the Conservatives in 1945 with comparative ease, holding Labour off with a 5,676 majority. Lloyd remained Conservative MP until 1959 and was succeeded by Betty Harvie Anderson, MP for the period 1959-79; even in the SNP election of October 1974 she held on with a majority of 8,710 over the Nationalists.

Allan Stewart first won the seat in 1979 with a majority of 13,238 over Labour; in the 1983 and 1987 elections, the Liberal-SDP Alliance established itself as the main challenger to the Conservatives, cutting Stewart's majority to first 8,595, then to 6,014. However, this challenge dissipated itself in 1992, as Labour re-established its claim to second place and Stewart doubled his majority to 11,688, presiding over a 7.3 per cent rise in the Conservative vote, four times the Scottish average.

Eastwood would possibly have remained Conservative in 1997, but for a series of unprecedented events. First, Allan Stewart announced his sudden retirement weeks before the election; the reasons included a damaging trial, in which he was charged with assaulting M77 protestors and fined £200 for breach of the peace, revelations of a long-standing affair and health problems. Second, the favoured successor, Michael Hirst, no sooner emerged than he withdrew amid allegations of a homosexual affair, still the kiss of death in Scottish Conservative circles. The Conservatives' third choice candidate, Paul Cullen, Solicitor-General for Scotland, presided over a collapse in his vote, polling 7,000 fewer votes and seeing his share decline by 13 per cent. Labour's Jim Murphy could not believe his luck as he became the constituency's first Labour MP for 74 years, increasing his vote by a staggering 8,000 and 16 per cent, to give him a 3,236 majority over the Conservatives.

The loss of Eastwood, previously the Conservatives' safest seat in Scotland, meant that for the first time in history no Tory MPs were returned for Scotland. Two years later, Labour held on to Eastwood, proof, if it were needed, of the party's continual ability to stretch its appeal to win seats and then hold them. Ken Macintosh, Labour candidate, saw his vote fall by 4,000, while a strong challenge from Jock Young, a long-time Glasgow Conservative councillor, saw his vote fall by 3,000 as a small swing back to the Conservatives occurred cutting Labour's lead back to 2,125. Labour never expected to win Eastwood in 1997, but it has proved that it was not entirely a fluke by winning it again. However, given the history and profile of the seat, Eastwood, along with Ayr and Edinburgh Pentlands, is the kind of territory the Conservatives need to start winning support in again to avoid permanent ghetto status.

MP Jim Murphy was born in 1967 in Glasgow and has represented the Eastwood seat from 1997. Educated at Bellarmine Secondary School, Glasgow, Milnerton High School, Cape Town and Strathclyde University, Murphy was President of the National Union of Students (Scotland) from 1992 until 1994 and the National Union of Students (UK) from 1994 to 1996. In the run-up to the 1997 election, he became Projects Manager of the Scottish Labour Party with special responsibility for the 'Partnership into Power' modernisation of the party. Many left-wingers felt that Murphy's work at party headquarters gave him the resources to run the Blairite Scottish Labour Forum pre-election plans to remove several left-wingers from the party Executive. He was as amazed as anyone to win Eastwood at the age of 29, without ever having had a real job, and is frequently on the TV raising his profile and defending the government in an attempt to save this unlikely Labour seat. In February 2001, he became Parliamentary Private Secretary to the new Secretary of State for Scotland, Helen Liddell.

MSP Ken Macintosh was born in 1962 in Inverness and educated at the Royal High School, Edinburgh, and Edinburgh University where he gained an MA in History. He began work at the BBC in 1987 and for the next twelve years worked in current affairs and news covering *Breakfast News*, *Breakfast with Frost* and the *Nine O'Clock News*. When he left the BBC in 1999 he was the producer responsible for Scottish network bulletins. He sat on the Education, Culture and Sport Committee, Subordinate Legislation Committee, and Finance Committee of the Parliament from May 1999 to December 2000 and in April 2000 was appointed its reporter to establish the costs of the burgeoning Holyrood Building Project. Since January 2001, he has also been a member of the Standards and Procedures Committees. He is also a member of the Cross Party Groups on Crofting, Gaelic, Information, Knowledge and Enlightenment, Media, and Sports.

EDINBURGH CENTRAL

Predecessor constituencies: created in 1983 from Edinburgh Central (1945-79) and Edinburgh North (1945–79).

1999

Electorate: 65,945
Turnout: 37,412 (56.73%)

Candidate	Party	Votes	Votes%	Change%
Sarah Boyack	Labour	14,224	38.02	- 9.07
Ian McKee	SNP	9,598	25.65	+ 9.85
Andy Myles	Liberal Democrat	6,187	16.54	+ 3.42
Jacqui Low	Conservative	6,018	16.09	- 5.10
Kevin Williamson	SSP	830	2.22	–
Brian Allingham	Independent Democrat	364	0.97	–
William Wallace	Braveheart	191	0.51	–

Labour majority: 4,626 (12.37%)
Swing: 9.46% Labour to SNP

1997

Electorate: 63,695
Turnout: 42,735 (67.09%)

Candidate	Party	Votes	Votes%	Change%
Alistair Darling	Labour	20,125	47.09	+ 8.56
Michael Scott-Hayward	Conservative	9,055	21.19	- 8.16
Fiona Hyslop	SNP	6,750	15.80	+ 0.57
Karen Utting	Liberal Democrat	5,605	13.12	- 1.72
Linda Hendry	Green	607	1.42	–
Austen Skinner	Referendum	495	1.16	–
Mark Benson	Independent Democrat	98	0.23	–

Labour majority: 11,070 (25.90%)
Swing: 8.36% Conservative to Labour

1945–92

	Lab%	Con%	SNP%	Lib%	Other%	Turnout%
1992	38.8	33.4	14.1	11.5	2.2	69.3
1987	40.2	34.7	6.2	17.9	1.0	68.9

	Lab%	Con%	SNP%	Lib%	Other%	Turnout%
1983	31.1	38.0	4.9	25.6	0.3	64.9
1979	47.8	29.5	9.8	12.2	0.7	67.5
1974O	40.3	26.0	24.8	8.9	–	67.5
1974F	37.9	34.6	13.6	13.9	–	73.6
1970	46.2	38.6	8.0	7.2	–	66.0
1966	58.9	41.1	–	–	–	69.4
1964	54.0	46.0	–	–	–	71.8
1959	51.0	49.0	–	–	–	72.7
1955	51.4	48.6	–	–	–	68.8
1951	52.2	47.8	–	–	–	76.7
1950	47.9	39.4	–	10.0	2.7	74.3
1945	54.3	33.3	–	11.2	1.2	59.5

Edinburgh North (1945–79)

	Lab%	Con%	SNP%	Lib%	Other%	Turnout%
1979	30.1	43.6	10.8	15.5	–	71.8
1974O	25.9	39.3	23.5	11.3	–	69.2
1974F	26.2	45.8	12.7	15.3	–	76.4
1973B	24.0	38.7	18.9	18.4	–	54.4
1970	37.1	52.8	–	10.1	–	70.1
1966	39.2	50.3	–	10.5	–	73.9
1964	41.8	58.2	–	–	–	73.6
1960B	30.3	54.2	–	15.5	–	53.8
1959	36.0	64.0	–	–	–	73.9
1955	38.3	61.7	–	–	–	72.0
1955B	40.6	59.4	–	–	–	46.4
1951	41.2	58.8	–	–	–	80.0
1950	39.3	51.2	–	9.5	–	78.7
1945	45.1	43.1	–	11.8	–	64.6

Edinburgh Central contains some of the most stunning panoramas in the Western world in urban settings, and some of the most famous landmarks and attractions in Edinburgh – the Castle, Royal Mile and High Street, Princes Street and its famous Gardens, Murrayfield rugby stadium and the Scottish Parliament itself. Boundary changes in 1983 cut Edinburgh representation from seven to six and brought together in one seat the stunning lay-outs and architecture of the Old and New Towns. Sadly, the 1997 boundary changes deprived Edinburgh Central of this claim to fame, with the New Town, along with Stockbridge, being hived off to the unlikely setting of Edinburgh North and Leith.

Central was first won by Labour in 1918, lost in 1931 and 1935, won by Andrew Gilzean in 1945 and 1950, then by Thomas Oswald from 1951 until 1974. It has always had the reputation as a marginal seat. Labour won it in 1959 by 51.0 per cent to the Conservatives' 49.0 per cent; Robin Cook won it three times in the 1970s as the seat slowly became more Labour, but the boundary changes of 1983 brought in Tory areas making it more marginal, with the result that Cook fled to the safety of nearby New Town Livingston. He was right in his calculations as Alex Fletcher won it for the Tories with 38.0 per cent and a majority of 2,566 over Labour.

His hold was but a brief interlude and in 1987 Alistair Darling retook the seat for Labour with 40.2 per cent, putting 5,000 votes on to Labour's support and resulting in a majority of 2,262. This fell in 1992 to 2,126, before rising dramatically to 11,070 in 1997. Darling put 4,000 votes on Labour's notional 1992 result, while the Conservative vote fell to 21.2 per cent in one of the most prosperous seats in the UK, an indication of how unpopular the Conservatives had become in Scotland.

Things did not change dramatically in 1999. Labour's Sarah Boyack lost nearly 6,000 votes on a reduced turnout, while the SNP gained nearly 3,000, establishing themselves in a respectable but distant second. The biggest shock was the Tory performance, finishing fourth with 16 per cent in a seat where they had (on different boundaries) polled 33 per cent in 1992 and finished a mere 5.4 per cent behind Labour. Edinburgh Central has swung too heavily towards Labour to be seen in the near future as a Labour-Tory marginal again.

MP Alistair Darling was born in 1953 in London and has been MP for Edinburgh Central since 1987. Educated at Loretto School, Edinburgh, a public school, and Aberdeen University, he served on Lothian Regional Council from 1982 to 1987 and Lothian and Borders Police Board from 1982 until 1986. He worked as a solicitor from 1978 until 1983 and an Advocate from 1984.

After his election in 1987, Darling rapidly rose up the Labour hierarchy and became Spokesman on Home Affairs from 1988 until 1992, and part of Labour's Treasury and Economic Affairs team with particular responsibility for the City from 1992 to 1996, before becoming Shadow Chief Secretary to the Treasury from 1996 to 1997. In government, he became Chief Secretary to the Treasury for Labour's first year, and in July 1998, in the first major reshuffle, was shifted to the post of Secretary of State for Social Security, replacing Harriet Harman. Darling is the great-nephew of William Darling, Conservative MP for Edinburgh South from 1945 to 1957, and his contribution to New Labour's search for respectability included shaving off his striking black beard (which dramatically contrasted with his white hair). More substantially, he was a key part of Gordon Brown's pre-election charm offensive in the City and board-rooms which has continued since Labour became the government.

MSP Sarah Boyack was born in 1961 and educated at the Royal High School, Edinburgh, and Glasgow University, graduating with a MA Hons in Modern History and Politics, and Heriot-Watt University with a Diploma in Town and Country Planning. Boyack is the daughter of the late Jim Boyack, and shares two of his central passions, town planning and Scottish home rule. She worked in planning for the London Borough of Brent from 1986 to 1988 and Central Regional Council from 1988 to 1992, before becoming a lecturer in Planning at Edinburgh College of Art and Heriot-Watt University from 1992 until 1999.

Boyack was active in student politics and was Chair of the National Organisation of Labour Students and a founder member of Scottish Labour Action, the pro-home rule Labour pressure group. She has been deeply involved in environmental issues and was Scottish co-ordinator of the Socialist Environmental Resource Association (SERA) and Convenor of the Royal Town Planning Institute Scotland. After her election as an MSP in May 1999, Boyack was part of Dewar's five-strong negotiating team with the Lib Dems on forming a coalition. She was subsequently appointed Minister for Transport and the Environment. In her first year and a half, on a number of occasions, Boyack has appeared more at home in the world of academia than politics, being pressured by the business lobby to reduce business costs in any transport strategies.

Following Henry McLeish's election as First Minister, Boyack was one of the most senior ministers who was considered by commentators to be vulnerable for the sack, but in a bloodless reshuffle in which no senior minister was removed, Boyack was effectively demoted to the post of Transport Minister, with the Environmental part of her brief hived off to Sam Galbraith. McLeish's government in its first weeks instigated a review of unpopular policies with the unofficial slogan 'dump the crap' which aimed to get rid of politically correct policies and return to bread and butter issues. Boyack in her new truncated role had to play a central part in this, abandoning the administration's proposals for workplace parking charges, which had met universal opposition from business groups such as the CBI. Whether Boyack can be a more successful minister with a reduced portfolio than before remains to be seen.

EDINBURGH EAST AND MUSSELBURGH

Predecessor Constituencies: Edinburgh East (1945–92).

1999

Electorate: 60,167
Turnout: 36,989 (61.48%)

Candidate	Party	Votes	Votes%	Change%
Susan Deacon	Labour	17,086	46.19	−7.38
Kenny MacAskill	SNP	10,372	28.04	+8.97
Jeremy Balfour	Conservative	4,600	12.44	−2.95
Marjorie Thomas	Liberal Democrat	4,100	11.08	+0.37
Derrick White	SSP	697	1.88	—
Michael Heavey	Independent Youth	134	0.36	—

Labour majority: 6,714 (18.15%)
Swing: 8.18% Labour to SNP

1997

Electorate: 59,648
Turnout: 42,118 (70.61%)

Candidate	Party	Votes	Votes%	Change%
Gavin Strang	Labour	22,564	53.57	+ 8.87
Derrick White	SNP	8,034	19.07	+ 1.14
Kenneth Ward	Conservative	6,483	15.39	− 8.63
Callum MacKellar	Liberal Democrat	4,511	10.71	− 0.82
James Sibbet	Referendum	526	1.25	—

Labour majority: 14,530 (34.50%)
Swing: 3.87% SNP to Labour

1945–92

	Lab%	Con%	SNP%	Lib%	Other%	Turnout%
1992	45.7	24.4	18.4	10.2	1.3	73.9
1987	50.4	24.7	9.5	15.4	—	74.1

	Lab%	Con%	SNP%	Lib%	Other%	Turnout%
1983	44.9	28.6	5.5	21.0	–	70.4
1979	53.7	33.5	12.1	–	0.7	76.1
1974O	44.9	23.1	25.6	5.9	0.5	76.2
1974F	43.7	31.6	15.4	8.7	0.6	81.1
1970	51.8	39.0	8.2	–	1.0	74.5
1966	60.5	39.5	–	–	–	77.4
1964	56.1	43.9	–	–	–	81.0
1959	50.4	49.6	–	–	–	80.7
1955	52.5	47.5	–	–	–	75.4
1954B	57.6	42.4	–	–	–	61.8
1951	54.1	45.9	–	–	–	83.8
1950	53.2	38.8	–	8.0	–	83.2
1947B	50.6	34.3	5.0	10.1	–	63.0
1945B	61.6	38.4	–	–	–	51.0
1945	56.4	37.3	6.3	–	–	69.4

Edinburgh East and Musselburgh is located around the visually striking Arthur's Seat, with a very diverse range of communities and socio-economic groups, from the middle-class, alternative atmosphere of Portobello and Joppa to the deprivation and poverty of Craigmillar and Niddrie, which sit underneath the southern side of Arthur's Seat.

Labour first won Edinburgh East in 1918 and has held it continuously since 1935. Labour's majority under Gavin Strang, MP since 1970, has never really been threatened, falling to 8,456 over the SNP high tide of October 1974. In 1983, when Labour were worried over the loss of Musselburgh, its lead fell to 5,866 over the Conservatives. Since then Labour has increased its majority, which rose from a notional 9,101 in 1992 to 14,530 in 1997 Strang putting on nearly 3,000 votes from the previous election – while the SNP remained static, but moved into second place as the Conservatives lost 4,000 votes.

Labour's vote dropped in the Scottish Parliament elections with Susan Deacon polling 5,000 votes less than Gavin Strang on a reduced turnout while the SNP's Kenny MacAskill made a strong showing in second place putting on over 2,000 extra votes and cutting Labour's majority to 6,714 its lowest since 1983. Edinburgh East has long provided Labour with a secure local base in good and bad times and this is a tradition which looks likely to continue.

MP Gavin Strang was born in 1943 in Dundee and has been MP for Edinburgh East from 1970 to 1997 and Edinburgh East and Musselburgh from 1997. He was educated at Morrison's Academy, Crieff, Edinburgh University, gaining both an honours degree and PhD; and Churchill College, Cambridge, where he attained a diploma in agricultural science. Strang was a Spokesman on Trade and Industry from 1973 to 1974, served in the 1974-9 Labour Government as a Parliamentary Secretary in the Department of Energy in 1974 and in Agriculture, Fisheries and Food from 1974 until 1979. In Labour's long years of opposition, Strang was a Spokesman on Agriculture, Fisheries and Food from 1979 to 1982, resigning from the front bench over Labour's support of the Falklands War. He became a member of the hard left Campaign Group in 1982, which usually precluded frontbench prospects, but he became Spokesman on Employment from 1987 to 1989 and Shadow Minister for Agriculture from 1992 to 1997. He also chaired the PLP Defence Committee from 1985 to 1987 and the Scottish Group of Labour MPs from 1986 to 1987. Upon Labour coming to power, Strang was surprisingly given the post of Minister for Transport in John Prescott's supra-Ministry which included a position at the Cabinet table. His ministerial career was never destined for great things or longevity; his face and politics did not fit the Blairite New Labour agenda of the times and he was sacked in the first ministerial reshuffle in July 1998. Strang has been as a back bencher, the leader of the revolt against the government's attempts to privatise air traffic control – a policy which has not had much support amongst Labour MPs. After leading three sizable revolts, the government eventually got its way when the House of Lords backed down at the end of 2000.

MSP Susan Deacon was born in 1964 in Musselburgh and educated at Musselburgh Grammar School and at Edinburgh University where she gained an MA Hons in Social Policy and Politics and an MBA. She has worked for West Lothian Council as a research officer from 1987 to 1989, East Lothian Council as a senior administrative officer from 1990 to 1992 and as a services manager from 1992 to 1994. Deacon became Director of MBA Programmes at Heriot-Watt University from 1994 to 1998 and worked for Neil Stewart Associates as a conference and events consultant from 1998 to 1999.

She has been a Labour Party activist from student days and was one of the founding members of Scottish Labour Action in 1988: Deacon played a leading part along with Ian Smart and Bob McLean in developing the home rule and neo-nationalist SLA. Neither Smart nor McLean was elected to the Scottish Parliament. Deacon herself nearly did not make it: excluded from the first round of Labour's panel selection, she appealed and was the only successful candidate re-admitted. In the 1999 elections, she was Labour's spokesperson on education and after the election was appointed Minister for Health and Community Care.

In her first year and a half as a minister, Deacon drew generally favourable notices advancing a progressive public health agenda and tackling head-on resistance over sex education from conservative circles such as pro-life campaigners and the Catholic Church, some of whom tried to label her 'nutcase Deacon', hardly a measured form of opposition. She was in this period seen as a potential candidate in a Labour leadership contest when Donald Dewar retired at some point in the distant future, but his tragic death in October 2000 came too soon for her to consider standing and she backed Henry

McLeish for Scottish Labour leader over Jack McConnell. She retained her post unchanged in the resulting ministerial reshuffle, and there followed speculation that either she or Wendy Alexander would put themselves forward for the post of Deputy Labour leader, but neither did, leaving the post to the relatively unknown Cathy Jamieson.

EDINBURGH NORTH AND LEITH

Predecessor Constituencies: Edinburgh Leith (1945–97).

1999

Electorate: 62,976
Turnout: 36,646 (58.19%)

Candidate	Party	Votes	Votes%	Change%
Malcolm Chisholm	Labour	17,203	46.94	+ 0.03
Anne Dana	SNP	9,467	25.83	+ 5.73
Jamie Sempill	Conservative	5,030	13.73	– 4.13
Sebastian Tombs	Liberal Democrat	4,039	11.02	– 2.01
Ronald Brown	SSP	907	2.48	+ 1.70

Labour majority: 7,736 (21.11%)
Swing: 2.85% Labour to SNP

1997

Electorate: 61,617
Turnout: 40,945 (66.45%)

Candidate	Party	Votes	Votes%	Change%
Malcolm Chisholm	Labour	19,209	46.91	+12.00
Anne Dana	SNP	8,231	20.10	– 0.24
Ewen Stewart	Conservative	7,312	17.86	– 6.98
Hilary Campbell	Liberal Democrat	5,335	13.03	+ 1.32
Alexander Graham	Referendum	441	1.08	–
Gavin Brown	SSA	320	0.78	–
Paul Douglas-Reid	NLP	97	0.24	–

Labour majority: 10,978 (26.81%)
Swing: 6.12% SNP to Labour

1945–92

	Lab%	Con%	SNP%	Lib%	Other%	Turnout%
1992	34.3	21.1	21.8	12.3	10.5	71.3
1987	49.3	22.9	9.5	18.3	–	70.8
1983	39.7	26.3	6.5	27.5	–	67.2
1979	46.3	31.9	9.7	12.1	–	75.2

	Lab%	Con%	SNP%	Lib%	Other%	Turnout%
1974O	39.7	28.0	26.1	6.2	–	74.8
1974F	40.6	38.3	21.1	–	–	79.3
1970	46.3	41.0	7.0	5.7	–	73.2
1966	56.8	42.2	–	–	1.0	76.1
1964	55.5	45.5	–	–	–	77.9
1959	47.8	38.0	–	14.2	–	79.5
1955	49.4	32.3	–	–	18.3	77.8
1951	50.1	49.9	–	–	–	84.0
1950	49.3	43.0	–	7.7	–	80.7
1945	60.9	–	–	31.4	7.7	69.1

In the last boundary changes Edinburgh North and Leith gained the middle-class, affluent areas of New Town and Stockbridge from Central, as well as Calton and Lochend from East; out went the council estate of Muirhouse to the West. These changes had very little political impact, cancelling each other out without threatening or strengthening Labour's hold. Leith includes the old port area which has been transformed through urban regeneration and yuppiefication in recent years to the extent that old harbour warehouses now contain fashionable, expensive restaurants and shops. The seat ranges socially from this booming waterfront, to the prosperous New Town and Stockbridge and the council estate of Pilton with major drug and crime problems.

Leith has for long celebrated its radical credentials. 1918 saw the election of an Independent Liberal against the Lloyd George Tory dominated coalition: Captain William Wedgwood Benn, who represented the seat until 1927, then switched to Labour and served in the 1929-31 and 1945 Labour Governments. Captain Benn was Tony Benn's father.

Leith only went Labour for the first time in 1945, like the rest of the city resisting Labour's charms longer than Glasgow and the West of Scotland. In 1951 James Hoy won the seat for Labour with 50.1 per cent against the Conservatives' 49.9 per cent and a majority of 72 on an 84 per cent poll. Ron Brown was first elected in 1979 with a Labour vote of 46.3 per cent and a majority of 4,017 over the Conservatives; this rose to 4,973 in 1983 over the Liberal/SDP Alliance and a Labour vote of 49.3 per cent and majority of 11,327 in 1987.

Ron Brown was an idiosyncratic hard left-winger who combined uncompromising principles with the reputation of a loner. More controversially, he visited Afghanistan post-Soviet invasion and visited Libya in 1984 and 1985, meeting Colonel Gaddafi. His left-wing beliefs were not out of tune with his constituency party, but his personal antics were. There were allegations of an affair with a female assistant and then disruption and misbehaviour at his mistress's London flat culminating in Brown throwing female underwear out of the window. He was consequently deselected by his local party in 1990 who replaced him with Malcolm Chisholm, someone with the same principled left views, but without the erratic behaviour.

Brown stood as independent Labour candidate in 1992 and polled 4,142 votes (10.3 per cent) finishing fifth; Chisholm polled 34.3 per cent, seeing Labour's vote drop 15 per cent and its majority reduced to 4,985. 1997 saw Chisholm put 4,000 votes back on Labour's support and its majority climb back to 10,978. The 1999 elections had Chisholm stand for Labour. Labour's vote fell by a mere 2,000 votes on a reduced turnout, while it actually rose in percentage terms – one of the few constituencies where this occurred. Also standing in these elections was Ron Brown, who polled a derisory 907 votes (2.5 per cent) and finished fifth again.

MP/MSP Malcolm Chisholm was born in 1949 in Edinburgh and was elected MP for Edinburgh Leith in 1992 and Edinburgh North and Leith as MP in 1997 and MSP in 1999. Educated at George Watson's College and Edinburgh University with an MA Hons and Diploma in Education, Chisholm was a teacher in Edinburgh secondary schools for sixteen years and as Chairman of Leith Constituency Labour Party was ideally placed to succeed Ron Brown after he was deselected in 1990.

Elected in 1992, Chisholm comes from the same political traditions as Ron Brown, and joined the hard left Campaign Group. Chairman of the Scottish Housing Group from 1994 to 1996, in 1996 he became Opposition Spokesman on Scotland, replacing his fellow left-winger John McAllion who resigned over Blair's announcement of a referendum. In 1997, he became Parliamentary Under-Secretary of State at the Scottish Office, but resigned a mere six months into office, in December 1997, when 47 Labour MPs rebelled over single-parent benefit cuts.

In the Scottish Parliament, Chisholm was deputy Convenor of the Health and Community Care Committee and a member of the Cross Party Groups on Information, Knowledge and Enlightenment, Older People, and Refugees and Asylum Seekers from May 1999 until October 2000.

In Henry McLeish's ministerial reshuffle upon being elected First Minister in October 2000, Chisholm was unexpectedly made Deputy Minister for Health and Community Care to Susan Deacon. This was seen as a reward for Chisholm for his generally constructive and unsectarian behaviour in the first year and a half, and just reward for a man with many talents and a passion about public health in Scotland. It was also in terms of 'Team McLeish', a politically astute appointment, recognising the need to keep the left of the party on board.

EDINBURGH PENTLANDS

Predecessor Constituencies: none.

1999

Electorate: 60,029
Turnout: 39,600 (65.97%)

Candidate	Party	Votes	Votes%	Change%
Iain Gray	Labour	14,343	36.22	-6.79
David McLetchie	Conservative	11,458	28.93	-3.45
Stewart Gibb	SNP	8,770	22.15	+9.14
Ian Gibson	Liberal Democrat	5,029	12.70	+2.70

Labour majority: 2,885 (7.29%)
Swing: 1.67% Labour to Conservative

1997

Electorate: 59,635
Turnout: 45,742 (76.70%)

Candidate	Party	Votes	Votes%	Change%
Lynda Clark	Labour	19,675	43.01	+11.84
Malcolm Rifkind	Conservative	14,813	32.38	-7.82
Stewart Gibb	SNP	5,952	13.01	-2.66
Jennifer Dawe	Liberal Democrat	4,575	10.00	-2.78
Malcolm McDonald	Referendum	422	0.92	—
Robin Harper	Green	224	0.49	—
Alistair McConnachie	UK Independence	81	0.18	—

Labour majority: 4,862 (10.63%)
Swing: 9.83% Conservative to Labour

1945–92

	Lab%	Con%	SNP%	Lib%	Other%	Turnout%
1992	31.1	40.7	15.4	12.6	0.2	80.2
1987	30.0	38.3	7.2	24.5	—	77.6
1983	23.9	39.2	6.1	29.3	1.6	73.3
1979	36.6	39.3	11.0	13.1	—	76.8
1974O	30.9	33.9	24.6	10.6	—	75.5

	Lab%	Con%	SNP%	Lib%	Other%	Turnout%
1974F	30.8	41.2	12.4	15.6	–	80.9
1970	39.4	46.1	5.9	8.6	–	77.0
1966	44.8	45.0	–	10.2	–	80.5
1964	40.6	46.0	–	13.4	–	81.6
1959	39.7	60.3	–	–	–	80.3
1955	40.5	59.5	–	–	–	77.3
1951	42.3	57.7	–	–	–	83.3
1950	39.2	50.5	–	10.3	–	82.0

Pentlands contains some of the most different areas it is possible to accomodate within the boundaries of one constituency. It has some of the most middle-class and prosperous parts of Edinburgh such as the detached villas of Colinton and Fairmilehead, as well as the stylish villages of Balerno and Currie. It also contains new private sector developments along the A70 as Edinburgh struggles to contain the fast growth of the last few years. The 'other side' of Edinburgh is just as present within the seat in the council scheme of Wester Hailes, which has witnessed extensive depopulation in the last two decades, both planned and unplanned, as well as smaller estates like Sighthill and Stenhouse.

Pentlands should be and has been a traditional, safe Conservative seat, but of course this is Scotland. The seat was Conservative from its creation in 1950, but Labour came near at its Wilsonian high point of 1966, winning 44.8 per cent to the Conservatives' 45.0 per cent. Malcolm Rifkind held it in October 1974 in a three-way contest with Labour and SNP by a mere 1,257 votes and in a two-way contest with Labour by 1,198 in 1979.

This was not an auspicious base with which to start an unpopular period of Conservative Government. Rifkind's majority grew to 4,309 in 1983 and held at 3,745 in 1987 and 4,290 in 1992. Rifkind had by this point served an illustrious career as a Cabinet Minister through the Thatcher-Major Governments including a stint as Scottish Secretary of State from 1986 to 1990, Transport Minister from 1990 to 1992 and Defence Minister from 1992 until 1997, before finally losing in 1997.

Lynda Clark, standing for the first time in 1997, put over 5,000 on Labour's vote, while the Conservatives' fell by nearly 4,000, giving Labour a majority of 4,862 in this most Conservative of seats. In 1999, Labour on a lower poll lost 5,000 voters, while the Conservatives polled 3,500 less reducing Labour's majority to 2,885. This translated into David McLetchie gaining a small swing of 1.67 per cent from Labour to Tory.

The fact Pentlands went Labour in the first place showed how far the Conservatives in Scotland had fallen by 1997 and that they had not dug themselves out of it by 1999. That it took Labour from 1979 to 1997 to win this seat shows the lack of conviction with which it has embraced Labour. When a Conservative revival begins in Scotland, Pentlands will be the kind of place where it will first register. The Conservative choice of candidate, Malcolm Rifkind, previously MP for the seat until he was defeated in 1997, increases the party's chances of making a quick recovery in this seat, which is likely to remain a key marginal in forthcoming UK and Scottish elections.

MP Lynda Clark was born in Dundee in 1949 and elected to Edinburgh Pentlands in 1997 defeating her fellow Queen's Counsel Malcolm Rifkind. Educated at Lawside Academy, Dundee, St Andrews University and Edinburgh University where she obtained her PhD, Clark became an Advocate in 1977, was called to the English Bar, Inner Temple, in 1988 and was appointed a Queen's Counsel in 1989. She became a member of the Scottish Legal Aid Board from 1991 until 1994.

Clark unsuccessfully contested North East Fife in 1992, before winning Edinburgh Pentlands in 1997. She subsequently became Advocate-General for Scotland in May 1999, the first woman Law Officer in Scotland. There were rumours at points that she was not happy with the life of a Scottish Labour Westminster MP and was considering not standing again at the next election. These proved to be totally groundless and Clark is standing in Pentlands again next time.

MSP Iain Gray was born in 1957 in Edinburgh and educated at Inverness Royal Academy, George Watson's College, Edinburgh, Edinburgh University, obtaining a degree in physics, and Moray House College with a certificate in education. Gray was a physics and maths teacher from 1978 until 1986 and Campaign Manager for Oxfam in Scotland from 1986 until 1999, living and working in Africa for two years. He was campaign spokesperson on housing in the Scottish Parliament elections. After being elected to the Scottish Parliament, he was appointed Deputy Minister for Community Care, as Deputy to the Minister for Health, a post he held from May 1999 to October 2000.

In Henry McLeish's first ministerial reshuffle, after his election as First Minister in October 2000, Gray was appointed Deputy Minister for Justice working under Jim Wallace. He has been seen by many observers as a competent minister in his period at community care, with good skills in presentation and grasp of detail, and may at some point be earmarked for further promotion.

EDINBURGH SOUTH

Predecessor Constituencies: none.

1999

Electorate: 64,100

Turnout: 40,135 (62.61%)

Candidate	Party	Votes	Votes%	Change%
Angus MacKay	Labour	14,869	37.05	−9.77
Margo MacDonald	SNP	9,445	23.53	+10.61
Mike Pringle	Liberal Democrat	8,961	22.33	+4.69
Iain Whyte	Conservative	6,378	15.89	−5.39
William Black	SWP	482	1.20	−

Labour majority: 5,424 (13.52%)

Swing: 10.19% Labour to SNP

1997

Electorate: 62,467

Turnout: 44,838 (71.78%)

Candidate	Party	Votes	Votes%	Change%
Nigel Griffiths	Labour	20,993	46.82	+5.30
Elizabeth Smith	Conservative	9,541	21.28	−10.88
Mike Pringle	Liberal Democrat	7,911	17.64	+4.45
John Hargreaves	SNP	5,791	12.92	+0.03
Ian McLean	Referendum	504	1.12	−
Bradley Dunn	NLP	98	0.22	−

Labour majority: 11,452 (25.54%)

Swing: 8.09% Conservative to Labour

1945–92

	Lab%	Con%	SNP%	Lib%	Other%	Turnout%
1992	41.5	31.2	12.8	13.4	0.2	72.7
1987	37.7	33.8	5.1	22.5	0.9	75.7
1983	28.6	36.8	5.0	28.6	1.0	71.1
1979	34.3	39.7	8.4	16.4	1.2	77.3
1974O	28.2	35.9	21.7	14.2	−	74.2

	Lab%	Con%	SNP%	Lib%	Other%	Turnout%
1974F	27.6	41.7	12.8	17.9	–	80.8
1970	36.5	48.2	6.9	8.4	–	74.1
1966	39.5	53.2	7.3	–	–	77.6
1964	33.7	53.2	–	13.1	–	80.3
1959	28.5	57.6	–	13.9	–	81.2
1957B	30.9	45.6	–	23.5	–	65.8
1955	32.5	67.5	–	–	–	77.2
1951	27.4	72.6	–	–	–	81.4
1950	24.6	65.0	–	10.6	–	82.1
1945	29.2	70.8	–	–	–	66.4

Edinburgh South combines some of the most exclusive neighbourhoods in urban Scotland. Areas such as Morningside, Merchiston and Newington are home to the Scottish establishment from the private sector finance houses, the legal profession and the city's universities. It also contains post-war council estates such as Gilmerton and Liberton.

South on the surface looks a rock-solid Conservative seat. William Darling was Conservative MP from 1945 until 1957 securing 70.8 per cent of the vote in 1945 and 72.6 per cent in 1951. He was followed by Michael Clark Hutchison from 1957 to 1979 whose majority fell to 3,226 in October 1974 over Labour. Michael Ancram was elected for the first time in 1979 defeating a young Gordon Brown; Labour managed a 1.1 per cent swing from the Conservatives reducing Ancram's majority to 2,460. Ancram held on in 1983 with an increased majority of 3,665 over the Liberal-SDP Alliance, before Nigel Griffiths jumped from third place putting 5,500 on Labour's vote to seize the seat in 1987 with a majority of 1,859. In 1992, a bad year for Labour and a relatively good year for the Conservatives in Scotland, Struan Stevenson could not win back any support and Labour held on, comfortably increasing its majority to 4,176.

In 1997 Nigel Griffiths increased Labour's vote by 4,500, while the Conservatives' fell by nearly 5,000 leaving Labour with an impressive majority of 11,452. In the 1999 elections, Angus MacKay held on easily for Labour despite seeing his vote fall by 6,000. The SNP, energised by a strong campaign by Nationalist hero Margo MacDonald, emerged from nowhere, rising from fourth to second putting on an extra 3,500 votes and 10.6 per cent. The Liberal Democrats, Mike Pringle, a popular local councillor, gained 1,000 votes after improving the Lib Dems' standing significantly in 1997. This left the Conservatives in a seat they had held continuously until the previous decade reduced to fourth place and their vote reduced by 3,000 from 1997.

Edinburgh as a city is ripe territory for a Conservative revival, and the economic and social times of the moment are conducive to such a possibility with a property and employment boom. Pentlands will need little persuasion to come back into the Tory fold, but South seems a different prospect, and the 1997 and 1999 elections seem to indicate that it has shifted away from the Conservatives permanently. A Tory revival without challenging in seats like South is not a revival worthy of the name, but can they or the SNP or Lib Dems challenge Labour's new dominance?

MP Nigel Griffiths was born in 1955 in Glasgow and has represented Edinburgh South since 1987 when he defeated Michael Ancram. Educated at Hawick High School, Edinburgh University and Moray College of Education, he has worked in a variety of advice and welfare rights posts, including a spell as Information and Welfare Rights Officer of the North Edinburgh Action Group for people with disabilities from 1979 to 1987.

Griffiths was an Edinburgh District Councillor from 1980 to 1987 and was Chair of the Housing Committee, a member of Edinburgh Council of Social Services from 1984 to 1987 and Edinburgh Health Council from 1982 until 1987. A committed devolutionist without ever being on the nationalist wing of the party, Griffiths was Secretary of Lothian Devolution Campaign in the 1979 referendum and a member of the cross-party Scottish Constitutional Convention, convening its Finance Committee.

On his election in 1987, he was a Labour Whip from 1987 to 1989, followed by Spokesman on Consumer Affairs from 1989 to 1997. Seen as an ally of Gordon Brown in opposition and part of Brown's charm offensive to win over the City and 'the forces of conservatism' to New Labour, in 1997 he became Trade and Industry Under-Secretary for Consumer Affairs. However, he never took to the trappings and pressures of office, and reportedly suffered from poor relations with officials. A week before the first Blair reshuffle in July 1998 he was railing against 'a civil service coup' to get him the sack; he was dismissed from office and subsequently became a member of the Public Accounts Committee from 1999 onward.

MSP Angus MacKay was born in 1964 in Edinburgh and educated at St Augustine's High School, Edinburgh, and Edinburgh University (where he was a good friend of the SNP's John Swinney) with a MA Hons in Politics and Modern History. MacKay worked for Shelter Scotland from 1987 to 1990, then became researcher to Adam Ingram MP and Mo Mowlam MP, while she was Spokesperson for City and Corporate Affairs from 1990 to 1992. He then worked as a policy adviser to Henry McLeish from 1992 until 1995 and Press Officer to George Robertson during the 1997 election.

Elected to Edinburgh City Council in 1995, he was Convenor of the Finance Committee from 1997 to 1999. In the 1999 Scottish Parliament election campaign, he was Labour spokesperson on the economy, industry and finance, and after the election, appointed Deputy Minister for Justice and given responsibility for land reform and drug policy co-ordination, a post he held from May 1999 to October 2000.

After Donald Dewar's death, MacKay became campaign manager for Henry McLeish in the contest to succeed Dewar and drew plaudits for a campaign that was widely over-optimistic and inaccurate in how it estimated McLeish's support, given the narrow 44:36 victory he secured over Jack McConnell. He secured his reward for being on the winning side with promotion to the post of Minister for Finance and Local Government, which had previously been Jack McConnell's post, combined with local government from the old Communities post. He is responsible in his new post for the overall Scottish budget, European structural funds, the 21st Century Government programme, including e-government, modernising government and civil service reform. Such a wide portfolio will give MacKay the chance to shine and establish a wider profile, but he will have to deal with numerous pressures and conflicting demands on the restricted Scottish budget.

EDINBURGH WEST

Predecessor Constituencies: none.

1999

Electorate: 61,747
Turnout: 41,583 (67.34%)

Candidate	Party	Votes	Votes%	Change%
Margaret Smith	Liberal Democrat	15,161	36.46	-6.74
James Douglas-Hamilton	Conservative	10,578	25.44	-2.54
Carol Fox	Labour	8,860	21.31	+2.52
Graham Sutherland	SNP	6,984	16.80	+9.96

Liberal Democrat majority: 4,583 (11.02%)
Swing: 2.10% Liberal Democrat to Conservative

1997

Electorate: 61,133
Turnout: 47,631 (77.91%)

Candidate	Party	Votes	Votes%	Change%
Donald Gorrie	Liberal Democrat	20,578	43.20	+13.31
James Douglas-Hamilton	Conservative	13,325	27.98	-10.23
Lesley Hinds	Labour	8,948	18.79	+1.42
Graham Sutherland	SNP	4,210	8.84	-3.70
Stephen Elphick	Referendum	277	0.58	-
Paul Coombes	Liberal	263	0.55	-
Anthony Jack	Anti-sleaze	30	0.06	-

Liberal Democrat majority: 7,253 (15.22%)
Swing: 11.77% Conservative to Liberal Democrat

1945–92

	Lab%	Con%	SNP%	Lib%	Other%	Turnout%
1992	18.0	37.0	8.4	35.2	1.3	82.7
1987	22.2	37.4	5.6	34.9	-	79.3
1983	20.1	38.2	4.6	37.1	-	75.0
1979	28.2	45.4	9.2	17.2	-	77.8
1974O	25.2	38.2	20.2	16.4	-	76.6

	Lab%	Con%	SNP%	Lib%	Other%	Turnout%
1974F	24.4	44.2	9.9	21.5	–	82.2
1970	35.8	49.2	6.8	8.2	–	75.0
1966	39.0	48.2	–	12.8	–	78.7
1964	35.3	50.6	–	14.1	–	80.9
1959	30.5	56.5	–	13.0	–	80.3
1955	33.0	67.0	–	–	–	75.7
1951	34.0	66.0	–	–	–	83.1
1950	32.0	60.0	–	8.0	–	82.2
1945	44.9	47.3	–	7.8	–	67.5

West sits on the outskirts of Edinburgh containing some of the finest areas of the Edinburgh middle classes and commuter towns outside the city. Its boundaries include Corstorphine, Cramond, Barnton and Blackhall, all highly exclusive and expensive. The slumbering, picturesque town of South Queensferry, perched as it is on the Firth of Forth between the Forth Road and Rail Bridges is also in West, having previously been in Linlithgow; Edinburgh Airport, prior to boundary changes in Livingston, is now also in West. The seat also includes the run-down council estate of Muirhouse with major economic, crime and drug problems, which provided the setting for Irvine Welsh's cult hit *Trainspotting*.

It is not surprising that the seat is a Conservative-Liberal Democrat battleground, but it is illustrative of how far Scotland has moved against the Tories that the Lib Dems have challenged so seriously for so long and eventually triumphed. West was Liberal until 1929, then briefly won by Labour in that year, before reverting to the Conservatives in 1931. Ian Clark Hutchison was Conservative MP from 1941 until 1959, holding it over Labour by only 1,054 votes in 1945; however by 1955 as Labour's star waned the Conservative vote increased to 67.0 per cent. Anthony Stodart (MP from 1957 until 1974) was followed by Lord James Douglas-Hamilton from October 1974 who first had a majority of 5,202 over Labour with a certain Donald Gorrie of the Liberals finishing fourth – he first stood in the constituency in 1970.

Post-1979, on three occasions, Douglas-Hamilton survived by narrow margins: in 1983 his majority fell from 7,351 to 498, rising to 1,234 in 1987 against the Liberal-SDP's Derek King. In 1992, Donald Gorrie returned to his previous haunts and reduced the majority to 879 and in 1997 finally triumphed, despite boundary changes helping the Tories. Gorrie beat Lord James gaining a Liberal Democrat majority of 7,253 – polling 5,000 extra votes and seeing the Conservative support drop by 6,500.

The 1999 elections were a good measure of the strength of the Lib Dems' support in terms of party versus Donald Gorrie's personal vote. Margaret Smith, an able, energetic councillor, had beaten Gorrie for the Lib Dems' nomination and held the seat with little difficulty. On a lower turnout, the Lib Dem vote fell by 5,000 and the Conservatives' by 3,000, producing a Lib Dem majority of 4,583.

Edinburgh West is a seat to watch in the future. Gorrie, after standing in the seat for three decades before winning is not standing again in the seat, but it will give the Lib Dems a decent chance to persuade this seat of their charms. If there is to be a Conservative recovery, even a mini one – and people have been talking about one since the 1960s – Edinburgh West is the kind of place where something has to happen.

MP Donald Gorrie was born in 1933 in India and was finally elected MP for Edinburgh West at the fifth attempt, having stood first in the seat in the distant days of 1970. Gorrie was educated at Hurst Grange, Stirling, Oundle School, Northampton, and Corpus Christi College, Oxford, where he gained a degree in Modern History. He was a schoolmaster at that northerly outpost of discipline Gordonstoun School from 1957 to 1960, followed by a period as adult education lecturer at Edinburgh University from 1966 to 1969. Having joined the Liberal Party in 1961, he was Director of Research of the Scottish Liberals from 1969 to 1971 and Director of Administration from 1971 to 1975. He was elected to Edinburgh City Council in 1971 in a by-election for the Corstorphine ward which he was to hold for the next 26 years; he was Leader of the Liberal Group on Lothian Regional Council from 1974 until 1996 and Edinburgh City Council from 1980 until 1997.

Gorrie was beaten to the Edinburgh West Liberal Democrat nomination for the Scottish Parliament elections by Margaret Smith and represents the Central Scotland region. In the Scottish Parliament, Gorrie has proved a stern critic of his party leadership on a number of issues, particularly the detail of the coalition negotiations between Labour and Liberal Democrats and the issue of student tuition fees, which the Lib Dems had pledged to abolish. Gorrie was one of three Lib Dem MSPs opposed to coalition with Labour, calling them 'Stalinist liars'. Along with Margo MacDonald, Nationalist MSP for the Lothians, he has been one of the most vocal opponents of the Holyrood project. In the Scottish Parliament, Gorrie sat on the Local Government Committee from May 1999 to December 2000 and on the Procedures Committee from May 1999 onwards, and now sits on the Finance Committee as well. He is also a member of the Cross Party Groups on Children, of which he is Convenor, Drug Misuse, Older People, Sports, and Refugees and Asylum Seekers, the last two of which he is Vice-Convenor of. He became Liberal Democrat Spokesperson on Finance in November 2000.

MSP Margaret Smith was born in 1961 in Edinburgh and educated at Broughton High School, Edinburgh, and Edinburgh University where she graduated with an MA in General Arts. She worked in pensions documentation in Guardian Royal Exchange from 1983 to 1984, as an Executive Officer of Registers of Scotland (Land Register) from 1984 to 1987 and as Scottish Officer of the United Nations Association from 1990 until 1996.

Elected to Edinburgh City Council in 1995, she was the Liberal Democrat spokesperson on transport from 1997 to 1999. Smith became Constituency Organiser of Edinburgh West Lib Dems in the run-up to the 1997 election and organised Gorrie's winning campaign. She then surprisingly defeated Gorrie for the Lib Dem nomination for the Scottish Parliament. She is Convenor of the Health and Community Care Committee and a member of the Public Petitions Committee and is also a member of the Cross Party Groups on Children, Older People, Care, Rail Services, and Tobacco Control. She was appointed Liberal Democrat Spokesperson on Equal Opportunities in November 2000.

FALKIRK EAST

Predecessor Constituencies: none.

1999

Electorate: 57,345
Turnout: 35,212 (61.4%)

Candidate	Party	Votes	Votes%	Change%
Cathy Peattie	Labour	15,721	44.65	-11.47
Keith Brown	SNP	11,582	32.89	+8.95
Alastair Orr	Conservative	3,399	9.65	-4.33
Gordon McDonald	Liberal Democrat	2,509	7.13	+1.95
Raymond Stead	Socialist Labour	1,643	4.67	–
Victor McGrain	Pensioners	358	1.02	–

Labour majority: 4,139 (11.76%)
Swing: 10.21% Labour to SNP

1997

Electorate: 56,792
Turnout: 41,595 (73.24%)

Candidate	Party	Votes	Votes%	Change%
Michael Connarty	Labour	23,344	56.12	+11.96
Keith Brown	SNP	9,959	23.94	-4.44
Malcolm Nicol	Conservative	5,813	13.98	-6.21
Rodger Spillane	Liberal Democrat	2,153	5.18	-2.09
Sebastian Mowbray	Referendum	326	0.78	–

Labour majority: 13,385 (32.18%)
Swing: 8.20% SNP to Labour

1983–92

	Lab%	Con%	SNP%	Lib%	Other%	Turnout%
1992	46.1	20.7	26.2	6.9	–	76.9
1987	54.2	18.7	15.4	11.7	–	74.8
1983	47.7	21.0	11.9	18.5	0.9	72.3

Despite its name, this seat does not really involve Falkirk at all as the boundary changes of the mid-1990s removed wards in Falkirk town from Falkirk East to Falkirk West. This constituency is centred on the towns of Grangemouth, Bo'ness (Borrowstounness) with its old railway line, Carron of Carron iron works fame, Polmont and Stenhousemuir. Despite some middle-class commuter areas such as Polmont, which is conveniently located on the Edinburgh-Glasgow rail line, Falkirk East is mainly a working-class constituency with a considerable but not overwhelming proportion of council housing (46.3 per cent in 1991). Economically, the area is dominated by the BP oil refinery at Grangemouth, a plant which also dominates the skyline, especially at night.

Politically, the seat is safely Labour, though the SNP has offered an important challenge in recent years. The SNP challenge was rooted in the predecessor constituencies to Falkirk East (and Falkirk West), with a strong performance in Stirling and Falkirk Burghs by former SNP leader Robert McIntyre at a by-election in 1971 and in the Stirling, Falkirk and Grangemouth seat at the general elections of 1974 (see Stirling for results). In the October 1974 election, Labour's Harry Ewing just held off the SNP with a majority of 1,766 in the Stirling, Falkirk and Grangemouth seat, though the break-up of that seat into three different constituencies ended the SNP surge at that time.

In the 1990s, the Nationalists suffered further from boundary changes to this seat at the 1997 Westminster election, as well as from the Labour landslide. But the SNP did recover support at the Scottish election in 1999. It is the only challenger to Labour, given the poor performances of the Conservatives and Liberal Democrats, but the SNP would have to make up an awful lot of ground to win this constituency at a Westminster election.

The SNP are, though, the most consistent challenger to Labour, as the Conservatives and Liberal Democrats are marginal forces in the seat. The Tories have declined in popularity in the seat, just as they have across Scotland, whilst the Liberal Democrats have a very limited history of competing in Falkirk East and its predecessor constituencies. Each has a very marginal role to play in the seat. The SNP, meantime, has slowly rebuilt considerable levels of support in the constituency following the party's collapse after 1979, when the party was in fourth place in the seat in 1983. At the next general election, the SNP will require a new candidate as its contestant in 1997 and 1999, Keith Brown, was selected for the marginal Ochil constituency. However, Labour and Michael Connarty are too well entrenched in this seat to see an upset. Labour's 1997 result was its second highest in the seat and its predecessors since 1945. The SNP may edge closer though, with hopes of future Scottish election success.

MP Michael Connarty was born in Coatbridge in 1947. He was educated at St Bartholomews and St Patricks High, Coatbridge and is a graduate of Stirling University, Glasgow University and Jordanhill College and worked as a special needs teacher from 1976 until 1992. He was a councillor on Stirling District from 1974 until 1990 and Labour leader from 1980 until 1990. He was also a founder member of the

Labour Co-ordinating Committee in Scotland. At Westminster he was Parliamentary Private Secretary to Tom Clarke at Culture from 1997 to 1998 and served on the European Directives Committee from 1993 to 1997. He was Chair of the Scottish Parliamentary Labour Group at Westminster from 1998 to 1999 and currently sits on the Information Committee and the European Scrutiny Committee and is Chair of the all-party group for chemical industries: a clear constituency interest given the BP refinery at Grangemouth. He was critical of the Scottish Executive over its abolition of Section 28/Clause 2A – a far cry from his days as a leading left-winger and his time as leader of Stirling Council where he was at the forefront of pioneering radical policies on equal opportunities and women's issues. He was also rejected by the Labour Party for its selection panel for the Scottish Parliament along with neighbouring Dennis Canavan and Ian Davidson.

MSP Cathy Peattie was born in 1952. She was educated at Beancross Primary and Moray Secondary School, Grangemouth and had a number of occupations before becoming an MSP. She was a shop worker, factory worker, training supervisor, field worker and training officer with SPPA, a Development Worker with the Volunteer Network in Falkirk, a Community Development Worker and then Manager of the Community Outreach organisation from 1991 to 1993 and Director of Falkirk Voluntary Action Resource Centre from 1993 until 1999. She was also Convenor of the Council of Voluntary Service Scotland. She joined the Labour Party in 1974 and was a former Chair of the Scottish Labour Women's Committee, in addition to serving on the party's Scottish Exectuive Committee. She sat on the Rural Affairs Committee of the Scottish Parliament from May 1999 to December 2000 and on the Education Committee from May 1999, and now sits on the Equal Opportunities Committee. She is also a member of the Cross Party Groups on Crofting, Children, Drug Misuse, Information, Knowledge and Enlightenment, Oil and Gas, Renewable Energy and Men's Violence Against Women. She is also Convenor of the Cross Party Group on the Media. She sang solo at Donald Dewar's funeral in Glasgow in 2000, singing at the request of Dewar's family Robert Burns' *Aye Waukin*.

FALKIRK WEST

Predecessor Constituencies: none.

Westminster By-election 21 December 2000

Electorate: 53,953
Turnout: 19,504 (36.15%)

Candidate	Party	Votes	Votes%	Change%
Eric Joyce	Labour	8,492	43.54	-15.81
David Kerr	SNP	7,787	39.93	+16.50
Craig Stevenson	Conservative	1,621	8.31	-3.78
Iain Hunter	SSP	989	5.07	–
Hugh O'Donnell	Liberal Democrat	615	3.15	-1.98

Labour majority: 705 (3.61%)
Swing: 16.16% Labour to SNP

1999

Electorate: 53,404
Turnout: 33,667 (63.04%)

Candidate	Party	Votes	Votes%	Change%
Dennis Canavan	MP for Falkirk West	18,511	54.98	–
Ross Martin	Labour	6,319	18.77	-40.58
Michael Matheson	SNP	5,986	17.78	-5.65
Gordon Miller	Conservative	1,897	5.63	-6.46
Andrew Smith	Liberal Democrat	954	2.83	-2.30

MP for Falkirk West majority: 12,192 (36.21%)
Swing: 47.78% Labour to MP for Falkirk West

1997

Electorate: 52,850

Turnout: 38,370 (72.6%)

Candidate	Party	Votes	Votes%	Change%
Dennis Canavan	Labour	22,772	59.35	+7.90
David Alexander	SNP	8,989	23.43	-0.10
Carol Buchanan	Conservative	4,639	12.09	-6.76
Derek Houston	Liberal Democrat	1,970	5.13	-1.03

Labour majority: 13,783 (35.92%)

Swing: 4.00% SNP to Labour

1983–92

	Lab%	Con%	SNP%	Lib%	Other%	Turnout%
1992	49.8	19.6	24.3	6.3	–	76.8
1987	53.2	17.6	16.5	12.7	–	76.6
1983	45.6	21.0	13.0	20.4	–	74.0

Until its recent controversies, Falkirk West has enjoyed a fairly undistinguished past as a safe Labour seat. Both of the Falkirk seats were created in 1983, out of the remains of the old Stirling, Falkirk and Grangemouth seat and in West's case, Stirlingshire West (see Stirling for results). Falkirk West contains the bulk of the town of Falkirk, along with the small towns of Denny, Larbert and Bonnybridge (Scotland's UFO capital). Before 1999, Falkirk West could be viewed as a safe Labour seat in which the SNP offered a sustained but somewhat distant challenge at recent elections. In 1999, it was the seat in which the Labour vote fell the furthest in the whole of Scotland, albeit in rather unique circumstances. The main political development within this constituency involved the selection battle between the Labour Party hierarchy and the local CLP over the ability of the sitting Westminster MP, Dennis Canavan, to stand as Labour's candidate at the Scottish election in 1999.

Canavan had been a Labour MP in the area since October 1974, first as MP for Stirlingshire West and then as MP for Falkirk West. Canavan defeated Donald Dewar for the Labour nomination of Stirlingshire West in October 1974, a result which left a bitter taste and sense of animosity between the two which was to come back to haunt Labour twenty-five years later.

Canavan had built up a substantial majority, was deeply popular within his constituency and local party, but had developed a reputation as a maverick left-winger at Westminster. Definitely 'off-message' within New Labour and prone to acts of rebellion in the division lobbies at Westminster, Canavan was one candidate the

Labour leadership did not want. After a protracted and very public selection battle in 1998 to 1999, Labour selected Ross Martin as its official candidate, with Canavan standing as an independent at the Scottish election in 1999: appearing as MP for Falkirk West on the ballot paper. Canavan's subsequent victory was overwhelming and a humiliation for Labour. Significantly, Canavan not only swept his constituency but polled extremely well in the regional list for Central Scotland in which he – as an individual – gained 7,000 more votes than the Liberal Democrats.

Canavan remained as a dual mandate member from his election in May 1999 until November 2000. During this period he had the power to call a troublesome Westminster by-election for Labour at a time of his choosing. However, his decision in October 2000 to call a by-election, then change his mind, and finally call it, changed things. From Labour being expected to automatically lose the seat, it was now seen to have a fighting chance, and after the Glasgow Anniesland results, Labour was viewed as the favourite to win the seat. It also took the opportunity post-Anniesland to hold the by-election quickly and in the immediate week before christmas: the first such Scottish by-election since Inverness in 1954.

Falkirk West was still a by-election Labour feared: the Canavan factor had cost Labour dear in the May 1999 elections and had also seen a number of Canavan's supporters elected as independent councillors. However, on the other hand, Labour's main opponents, the SNP did not have a strong base in the constituency and one had to go as far back as October 1974 for when the SNP last challenged Labour reducing Canavan's majority when he was first elected by a mere 367 votes in the then Stirlingshire West.

In the event, Labour held on to the seat by the narrow margin of 705, a much less emphatic margin than had been widely predicted. Labour's vote fell by 14,000 from 1997 on a turnout reduced by half, while the SNP's vote fell by over 1,000. In percentage terms, Labour's vote fell 15.8%, substantially more than in Glasgow Anniesland, but nowhere near the drastic fall of Hamilton South, while the SNP's increase of 16.5% was a remarkable comeback after the Anniesland results. The Scottish Socialists polled a respectable 5.07% – their fourth saved deposit in five contests – signalling that they may have become a permanent fixture on the Scottish political landscape.

Labour were content to hold Falkirk West in difficult circumstances, but the low turnout and close result must worry the party about how it can best mobilise its vote. The SNP's post-election reaction was revealing arguing that the pattern of Scottish politics in the last 27 by-elections was of the SNP going up and Labour down: a timeframe that goes back to Hamilton in 1967: a perspective which assumes that modern Scottish politics began at that point.

Labour have taken a considerable amount of political damage in Falkirk West in the last few years, and they can only hope that things will improve from now on. They will be odds-on favourites to hold the seat at the UK election, but Canavan seems entrenched for the foreseeable future as an independent MSP: a reminder of the pitfalls of 'control freakery' politics.

MP Eric Joyce was born in 1960 in Perth and is an ex-major in the British Army and worked for the Commission for Racial Equality in Scotland as a public affairs consultant from 1999 to 2000. Joyce first hit public attention when he was sacked from the army in February 1998 and threatened with a court martial for writing a Fabian Society pamphlet 'Arms and the Man: Renewing the Armed Forces', accusing the army of sexism, racism and class discrimination.

Joyce made it on to Labour's panel of approved candidates for the Scottish Parliament in 1998 and was a list candidate for Central Scotland. He has been a member of the Fabian Society National Executive from 1998 and was also editor of the Fabian pamphlet 'Now's the Hour: New Thinking for Holyrood'. He is a Blairite moderniser and an arch-Labour anti-nationalist who sees the SNP as an irrelevance in post-devolution politics. He criticised Yasmin Alibhai-Brown, the writer in the New Statesman in November 2000 for her 'superficial and confused analysis' which excluded other black voices in the media.

In the by-election campaign, Joyce presented himself as an independent voice, emphasising his criticisms of the army and bringing to attention getting into trouble at school at the age of 15 for violent behaviour. The SNP tried to annoy him, constantly calling him 'Major Joyce', but he ignored this and is clearly a man of talent and much ambition who should be destined for higher things at Westminster.

MSP Dennis Canavan was MP for Stirlingshire West from 1974 until 1983 and then became the member for Falkirk West. He was also famously elected as the constituency's MSP in 1999. He was born in Cowdenbeath in 1942, educated at St Bride's primary school and St Columbia's High School, Cowdenbeath and graduated from Edinburgh University with a BSc (Hons) and a diploma in education, after which he entered the teaching profession as a maths teacher. He taught at St Modan's in Stirling from 1970 to 1974 and then was assistant head of Holyrood High School, in Edinburgh. He was a councillor in Stirling from 1973 to 1974 and became Labour group leader in 1974, before his election to Parliament in later that year. At Westminster, Canavan was a member of the Foreign Affairs Select Committee from 1982 until 1997 and then the International Development Select Committee from 1997 to 1999. In the Scottish Parliament this specialism in international affairs was continued as he became a member of the European Committee. He is also a member of the Cross Party Groups on Animal Welfare, Palliative Care, Refugees and Asylum Seekers and is Convenor of the Sports Group. In his biographies his clubs are listed as Camelon Labour and Bannockburn Miners' Welfare – not exactly the New Club or the Garrick. Before standing as an Independent, Canavan conducted a ballot of Falkirk West Constituency Labour Party and a staggering 95 per cent of party members wanted him to be able to stand as the Labour candidate. On the second day of the Parliament, Canavan put himself forward as a candidate for First Minister, gaining three votes. After Donald's Dewar's election to the post, Canavan strode across the floor of the Parliament and shook hands with Dewar, much to the latter's obvious discomfort. Canavan, like Ken Livingstone in London, has found out that there is a blossoming life outside Labour; independence has only enhanced, rather than diminished him and he seems a safe bet for election to Falkirk West for as long as he wishes to stand.

A bizarre chain of events eventually led to Canavan resigning his Westminster seat. In October 2000, he announced his intention to resign his seat and force a Westminster by-election on Labour. However, events took an unexpected turn following Donald Dewar's death. In the subsequent election for a First Minister, Canavan stood again and won three votes, but engaged in a series of respectful asides with Henry McLeish. Within weeks, after behind-the-scenes negotiations, Canavan called off his threat to force a by-election and reapplied to join the Labour Party. Two weeks later in November, Canavan announced he had changed his mind and was not re-applying to Labour and invoked a difficult by-election on them. The reason he gave was that he had found 'additional information' on why he was excluded from the list of approved candidates for the Scottish Parliament. Another, as plausible a reason, could have been that Canavan was genuinely shocked by many voters' reaction to his intention to rejoin Labour, which was one of regret and feeling let down at losing one of the few independent voices in the Parliament. Whatever the reasons in this strange chapter of events, Canavan emerged from it slightly damaged and diminished by the whole process.

FIFE CENTRAL

Predecessor Constituencies: Fife West (1945–70).

1999

Electorate: 58,850
Turnout: 32,852 (55.82%)

Candidate	Party	Votes	Votes%	Change%
Henry McLeish	Labour	18,828	57.31	-1.35
Tricia Marwick	SNP	10,153	30.91	+5.89
Jane Ann Liston	Liberal Democrat	1,953	5.94	-0.46
Keith Harding	Conservative	1,918	5.84	-3.16

Labour majority: 8,675 (26.4%)
Swing: 3.62% Labour to SNP

1997

Electorate: 58,315
Turnout: 49,765 (69.9%)

Candidate	Party	Votes	Votes%	Change%
Henry McLeish	Labour	23,912	58.66	+7.94
Tricia Marwick	SNP	10,199	25.02	+0.08
Jacob Rees-Mogg	Conservative	3,669	9.00	-8.45
Ross Laird	Liberal Democrat	2,610	6.40	-0.49
J. Scrymgeour-Wedderburn	Referendum	375	0.92	—

Labout majority: 13,713 (33.64%)
Swing: 3.93% SNP to Labour

1945–92

	Lab%	Con%	SNP%	Lib%	Other%	Turnout%
1992	50.4	17.6	25.1	6.9	—	74.3
1987	53.4	16.7	14.7	15.2	—	76.2
1983	43.1	22.5	10.2	23.4	0.8	72.5
1979	58.0	20.2	19.3	—	2.5	77.4
1974O	51.9	12.3	33.4	—	2.4	73.9
1974F	53.3	19.8	22.5	—	4.4	79.2
1970	61.6	26.2	11.0	—	1.7	74.3

	Lab%	Con%	SNP%	Lib%	Other%	Turnout%
1966	63.0	19.3	14.1	–	3.6	76.8
1964	65.6	27.0	–	–	7.4	78.6
1959	56.2	24.7	–	–	19.1	81.3
1955	62.6	24.8	–	–	12.6	80.3
1951	64.9	24.6	–	–	10.5	85.5
1950	54.8	23.6	–	–	21.6	84.9
1945	37.7	20.6	–	–	42.1	75.4

Geographically, this seat covers Glenrothes, the main town in the constituency, as well as Leslie, Leven, Markinch, Methil and Windygates. Former heavy industrial areas are mixed with the New Town service sector economy of Glenrothes, also home to light industry. Despite the existence of the New Town, male claimant unemployment was 10.1 per cent in June 2000.

Politically, this constituency has seldom seen a challenge to Labour. The SNP came closest in 1974, but even then, Labour retained over 50 per cent of the vote and had a majority of 7,986 votes. Parts of this seat were also in Communist Willie Gallacher's constituency, but support for the far left folded in the 1950s to the benefit of Labour, though the Communists kept standing candidates into the early 1980s. The boundary changes to the old Central Fife seat, which removed the ex-mining core of the constituency to Dunfermline East, significantly undermined the far left presence in the constituency and it never recovered (see Dunfermline East profile).

Though the SNP vote has risen in percentage terms from 1992 to 1999, its numerical support remains static at around the 10,000 mark: clear signs of a plateau effect. As the SNP candidate at recent elections, Tricia Marwick, is now a list MSP for Mid-Scotland and Fife, the Nationalists will field a new candidate at the UK general election. However, success is highly unlikely though through Ms Marwick and the SNP Scottish Parliamentary office in Glenrothes the party's profile in Fife Central will be raised. The SNP has also had some local election success in the constituency in Glenrothes and some of the surrounding small towns, winning the council ward of Macedonia and South Parks from Labour in October 2000; but it would take a substantial change in political fortunes for the SNP to turn Fife Central into a marginal seat.

Labour's support has fluctuated, but stays substantial, and the seat has remained safe in both recent years and the long term. Though the sitting MP, Henry McLeish, is retiring from Westminster to concentrate on the Scottish Parliament, where he is now First Minister, his successor, Fife Council leader John McDougall, will inherit a safe seat. Recent elections have also shown that the Conservatives and Liberal Democrats are practically non-existent in the constituency, so Labour should triumph again fairly comfortably in spite of the enhanced SNP presence.

MP/MSP Henry McLeish was born in Methil in 1948, educated at Buckhaven High School, Methil and gained a BSc (Hons) in Urban Planning at Heriot-Watt University. A schoolboy signing for Leeds United at the age of 15, he ended up playing for his local team and no-hopers East Fife as well as being capped by Scotland under-18s. He was employed as a planning officer with Fife County Council from 1974 to 1975 and with Dunfermline District Council from 1975 to 1987. He also worked as a part-time lecturer at Heriot-Watt University from 1973 to 1987 and as a part-time employment consultant from 1984 to 1987. He was a councillor on Kirkcaldy District Council from 1974 to 1977, where he was Chairman of the Planning Committee, and on Fife Regional Council from 1978 to 1987, where he was chair of the Further Education Committee from 1978 to 1982, before becoming council leader from 1982 to 1987.

As leader of Fife Regional Council, McLeish was responsible for developing popular policies such as free TV licences and bus passes for the elderly, free home helps and comprehensive nursery places for all four-year-olds. He first stood for Westminster in Fife East in the 1979 election winning 19.9 per cent and coming third, before attempting as a young anti-Common Market, unilateral disarmer to unseat the aging right-winger Willie Hamilton in Fife Central prior to the 1983 election, narrowly failing. Willie Hamilton retired after the 1983 election, and McLeish was selected to fight the seat and won it in 1987.

After his election to Westminster, McLeish became Vice-Chair of the Parliamentary Labour Party Scottish Committee from 1987 to 1988 and a member of the Public Accounts Committee from 1988 to 1989. He then was appointed Scottish Education and Employment Spokesperson from 1988 to 1989, Assistant Spokesman on Employment from 1989 to 1992, Scottish Local Government Spokesman from 1992 to 1994, Transport Spokesman 1994–95, Health Spokesman 1995–96 and Deputy Spokesman on Social Security 1996–97. After the 1997 election, he became Minister for State in the Scottish Office with responsibility for home affairs, local government and devolution and was effectively Donald Dewar's deputy in the Scottish Office. He played a significant part in the preparations for a Scottish Parliament, contributing to negotiations with the SNP to allow them to come aboard the cross-party Scotland Forward campaign in the run-up to the 1997 referendum. He also chaired the influential Consultative Steering Group which produced the report *Shaping Scotland's Parliament*, the intention of which was to draw up plans for a different kind of Parliament to Westminster.

In the election to the Scottish Parliament, McLeish was campaign spokesperson on Home Affairs and Government and subsequently became a member of Dewar's five-strong coalition negotiating team with the Liberal Democrats and was appointed Minister for Enterprise and Lifelong Learning. This gave him a key role in the policy debate over tuition fees, which had proved one of the main issues in the election and in discussions with the Lib Dems over forming a government. This resulted in the establishment of the Cubie Committee and once it reported, the Executive's acceptance of a diluted form of its proposals in January 2000. This was seen as one of the first really significant policy developments under devolution. He was also identified as one of 'the Big Macs', along with Tom McCabe and Jack McConnell, who urged caution on Section 28/Clause 2A.

Prior to the Scottish Parliament elections, McLeish had been widely promoted for the formal post of Donald Dewar's Deputy in the Labour Group, but this did not happen and when Dewar underwent heart surgery in the summer of 2000, there was never any doubt that Wallace would be Acting First Minister. When Donald Dewar died in office in October 2000, there was an attempt to anoint Henry McLeish without an election which backfired with Jack McConnell standing and initially catching the McLeish camp off-guard. Despite being out-manoeuvred in the campaign, 'Team McLeish' with the backing of 17 out of 18 Labour members of the Executive saw their man elected over Jack McConnell by the narrow margin of 44:36. He was then elected First Minister and engaged in his first ministerial reshuffle, rewarding supporters (MacKay, McCabe), moving problem ministers (Galbraith, Boyack) and keeping the party's left and trade union wings content.

The first months of the new McLeish administration saw some confusion about its direction. First, there was 'dump the crap', dropping unpopular policies and returning to bread and butter issues. Then there was 'progressive pragmatism': a phrase as vacuous as 'the third way' and destined to go in the bin. McLeish has also promised 'a bonfire of the quangos', funding for long-term care, and proportional representation for local government: marking a distinct shift from the tone of Donald Dewar. McLeish was meant to face a full electoral college contest in December 2000, but like most interim Labour leaders, he has become permanent and did not face a fuller contest. McLeish got himself into all kinds of problems in January 2001 when he floated the possibility of renaming the Scottish Executive, 'the Scottish Government', only to be slapped down by Tony Blair. He then encountered difficulties over the implementation of the Sutherland Commission on care for the elderly, which he had initially indicated he was in favour of, then, changed his mind. Forced by his Liberal Democrat colleagues to climb down and accept the principle of free care, questions have been raised about the competencies and political direction of 'Team McLeish' which it is still too early to answer.

FIFE NORTH EAST

Predecessor Constituencies: Fife East (1945–79).

1999

Electorate: 60,886
Turnout: 35,941 (59.03%)

Candidate	Party	Votes	Votes%	Change%
Iain Smith	Liberal Democrat	13,590	37.81	-13.41
Edward Brocklebank	Conservative	8,526	23.72	-2.75
Colin Welsh	SNP	6,373	17.73	+6.87
Charles Milne	Labour	5,175	14.40	+4.12
Donald MacGregor	Independent	1,540	4.28	—
Robert Beveridge	Independent	735	2.05	—

Liberal Democrat majority: 5,064 (14.09%)
Swing: 5.33% Liberal Democrat to Conservative

1997

Electorate: 58,794
Turnout: 41,839 (71.16%)

Candidate	Party	Votes	Votes%	Change%
Menzies Campbell	Liberal Democrat	21,432	51.22	+4.82
Adam Bruce	Conservative	11,076	26.47	-12.05
Colin Welsh	SNP	4,545	10.86	+2.27
Charles Milne	Labour	4,301	10.28	+4.70
William Stewart	Referendum	485	1.16	—

Liberal Democrat majority: 10,356 (24.75%)
Swing: 8.44% Conservative to Liberal Democrat

1945–92

	Lab%	Con%	SNP%	Lib%	Other%	Turnout%
1992	5.5	38.5	8.6	46.4	—	77.8
1987	7.4	41.2	6.6	44.8	—	76.2
1983	6.5	46.1	6.6	40.2	0.7	73.7
1979	19.9	43.0	14.1	23.0	—	79.0
1974O	16.9	38.8	31.7	12.6	—	73.7
1974F	15.0	47.9	19.5	17.6	—	78.8

	Lab%	Con%	SNP%	Lib%	Other%	Turnout%
1970	24.6	54.6	11.8	9.0	–	74.5
1966	24.6	51.5	14.4	9.5	–	76.1
1964	25.2	54.2	6.8	13.1	0.7	77.8
1961B	26.4	47.5	–	26.1	–	67.3
1959	30.1	69.9	–	–	–	75.2
1955	29.4	70.6	–	–	–	73.2
1951	29.4	70.6	–	–	–	78.7
1950	26.5	63.7	–	9.8	–	81.6
1945	30.6	69.4	–	–	–	70.8

Fife North East covers St Andrews, the coastal towns of Anstruther, Crail and Elie, and the inland market towns of Auchtermuchty, Cupar and Falkland. The constituency was consistently held by the Conservatives until 1987, when the Liberal Democrats won the seat. When the Tories dominated this seat in the past, the Liberals did not contest it, with the Conservatives often standing as National Liberal and Conservative candidates. When the Liberals began to fight the constituency again in the 1960s and the National Liberal label disappeared, the Conservative vote dropped.

The current Liberal Democrats therefore benefited from a Liberal legacy within the constituency, which was evident from the party's by-election performance in 1961. However, the Liberal electorate required careful rebuilding over the years, and the party only made progress in this area in post-1979 elections. Having said that, the party made extremely swift progress towards winning Fife North East after the 1979 election, with impressive increases in support, particularly at the 1983 election, to turn the constituency into a two-party marginal and build a coherent anti-Conservative coalition of supporters.

The Liberal/Liberal Democrats' ability to consistently field a high calibre candidate in the seat, Menzies Campbell, was also part of the party's success. His victory in 1987 was preceded by Liberal Democrat electoral success on North East Fife District Council in 1984, before its abolition with reorganisation, and then with a substantial contingent of councillors from the constituency on the new Fife Council. 21 Liberal Democrat councillors were elected to Fife Council in 1999, almost all from the Fife North East constituency.

At the same time, local support for the Conservatives has faded at all electoral levels. The Tories have only one councillor in the constituency, in the Leuchars, Balmullo and Guardbridge ward (one of only two Conservative councillors on Fife Council) and support dipped at the 1997 and 1999 elections to its lowest ever levels. The prognosis for a Conservative recovery is not bright, given the party's decline nationally and locally, and the growth in support for the Liberal Democrats at all levels in the seat, as well as the popularity of the local MP, Ming Campbell. The SNP has seldom been a contender in this seat. Its 31.7 per cent of the vote in October 1974 disappeared as rapidly as it appeared at that election. SNP and Labour are both effectively squeezed out by the Conservative-Liberal Democrat contest.

MP Menzies Campbell was born in 1941 in Glasgow. He was educated at Hillhead High School, Glasgow, and has an MA and LLB from Glasgow University and also studied at Stanford in the USA. He was an advocate before his election, but also distinguished himself as a sportsman. Campbell competed in the 100 metres at the Tokyo Olympics in 1964 and the Commonwealth Games in Jamaica in 1966. He was also UK athletics captain from 1965 to 1966. Politically, he was a long-standing member of the Liberal Party and chaired the Scottish Liberals from 1975 to 1977. Since his election in 1987 he has been a party spokesperson on Arts, Broadcasting and Sport, Scotland, Defence and Foreign Affairs. He was a member of the Trade and Industry Select Committee from 1990 to 1992 and the Defence Select Committee from 1992 until 1999.

MSP Iain Smith was born in 1960 and went to school locally in Cupar. He is a graduate of Newcastle University in politics and economics and worked for Northumberland County Council in 1981. He became an advice worker and then manager at Bonnethill Advice Centre in Dundee from 1982 to 1985 and was subsequently research assistant and agent for local MP Menzies Campbell before becoming an MSP. He was also a councillor on Fife Region from 1986 until 1996, where he was opposition leader, and then a councillor on Fife Council from 1995 until 1999, where he was also opposition leader. From 1999 to October 2000 he was the Deputy Minister for Parliament and thus a junior member of the Scottish Executive, as well as Liberal Democrat Business Manager, with a key role on the Parliamentary Bureau and the Procedures Committee. However he was effectively sacked from this post in 2000 due to dissatisfaction amongst party colleagues over his role in reforms to the committee system. He was appointed Liberal Democrat Spokesman for Local Government in November 2000, and joined the Local Government Committee of the Scottish Parliament in January 2001.

GALLOWAY AND UPPER NITHSDALE

Predecessor Constituencies: Galloway (1945–79).

1999

Electorate: 53,057
Turnout: 35,316 (66.56%)

Candidate	Party	Votes	Votes%	Change%
Alasdair Morgan	SNP	13,873	39.28	-4.63
Alex Fergusson	Conservative	10,672	30.22	-0.30
Jim Stevens	Labour	7,209	20.41	+4.08
Joan Mitchell	Liberal Democrat	3,562	10.09	+3.66

SNP majority: 3,201 (9.06%)
Swing: 2.16% SNP to Conservative

1997

Electorate: 52,721
Turnout: 42,018 (79.65%)

Candidate	Party	Votes	Votes%	Change%
Alasdair Morgan	SNP	18,449	43.91	+7.46
Ian Lang	Conservative	12,825	30.52	-11.47
Katy Clark	Labour	6,861	16.33	+3.37
John McKerchar	Liberal Democrat	2,700	6.43	-2.17
Roger Wood	Independent	566	1.35	–
Alan Kennedy	Referendum	428	1.02	–
Joseph Smith	UK Independence	189	0.45	–

SNP majority: 5,624 (13.39%)
Swing: 9.47% Conservative to SNP

	Lab%	Con%	SNP%	Lib%	Other%	Turnout%
1992	13.0	42.0	36.4	8.6	–	81.7
1987	12.9	40.4	31.5	14.6	0.6	76.8
1983	11.4	44.7	30.8	13.1	–	75.8
1979	8.5	45.9	37.1	8.5	–	81.2
1974O	9.0	40.2	40.3	10.5	–	77.1
1974F	10.2	43.9	30.6	15.3	–	77.8
1970	20.3	50.4	20.5	8.8	–	72.0
1966	38.0	62.0	–	–	–	66.6
1964	23.2	52.8	–	24.0	–	73.8
1959	20.4	56.2	–	23.4	–	75.6
1959B	23.9	50.4	–	25.7	–	72.7
1955	33.1	66.9	–	–	–	69.1
1951	26.3	61.7	–	12.0	–	75.6
1950	34.4	65.6	–	–	–	63.0
1945	35.3	24.0	–	–	40.7	69.9

Galloway is positioned in the south-west of Scotland, to the south of Carrick, Cumnock and Doon Valley and to the west of Dumfries. It combines the old Scottish counties of Kirkcudbrightshire and Wigtown which existed up until the 1974 local government reorganisation. The largest towns in the seat are Stranraer, Kirkcudbright, Dalbeattie, Newtown Stewart, and Wigtown, with a large number of the population employed in agriculture, fishing and forestry.

Galloway has a long tradition of Conservative representation and in the last three decades has seen a Conservative-SNP battle for supremacy, typical of much of rural Scotland. Conservative for most of the inter-war period, Galloway was won by the Liberals in 1922, 1923 and 1929, by John Mackie for the Conservatives in 1931 and held by him in 1945 as an Independent Unionist against the official Conservatives when he won with a 1,825 lead over Labour; he was returned as an official Conservative from 1950 until 1959. John Brewis held the seat from 1959 facing a challenge from the SNP from 1970 onwards. In October 1974, the Nationalists, standing for only the third successive time in the seat, broke through and took the seat, George Thompson winning over the Conservatives by a mere 30 votes.

Galloway was the second most marginal SNP seat and Ian Lang won it back with a majority of 2,922 – one of seven SNP seats won back by the Conservatives in 1979. The SNP kept their vote at 30 per cent in 1983 and 1987, clearly remaining the main challengers to the Tories; in 1992, Lang's majority was cut to 2,468 as the SNP's Matt Brown put 3,000 votes on his party's support.

In 1997, the SNP's Alasdair Morgan increased his vote by a further 3,000, while the Conservatives fell by 3,000; there was some evidence of tactical voting as Labour's vote increased by a mere 1,000 votes and rose by half the Scottish average. Morgan easily held the seat in 1999 despite the SNP slipping back by 4,500 as the Conservatives fell as well by 2,000 on a lower turnout to give an SNP lead of 3,201. Labour polled credibly in third place increasing their support by over 300 votes. Galloway and Upper Nithsdale will remain as far as one can see a SNP-Conservative marginal, but the SNP have a much stronger grip on it than they managed in the heady days of the 1970s, and their chances of holding it at UK and Scottish elections are commensurately greater.

MP and MSP Alasdair Morgan was born in 1945 in Aberfeldy and elected MP for Galloway and Upper Nithsdale in 1997 and MSP in 1999. Morgan was educated at Breadalbane Academy, Aberfeldy, and the University of Glasgow where he obtained a MA in Mathematics and Political Economy, before going to Moray House College of Education and the Open University where he studied for a BA Hons in History.

A maths teacher from 1973 to 1974, Morgan then switched to being a computer analyst with Shell from 1974 until 1980 and with GEC from 1980 to 1984. He was then a computer systems team leader with Fife Regional Council 1984 to 1986 and West Lothian Council and Lothian Regional Council from 1986 until 1997. Morgan was National Treasurer of the SNP from 1983 until 1990 and Senior Vice-Convenor 1990 to 1991, and was seen as a safe pair of hands and pro-leadership loyalist. He was the SNP leadership's preferred choice as candidate in the important 1995 Perth and Kinross by-election instead of Roseanna Cunningham, but she was selected. Elected to the House of Commons in 1997, he has become a one-term MP by choice and currently sits on the Select Committee on Trade and Industry. He clashed at the 1997 conference with Roseanna Cunningham, opposing her call for the abolition of the monarchy in an independent Scotland.

At Westminster, Morgan became leader of the SNP Westminster Parliamentary Group in 1999. In the Scottish Parliament, he is SNP Spokesperson on Rural Affairs, was Deputy Convenor of the Rural Affairs Committee and is now Convenor of the Justice Committee. He is a member of the Cross Party Groups on Borders Rail, Crofting, Information, Knowledge and Enlightenment, Rail Services, and Agriculture and Horticulture, of which he is Joint Convenor.

GLASGOW ANNIESLAND

Predecessor Constituencies: Glasgow Partick (1945), Scotstoun (1950–70) and Garscadden (1974–92).

Scottish Parliament By-election 23 November 2000

Electorate: 52,809
Turnout: 20,221 (38.29%)

Candidate	Party	Votes	Votes%	Change%
William Butler	Labour	9,838	48.65	-10.16
Tom Chalmers	SNP	4,462	22.07	+1.86
Kate Pickering	Conservative	2,148	10.62	-0.03
Rosie Kane	SSP	1,429	7.07	+3.56
Judith Fryer	Liberal Democrat	1,384	6.84	+0.51
Alastair Whitelaw	Green	662	3.27	–
Murdo Ritchie	Socialist Labour	298	1.47	+0.98

Labour majority: 5,376 (26.58%)
Swing: 6.01% Labour to SNP

Westminster By-election 23 November 2000

Electorate: 52,609
Turnout: 20,212 (38.42%)

Candidate	Party	Votes	Votes%	Change%
John Robertson	Labour	10,539	52.14	-9.70
Grant Thoms	SNP	4,202	20.79	+3.68
Dorothy Luckhurst	Conservative	2,188	10.83	-0.63
Christopher McGinty	Liberal Democrat	1,630	8.06	+0.82
Charlie McCarthy	SSP	1,441	7.13	+6.45
William Lyden	Family	212	1.05	–

Labour majority: 6,337 (31.35%)
Swing: 6.69% Labour to SNP

1999

Electorate: 54,378
Turnout: 28,480 (52.37%)

Candidate	Party	Votes	Votes%	Change%
Donald Dewar	Labour	16,749	58.81	-3.03
Kaukab Stewart	SNP	5,756	20.21	+3.10
William Aitken	Conservative	3,032	10.65	-0.81
Iain Brown	Liberal Democrat	1,804	6.33	-0.91
Ann Lynch	SSP	1,000	3.51	+2.83
Edward Boyd	Socialist Labour	139	0.49	–

Labour majority: 10,993 (38.60%)
Swing; 3.07% Labour to SNP

1997

Electorate: 52,995
Turnout: 33,879 (63.98%)

Candidate	Party	Votes	Votes%	Change%
Donald Dewar	Labour	20,951	61.84	+8.77
William Wilson	SNP	5,797	17.11	+0.10
Robert Brocklehurst	Conservative	3,881	11.46	-4.18
Christopher McGinty	Liberal Democrat	2,453	7.24	-6.47
Akhtar Majid	Pro-Life	374	1.10	–
William Bonnar	SSA	229	0.68	–
Alan Milligan	UK Independence	86	0.25	–
Gillian McKay	Referendum	84	0.25	–
Thomas Pringle	NLP	24	0.07	–

Labour majority: 15,154 (44.73%)
Swing: 4.34% SNP to Labour

1945–92

	Lab%	Con%	SNP%	Lib%	Other%	Turnout%
1992	64.4	11.5	19.0	4.9	0.2	71.3
1987	67.7	10.7	12.2	3.4	–	71.4
1983	56.2	15.4	10.2	17.6	0.6	69.1
1979	61.5	21.8	15.7	–	1.0	73.2
1978B	45.4	18.5	32.9	–	3.2	69.1
1974O	50.9	12.9	31.2	5.0	–	70.8

	Lab%	Con%	SNP%	Lib%	Other%	Turnout%
1974F	52.3	24.3	21.8	–	1.6	74.1
1970	57.5	31.4	9.3	–	1.8	70.5
1966	61.8	32.8	–	–	5.4	74.3
1964	61.6	38.4	–	–	–	77.2
1959	53.7	46.3	–	–	–	81.8
1955	49.4	50.6	–	–	–	79.5
1951	49.3	50.7	–	–	–	85.1
1950B	47.3	50.8	–	–	1.9	73.7
1950	46.0	46.5	–	4.9	2.6	84.6
1945	48.4	51.6	–	–	–	69.0

Anniesland has a fairly homogeneous social composition centred on the massive post-war council estate of Drumchapel built in the 1950s Macmillan housing boom, with smaller estates such as Knightswood and Yoker alongside. It is the Drum which defines the seat, as a community it sits on Glasgow's north west frontier cheek-to-cheek with Bearsden with whom it shares little in common: economic prosperity, opportunities and even life expectancy are dramatically different in the two areas.

Anniesland is the fifth most unhealthy constituency in Britain – only beaten by four other Glasgow constituencies; 34 per cent of the population live in poverty and the male unemployment rate of 11.8 per cent in June 2000 is the fourth highest in Scotland. The seat has had a deep political attachment to the Labour Party through its many different variants, but it has at points wavered. In 1950 the then new seat of Scotstoun was captured with a 239 majority over Labour by the Conservative A. S. L. Young who promptly died eight months later; in the subsequent by-election Conservative Col J. R. H. Hutchison held on with a majority of 1,319 over Labour and retained the seat for the next two general elections before Labour won it in 1959.

Donald Dewar became MP for Garscadden in the famous 1978 by-election when Labour and the SNP were battling for the political supremacy of Scotland with Dewar campaigning on the implausible slogan 'Score with Dewar'. The by-election saw the SNP candidate Kevin Bovey court controversy with his pro-abortion and pro-CND views and Dewar restricted the swing to the SNP to 3.6 per cent. This, along with the Hamilton by-election a few months later in which George Robertson was elected, was seen as halting the SNP electoral bandwagon in the 1970s.

In the early 1990s, a new electoral threat arose to challenge the supremacy of Labour – Scottish Militant Labour, which made brief inroads at council level in 1992, nearly winning the Summerhill ward in that year's elections when Labour won 38.5 per cent to SML's 35.4 per cent.

In 1997, the reconfigurated seat saw Dewar put 8.8 per cent on Labour's support and the SNP marginally advance in percentage terms while losing support in actual votes. The Conservatives continued to fall back losing 2,000 voters and declining to 11.5 per cent. In 1999, Labour's majority fell from 15,154 to 10,993, while the party's support fell by 4,000 votes on a reduced turnout. The SNP in a distant second place lost 241 votes and the swing from Labour to SNP of 3.1 per cent was the second lowest in Glasgow and one of the lowest in the country.

The sudden death of Donald Dewar in October 2000 not only flung Labour into political and constitutional crisis, but left it facing two by-elections in the Anniesland seat, as Dewar represented the seat at both Westminster and Holyrood. The resulting by-elections in November 2000 saw Labour comfortably hold both seats but with drastically reduced majorities and turnouts. Labour's vote fell by over 10,000 in the Westminster by-election and by nearly 7,000 in the Scottish Parliament by-election, but on reduced turnouts these represented falls of respectively 9.7 per cent and 10.2 per cent, a considerable improvement on the Hamilton South and Ayr by-elections. This, along with the failure of the SNP to make any headway whatsoever, gave Labour cause for celebration; the two results were the worst performances by the SNP in by-elections where it was the main challenger to Labour since Hamilton in 1978, a fact the SNP must hope is down to the Donald Dewar factor, rather than weaknesses in party strategy; they were aided in hoping this by their good showing in the Falkirk West Westminster by-election in December 2000.

MP John Robertson was born in 1952 in Glasgow and was elected Labour MP for the seat in the November 2000 by-election caused by the death of Donald Dewar. He had previously been selected as the Labour candidate to fight the Westminster seat before Dewar's death, and was Dewar's election agent in the 1997 election. He had prior to his election worked as an engineer for BT Scotland.

MSP Bill Butler was born in 1956 in Glasgow and was elected Labour MP for the seat in the November 2000 by-election following the death of Donald Dewar. Butler has been a Labour councillor on Glasgow City Council, until recently representing the Tollcross Ward which he won in 1999 with 56.0 per cent of the vote. In his period on the city council, he was identified with the anti-Pat Lally faction during Lally's reign as leader of the council, and was suspended from the Labour group for six months in 1991 for poll tax non-payment.

Butler has been a prominent member of the hard left Campaign for Socialism group, which grew up out of the Labour left's opposition to Tony Blair's campaign to abolish Clause Four, and is currently its Secretary. He has opposed a whole raft of policies associated with the Blair Government and the Scottish Executive, including the housing stock transfer of council houses and the introduction of electoral reform into local government. Butler won the selection contest for the Labour nomination, fairly easily defeating Donnie Munro, the ex-lead singer of Runrig, and Ian Smart. However, he had, with some difficulty and embarrassment, to follow the official party line in the by-election campaign, declaring 'I am not New Labour. I am not Old

Labour. I am middle-aged Labour.' He is married to Patricia Ferguson, Labour MSP for Glasgow Maryhill, making them the first husband and wife team on the Labour benches. She is seen as an arch-party loyalist, something which until now has never been claimed of Butler. He became a member of the Enterprise and Life-Long Learning Committee and the Subordinate Legislation Committee of the Scottish Parliament in January 2001.

GLASGOW BAILLIESTON

Predecessor Constituencies: Glasgow Camlachie (1945–55) and Provan (1959–92).

1999

Electorate: 49,068
Turnout: 23,709 (48.32%)

Candidate	Party	Votes	Votes%	Change%
Margaret Curran	Labour	11,289	47.61	−18.08
Dorothy-Grace Elder	SNP	8,217	34.66	+15.56
James McVicar	SSP	1,864	7.86	+4.04
Kate Pickering	Conservative	1,526	6.44	−1.31
Judith Fryer	Liberal Democrat	813	3.43	−0.39

Labour majority: 3,072 (12.95%)
Swing: 16.82% Labour to SNP

1997

Electorate: 51,152
Turnout: 31,853 (62.27%)

Candidate	Party	Votes	Votes%	Change%
James Wray	Labour	20,925	65.69	+2.47
Patsy Thomson	SNP	6,085	19.10	−3.47
Malcolm Kelly	Conservative	2,468	7.75	−2.14
Sheila Rainger	Liberal Democrat	1,217	3.82	−0.50
James McVicar	SSA	970	3.05	—
John McClafferty	Referendum	188	0.59	—

Labour majority: 14,840 (46.59%)
Swing: 2.97% SNP to Labour

1945–92

	Lab%	Con%	SNP%	Lib%	Other%	Turnout%
1992	66.5	7.8	21.7	4.0	—	65.3
1987	72.9	7.7	12.1	7.2	—	69.1
1983	64.4	10.8	8.8	15.0	0.9	65.2
1979	69.5	15.1	13.7	—	1.7	66.0
1974O	58.6	9.8	30.2	—	1.4	64.0

	Lab%	Con%	SNP%	Lib%	Other%	Turnout%
1974F	61.6	16.8	19.6	–	2.0	69.0
1970	60.9	27.9	9.8	–	1.4	65.6
1966	66.9	30.8	–	–	2.3	70.8
1964	65.8	30.8	–	–	–	75.7
1959	55.6	44.4	–	–	–	78.8
1955	50.3	49.7	–	–	–	74.7
1951	51.3	48.7	–	–	–	82.4
1950	51.5	48.5	–	–	–	80.7
1948B	42.1	43.7	–	1.2	13.0	56.8
1945	–	42.3	–	–	57.7	65.0

Baillieston can be found in the north-east corner of Glasgow and is divided in two by the massive M8 Glasgow-Edinburgh motorway. It is dominated by the vast post-war estate of Easterhouse and includes smaller estates such as Barlanark, Queenslie and Gartloch – all of which were previously in Provan; Carntyne and Mount Vernon come from the old Shettleston. Easterhouse is one of the monuments to post-war planning that cover Glasgow. Built several miles outside the city centre with few leisure or social facilities, life on it has always been grim even in times of full employment. It has now had high levels of unemployment, crime and poverty for three decades and its population has been in decline for the same period.

The seat had 61.4 per cent council housing in the 1991 census – the third highest in Scotland and the UK, only beaten by Airdrie and Shotts and Motherwell and Wishaw; it is the sixth most unhealthy constituency in Britain, with five other Glasgow seats outscoring it in terms of ill-health; 39 per cent of the population live in poverty and in June 2000 its 11.5 per cent male unemployment rate was the fifth highest in Scotland.

Pre-Easterhouse, Glasgow's East End was represented by Camlachie, which was first won by Labour in the breakthrough election of 1922 by the Rev. Campbell Stephen, who held it until his death in 1948 (with the exception of the 1931 debacle). In 1935 and 1945 Stephen had stood on the Independent Labour Party ticket, following its breakaway from official Labour in 1932; in the by-election after his death the Conservatives squeaked home in what was previously inhospitable territory as both Labour and the ILP put up candidates. The Conservative C. S. McFarlane won Camlachie with a 395 majority, but Labour won back the seat in 1950.

The seat became Glasgow Provan from 1959 and has grown increasingly Labour since. Labour faced some opposition in the early 1990s from Scottish Militant Labour who elected two Independent Labour councillors in the 1992 council elections in Baillieston and Queenslie with 37.4 per cent and 64.1 per cent respectively; both were defeated in 1995.

1997 showed no real surprises with Labour increasing its majority from a notional 14,165 to 14,480, but 1999 illustrated the fragility of Labour's hold on the constituency's political preferences. Labour's majority fell from 14,840 to 3,072, while its vote was nearly cut in half on a much reduced turnout – 20,925 down to 11,289. Labour's fall in its vote was the third highest in Scotland (after Falkirk West and Shettleston) – declining 18.1 per cent, while the swing from Labour to SNP was the highest in the country – 16.8 per cent. The SNP increased their vote by 2,000 votes, while James McVicar, the Scottish Socialist candidate and previously one of the Scottish Militant Labour supported councillors, put on nearly 1,000 votes compared to 1997. Baillieston should return to unchallenged Labour dominance in the UK election, but Scottish Labour was given a nasty shock in Baillieston in the Scottish Parliament elections as generations of political atrophy and complacency came home to roost.

MP Jimmy Wray was born in 1938 in the Gorbals area of Glasgow. He has been MP for Glasgow Provan from 1987 until 1997 and for its successor Baillieston from 1997. Educated at St Bonaventure's School in the Gorbals, Wray was a heavy goods vehicle driver and served as a Glasgow Corporation councillor from 1972 to 1974 and on Strathclyde Region from 1974 until 1987.

As a member of the hard left Campaign Group, Wray stood up for retaining the old socialist Clause Four, opposed the Gulf War, and his Irish republican sympathies have led to the nickname 'I. R. Wray' in *Private Eye*. He combines this with an authoritarian conservatism on social issues such as abortion and gay rights – calling the Blair Government 'a gay mafia' over its proposals to abolish Section 28. Wray has often been in the public eye in recent years due to his personal life, sacking his second wife as his constituency secretary, facing an industrial tribunal from her, and then suing her and winning over allegations she made that he was a wife-beater. He welcomed Mike Tyson's decision to come to Glasgow for a boxing contest in May 2000, putting him at odds with the MSP for the seat, Margaret Curran.

MSP Margaret Curran was born in 1958 in Glasgow and was educated at Our Lady and St. Francis School, Glasgow, and Glasgow University, with a degree in History and Economic History and a certificate in Community Education. She has been a welfare rights officer and community worker at Strathclyde Region, before becoming a lecturer in Community Education at Strathclyde University.

Curran was a member of the left-wing Labour Co-ordinating Committee (Scotland) in the early 1980s and a founding member of the Scottish Labour Women's Caucus which advocated gender balance in the Scottish Parliament. She was the third candidate in the first bitter ballot between Mike Watson and Mohammed Sarwar for the Glasgow Govan Labour nomination and eventually became Sarwar's election agent in an attempt to heal party wounds. This move only brought her grief as a one-and-a-half-year investigation led to Sarwar being tried and acquitted; with charges also considered against her for election expense irregularities, thought these were dropped. In the Scottish Parliament, she became Convenor of the Social Inclusion Committee as well as Co-convener of the Cross Party Group on Women. In the Scottish Parliament debate on Mike Tyson's coming to Scotland in May 2000, Curran's contribution was acknowledged by all sides as an excellent one, raising the issue of male violence against women while refusing to make cheap political points out of it.

Curran combines a fierce passion and drive to bring about change with an ability to do things and to compromise without losing sight of her principles; she received due recognition when Henry McLeish in his first ministerial reshuffle in October 2000 gave Curran the post of Deputy Minister for Social Justice, working under Jackie Baillie. This was a very astute political move by McLeish, recognising Curran's standing not only on the pragmatic Labour left, but also amongst Labour women. With the death of Donald Dewar and demotion of Frank McAveety, Curran is the only one of Glasgow's ten Labour MSPs to hold a ministerial post.

GLASGOW CATHCART

Predecessor Constituencies: none.

1999

Electorate: 51,338
Turnout: 26,976 (52.55%)

Candidate	Party	Votes	Votes%	Change%
Michael Watson	Labour	12,966	48.06	-7.89
Maire Whitehead	SNP	7,592	28.14	+7.84
Mary Leishman	Conservative	3,311	12.27	-0.18
Callan Dick	Liberal Democrat	2,187	8.11	+1.36
Roddy Slorach	SWP	920	3.41	–

Labour majority: 5,374 (19.92%)
Swing: 7.87% Labour to SNP

1997

Electorate: 49,312
Turnout: 34,110 (69.17%)

Candidate	Party	Votes	Votes%	Change%
John Maxton	Labour	19,158	56.17	+6.82
Maire Whitehead	SNP	6,913	20.27	+1.17
Alastair Muir	Conservative	4,248	12.45	-9.08
Callan Dick	Liberal Democrat	2,302	6.75	-0.45
Sofia Indyk	Pro-Life	687	2.01	–
Ronnie Stevenson	SSA	458	1.34	–
Strang Haldane	Referendum	344	1.01	–

Labour majority: 12,245: (35.90%)
Swing: 2.83% SNP to Labour

1945–92

	Lab%	Con%	SNP%	Lib%	Other%	Turnout%
1992	48.3	24.5	18.1	7.8	1.3	75.4
1987	52.1	22.4	10.3	15.2	–	76.3
1983	41.4	30.5	5.6	22.5	–	75.7
1979	45.9	41.8	6.9	5.4	–	78.6

	Lab%	Con%	SNP%	Lib%	Other%	Turnout%
1974O	38.1	42.7	16.5	2.7	–	76.7
1974F	40.6	45.8	13.6	–	–	80.6
1970	45.0	54.2	–	–	0.8	74.6
1966	48.3	50.7	–	–	1.0	79.7
1964	47.1	52.9	–	–	–	79.3
1959	40.8	59.2	–	–	–	80.2
1955	27.4	72.6	–	–	–	75.7
1951	29.5	70.5	–	–	–	82.5
1950	27.3	64.8	–	7.9	–	83.8
1946B	37.1	52.5	10.4	–	–	55.6
1945	41.2	58.8	–	–	–	67.6

The Glasgow Southside seat is dominated by the council estate of Castlemilk which sits on a hill overlooking most of the rest of the seat. It also contains some of the most affluent areas of the city: King's Park, Mount Florida, Newlands and Cathcart. These areas include some of the most desirable and expensive detached bungalows to be found anywhere in Glasgow.

Cathcart has the highest owner-occupation tenure rates in the city at 48.6 per cent in 1991 and a council housing rate of 40.6 per cent. It is also the healthiest constituency in Glasgow to live in – rated at the dizzy heights of the nineteenth most unhealthy in Britain; it has 31 per cent of its population living in poverty and with a male unemployment rate of 8.1 per cent in June 2000 it has the eighteenth highest rate in Scotland.

Cathcart was once a safe Conservative seat with Conservative representation from 1918 until 1979. In 1955 in the Tories' peak year in Scotland they polled 72.6 per cent in Cathcart to Labour's 27.4 per cent – a majority of 15,751. Slowly Labour began to eat into this majority as Scotland and more so Glasgow swung to the left, culminating in 1979 when Labour's John Maxton, nephew of Jimmy Maxton, ILP firebrand, won the seat from Teddy Taylor, the man who would have been Mrs Thatcher's Secretary of State for Scotland.

Cathcart has become a secure Labour seat since then. Labour turned a Conservative majority of 1,757 in October 1974 into a Labour one of 1,600 in 1979; this increased in 1983 to 4,230 and to 11,203 in 1987. The Conservative vote fell 41.8 per cent in 1979 to 22.4 per cent in 1987, although they recovered slightly in 1992 to win 24.5 per cent and reduce Labour's majority to 8,001.

In 1992 the Tories still held the wards of Newlands and King's Park on the local council with longstanding councillor Jock Young winning 58.7 per cent in Newlands; in 1995 he won 42.4 per cent in Cathcart, but, in 1999 with Young standing for the Scottish Parliament, no Tories were returned in the parliamentary seat of Cathcart. In the 1997 election, Maxton increased his vote to 56.2 per cent and his majority to 12,245 over the SNP. This once rock-solid Conservative seat now saw the Tory vote plummet to 12.4 per cent, down 9.1 per cent on the notional 1992 result. Mike Watson standing for Labour for the Scottish Parliament saw 6,000 votes fall off his support, but even a 7.9 per cent swing from Labour to SNP could not do more than dent the party's majority. With Maxton now retiring from the Commons after a 22-year stint, Cathcart has been turned from a Labour-Conservative marginal into a safe, unexciting Labour stronghold with little SNP threat and the Tories reduced to marginal appeal at UK, Scottish and local level.

MP John Maxton was born in Oxford in 1936. MP for Glasgow Cathcart from 1979 after winning it from Teddy Taylor, Maxton is retiring at the next election. Educated at Lord Williams Grammar School, Thame, Oxfordshire, and University College, Oxford, he became a lecturer in social studies at Hamilton College of Education and was Chairman of the Association of Lecturers in Colleges of Education in Scotland from 1974 to 1978.

Maxton is nephew of the legendary Jimmy Maxton, ILP MP for Glasgow Bridgeton from 1922 until 1946. He was a member of the Scottish Affairs Select Committee from 1979 to 1981, before becoming a Scottish and Treasury Whip from 1984 to 1985 and then a spokesman on Scotland, covering first health, local government and transport from 1985 to 1987, and then industry and local government finance from 1987 until 1992. His role as part of Dewar's Scottish team was to hold the party line from the more radical and nationalist perspectives being pushed from certain quarters. He has also been a member of the National Heritage Committee from 1992 until 1997 and Culture Select Committee from 1997 onwards.

A member of what James Callaghan has called 'the lost generation' of Labour MPs first elected in 1979, he was increasingly out of kilter with the sympathy of Scottish Labour during the Tory years. At a Fabian Society post-election event in 1983 he drew cries of 'Rubbish' from the audience for opposing any strategy involving parliamentary disruption or co-operation with other opposition parties: key pointers for discussion during the long opposition years. Maxton was an old left type of Labour politician who was neither new left nor New Labour and who never quite lived up to his billing or romantic associations.

Maxton was investigated by the House of Commons Commissioner for Standards, Elizabeth Filkin, along with John Reid. She found that they had acted improperly in misusing Westminster parliamentary allowances for Scottish Labour Party purposes. A subsequent enquiry by the Standards Committee in December 2000 did not 'uphold' the complaints against the two.

MSP Mike Watson was born in Cambuslang in 1949. MP for Glasgow Central from 1989 until 1997, having first won the seat in a by-election, he then lost the Glasgow Govan Labour nomination to Mohammed Sarwar in June 1996 in a bitter internal party struggle. Educated at Dundee High School, Watson graduated from

Heriot-Watt University in Economics and Industrial Relations. He was a tutor and organiser with the Workers' Educational Association from 1974 until 1977 and a full-time organiser with ASTMS, then Manufacturing Science Finance, from 1978 until 1989. Watson was made a life peer – Lord Watson of Invergowrie – after the 1997 election and became a director of a public affairs company, PS Communications. As an MP, Watson opposed the Gulf War in 1991 and the Maastricht Treaty in 1993.

In the Scottish Parliament, he is Convenor of the Finance Committee and was a member of the Social Inclusion, Housing and the Voluntary Sector Committee from May 1999 to December 2000. He is also Joint Convenor of the Cross Party Group on Epilepsy. In the first year and a half he has advanced a backbench bill – the Protection of Wild Mammals Bill – to ban foxhunting, which has caused much controversy. Watson is author of two books on Dundee United, *Rags to Riches* and *The Tannadice Encyclopedia*, and has played a leading role in the United for Change supporters' group. He has also written a book on his experiences of the first year of the Scottish Parliament: *Year Zero: An Inside View of the Scottish Parliament* which was published in 2001.

GLASGOW GOVAN

Predecessor Constituencies: Glasgow Tradeston (1945–51) and Craigton (1955–79).

1999

Electorate: 53,257
Turnout: 26,373 (49.52%)

Candidate	Party	Votes	Votes%	Change%
Gordon Jackson	Labour	11,421	43.31	−0.78
Nicola Sturgeon	SNP	9,665	36.65	+1.60
Tasmina Ahmed-Sheikh	Conservative	2,343	8.88	+0.08
Mohammed Aslam Khan	Liberal Democrat	1,479	5.61	−0.33
Charlie McCarthy	SSP	1,275	4.83	+2.49
John Foster	Comm Brit	190	0.72	—

Labour majority: 1,756 (6.65%)
Swing: 1.19% Labour to SNP

1997

Electorate: 49,836
Turnout: 32,242 (64.70%)

Candidate	Party	Votes	Votes%	Change%
Mohammed Sarwar	Labour	14,216	44.09	+1.05
Nicola Sturgeon	SNP	11,302	35.05	+7.42
William Thomas	Conservative	2,839	8.81	−10.88
Robert Stewart	Liberal Democrat	1,915	5.94	+0.35
Alan McCombes	SSA	755	2.34	—
Peter Paton	SLU	325	1.01	—
Islam Badar	SLI	319	0.99	—
Zahid Abbasi	SCU	221	0.69	—
Kenneth MacDonald	Referendum	201	0.62	—
James White	BNP	149	0.46	—

Labour majority: 2,914 (9.04%)
Swing: 3.19% Labour to SNP

	Lab%	Con%	SNP%	Lib%	Other%	Turnout%
1992	48.9	9.9	37.1	3.5	0.5	76.0
1988B	37.0	7.3	48.8	4.1	2.8	60.4
1987	64.8	11.9	10.4	12.3	0.6	73.4
1983	55.0	19.7	6.0	19.4	–	71.7
1979	67.9	18.5	13.6	–	–	69.1
1974O	49.5	7.1	41.0	1.9	0.5	71.7
1974F	43.2	12.7	40.9	3.2	–	74.9
1973B	38.2	11.7	41.9	8.2	–	51.7
1970	60.0	28.2	10.3	–	1.5	63.3
1966	67.9	28.1	–	–	4.0	67.5
1964	65.0	30.6	–	–	4.4	70.3
1959	60.3	34.8	–	–	4.9	75.0
1955	62.0	38.0	–	–	–	71.8
1951	49.7	50.3	–	–	–	84.9
1950	45.7	46.7	–	3.9	3.7	84.0
1945	66.1	33.9	–	–	–	63.9

Glasgow Craigton (1955–79)

	Lab%	Con%	SNP%	Lib%	Other%	Turnout%
1979	59.9	28.5	11.6	–	–	75.2
1974O	50.5	20.1	24.3	5.1	–	75.8
1974F	51.3	30.8	17.9	–	–	80.0
1970	55.7	36.4	7.9	–	–	75.1
1966	57.9	32.7	9.4	–	–	80.4
1964	58.4	41.6	–	–	–	80.9
1959	50.8	49.2	–	–	–	82.7
1955	49.7	50.3	–	–	–	79.1

Glasgow Tradeston (1945–51)

	Lab%	Con%	SNP%	Lib%	Other%	Turnout%
1951	63.1	36.9	–	–	–	80.0
1950	62.9	37.1	–	–	–	78.8
1945	59.7	40.3	–	–	–	62.0

Govan is the most well-known of Glasgow constituencies having reached in some circles near legendary status due to countless bitter Labour-SNP battles, sensational by-elections and internal party struggles. Govan's history is even more interesting and varied than it now seems. Daniel Turner Holmes, Tony Benn's maternal grandfather was Liberal MP for the seat from 1910-18; while the Tories won the seat in 1950 and 1951 by respectively 373 and 241 votes over Labour, returning Jack Nixon Browne. Govan's claim to legendary status began in 1973 when Margo MacDonald overturned Labour's majority of 7,142 over the Conservatives to produce a SNP majority of 571 over Labour's Harry Selby; with significant boundary redistribution in the February 1974 election, MacDonald narrowly failed to hold the seat against Selby. The first Govan by-election was a watershed in Scottish politics exposing the frailty of Labour's hold over the West of Scotland. Jim Sillars recalled in his autobiography, canvassing as a Labour MP in the 1973 campaign and see Labour blame everything on 'the boss class' leading to the comedy of Willie Ross touring the seat with a loudhailer proclaiming: 'Noo's the day and noo's the hour for Govan to kick out Tory power' in a seat where the Tories were very much a minority. Govan then reverted to being a safe Labour seat with Labour's vote in 1987 under Bruce Millan rising to 64.8 per cent, its majority over the Liberal-SDP Alliance to 19,509, while the SNP were reduced to 10.4 per cent. However, all that changed when Millan resigned to take over as one of the two UK European Commissioners in 1988. Scottish politics were at this point in a combustible shape following 'the Doomsday Scenario' of the 1987 election when the Tories had lost half their Scottish seats, but been returned to government on English votes.

Jim Sillars, ex-Labour MP and one-time founder of the ill-fated Scottish Labour Party, had joined the SNP, became one of its leading lights and married Margo MacDonald. His decision to stand in Govan in November 1988 made a high-profile by-election even more so. Labour's candidate Bob Gillespie, an old-fashioned trade unionist, was no match for Sillars on the hustings and various TV debates, where he was spectacularly out-manoeuvred by Sillars on the finer points of European funding. Sillars turned a Labour majority of 19,509 into an SNP one of 3,500. Tony Benn, reflected on Sillars victory in his diaries: 'It revealed that if you don't offer people analysis they go for separatism, and it was also a reflection of our failure to discuss constitutional questions, which are at the core of the devolution argument.' However, Sillars like Margo before could not hold on in the resulting election, losing in 1992 by 4,125 to Labour's Ian Davidson.

In 1997 Govan was once again faced with far-reaching boundary changes involving the abolition of Glasgow Central, whose MP was Mike Watson. Several of its wards came into Govan while Pollokshields, an area with a large Pakistani community and the base for Glasgow councillor Mohammed Sarwar, was added from Pollok. There was a long and bitter Labour selection battle between the two, resulting in Sarwar eventually winning a re-run ballot. In the 1997 election, Sarwar faced the young, energetic SNP candidate Nicola Sturgeon, who nearly halved Labour's majority from the notional 5,609 of 1992 to 2,914, winning a 3.2 per cent swing from Labour – one of the best SNP results in the election.

That was not the end, but only a pause in the controversy. Two weeks after the 1997 election, allegations were published of Sarwar trying to bribe an election opponent. Sarwar insisted the money was a loan and in the resulting trial in March 1999 he was cleared of all charges. After two years of adverse publicity, no one thought Labour had much of a chance holding the seat in the Scottish Parliament election, but hold it they did, Gordon Jackson winning with a reduced majority of 1,756 over the SNP's Nicola Sturgeon: the 1.2 per cent swing to the SNP was the lowest in Glasgow and one of the lowest in the country. At the next UK election Govan will again be an important gauge of the respective fortunes of Labour and the SNP. The special circumstances of 1997 and 1999 were the worst possible backdrops for Labour to defend the seat – yet it did so in the end with relative ease. Given this, Labour's chances of holding the seat in future years must look very good indeed, but Govan has always prided itself on its ability to shock.

MP Mohammed Sarwar was born in Faselabad, Pakistan, in 1952. Educated at Faselabad University where he graduated with a BA in Political Science, English and Urdu, he emigrated to Glasgow in 1976. He built up his businesses to become a cash and carry millionaire and company director, and was elected to Glasgow District Council, winning the Pollokshields ward from the Tories in 1992 (Labour's only gain that year in the whole of Scotland) then continuing on Glasgow City Council from 1995 to 1997. Sarwar was selected as Labour candidate after a bitter selection battle with Mike Watson, then MP for Glasgow Central, which involved allegations from both sides of malpractice by the other.

Sarwar's election as MP brought forth allegations that he had bribed a fellow Pakistani election opponent with a £5,000 'bung' to 'ease off' his campaign. Sarwar's defence was that the money was merely a loan and part of Pakistani culture. He was suspended from the PLP and the Procurator-Fiscal launched an investigation which led to him being charged, tried and acquitted in March 1999. Sarwar has been severely damaged by this long-drawn-out process and his political judgement brought into question; Sarwar and his supporters, who include George Galloway MP, see the above as evidence of widespread Islamaphobia in Scotland.

MSP Gordon Jackson was born in Saltcoats in 1948 and was educated at Ardrossan Academy and St Andrews University where he gained his LLB. Jackson is a Queen's Counsel, a member of the prestigious and predominantly male Faculty of Advocates and was previously an Advocate and Deputy and private solicitor. Jackson has been described as the highest-paid QC in Scotland, and he was a surprise choice for Labour in Govan and an even more surprise victor. He sat on the Justice and Home Affairs Committee as well as the Procedures Committee from May 1999 to December 2000, before joining the Justice I Committee in January 2001. He is Convenor of the Cross Party Group on Shipbuilding. He has incurred widespread criticism from all parties, including his own, for continuing his lucrative legal work while being an MSP and for his missing many of the debates prior to voting. His habit of turning up at 5.00 p.m. to vote has brought him the nickname 'Crackerjack' after the TV programme of the same name.

GLASGOW KELVIN

Predecessor Constituencies: Glasgow St Rollox (1945), Glasgow Woodside (1950–70), Glasgow Kelvingrove (1945–79) and Glasgow Hillhead (1945–92).

1999

Electorate: 61,207
Turnout: 28,362 (46.34%)

Candidate	Party	Votes	Votes%	Change%
Pauline McNeill	Labour	12,711	44.82	-6.15
Sandra White	SNP	8,303	29.28	+7.91
Moira Craig	Liberal Democrat	3,720	13.12	-1.06
Assad Rasul	Conservative	2,253	7.94	-2.90
Heather Ritchie	SSP	1,375	4.85	+3.67

Labour majority: 4,408 (15.54%)
Swing: 7.03% Labour to SNP

1997

Electorate: 57,438
Turnout: 32,654 (56.85%)

Candidate	Party	Votes	Votes%	Change%
George Galloway	Labour	16,643	50.97	+4.11
Sandra White	SNP	6,978	21.37	+2.09
Elspeth Buchanan	Liberal Democrat	4,629	14.18	-4.73
Duncan McPhie	Conservative	3,539	10.84	-2.32
Allan Green	SSA	386	1.18	–
Robert Grigor	Referendum	282	0.86	–
Victor Vanni	SPGB	102	0.31	–
George Stidolph	NLP	95	0.29	–

Labour majority: 9,665 (29.60%)
Swing: 1.01% SNP to Labour

Glasgow Hillhead (1945–92)

	Lab%	Con%	SNP%	Lib%	Other%	Turnout%
1992	38.5	17.1	16.5	26.2	1.8	68.8
1987	42.9	14.4	6.5	35.1	1.1	72.3
1983	33.3	23.6	5.4	36.2	1.5	71.9
1982B	25.9	26.6	11.3	33.4	2.8	76.4
1979	34.4	41.1	10.1	14.4	–	75.7
1974O	28.2	37.1	22.8	11.9	–	72.4
1974F	24.4	44.0	11.3	20.3	–	78.7
1970	30.5	61.3	8.2	–	–	69.6
1966	37.1	62.9	–	–	–	73.5
1964	36.0	64.0	–	–	–	74.7
1959	31.7	68.3	–	–	–	77.1
1955	32.4	67.6	–	–	–	72.9
1951	35.1	64.9	–	–	–	82.2
1950	33.8	60.8	–	5.4	–	82.2
1948B	31.6	68.4	–	–	–	56.7
1945	33.6	58.5	–	7.9	–	65.8

Glasgow Kelvingrove (1945–79)

	Lab%	Con%	SNP%	Lib%	Other%	Turnout%
1979	50.3	28.8	10.0	10.9	–	65.6
1974O	42.8	27.6	23.2	6.4	–	63.4
1974F	44.5	36.3	19.2	–	–	69.4
1970	53.7	46.3	–	–	–	60.2
1966	57.8	42.2	–	–	–	66.3
1964	54.0	46.0	–	–	–	67.3
1959	46.2	50.8	–	–	3.0	70.9
1958B	48.0	41.6	–	7.6	2.8	60.5
1955	44.6	55.4	–	–	–	67.6
1951	47.6	52.4	–	–	–	78.6
1950	45.6	49.6	–	2.7	2.1	78.8
1945	46.0	45.7	4.9	3.4	–	61.7

Glasgow St Rollox (1945), Glasgow Woodside (1950–70)

	Lab%	Con%	SNP%	Lib%	Other%	Turnout%
1970	47.4	41.5	8.4	–	2.7	63.8
1966	50.5	41.8	7.2	–	0.5	73.0
1964	45.6	40.4	5.4	8.3	0.3	74.0

	Lab%	Con%	SNP%	Lib%	Other%	Turnout%
1962B	36.1	30.1	11.1	21.7	1.0	54.7
1959	43.1	49.2	–	7.7	–	75.2
1955	43.9	56.1	–	–	–	72.8
1951	46.6	53.4	–	–	–	80.9
1950	45.6	48.7	–	5.7	–	80.2
1945	62.9	37.1	–	–	–	61.1

Glasgow Kelvin is Scotland's nearest equivalent to Hampstead and Highgate, or so the Glasgow West End cognoscenti would like to believe. The transition from Hillhead to Kelvin has seen the seat move eastward into the city centre, losing parts of its west side to Anniesland. Kelvin now includes within its boundaries some of the great cultural and civic symbols of Glasgow's wealth, past and present: BBC Scotland's headquarters at Queen Margaret Drive, Glasgow University, Kelvingrove Park, George Square and the marble opulence of the City Chambers.

Hillhead was a traditional Conservative seat represented continuously by the Conservatives through the inter-war years, easily, for example, surviving the Red Clydeside election of 1922. James Reid, MP from 1937 until 1948, held the seat in 1945 with a majority of 6,364. Thomas Galbraith won the 1948 by-election with a 8,641 majority over Labour and represented the seat until 1982. He won Hillhead in 1959 with a Tory vote of 68.3 per cent, which had fallen by 1979 to 41.1 per cent and a 2,002 lead over Labour: the last Tory seat in Glasgow and the last time they have won a seat in the city.

Hillhead's name was put on the map of British politics with the 1982 by-election. After the establishment of the Social Democratic Party in March 1981, Roy Jenkins had stood in Warrington and nearly won the once safe Labour seat; subsequently in conjunction with the Liberals they won spectacular by-election victories in Croydon North-West and Crosby (with Shirley Williams). Jenkins stood again in Hillhead and, in a genuine three-way contest with the Tories' Gerry Malone and Labour's David Wiseman, he came out the winner with 33.4 per cent and a majority of 2,038 over the Conservatives.

1983 boundary changes abolished the Labour seat of Kelvingrove and the southern parts of the seat were joined to a more pro-Labour Hillhead. The contest for the new seat pitted Jenkins, now leader of the Social Democrats and the Alliance's candidate for Prime Minister, against Neil Carmichael, MP for Kelvingrove; Jenkins won with 36.2 per cent and a majority of 1,164 over Labour. However, in 1987 Jenkins faced Labour's George Galloway, and in a year in which Labour made gains all across Scotland, there was little Jenkins could do to stop Galloway winning with a majority of 3,251.

Post-Jenkins Labour have tightened their hold, Galloway gaining over half the vote in 1997 and the SNP establishing themselves in second place over the Lib Dems.

Labour's Pauline McNeill held the seat comfortably in the first Scottish Parliament elections despite losing nearly 4,000 votes on a lower turnout; the SNP gained nearly 1,500 votes and secured their claim to second place. It is a measure of the changed political allegiances of the West of Scotland and Labour's current breadth of support that the two non-Labour parties which recently held Hillhead now poll derisory votes, the Lib Dems with 13 per cent and the Tories with 8 per cent. Hillhead has become that common thing in the West of Scotland, a safe Labour seat.

MP George Galloway was born in Dundee in 1954 and was MP for Glasgow Hillhead from 1987 until 1997 after winning the seat from Roy Jenkins, and for the successor seat of Glasgow Kelvin from 1997. Educated at Harris Academy, Dundee, Galloway never went to university, but instead worked for a brief period as a production worker in a Michelin Tyre factory before becoming a party apparatchik.

At the age of 23, Galloway became Secretary Organiser of Dundee Labour Party and at the same time stood in the 1977 council elections, losing a safe Labour ward with a sizeable Catholic community because he was co-habiting with his girlfriend. He aligned himself with the Bennite left, and was responsible for Dundee District Council flying the Palestinian flag and twinning with Nablus. Galloway is an Arab in a city where the word has two meanings, pro-Palestinian and a Dundee United fan, he being the former.

Known to friends and foes alike as 'gorgeous George', he became Chair of the Scottish Labour Party in 1981 to 1982, and went south to become General Secretary of War on Want from 1983 until 1987 where his flamboyant character led to accusations of expense irregularities and his admission of 'carnal knowledge' of two women at a conference in Greece. After his election in 1987, he was nearly deselected in 1992, losing the ballot of party members and only scraping through due to the trade union block vote. In 1994, on a visit to Iraq, he praised on national TV Saddam Hussein's 'indefatigability' and has been a consistent opponent of the West's policy of sanctions against Iraq. A frequent globetrotter, Galloway has travelled the world opposing American hegemony and undertaking much criticised humanitarian trips to Romania and Iraq.

MSP Pauline McNeill was born in 1962 and educated at Our Lady's High School, Cumbernauld, and Glasgow College of Building and Printing where she qualified with a Diploma in Design for Print, and City and Guilds Graphic Illustration, as well as gaining an LLB at Strathclyde University. McNeill was President of the National Union of Students (Scotland) in 1986 to 1988 (forever immortalised in student circles as Poll Tax McKnife for her non-payment position on that issue) and National Organiser for GMB Scotland from 1988 until 1999. She has been part of Labour's vocal home rule wing, active in the Campaign for a Scottish Parliament and a founding member of Scottish Labour Action, the nationalist pressure group formed after the 1987 election defeat.

She was Deputy Convenor of the Public Petitions Committee of the Parliament and a member of the Justice and Home Affairs Committee from May 1999 to December 2000, before joining the Justice II Committee and becoming its Convenor. She is also a member of the Cross Party Groups on Epilepsy and Information, Knowledge and Enlightenment. McNeill is seen as a potential future talent, and as Deputy Convenor of the Scottish Parliamentary Labour Group, an important conduit between an Executive which was too prone to top-down control politics and a disenfranchised group of backbench MSPs. McNeill is likely to play a crucial role with Henry McLeish as First Minister, particularly considering the widespread desire by ministers and MSPs to develop more effective means of communication between each other.

GLASGOW MARYHILL

Predecessor Constituencies: none.

1999

Electorate: 56,469
Turnout: 23,010 (40.75%)

Candidate	Party	Votes	Votes%	Change%
Patricia Ferguson	Labour	11,455	49.78	−15.16
Bill Wilson	SNP	7,129	30.98	+14.03
Clare Hamblen	Liberal Democrat	1,793	7.79	+0.66
Gordon Scott	SSP	1,439	6.25	+4.87
Michael Fry	Conservative	1,194	5.19	−0.69

Labour majority: 4,326 (18.80%)
Swing: 14.59% Labour to SNP

1997

Electorate: 52,523
Turnout: 29,721 (56.59%)

Candidate	Party	Votes	Votes%	Change%
Maria Fyfe	Labour	19,301	64.94	+2.34
John Wailes	SNP	5,037	16.95	−2.48
Elspeth Attwooll	Liberal Democrat	2,119	7.13	+0.47
Stuart Baldwin	Conservative	1,747	5.88	−3.76
Lorna Blair	NLP	651	2.19	−
Mandy Baker	SSA	409	1.38	−
Jahangir Hanif	Pro-Life	344	1.16	−
Roderick Paterson	Referendum	77	0.26	−
Stephen Johnstone	SEP	36	0.12	−

Labour majority: 14,264 (47.99%)
Swing: 2.41% SNP to Labour

1945–92

	Lab%	Con%	SNP%	Lib%	Other%	Turnout%
1992	61.6	10.3	19.1	7.0	1.9	65.2
1987	66.4	9.4	11.0	11.7	1.5	67.5

	Lab%	Con%	SNP%	Lib%	Other%	Turnout%
1983	55.2	14.8	7.1	22.2	0.9	65.4
1979	66.2	15.0	11.2	6.8	0.8	67.7
1974O	57.7	9.3	29.9	3.1	–	65.9
1974F	56.6	18.5	24.9	–	–	69.9
1970	65.6	23.0	11.4	–	–	63.9
1966	67.8	20.7	11.5	–	–	68.5
1964	68.4	27.6	–	–	4.0	70.5
1959	64.0	36.0	–	–	–	73.7
1955	62.8	37.2	–	–	–	69.9
1951	63.0	36.0	–	–	1.0	80.7
1950	61.2	32.2	–	6.6	–	80.0
1945	60.1	39.9	–	–	–	66.8

Glasgow Maryhill has been one of Scottish Labour's safest seats, even by the standards of Scottish politics, Labour winning it first in 1922, and holding it continuously since 1935. Maryhill in social mix is mostly a traditional working-class area with 58.9 per cent council housing tenure and it includes the outlying council estates of Possil, Milton and Summerton, but is centred around the older working-class area of Maryhill itself with the Maryhill corridor of urban regeneration and housing association infill. It encroaches into the West End of the city in the shape of the multi-cultural and student mix of Woodlands near to Glasgow University. It has overall the third worst health record in Britain, only beaten by Shettleston and Springburn; 42 per cent of its population live in poverty, while its male unemployment rate in June 2000 was 11.9 per cent, the third highest in Scotland.

Maryhill may have been Labour since time began, but other areas incorporated into Maryhill have more diverse traditions. Woodside was a parliamentary seat from 1950 until 1970 and was represented by the Conservatives from 1950 until Labour's Neil Carmichael won it in a 1962 by-election. Labour's vote in Maryhill reached a staggering 68.4 per cent in 1964, 66.2 per cent in 1979 and 66.4 per cent in 1987, the last two in four-party contests. Maria Fyfe was first elected in 1987, and saw her vote slip back in 1992, before climbing back in 1997 to 64.9 per cent and a majority of 14,242. The only exceptional thing about Maryhill in this election was the 2.19 per cent vote recorded by Lorna Blair, the Natural Law Party candidate. This was the highest vote recorded anywhere by the NLP in the UK, and twice the level of their next highest vote for no obvious reason.

Labour had a poor result here in the Scottish Parliament elections with Patricia Ferguson seeing nearly 8,000 disappear from Labour's vote and its share decline by 15.2 per cent – the seventh worst in the whole of Scotland. Labour's vote was the lowest it had ever been in a post-war election in Maryhill, but Labour look secure in

Maryhill in the long run. The equivalent of a political earthquake will be needed to remove Labour in Maryhill, and the shock waves of 1999 were only enough to weaken, not demolish Labour's historic dominance.

MP Maria Fyfe was born in 1938 in the Gorbals area of Glasgow. First elected MP for Glasgow Maryhill in 1987, she has been returned for the seat three times. Educated at Notre Dame High School, Glasgow, and Strathclyde University, Fyfe went on to be a lecturer in Trade Union Studies at the Central College of Commerce, Glasgow, from 1977 until 1987. She also served as a councillor on Glasgow District Council from 1980 until 1987 where she was Convenor of the Personnel Committee, and was elected on to the Scottish Labour Executive in the 1980s.

Fyfe was a spokesperson on women's issues from 1988 to 1991, resigning over Labour's support of the Gulf War. She was Convenor of the Scottish Labour MPs from 1991 to 1992 and a spokeswoman on Scotland from 1992 to 1995. Given the advent of New Labour, Fyfe, who was vocal in defence of Clause Four and aligned with the hard left Campaign for Socialism (as was her CLP), was never going to progress. However, Fyfe is more than a stereotypical left-winger and has given her support to a variety of causes ranging from Scottish devolution to women's rights and disarmament. A hard-working, conscientious MP, she put down an Early Day Motion in the Commons opposing Mike Tyson's coming to Scotland in May 2000, gaining more than 100 signatures. Fyfe announced her intention in January 2001 to not stand again at the forthcoming Westminster election, a decision which because of its proximity to the election increases the chances of the NEC imposing a central shortlist for any Labour selection.

MSP Patricia Ferguson was born in 1958 in Glasgow and educated at Garnethill Convent Secondary School, Glasgow and Glasgow, College of Technology where she gained a SHNC in Public Administration. She subsequently worked as a health administrator in a variety of posts in Greater Glasgow Health Board and Lanarkshire Health Board, before becoming an administrator at the Scottish Trades Union Congress from 1990 until 1994. Ferguson then became an organiser for the Scottish Labour Party in the South-West of Scotland from 1994 to 1996, before moving to Keir Hardie House to become Scottish Officer of the party from 1996 to 1999. Upon election to the Parliament, she became one of the two Deputy Presiding Officers and is also a member of the Cross Party Groups on Drug Misuse and Tobacco Control. An archetypical party bureaucrat she is married to Bill Butler, Secretary of the hard-left, arch anti-loyalist Campaign for Socialism, the newly elected MSP for Glasgow Anniesland which either suggests an interesting political marriage or that there is more to Ferguson than meets the eye.

GLASGOW POLLOK

Predecessor Constituencies: none.

1999

Electorate: 47,970
Turnout: 26,080 (54.37%)

Candidate	Party	Votes	Votes%	Change%
Johann Lamont	Labour	11,405	43.73	-16.18
Kenneth Gibson	SNP	6,763	25.93	+8.06
Thomas Sheridan	SSP	5,611	21.51	+10.42
Rory O'Brien	Conservative	1,370	5.25	-0.78
James King	Liberal Democrat	931	3.57	-0.10

Labour majority: 4,642 (17.80%)
Swing: 12.12% Labour to SNP

1997

Electorate: 49,284
Turnout: 32,802 (66.56%)

Candidate	Party	Votes	Votes%	Change%
Ian Davidson	Labour	19,653	59.91	+10.06
David Logan	SNP	5,862	17.87	-7.11
Thomas Sheridan	SSA	3,639	11.09	—
Edwin Hamilton	Conservative	1,979	6.03	-2.15
David Jago	Liberal Democrat	1,137	3.47	-0.87
Monica Gott	Pro-Life	380	1.16	—
Derek Haldane	Referendum	152	0.46	—

Labour majority: 13,791 (42.04%)
Swing: 8.59% SNP to Labour

1945–92

	Lab%	Con%	SNP%	Lib%	Other%	Turnout%
1992	43.4	15.8	15.6	5.9	19.3	70.7
1987	63.1	14.3	9.6	12.1	1.0	71.6
1983	52.3	20.5	9.9	17.4	—	67.2
1979	49.3	29.7	9.6	9.1	2.3	73.7

	Lab%	Con%	SNP%	Lib%	Other%	Turnout%
1974O	43.4	27.0	24.3	5.3	–	72.3
1974F	46.1	38.7	14.4	–	0.8	77.5
1970	46.3	44.8	8.9	–	–	72.6
1967B	31.2	36.9	28.2	1.9	1.8	75.7
1966	52.4	47.6	–	–	–	79.0
1964	44.6	43.9	–	11.5	–	77.8
1959	41.2	58.8	–	–	–	78.9
1955	38.7	61.3	–	–	–	75.5
1951	44.6	55.4	–	–	–	82.5
1950	38.8	56.4	–	4.8	–	81.3
1945	33.6	63.5	–	–	2.9	68.2

Glasgow Pollok occupies the south-west corner of the city dominated by the post-war council estate of the same name. The new 1997 seat includes Pollok, Nitshill, Cowglen and Arden from the old Pollok, and Cardonald and Mosspark from the old Govan. The new Pollok seat has a mixture of affluence and poverty: the beauty of Pollok Park and House with the tourist attraction of the Burrell Collection, combined with some of Scotland's worst unemployment spots. Pollok is the fourth most unhealthy constituency in Britain; 36 per cent of its population live in poverty and it had the second highest male unemployment in Scotland in June 2000 with 13.1 per cent.

Pollok has a reputation as a safe Labour seat, but that is an unfair reading of its past and present. It was in fact a Conservative seat continuously from 1918 until 1964, when it was first won by Labour in Wilson's first election victory; it was then rewon in spectacular fashion in 1967 by the Conservatives' Esmond Wright thanks to an increase in the SNP vote damaging Labour; this was only months before Hamilton set Scottish politics alight and it played a contribution in those famous events. Pollok returned to the safe Labour fold in 1970 under James White who remained MP until 1987. Jimmy Dunnachie followed in 1987 by which point Labour's vote had risen to 63.1 per cent and a 17,983 majority over the Conservatives.

However, everything was not happy within Scottish Labour. In 1992, Tommy Sheridan stood under the banner Scottish Militant Labour (while in prison) and scored a significant success winning 6,287 votes and 19.3 per cent, causing Labour's vote under the dour Dunnachie to fall to 43.4 per cent and cutting Labour's lead to 7,883. The subsequent council elections were relatively bad results for Scottish Labour, coming one month after the unexpected re-election of the Conservative Government and two SML councillors were returned in Glasgow, both in the Pollok seat: Sheridan in Pollok with 52.5 per cent and Nicky Bennett in South Nitshill with 44.3 per cent. Sheridan is still a sitting Glasgow councillor returned with 44.0 per cent in the Pollok ward in the 1999 elections. Sheridan's vote could be compared with that of Jimmy Reid standing in Central Dunbartonshire for the Communists in February 1974 after the Upper Clyde Shipworkers, work-in; it was the highest vote in post-war politics at that point gained by an independent who had not previously been an MP (beaten by Martin Bell in the 1997 election). It was thought Sheridan's star would wane, and in 1997 with boundary changes his vote fell to 11.1 per cent and Labour's majority climbed back to a respectable 13,791.

Such a judgement would have underestimated Sheridan, who remained a hard-working, charismatic councillor, and who nearly doubled his vote to 21.5 per cent in the 1999 Scottish Parliament elections, while Labour's vote fell by 8,000 and 16.2 per cent – Labour's fifth worst performance in the whole of Scotland – leaving Labour with a majority of 4,642 over the SNP. Both Sheridan and Kenny Gibson, the SNP candidate, were elected on the Glasgow list vote and Labour's saving grace in this seat is that the opposition to it is equally divided, allowing Labour to come through the middle.

MP Ian Davidson was born in 1950 in Jedburgh and was MP for Glasgow Govan from 1992 until 1997, defeating the SNP's Jim Sillars in 1992, then won Pollok in 1997. Educated at Jedburgh Grammar School and Galashiels Academy, Davidson went on to Edinburgh University and Jordanhill College of Education.

Prior to becoming an MP, Davidson was a senior Strathclyde Region councillor from 1978 until 1992 and served as Convenor of the Education Committee, while also being Chair of COSLA's Education Committee and on its Negotiating Committee on Teachers' Pay. He also worked as a researcher to Janey Buchan, MEP for Glasgow from 1978 until 1985, and for Community Service Volunteers from 1985 until 1992.

Davidson positioned himself as a sensible critic of the Labour leadership, but it won him no favours when in 1998 the Labour leadership excluded him from the panel for consideration for the Scottish Parliament. Davidson took this exclusion badly and with fellow excluded colleague Dennis Canavan lodged unsuccessful appeals. The end result has been to leave Davidson as damaged political goods, but this should not affect his chances of being re-elected in Pollok.

MSP Johann Lamont was born in 1958 in Glasgow and was educated at Woodside Secondary School, Glasgow, Glasgow University and Jordanhill College of Education. She worked as a history teacher in Rothesay and Glasgow and has been involved in a number of community projects including Education and Social Work developments in Castlemilk.

Lamont has long been identified as on the left of the Labour Party and as a campaigner on women's issues. She was involved in the Labour Co-ordinating Committee (Scotland) and as founder member of Scottish Labour Women's Caucus (along with her friend Margaret Curran). As a member of Hillhead Labour Party in the run-up to the 1992 election, she was a vocal opponent of sitting MP George

Galloway and played a leading part in the unsuccessful attempt to deselect him. Lamont was Deputy Convenor of the Local Government Committee of the Parliament and a member of the Equal Opportunities Committee from May 1999 to December 2000, before becoming Convenor of the Social Justice Committee in January 2001. She is also a member of a number of Cross Party Groups including those on Animal Welfare, Children, Drug Misuse, Older People, Shipbuilding, Media, Women, Sports, and Men's Violence Against Women and Children. In the debate on the Abolition of Warrant Sales in April 2000, Lamont made what many observers regarded as one of the most impressive contributions to the debate, supporting the bill and indicating the strength of opinion amongst Labour MSPs: an important speech given that Tommy Sheridan was the Bill's sponsor.

GLASGOW RUTHERGLEN

Predecessor Constituencies: none.

1999

Electorate: 51,012
Turnout: 29,023 (56.89%)

Candidate	Party	Votes	Votes%	Change%
Janis Hughes	Labour	13,442	46.31	-11.21
Tom Chalmers	SNP	6,155	21.21	+5.94
Robert Brown	Liberal Democrat	5,798	19.98	+5.43
Iain Stewart	Conservative	2,315	7.98	-1.28
William Bonnar	SSP	832	2.87	+2.16
James Nisbet	Socialist Labour	481	1.66	–

Labour majority: 7,287 (25.10%)
Swing: 8.58% Labour to SNP

1997

Electorate: 50,646
Turnout: 35,521 (70.14%)

Candidate	Party	Votes	Votes%	Change%
Thomas McAvoy	Labour	20,430	57.52	+4.14
Ian Gray	SNP	5,423	15.27	-0.30
Robert Brown	Liberal Democrat	5,167	14.55	+2.89
David Campbell Bannerman	Conservative	3,288	9.26	-9.89
George Easton	Independent Labour	812	2.29	–
Rosie Kane	SSA	251	0.71	–
Julia Kerr	Referendum	150	0.42	–

Labour majority: 15,007 (42.50%)
Swing: 2.22% SNP to Labour

1945–92

	Lab%	Con%	SNP%	Lib%	Other%	Turnout%
1992	55.4	16.9	16.3	11.3	0.2	75.2
1987	56.0	11.5	8.1	24.4	–	77.2
1983	48.3	18.0	5.5	27.8	0.3	75.1

	Lab%	Con%	SNP%	Lib%	Other%	Turnout%
1979	46.7	26.5	8.4	18.4	–	80.4
1974O	44.4	24.0	25.3	6.3	–	78.8
1974F	47.6	37.2	15.2	–	–	82.6
1970	52.3	43.3	–	–	4.4	79.7
1966	54.1	39.5	6.4	–	–	84.2
1964	52.6	42.8	4.6	–	–	86.0
1964B	55.5	44.5	–	–	–	82.0
1959	47.9	52.1	–	–	–	85.8
1955	47.1	52.9	–	–	–	84.1
1951	49.5	50.5	–	–	–	87.7
1950	49.5	47.7	–	2.8	–	86.1
1945	59.6	40.4	–	–	–	76.4

Rutherglen was until recently an independent burgh, entirely separate from Glasgow; it became part of the city council of Glasgow in the local reorganisation of 1974. It has not entirely lost its independent state of mind and in the 1995 local government reorganisation part of the parliamentary seat was put into South Lanarkshire.

Labour first won Rutherglen in the breakthrough year of 1922, before losing it in 1931, and in 1945 Gilbert McAllister won it back for Labour, holding it in 1950; Richard Brooman-White won it back for the Conservatives with a slender majority of 352 in 1951. George MacKenzie then regained it for Labour in a May 1964 by-election, just months before the October 1964 election, and held it continuously until his retirement in 1987.

Thomas McAvoy in 1987 increased Labour's vote to 56.0 per cent and this rose to 57.5 per cent in 1997. Labour polled 7,000 fewer votes in the Scottish Parliament elections, while the SNP closed the gap between the two parties from 15,007 to 7,287 without showing any possibility of threatening Labour. Rutherglen has long had a strong Liberal tradition, reflecting the independent mind of the ancient burgh, but between 1983 and 1992 the Lib Dems saw their vote fall from 28 per cent to 11 per cent, before seeing it rise to 14.5 per cent in 1997 and 20 per cent in 1999.

MP Tommy McAvoy was born in 1943 in Rutherglen and has been MP for Rutherglen since 1987. Educated at St Columbkills junior secondary school, he worked as an engineering storeman and became a Strathclyde Region councillor from 1982 until 1987. In opposition, he was a Whip from 1990 to 1993 and 1996 to 1997 and in government became third in the Whips' Office in 1997. Like several Catholic Scottish Labour MPs from the West of Scotland he has an innate conservatism across a range of social issues, in his case restricted to the issue of abortion time limits.

MSP Janis Hughes was born in 1958 in Glasgow and educated at Queen's Park School, Glasgow, and Glasgow Western School of Nursing. She subsequently became a nurse working in a variety of settings in Greater Glasgow Health Board area including the Victoria Infirmary, Royal Hospital for Sick Children, Western Infirmary and Belvidere Hospital from 1980 until 1988 and then as an administrator in the Renal Unit of the Glasgow Royal Infirmary from 1988 until 1999. Hughes was Deputy Convenor of the Procedures Committee of the Parliament and a member of the Transport and Environment Committee from May 1999 to December 2000, before becoming a member of the Health and Community Care Committee in January 2001. She is also a member of the Cross Party Groups on Epilepsy, Shipbuilding and Renewable Energy.

GLASGOW SHETTLESTON

Predecessor Constituencies: Glasgow Bridgeton (1945–70), Glasgow Gorbals (1945–70), Glasgow Queen's Park (1974–82) and Glasgow Central (1945–92).

1999

Electorate: 50,592
Turnout: 20,532 (40.58%)

Candidate	Party	Votes	Votes%	Change%
Frank McAveety	Labour	11,078	53.95	-19.21
Jim Byrne	SNP	5,611	27.35	+13.35
Rosie Kane	SSP	1,640	7.99	+6.19
Colin Bain	Conservative	1,260	6.14	+0.21
Laurence Clarke	Liberal Democrat	943	4.59	+0.63

Labour majority: 5,467 (26.62%)
Swing: 16.28% Labour to SNP

1997

Electorate: 47,990
Turnout: 26,813 (55.87%)

Candidate	Party	Votes	Votes%	Change%
David Marshall	Labour	19,616	73.16	+7.66
Humayun Hanif	SNP	3,748	13.98	-2.18
Colin Simpson	Conservative	1,484	5.53	-6.70
Kerry Hiles	Liberal Democrat	1,061	3.96	-2.16
Christine McVicar	SSA	482	1.80	–
Robert Corrie	BNP	191	0.71	–
Thomas Montguire	Referendum	151	0.56	–
John Graham	WRP	80	0.30	–

Labour majority: 15,868 (59.18%)
Swing: 4.92% SNP to Labour

1945–92

	Lab%	Con%	SNP%	Lib%	Other%	Turnout%
1992	60.6	15.0	19.1	5.3	–	68.9
1987	63.6	13.3	12.7	10.4	–	70.4
1983	54.2	19.1	7.9	18.5	0.3	67.4
1979	64.1	22.0	–	13.9	–	68.2
1974O	54.3	14.4	28.5	2.8	–	64.4
1974F	53.6	24.4	22.0	–	–	69.4
1970	59.9	26.7	13.4	–	–	63.7
1966	65.6	22.3	12.1	–	–	68.6
1964	68.0	32.0	–	–	–	71.4
1959	60.9	39.1	–	–	–	75.3
1955	57.8	42.2	–	–	–	69.3
1951	59.8	37.4	–	–	2.8	81.2
1950	56.6	36.8	–	–	6.6	79.9
1945	20.6	31.1	–	–	48.3	66.6

Glasgow Central (1945–92)

	Lab%	Con%	SNP%	Lib%	Other%	Turnout%
1992	57.2	13.9	20.8	6.3	1.8	63.1
1989B	54.6	7.6	30.2	1.5	6.0	52.8
1987	64.5	13.0	9.9	10.5	2.0	65.6
1983	53.0	19.0	10.3	16.7	1.1	62.9
1980B	60.4	8.8	26.3	–	4.1	42.8
1979	72.5	16.4	11.1	–	–	59.5
1974O	63.6	13.0	19.2	4.2	–	56.9
1974F	58.7	21.4	13.8	6.1	–	63.0
1970	66.1	19.9	14.0	–	–	59.2
1966	74.8	25.2	–	–	–	58.7
1964	70.1	29.9	–	–	–	62.4
1959	64.6	35.4	–	–	–	67.4
1955	61.8	38.2	–	–	–	64.1
1951	58.3	40.2	–	–	1.5	74.3
1950	54.6	43.6	–	–	1.8	74.0
1945	36.9	44.0	–	5.0	14.1	59.6

Glasgow Gorbals (1945–70), Glasgow Queen's Park (1974–82)

	Lab%	Con%	SNP%	Lib%	Other%	Turnout%
1982B	56.0	12.0	20.0	9.4	2.6	47.0
1979	64.4	24.0	9.7	–	1.9	68.4
1974O	56.1	17.0	21.8	3.7	1.4	67.0
1974F	56.2	26.6	15.6	–	1.6	73.3
1970	69.3	20.8	7.4	–	2.5	59.8
1969B	53.4	18.6	25.0	–	3.0	58.5
1966	73.1	22.8	–	–	4.1	61.7
1964	71.4	23.0	–	–	5.6	64.5
1959	63.3	30.8	–	–	5.9	68.2
1955	61.1	32.1	–	–	6.8	65.2
1951	61.9	31.9	–	–	6.2	76.0
1950	58.0	31.4	–	–	10.6	77.3
1948B	54.5	28.6	–	–	16.9	50.0
1945	80.0	20.0	–	–	–	56.8

Glasgow Bridgeton (1945–70)

	Lab%	Con%	SNP%	Lib%	Other%	Turnout%
1970	62.9	21.6	8.8	–	6.7	56.3
1966	74.3	25.7	–	–	–	58.8
1964	71.6	28.4	–	–	–	63.6
1961B	57.5	20.7	18.7	–	3.1	41.9
1959	63.4	36.6	–	–	–	68.5
1955	57.7	34.9	–	–	7.4	66.0
1951	63.6	31.0	–	–	5.4	76.9
1950	59.4	32.3	–	–	8.3	76.9
1946B	28.0	21.6	13.9	–	36.5	53.3
1945	–	33.6	–	–	66.4	58.2

Glasgow Shettleston is only half the seat it was previously. The 1997 boundary redistribution savagely reconfigurated the seat and the new Shettleston is made up of exactly half of the old Central seat (24,693 voters) and half from Shettleston (24,665). Shettleston was previously the seat of the historic East End of Glasgow with its traditions of hard-working, radical and respectable working-class communities and culture. It is also the home of the legendary Glasgow Celtic FC, a team connected to the predominantly Catholic communities of the East End. The new Shettleston has now moved westward into the city centre and across the River Clyde taking in some of the most famous and evocative areas of Glasgow – the Gorbals and Hutchesontown – and reaching as far south as the once Tory and still gentrified terraces of Queen's Park.

Shettleston has the dubious honour of being rated the most unhealthy constituency in the whole of Britain, just ahead of nearby Springburn and four other Glasgow seats which make up the top six; 42 per cent of its population live in poverty, while its male unemployment rate in June 2000 was 10.6 per cent, the eighth highest in Scotland. Despite these grim statistics there are signs of life in the new Shettleston. The legendary Gorbals now carries the word 'new' in front of it as a symbol of its comprehensive urban regeneration for the second time in just over a generation, as tenements, shops and tree-lined streets have been reintroduced. For the first time in decades, Glasgow's inner core has been reversing its population decline, seeing people and businesses come back into once declining areas – a symbol of Glasgow's capacity to endlessly reinvent itself.

Shettleston's Labour roots go back to the days of the Independent Labour Party. John Wheatley stood in the 'coupon' election of 1918 and just failed to defeat Rear Admiral Adair by 74 votes; he won the seat in Labour's watershed year of 1922 and went on to serve in the first Labour Government of 1924 as Minister for Health. He bequeathed Labour's claim to its first piece of significant legislation with the Housing Act 1924 which brought in subsidies for council house building.

Wheatley's death in 1930 saw John McGovern become Labour MP from 1930 until 1959, even managing to hold the seat in the debacle of 1931 when Labour was reduced to a mere seven seats across Scotland. Myer Galpern, MP from 1959 until 1979, saw Labour's vote rise to 68.0 per cent in 1964; subsequently David Marshall became MP in 1979 winning 64.1 per cent in 1979 and a majority of 9,161; in 1987 this rose back up to 63.6 per cent, after dipping in 1983, while his majority increased to 18,981.

Labour's vote rose in 1997 to 73.2 per cent, while its majority rose from a notional 15,644 in 1992 to 15,868 in 1997. No significant opposition emerged as all the mainstream parties lost ground and the Scottish Socialists made little headway. The 1999 elections caused Labour a few problems. Frank McAveety, a young, popular and energetic city councillor, became leader of the city council at the ridiculously early age by Glasgow standards of 35. This involved him presiding over a series of year-on-year cuts in jobs and services, which attracted unpopularity, so his candidature in Shettleston was never going to be universally popular. McAveety was never going to lose Shettleston, but he presided over Labour's worst result in the elections (outside of Falkirk West) with Labour's vote falling 19.2 per cent and its majority slashed from 15,868 to 5,467. The swing of 16.3 per cent was the second highest in the country. However, Labour held on in Shettleston and its hold should become more solid in the forthcoming UK election; it is difficult to see the SNP making the headway needed for success at forthcoming Scottish Parliament elections either.

MP David Marshall was born in 1941 in Glasgow. Educated at Larbert, Denny and Falkirk High Schools and Woodside Senior Secondary School, Glasgow, he has been MP for Glasgow Shettleston since 1979. Previously a transport worker and shop steward, he joined the Labour Party in 1962, became Labour Organiser for Glasgow in 1969, before serving on Glasgow Corporation from 1972 to 1974 and Strathclyde Regional Council from 1974 until 1979 where he was Convenor of its Manpower Committee.

As MP, he introduced a backbench bill which became the Solvent Abuse (Scotland) Act 1983, has served on the Scottish Affairs Select Committee from 1981 to 1983 and 1992 to 1997 and the Transport Select Committee from 1985 until 1992 and was its Chair from 1987 to 1992. Marshall combines a mix of radical and conservative views not unusual amongst Scottish Labour MPs, being anti-European Union, voting against the Maastricht Treaty and also opposed to the Gulf War, while opposing any reduction in the age of consent for male homosexuals in 1994 and again in 1998.

MSP Frank McAveety was born in 1962 in Glasgow and educated at All Saints Secondary School, Glasgow, and Strathclyde University, gaining a BA in English and History then going on to St Andrew's College of Education. McAveety has been an English teacher and was a full-time Glasgow councillor from 1988, at the youthful age of 25 among the generationally challenged ranks of Glasgow councillors. He became Convenor of the Arts and Culture Committee from 1994 to 1997, and in 1997 at the age of 35 he became the youngest leader the council has ever had, after Bob Gould was forced to resign following his 'junkets for votes' allegations. McAveety has also been a board member of Glasgow Development Agency and Chair of the Glasgow Alliance. Nicknamed 'Frankie goes to Holyrood' upon his election to the Scottish Parliament, due to his obsessional Nick Hornbyesque interest in rock music, he became Minister for Local Government, having previously been the Labour Party's spokesperson on housing in the 1999 elections.

McAveety's career as a minister was short-lived: he was sacked in Henry McLeish's first ministerial reshuffle on being elected First Minister in October 2000 – one of only two Labour sackings in the reshuffle. This seemed to be less to do with McAveety's failings as a minister – which were well known and included his inability to work underneath a women minister, Wendy Alexander, and his lack of attention to detail – and more about his behaviour during the Labour leadership contest following Donald Dewar's death. McAveety started out publicly as a Jack McConnell supporter, while all other ministers came out in favour of Henry McLeish in best North Korean practice. McAveety, suddenly, defected to the McLeish camp, raising the animosity of both sides. As a Labour backbench MSP, McAveety is now a member of the Health and Community Care Committee. Whether this is the end of the political career of a man whose burning ambition was to be the first elected mayor of Glasgow, and who was part of a Scottish Executive which under pressure from trade unions and conservative elements of Labour ruled out mayors, remains to be seen. He became a member of the Standards Committee in January 2001.

GLASGOW SPRINGBURN

Predecessor Constituencies: none.

1999

Electorate: 55,670
Turnout: 24,365 (43.77%)

Candidate	Party	Votes	Votes%	Change%
Paul Martin	Labour	14,268	58.56	-12.80
John Brady	SNP	6,375	26.16	+9.67
Murray Roxburgh	Conservative	1,293	5.31	-0.68
Matthew Dunningan	Liberal Democrat	1,288	5.29	+1.02
James Friel	SSP	1,141	4.68	+3.39

Labour majority: 7,893 (32.40%)
Swing: 11.23% Labour to SNP

1997

Electorate: 53,473
Turnout: 31,577 (59.05%)

Candidate	Party	Votes	Votes%	Change%
Michael Martin	Labour	22,534	71.36	+6.44
John Brady	SNP	5,208	16.49	-3.39
Mark Holdsworth	Conservative	1,893	5.99	-4.88
James Alexander	Liberal Democrat	1,349	4.27	-0.06
John Lawson	SSA	407	1.29	—
Andrew Keating	Referendum	186	0.59	—

Labour majority: 17,326 (54.87%)
Swing: 4.92% SNP to Labour

1945—92

	Lab%	Con%	SNP%	Lib%	Other%	Turnout%
1992	67.7	8.7	19.5	4.1	—	65.7
1987	73.6	8.3	10.2	7.9	—	67.5
1983	64.7	13.1	8.1	14.1	—	65.1
1979	66.1	21.3	12.6	—	—	67.8

	Lab%	Con%	SNP%	Lib%	Other%	Turnout%
1974O	54.6	13.3	28.3	2.7	1.1	66.5
1974F	53.7	22.1	22.8	–	1.4	70.4
1970	64.3	19.6	14.3	–	1.8	61.3
1966	67.8	19.1	9.4	–	3.7	66.6
1964	65.3	21.8	9.2	–	3.7	69.2
1959	58.8	36.7	–	–	4.5	72.6
1955	57.5	37.0	–	–	5.0	69.1
1951	62.4	37.6	–	–	–	78.0
1950	59.7	31.9	–	4.3	4.1	76.9
1945	65.0	35.0	–	–	–	63.6

Springburn stretches from the northern boundary of the city to close to the city centre and East End. It includes areas like Riddrie and Lethamhill, the striking tower blocks known as the 'Red Road' flats, which recently used to house Kosovo Albanian refugees, and the tenements and parks of Dennistoun and Alexandra Parade. It is rated the second most unhealthy constituency in Britain after Shettleston; 41 per cent of the population live in poverty and in June 2000 the male unemployment rate was 13.4 per cent, the highest in Scotland.

Springburn, like several of the Glasgow seats, was first won by Labour in 1922, by George Hardie, half-brother of Labour leader and legend, Keir Hardie, lost by him in the National landslide of 1931 by the most slender of margins (34 votes) and rewon in 1935. Post-war Springburn was represented first by John Forman, from 1945 until 1964, and then by Richard Buchanan from 1964 until 1979, followed by Michael Martin from 1979 to the present day. Martin drove Labour's vote up to 73.6 per cent in 1987 – the highest in Glasgow and one of the highest in the UK. In 1997, Martin polled 71.4 per cent, just being outpolled by neighbouring Shettleston for the highest Labour vote in Scotland.

The 1999 elections saw the unusual situation of a father handing on to his son. In this case the father remained a Westminster MP, while his son, Paul Martin, a local councillor, became an MSP. Martin Junior was elected with 8,000 fewer votes on a lower turnout and a majority reduced from 17,326 to 7,893; the SNP established a respectable second place, but still 32 per cent behind Labour. Springburn, like all the Glasgow seats (with the exception of Govan) is one Labour can count on winning and where the only doubt is the size of the Labour vote. The election of Michael Martin as Speaker of the House of Commons has provided practically the only imaginable circumstances in which Springburn would not return a Labour MP at the next election.

MP Michael Martin was born in Glasgow on 3 July 1945, two days before the 1945 general election, and has been MP for Glasgow Springburn since 1979.

Educated at St Patrick's Boys' School, Glasgow, he served on Glasgow Corporation from 1973 to 1974 and Glasgow District Council from 1974 until 1979. Originally a sheet metal worker, he was active in the 1970s campaigns against the closures of the Upper Clyde Shipyard and Hillington Rolls Royce plant where he was an AUEW shop steward from 1970 to 1974 before becoming a NUPE full-time organiser from 1976 to 1979.

After being elected an MP in 1979, he became Parliamentary Private Secretary to Denis Healey, when Healey was Deputy Leader of the Labour Party from 1981 to 1983, a member of the Services Committee from 1987 until 1991 and Finance and Services Committee from 1992 until 1997 as well as Chair of the Administrative Committee from 1992 until 1997. In 1997, he became a Deputy Speaker and Deputy Chair of Ways and Means. One of Scottish Labour's many Catholic MPs, he is openly conservative on social issues such as abortion and homosexuality, voting against the lowering of the age of consent for male homosexuals in 1994 and abstaining in 1998.

When Betty Boothroyd announced her intention to retire as Speaker of the House of Commons, Martin became one of the leading candidates to succeed her. In the contest, arranged on the first day of the new Parliamentary session on 23 October 2000, and presided over by the father of the house, Ted Heath, a dozen candidates competed for the honour of the post. The main contest was between Martin, supported by many Labour members, and Sir George Young, the Eton-educated Tory MP, who was supported by Tony Blair and several prominent ministers. Martin won the vote easily, a result many of the London tabloids did not like, attacking Martin's intelligence and credentials for the job. He faces a tough task, with MPs of all persuasions looking for the Speaker to help reverse the decline in Parliament's influence and resist the ease with which the government can sideline Parliament.

MSP Paul Martin was born in 1967 in Glasgow and educated at All Saints Secondary School, Glasgow, and Barmulloch College, Glasgow. Elected a councillor on Glasgow District Council in a December 1993 by-election for the Alexandra Park ward, he became a councillor on Glasgow City Council in 1995 for Royston. On the council, Martin held a variety of economic development posts such as Chair of the Glasgow Council Local Economic Initiatives Sub-Committee, Vice-Chair of Glasgow Council Economic Development and Industrial Development Committee. In the Scottish Parliament, Martin sits on the Audit Committee and the Cross Party Group on Children and joined the Justice I Committee in January 2001.

His election to Glasgow District Council in 1993 opened Labour to charges of nepotism, given his father was the local MP, and allowed Scottish Militant Labour to mount a strong challenge. His election to the Scottish Parliament has seen the emergence of the first father-son double act for the same constituency at different levels. In his first year, Martin's most significant achievement was to successfully campaign against Greater Glasgow Health Board's decision to put a secure unit at Stobhill Hospital in his constituency.

GORDON

Predecessor Constituencies: Aberdeenshire and Kincardineshire Central (1945) and Aberdeenshire West (1950–79).

1999

Electorate: 59,497
Turnout: 33,622 (56.51%)

Candidate	Party	Votes	Votes%	Change%
Nora Radcliffe	Liberal Democrat	12,353	36.74	-5.87
Sandy Stronach	SNP	8,158	24.26	+4.29
Alex Johnstone	Conservative	6,602	19.64	-6.40
Gillian Carlin-Kulwicki	Labour	3,950	11.75	+1.45
Hamish Watt	Independent	2,559	7.61	–

Liberal Democrat majority: 4,195 (12.48%)
Swing: 5.08% Liberal Democrat to SNP

1997

Electorate: 58,767
Turnout: 42,245 (71.89%)

Candidate	Party	Votes	Votes%	Change%
Malcolm Bruce	Liberal Democrat	17,999	42.61	+15.42
John Porter	Conservative	11,002	26.04	-21.92
Richard Lochhead	SNP	8,435	19.97	+1.39
Lindsey Kirkhill	Labour	4,350	10.30	+4.03
Fred Pidcock	Referendum	459	1.09	–

Liberal Democrat majority: 6,997 (16.57%)
Swing: 18.67% Conservative to Liberal Democrat

1945–92

	Lab%	Con%	SNP%	Lib%	Other%	Turnout
1992	11.3	37.0	14.3	37.4	–	73.9
1987	11.5	31.9	7.2	49.5	–	73.7
1983	8.5	42.0	5.7	43.8	–	69.4
1979	15.3	40.9	8.3	35.5	–	75.9
1974O	12.2	35.7	22.2	29.9	–	76.5

	Lab%	Con%	SNP%	Lib%	Other%	Turnout%
1974F	10.5	38.9	15.4	35.2	–	81.0
1970	15.5	46.7	5.3	32.5	–	75.8
1966	17.1	39.7	–	43.2	–	76.3
1964	20.4	46.4	–	33.2	–	77.4
1959	31.5	68.5	–	–	–	72.1
1955	27.2	59.0	–	13.8	–	72.6
1951	22.6	55.2	–	22.2	–	78.3
1950	23.1	55.5	–	21.4	–	80.9
1945	26.6	52.3	–	21.1	–	68.3

Gordon constituency takes in the towns of Ellon, Huntly, Inverurie, Keith, Old Meldrum and Turriff to the north-west of Aberdeen. It has had a long Liberal tradition. The party won this seat in a 1919 by-election when Major M. M. Wood won with a majority of 186 over the Unionists and held the seat until the 1924 election. The Liberals contested it until 1945, gaining a sizeable vote in the constituency. Moreover, and unusually for the Liberals, the party then contested this seat at every election from 1945 to 1999, except for 1959.

Electorally, the constituency has been a Conservative-Liberal contest since 1964. Indeed, the Liberals won the seat at the 1966 general election through James Davidson and were a good second to the Tories from 1970 onwards until they regained the seat in 1983. The rise of the SNP in the mid-1970s probably undermined Liberal attempts to regain the seat until 1983, with the Nationalists polling an impressive 9,409 votes in October 1974. When the Liberals did win Gordon in 1983, in alliance with the SDP, they did so very narrowly by a majority of 850 votes.

The seat was safely held in 1987, with a large majority of 9,519 votes, but nearly lost in 1992 with the Conservative revival, Malcolm Bruce only just holding on with another slim majority of 274. After 1992, following extensive boundary changes to Gordon because of the rapid growth of the population in the seat, it was expected that Gordon would become safely Conservative in 1997. The boundary changes involved the transfer of around 20,000 Gordon voters in the Liberal Democrat voting Aberdeen suburbs to the Aberdeen North constituency, while, Turiff, with no Liberal Democrat tradition and a predominantly Conservative electorate, was transferred into Gordon.

However, a notional Conservative majority of approximately 8,500 was turned on its head by the Tory wipeout at the 1997 elections. The Liberal Democrats emerged as winners again, with Malcolm Bruce triumphing comfortably with a majority of 6,997. John Major commented in his autobiography of a visit to this constituency in 1997: 'After a few minutes in the town I was certain we would not win there – and if not Gordon, what would be won in Scotland?'. The Conservative decline continued at the 1999 election, and the party's fall from grace was underlined by the fact that it came third behind the SNP and saw the Tory vote fall to just under 11 per cent. The last two election results and the Liberal Democrat strength in local, Scottish and general elections in the constituency should make this seat safely Liberal Democrat, though it does appear open to a Conservative revival, albeit a substantial one.

Neither the Nationalists nor Labour have had much of a chance in Gordon, given the dominance of the Conservatives and Liberal Democrats. The SNP achieved its best ever result in the constituency in 1999, and if it can emulate this performance at the forthcoming general election and retain second place over the Conservatives it will be extremely pleased. Both the SNP and Conservatives will seek to exploit any dissatisfaction with the performance of the Labour-Liberal Democrat coalition in the Scottish Executive, especially as Malcolm Bruce was prey to defections to the Tories in 1992 over political co-operation with Labour in the Scottish Constitutional Convention. However, the seat looks likely to remain Liberal Democrat for some time.

MP Malcolm Bruce was born in Birkenhead in 1944. He was educated at Wrekin college and has an MA from St Andrews in Economics and Political Science as well as an MSc in Marketing from Strathclyde. In the 1990s, perhaps foreseeing the potential loss of his seat with the boundary changes, he studied Law at the Inns of Court in London and became a barrister, though the voters of Gordon saved him from the second oldest profession. Before his election in 1983, he had a varied business background, with the *Liverpool Daily Post and Echo*, Boots, Goldbergs, the North East of Scotland Development Agency, Noroil Publishing and Aberdeen Petroleum Publishing. He was first elected in 1983 and has held a variety of Liberal, Alliance and then Liberal Democrat portfolios at Westminster. He has been a spokesperson for energy, education, employment, trade and industry, environment, Scotland and latterly Treasury issues. He was a member of the Treasury Select Committee from 1997 to 1999 and now sits on the Select Committee on Standards and Privileges. He was Scottish Liberal Democrat leader between 1988 and 1992 and also elected to the Rectorship of Dundee University from 1986 to 1989.

MSP Nora Radcliffe was born in Aberdeen in 1946. She was educated at Aberdeen High School for Girls and is a graduate of Aberdeen University and worked in both the hotel and catering industry and for Grampian Health Board before her election. She was also a councillor on Gordon District from 1988 until 1995, and was vice-chair of the Environmental Health and Economic Development Committees. In the Parliament, she is Liberal Democrat Spokesperson for the Environment and Europe, was Deputy Convenor of the Transport and Environment Committee and also sat on the Equal Opportunities Committee from May 1999 to December 2000, before joining the European Committee in January 2001. In the Equal Opportunities Committee she was a reporter on the group on sexual orientations and took a prominent role in the debate over the repeal of Section 28. She is a member of Cross Party Groups on Epilepsy, Information, Knowledge and Enlightenment, Older People, Age and Aging, Strategic Rail Services, Palliative Care, the Media, Agriculture and Horticulture, Renewable Energy and Men's Violence Against Women. She is also Joint Convenor of the Cross Party Group on Women.

GREENOCK AND INVERCLYDE

Predecessor Constituencies: Greenock (1945–70) and Greenock and Port Glasgow (1974–92).

1999

Electorate: 48,584
Turnout: 28,639 (58.95%)

Candidate	Party	Votes	Votes%	Change%
Duncan McNeil	Labour	11,817	41.26	-14.90
Ross Finnie	Liberal Democrat	7,504	26.20	+12.39
Ian Hamilton	SNP	6,762	23.61	+5.04
Richard Wilkinson	Conservative	1,699	5.93	-5.53
David Landels	SSP	857	2.99	–

Labour majority: 4,313 (15.06%)
Swing: 13.64% from Labour to Liberal Democrat

1997

Electorate: 48,818
Turnout: 34,687 (71.05%)

Candidate	Party	Votes	Votes%	Change%
Norman Godman	Labour	19,480	56.16	+8.39
Brian Goodall	SNP	6,440	18.57	+1.30
Rod Ackland	Liberal Democrat	4,791	13.81	-0.07
Hugo Swire	Conservative	3,976	11.46	-9.61

Labour majority: 13,040 (37.59%)
Swing: 3.55% SNP to Labour

1945–92

	Lab%	Con%	SNP%	Lib%	Other%	Turnout%
1992	58.0	11.7	19.0	11.4	–	73.7
1987	63.9	9.6	8.5	17.9	–	75.4
1983	46.8	9.8	6.8	36.3	0.3	74.2
1979	53.0	10.8	7.6	28.2	0.4	73.7
1974O	48.2	11.3	21.1	19.4	–	71.1
1974F	48.3	18.5	11.5	20.6	1.1	69.3

	Lab%	Con%	SNP%	Lib%	Other%	Turnout%
1970	53.7	–	–	44.7	1.6	76.0
1966	57.2	17.5	–	23.2	2.1	73.6
1964	55.1	18.2	–	25.4	1.3	76.5
1959	50.6	22.6	–	26.8	–	78.9
1955B	53.7	46.3	–	–	–	75.3
1955	51.4	48.6	–	–	–	77.9
1951	57.1	42.9	–	–	–	83.0
1950	50.6	–	–	28.7	20.7	83.2
1945	47.0	23.6	–	17.2	17.2	68.0

Found at the mouth of the River Clyde, Greenock and Inverclyde is centred around the working-class town of Greenock, built in the plain between the Clyde and nearby hills; other towns in the seat include Port Glasgow, Gourock and Wemyss Bay. Greenock has in the last twenty years suffered high unemployment, poor housing and health levels, and has tried to reinvent itself by bringing new industries into the area such as IBM and National Semi-conductors, as well as building a yacht marina. The seat is the eleventh most unhealthy parliamentary constituency in Britain and eighth in Scotland – the most unhealthy seat in Scotland outside Glasgow. 31 per cent of its population live in poverty and in June 2000 its male unemployment rate was 7.2 per cent.

Greenock was first won by Labour in a 1936 by-election, having previously been a Liberal seat. Hector McNeil represented the seat for Labour from 1941 to 1955, winning it in 1945 with a majority of 8,089 over the Conservatives as the Communists polled a respectable 5,900 votes (17.2 per cent). Dickson Mabon held the seat for Labour in a 1955 by-election with 53.7 per cent to the Conservatives' 46.3 per cent, but fifteen years later in 1970 the Conservatives unusually allowed the Liberals a free run against Mabon, who saw his majority fall to 3,000. In October 1974, Mabon survived the challenge of the SNP with a lead of 11,955, and in 1979 this became a 11,282 majority over the Liberals, who increased their vote by 3,500.

Dickson Mabon defected to the Social Democrats and stood in the Renfrew West and Inverclyde seat in 1983; Norman Godman became Labour candidate in Greenock and Port Glasgow, holding it with a majority of 4,625 over the Liberal-SDP Alliance who mounted a strong challenge, increasing their vote by 3,000; however, in 1987 the Alliance could not keep up this momentum and their vote collapsed, falling by more than half to leave Labour with a colossal 20,055 majority. By 1992, Godman's main challenger was the SNP who moved into second place 14,979 behind Labour, with the Liberal Democrats now in fourth place.

Boundary changes prior to 1997 gave Labour a notional 10,238 lead over the Conservatives, but the resulting election saw Godman increase Labour's vote by 1,000, while the SNP held their vote and retained second place 13,040 votes behind

Labour, and the Conservatives slipped into fourth place losing 4,000 votes. Two years later and Ross Finnie, for the Lib Dems, resuscitated his party's cause by cutting the Labour majority to 4,313 in the Scottish Parliament. In the process, he increased the Lib Dem vote by 2,500 and saw Labour's support fall by 7,500, while the SNP vote remained static. Whether Finnie, now a Regional list MSP and a Scottish Executive Minister, can at future Scottish elections build a wider Lib Dem base and challenge Labour remains an open question, but at UK elections this will remain for the moment a safe Labour seat.

MP Norman Godman was born in 1938 in Hull and elected Labour MP for Greenock and Port Glasgow in 1983. He was educated at Westbourne Street Boys' School, Hull, at Hull University where he graduated with a BA in Psychology and Sociology, and Heriot-Watt University where he obtained a PhD.

An ex-shipyard worker in Humberside, Godman went to university late in life and then became a lecturer in Industrial Relations at Heriot-Watt University. He unsuccessfully contested Aberdeen South in 1979 before becoming an MP in 1983. He was a member of the Scottish Affairs Select Committee from 1983 to 1987 and a Spokesman on Agriculture and Rural Affairs from 1987 to 1990. Godman sat on the European Legislation Select Committee from 1990 to 1992, the Northern Ireland Select Committee from 1996 to 1997 and Select Committee on Foreign Affairs from 1997. He is a soft left Labour loyalist, who rebelled against the leadership and voted against the Maastricht Treaty in 1993 and voted for John Prescott as leader in 1994. Godman is married to Patricia Godman, MSP for West Renfrewshire.

MSP Duncan McNeil was born in 1950 and worked as an apprentice in Cartsdyke shipyard and as a shipbuilder, before becoming a full-time officer in the GMB union where he was responsible for membership in the construction, distribution and whisky industries. McNeil has been Chair of Inverclyde Rights and Advice Centre, Chair of the Scott Lithgow Charity Committee and a member of the Scottish Labour Executive. He is a deputy member of the Scottish Parliamentary Bureau, and was a member of the Enterprise and Lifelong Learning Committee from May 1999 to December 2000 as well as the Cross Party Groups on Epilepsy and Shipbuilding.

HAMILTON NORTH
AND BELLSHILL

Predecessor Constituencies: Bothwell (1945-79), Lanarkshire North (1945-79) and
Motherwell North (1983-92).

1999

Electorate: 53,992
Turnout: 31,216 (57.82%)

Candidate	Party	Votes	Votes%	Change%
Michael McMahon	Labour	15,227	48.78	-15.23
Kathleen McAlorum	SNP	9,621	30.82	+11.73
Stuart Thomson	Conservative	3,199	10.25	-0.13
Jane Struthers	Liberal Democrat	2,105	6.74	+1.68
Katherine McGavigan	Socialist Labour	1,064	3.41	–

Labour majority: 5,606 (17.96%)
Swing: 13.48% from Labour to SNP

1997

Electorate: 53,607
Turnout: 37,999 (70.88%)

Candidate	Party	Votes	Votes%	Change%
John Reid	Labour	24,322	64.01	+5.72
Michael Matheson	SNP	7,255	19.09	-0.65
Gordon McIntosh	Conservative	3,944	10.38	-4.84
Keith Legg	Liberal Democrat	1,924	5.06	-1.70
Ray Conn	Referendum	554	1.46	–

Labour majority: 17,067 (44.92%)
Swing: 3.19% SNP to Labour

Motherwell North (1983–92)

	Lab%	Con%	SNP%	Lib%	Other%	Turnout%
1992	63.4	11.4	20.3	4.9	–	76.7
1987	66.9	11.1	14.0	8.0	–	77.3
1983	57.8	15.5	12.6	14.1	–	74.9

Bothwell (1945–79)

	Lab%	Con%	SNP%	Lib%	Other%	Turnout%
1979	55.0	23.4	10.8	10.8	–	78.6
1974O	47.8	17.9	24.5	8.9	–	76.5
1974F	46.8	26.7	14.1	11.2	1.2	81.2
1970	54.8	32.5	12.7	–	–	75.5
1966	61.0	36.3	–	–	2.7	78.0
1964	60.4	39.6	–	–	–	80.4
1959	54.7	45.3	–	–	–	82.2
1955	54.2	45.8	–	–	–	78.9
1951	56.3	43.7	–	–	–	86.0
1950	56.7	43.3	–	–	–	84.5
1945	65.8	34.2	–	–	–	73.0

Lanarkshire North (1945–79)

	Lab%	Con%	SNP%	Lib%	Other%	Turnout%
1979	55.5	31.5	13.0	–	–	79.7
1974O	46.2	22.5	26.9	4.4	–	79.5
1974F	48.4	33.1	18.5	–	–	82.7
1970	51.8	40.0	8.2	–	–	77.9
1966	60.9	30.1	–	–	–	79.2
1964	60.6	39.4	–	–	–	82.0
1959	58.7	41.3	–	–	–	82.8
1955	57.9	42.1	–	–	–	81.5
1951	58.2	41.8	–	–	–	85.4
1950	58.3	39.0	–	2.7	–	84.7
1945	59.6	40.4	–	–	–	73.3

Hamilton North was created from two existing constituencies in 1997 – Hamilton and Motherwell North – each of which was strongly Labour. The seat contains a small part of Hamilton and the towns of Bellshill, Bothwell, Holytown, New Stevenston and Uddingston amongst others, so is not really Hamilton at all: much like the fact that the former Motherwell North contained very little of Motherwell. The constituency has a mining and steel-working tradition, even though these industries declined many years ago. In 1991, 53.4 per cent of the housing was under local authority control.

Politically, it has been safely Labour for years, but it was not always so. Hamilton was first won by Labour in 1918 and even held in 1931 – the year of Labour's wipeout when it was reduced across Scotland to a mere seven seats. Jennie Lee, as a young, energetic left-winger was elected Labour MP for North Lanarkshire in a 1929 by-election, winning the seat from the Conservatives. She lost it in the 1931 debacle and stood again unsuccessfully in 1935 under the Independent Labour Party banner as Mrs Aneurin Bevan, splitting the Labour vote. Lee went on with her husband Nye to establish the left-wing paper *Tribune* in 1937, which exists to this day, and served as Minister of Arts in the 1964 – 70 Wilson Government.

Winnie Ewing's by-election victory in Hamilton in 1967 for the SNP was a sensational earthquake of epic proportions across Scotland and in particular in this part of the West of Scotland – difficult now to fully comprehend given the extent to which we have become used to by-election sensations – though that was largely in the constituency now called Hamilton South. Labour's hegemony has been seldom brought into question in these parts since then and Labour's majority in recent years has usually been upwards of 15,000 until the Scottish election in 1999; low turnout and an improved showing for the SNP were responsible for the fall in the Labour share of the vote at that election. At the Scottish election the SNP added around 2,500 votes to its 1997 performance as well as increasing its share of the vote in percentage terms.

The 1999 result was an improvement on earlier SNP challenges in the other predecessor constituencies to Hamilton North, when it was a distant second to Labour. In Bothwell, the SNP's best result was only 24.5 per cent in October 1974, which left it 10,948 votes behind Labour. In Lanarkshire North, the SNP's best result was 26.9 per cent in October 1974, which was 8,341 votes behind Labour's John Smith.

Hamilton North is definitely one of the safest Labour seats in Scotland and unlikely to change, unless there is a future by-election of Hamilton 1967 proportions! None of Labour's competitors has extensive local support in the constituency, evident from their poor showing at the council elections of 1999 in which Labour succeeded in both the working-class and the middle-class areas of the constituency. The SNP will look to improve on their 1999 showing though, and attempt to cut the Labour majority as they did at the Scottish election.

MP Dr John Reid was born in Bellshill in 1947, won the Motherwell North seat in 1987 and Hamilton North and Belshill in 1997. He was educated at St Patrick's Secondary School, Coatbridge and has degrees in history from Stirling University, including a doctorate on economic history ('Warrior Aristocrats in Crisis: The political effects of the transition from the slave trade to palm oil commerce in the Kingdom of Dahomey'). He was briefly a member of the Communist Party from 1973–5, joined the Labour Party in 1976 and was Research Officer of the Scottish Labour Party from 1979–83. He was involved in Neil Kinnock's successful campaign for the leadership in 1983, having been convinced by the party's 1983 humilation of its need to renew and modernise. Reid then worked for two years in Kinnock's office as a Political Adviser, before becoming Scottish Organiser of Trade Unionists for Labour from 1985–7. He was Minister of State at Defence from 1997 to 1998, then

Minister of Transport from 1998 to 1999 and then moved to the post of Secretary of State for Scotland. There he has attempted to breathe life into the position of Scottish Secretary, which initially led him into turf wars with the Scottish Executive in 1999 over the proposed closure of Kvaerner Govan shipyard. This passage with Donald Dewar created bad feeling and was not helped by the revelations of 'Lobbygate', in which Reid's son Kevin was implicated. There was significant tension and disagreement between Reid and Dewar over this, and it led to a much quoted public scene between the two at Scots night at the UK Labour conference in 1999.

Reid's tough demeanour and combative nature hide a formidable intellectual and political brain. He was convinced of the need for Labour to transform itself long before the words 'New Labour' were ever invented. He is capable of putting forward a compelling case for the need to modernise and for the rationale of New Labour, combining traditional principles with a revisionist understanding in a manner that is a combination of Blair and Brown. As the Secretary of State for Scotland in a much reduced Scotland Office, Reid was given the role of 'Minister for Crisis', and was frequently on TV presenting the Government on difficult issues, such as the petrol blockade, and able to put his head above the parapet on such issues as a strong TV performer who did not have a marginal seat or demanding ministerial responsibilities.

Reid was investigated by the House of Commons Commissioner for Standards, Elizabeth Filkin, along with fellow Labour MP, John Maxton. She found that they had acted improperly in misusing Westminster parliamentary allowances for Scottish Labour purposes in the Scottish Parliament elections. A subsequent enquiry by the Standards Committee reported in December 2000 and did not 'uphold' the complaints against Reid and Maxton. Labour spin doctors presented this as both of them being 'cleared', much to the anger of opposition MPs on the committee who insisted their verdict was more accurately one of 'not proven'.

After Peter Mandleson's unexpected resignation in January 2001, John Reid became Secretary of State for Northern Ireland: an indication of the esteem with which Tony Blair views his political abilities given the difficulties involved in keeping the Northern Ireland peace process on track.

MSP Michael McMahon was born in 1961. He was educated at Our Lady's High School, Motherwell, worked as a welder with Terex Equipment in Motherwell from 1977 until 1992 before entering University in 1992 and gaining a degree in Social Sciences from Glasgow Caledonian University in 1996. He worked as a political researcher from 1996 to 1999, and held various offices in his local Labour Party including CLP Secretary. In the Scottish Parliament, he serves on the Equal Opportunities and Local Government Committees. McMahon played a crucial role in the Section 28 debate, proposing in the Education Committee in May 2000 an amendment recognising the importance of 'marriage'. This specific proposal was defeated, but McMahon was seen as one of the Lanarkshire group of Labour MSPs who were very unhappy about the Section 28 debate; others saw McMahon as being far too sympathetic to the agenda of the Catholic Church in Scotland, evident when he refused to criticise Cardinal Winning's condemnation of homosexuals as 'perverted'. He sits on the Cross Party Groups for Shipbuilding, Tobacco Control and Sports and is Convenor of the group on Palliative Care.

HAMILTON SOUTH

Predecessor Constituencies: Hamilton (1945–92).

Westminster By-election 23 September 1999

Electorate: 46,765
Turnout: 19,449 (41.59%)

Candidate	Party	Votes	Votes%	Change%
Bill Tynan	Labour	7,172	36.88	−28.72
Annabelle Ewing	SNP	6,616	34.02	+16.40
Shareen Blackall	SSP	1,847	9.50	−
Charles Ferguson	Conservative	1,406	7.23	−1.41
Stephen Mungall	Hamilton Accies	1,075	5.53	−
Marilyne McLaren	Liberal Democrat	634	3.26	−1.86
Monica Burns	Pro-Life	257	1.32	−0.75
Tom Dewar	Socialist Labour	233	1.20	−
James Reid	Scottish Unionist	113	0.58	−
Alistair McConnachie	UK Independence	61	0.31	−
George Stidolph	NLP	18	0.09	−
Drummond Murray	Status Quo	17	0.09	−

Labour majority: 556 (2.86%)
Swing: 22.56% from Labour to SNP

1999

Electorate: 46,765
Turnout: 25,920 (55.43%)

Candidate	Party	Votes	Votes%	Change%
Tom McCabe	Labour	14,098	54.39	−11.21
Adam Ardrey	SNP	6,922	26.71	+9.09
Margaret Mitchell	Conservative	2,918	11.26	+2.62
John Oswald	Liberal Democrat	1,982	7.65	+2.53

Labour majority: 7,176 (27.68%)
Swing: 10.15% from Labour to SNP

Electorate: 46,562
Turnout: 33,091 (71.07%)

Candidate	Party	Votes	Votes%	Change%
George Robertson	Labour	21,709	65.60	+8.65
Ian Black	SNP	5,831	17.62	-2.71
Robert Kilgour	Conservative	2,858	8.64	-7.44
Richard Pitts	Liberal Democrat	1,693	5.12	-1.51
Colin Gunn	Pro-Life	684	2.07	–
Stuart Brown	Referendum	316	0.95	–

Majority: 15,878 (47.98%)
Swing: 5.68% SNP to Labour

Hamilton 1945–92

	Lab%	Con%	SNP%	Lib%	Other%	Turnout%
1992	55.2	17.6	19.7	7.5	–	76.2
1987	59.7	14.4	12.7	13.2	–	76.9
1983	52.4	19.2	8.2	20.1	–	75.7
1979	59.6	23.8	16.6	–	–	79.6
1978B	51.0	13.0	33.4	2.6	–	72.1
1974O	47.5	9.5	39.0	4.0	–	77.2
1974F	48.0	20.1	31.9	–	–	79.7
1970	52.9	11.4	35.1	0.6	–	80.0
1967B	41.5	12.5	46.0	–	–	73.7
1966	71.2	28.8	–	–	–	73.3
1964	71.0	29.0	–	–	–	77.5
1959	66.1	27.7	6.2	–	–	79.9
1955	67.4	32.6	–	–	–	76.1
1951	68.7	31.3	–	–	–	80.6
1950	70.0	30.0	–	–	–	81.7
1945	73.5	26.5	–	–	–	70.0

Hamilton South contains the majority of the town of Hamilton itself. This is a safe Labour seat but has a tradition of dramatic by-elections involving the SNP, which have occurred on three separate occasions, giving it something of the status of Govan. Winnie Ewing won here in 1967, overturning a substantial Labour majority after the retirement of Tom Fraser. This result gave the SNP its first electoral success since the brief Motherwell victory by Robert McIntyre in 1945, and entered the seat and Mrs

Ewing into Nationalist mythology. Richard Crossman wrote in his diary in November 1967 immediately after the Hamilton result: 'Tam [Dalyell] had been working here a great deal and said that the way Tom Fraser, like Bowden [Labour MP for Leicester 1945–67], went off to a highly-paid job had caused great resentment among the miners and a boost for the Scot. Nat. movement. This, of course, follows the Scot. Nat. success in Pollok, more Welsh nationalist success in Rhondda and absolute success in Carmarthen. I was reminded of how Ted Heath had said last week at the Broadcasting Committee meeting that nationalism is the biggest single factor in our politics today.' Scottish politics were never to be the same again, and no SNP by-election was ever to have such a dramatic impact. Crossman, unlike nearly all his other Labour ministerial colleagues' understood that something fundamental was afoot in Scotland and Wales; Benn, for example, his competitor as a comprehensive recorder of every mood and nuance in Cabinet, made no mention of Hamilton.

Two other by-elections were to have far-reaching consequences beyond the streets of Hamilton and its surrounding Lanarkshire towns. Margo MacDonald contested the seat at the 1978 by-election, which Labour won convincingly. Finally, Winnie Ewing's daughter, Annabelle, nearly snatched the Westminster seat from Labour in 1999 after the Scottish election as the SNP tried to get history to repeat itself with another Ewing.

Both the 1967 and 1999 results were a shock, given the safeness of the seat. The former MP for the seat from 1978 until 1999, George Robertson, had first won here at the by-election in 1978, an intense campaign fought at a time of unpopularity for the Labour Government. His victory, like Dewar's at Glasgow Garscadden in the same year, were decisive defeats for the SNP and demonstrated that Labour had turned the Nationalist tide that ran from 1974 onwards. Robertson's appointment as Secretary-General of NATO in 1999 brought elevation to the House of Lords and yet another by-election to the constituency.

Robertson had held this working-class seat for many years fairly comfortably with majorities of 15,000 to 20,000, but the by-election of 1999 gave Labour a real scare: in 1997 and at the 1999 Scottish election, after safe Labour wins the Nationalists came within 556 votes of taking the seat. The Labour leadership had chosen the by-election date to coincide with the SNP's annual conference in Inverness to prevent the SNP's horde of activists from descending on the constituency Govan-style. This tactic was not entirely successful for Labour as the narrowness of the result showed. However, it prevented an activist-led SNP bandwagon from developing in Hamilton that would have brought an SNP victory and Labour just held on.

Despite the by-election performance, the SNP's popularity in the constituency will likely prove shortlived. The SNP candidate at the 1999 by-election, Annabelle Ewing, was later selected to fight the more promising Perth seat at the next general election and the party's performance in 1999 will probably slip away into history as a near-victory. Labour should win this seat comfortably come the general election.

From the Ewing victory of 1967 to Margo's contest in 1978, support for the SNP in the constituency was extemely strong, at over 31 per cent at each election until the 1979 general election. Since then, barring the 1999 by-election, the SNP's perform-ance in the seat has been extremely disappointing.

MP Bill Tynan was born in 1940 in Glasgow and educated at Stow College as a mechanical engineer. He was a toolmaker and union official with the AEEU before his election in 1999. Tynan had lost out to Jack McConnell in the candidate selection for Motherwell and Wishaw at the Scottish election in 1999, and this seat was very much second best for him. In the circumstances of the by-election, he was fortunate to be elected at all. He is a member of the Scottish Affairs Committee in the Commons.

MSP Tom McCabe was born in Hamilton in 1954. He was educated at Bell College of Technology, Hamilton, and gained a Diploma in Public Sector Management, before working for Hoover plc from 1974 to 1993 where he was a senior shop steward. He then worked as a Welfare Rights Officer for Strathclyde Regional Council from 1993 to 1996 and in North Lanarkshire from 1996-99. He was a councillor in Hamilton District Council from 1988 to 1996 where he was Chair of Housing from 1990-92 and leader of the council from 1992 to 1996. Following the reorganisation of local government in 1995, he was elected to South Lanarkshire Council in 1995 and was its leader from 1995 to 1999. He also served as Vice-Convenor of Strathclyde Joint Police Board and was a member of Lanarkshire Development Agency over this period.

McCabe's seat Hamilton South was twinned with neighbouring Clydesdale and both he and Karen Gillon were selected from shortlists of one: an unusual occurrence in the Labour selections for the Scottish Parliament. McCabe's leadership of Hamilton and South Lanarkshire councils was filled with controversy, such as the decision in the latter to introduce curfews for young people in the town of Hamilton. He was also involved in South Lanarkshire in a major scandal in January 1999 when allegations of widespread bullying and intimidation were made against him. Stuart McQuarrie, then Secretary of the Labour Group, accused McCabe and his deputy, Eddie McAvoy, of 'the most vicious foul-mouthed verbal threats I have ever experienced'. The matter was investigated by Alex Rowley, then Labour General Secretary, and McCabe was completely cleared, but there were several resignations from the party and McQuarrie stood down at the 1999 council elections.

During the Scottish Parliament election McCabe was one of the campaign spokespeople on Home Affairs and Government and then became a member of Labour's five-strong coalition negotiating team, the only member, apart from Sarah Boyack, who was not a Westminster MP. He was then appointed Minister for Parliament and Labour Business Manager. His role in the Section 28/Clause 2A debate came under scrutiny, with McCabe seen as one of the influential 'Big Macs' who was acutely sensitive to the concerns of the Keep the Clause campaign, partly driven by vocal forces within Hamilton South CLP who opposed the Scottish Executive's policy. His contribution in September 2000 when he tried to prevent a debate in Parliament on the Scottish Qualifications Authority crisis was widely seen as misjudged. McCabe tried to prevent a full debate, and restrict Parliament to a 45-minute Question and Answer session. Even though he had the numbers to win the vote, his contribution was widely seen as arrogant and partisan in tone and more appropriate to a West of Scotland council chamber than Parliament.

After the death of Donald Dewar, McCabe was one of the prime movers in Henry McLeish's successful campaign to become Labour leader and First Minister. After McLeish's election, McCabe was given responsibility for strategic communications and presentation while retaining his post as Minister for Parliament. He has overseen the Executive's policy review, unofficially titled 'dump the crap'. McCabe's influence in this, negotiating bilaterally with ministers, gives him the discretion to decide what policies are kept and gives him a role as 'a new enforcer'. McCabe has been criticised by some as an old-time Labour fixer with a 'cooncil' mentality who is out of place in 'the new politics', but this underestimates McCabe's undoubted abilities. Behind closed doors, his skills have unarguably contributed towards keeping the coalition together and he has worked hard at developing good relations across the Labour Group of MSPs and keeping communications open with key elements: ex-councillors, trade unionists, women MSPs and others. These are important political skills to any administration.

INVERNESS EAST, NAIRN AND LOCHABER

Predecessor Constituencies: Inverness (1945–79) and Nairn and Lochaber (1983–92).

1999

Electorate: 66,285
Turnout: 41,824 (63.1%)

Candidate	Party	Votes	Votes%	Change%
Fergus Ewing	SNP	13,825	33.06	+4.07
Joan Aitken	Labour	13,384	32.00	-1.89
Donnie Fraser	Liberal Democrat	8,508	20.34	+2.83
Mary Scanlon	Conservative	6,107	14.60	-2.89

SNP majority: 441 (1.06%)
Swing: 2.98% Labour to SNP

1997

Electorate: 65,701
Turnout: 47,768 (72.71%)

Candidate	Party	Votes	Votes%	Change%
David Stewart	Labour	16,187	33.89	+10.72
Fergus Ewing	SNP	13,858	28.99	+3.90
Stephen Gallagher	Liberal Democrat	8,364	17.51	-9.18
Mary Scanlon	Conservative	8,355	17.49	-5.99
Winona Wall	Referendum	436	0.91	—
Murray Falconer	Green	354	0.74	—
Daniel Hart	Christian Union	224	0.47	—

Labour majority: 2,339 (4.90%)
Swing: 9.95% Liberal Democrat to Labour

1945–92

	Lab%	Con%	SNP%	Lib%	Other%	Turnout%
1992	25.1	22.6	24.7	26.0	1.5	73.3
1987	25.3	23.0	14.8	36.8	—	70.9
1983	14.4	29.8	9.8	46.1	—	70.6

	Lab%	Con%	SNP%	Lib%	Other%	Turnout%
1979	20.6	24.8	20.6	33.8	0.2	74.4
1974O	15.6	22.0	29.6	32.4	0.4	70.5
1974F	16.6	26.8	17.9	38.7	–	76.7
1970	23.0	31.5	7.1	38.4	–	72.3
1966	27.7	32.9	–	39.4	–	72.1
1964	26.3	33.9	–	39.8	–	71.4
1959	22.8	44.3	–	32.9	–	71.6
1955	19.9	41.4	–	38.7	–	67.6
1954B	22.6	41.4	–	36.0	–	49.2
1951	35.5	64.5	–	–	–	69.3
1950	31.8	45.5	–	22.7	–	68.6
1945	34.6	–	–	22.2	43.2	59.0

A fascinating seat with a changing political history in recent years. Once safely Liberal Democrat, this constituency became a four-way marginal in 1992 when only 1,616 votes separated the four main parties, then a Labour held-seat in 1997 followed by the SNP's victory at the Scottish election in 1999. Such changes make choosing between these two parties at the next Westminster election a difficult task. Historically, this seat was a happy hunting ground for the Liberals. The Conservatives did not contest the constituency from 1918 to 1945, and left the seat to the Liberals and National Liberals, so there was a strong historic Liberal vote at all elections from 1918 to 1999, with the exception of 1951. Also of historical interest was the fact that John MacCormick of the SNP contested this seat on a number of occasions in the inter-war period, giving the SNP a very early presence in the constituency.

Murdo Macdonald won the seat as an Independent Liberal in 1945 with a majority of 2,435 over Labour with the official Liberals polling significantly. Lord Malcolm Douglas Hamilton then won the seat for the Conservatives in 1950 and held it in 1951, but in a December 1954 by-election, Neil McLean only just won the seat for the Conservatives seeing his majority slashed to 1,331 over the Liberals who won 36 per cent of the vote. In the 1950s and 1960s, Inverness was very much a two-party marginal between the Conservatives and Liberals. The SNP came into second place only 1,134 votes behind the Liberals in October 1974, and Labour also polled some decent results in recent years in advance of victory in 1997. However, for most of the last thirty years it was the Liberals who held the seat through Russell Johnston, who won the seat in 1964 and held it until his retirement at the 1997 election. For most of this period the Liberals won against a divided opposition vote. Johnston's relatively comfortable victories came to an end in 1992, when he crept home with a majority of 458 over Labour. Since then, the seat has altered to become a contest between Labour and the SNP, with the Liberal Democrats confined to a distant third place in 1997 and 1999 from which they show little sign of recovering.

Labour and the SNP have benefited most from the decline of the Liberal vote following Russell Johnston's retirement. Indeed, the changing complexion of the seat suggests how much Johnston relied on a personal vote that did not automatically transfer to his party – unlike David Steel's seat in Tweeddale. Labour and the SNP also benefited from having familiar candidates who were committed to the constituency over several elections, with the prospect of building their own personal votes. Current Westminster MP Dave Stewart had fought the constituency in 1987 and 1992 before triumphing in 1997. SNP MSP Fergus Ewing had contested the seat in 1992 and 1997 before his victory in 1999. It was not just the Ewing name that assisted his victory.

Both Labour and the SNP have effective organisations in this seat and it will be an important individual battleground between the two parties as Labour seeks to retain its only Highlands seat outside of the Western Isles against the SNP's challenge. The fact that Fergus Ewing is now an MSP has two consequences. Most obviously, he cannot contest the Westminster seat, so the SNP requires a new candidate. Second, Ewing's election in 1999 has markedly raised the SNP's profile in a constituency it has never held. However, one could also make this latter observation about Dave Stewart and Labour. A fascinating two-party battle lies ahead at the general election, with the other two parties seemingly irrelevant to the electoral outcome.

MP David Stewart was born in 1956 and educated at Hyndland Secondary School, Glasgow and Paisley College in Social Science, followed by Social Work at Stirling and Management with the Open University. He was a social worker from 1981 to 1987 in first Dumfries and then Dingwall and then a social work manager with Highland Council from 1987 to 1997. He served as a councillor in Nithsdale from 1984 to 1986 and subsequently in Inverness from 1988 to 1996. He was a member of the Scottish Affairs Select Committee from 1997 to 1999.

MSP Fergus Ewing was born in Glasgow in 1957. He was educated at Loretto School, Edinburgh and is a graduate in law from Glasgow University and was employed as a solicitor until his election in 1999. He is the latest Ewing to achieve electoral success, following his mother, Winnie, and his wife, Margaret, who is MP and MSP for the neighbouring seat of Moray. He held a number of offices within the SNP and was active in the small business area, an issue he has pursued within the Parliament. In the Scottish Parliament he became infamous for asking the largest number of written questions, especially on environmental issues which affected his constituency. He was a member of the Enterprise and Lifelong Learning and Rural Affairs Committees from May 1999 to December 2000, and now sits on the Rural Development Committee. He also sits on the Cross Party Groups for Crofting, Epilepsy, Oil and Gas and Sport. He is a keen hill walker and a member of Lochaber mountain rescue team. He also used to take holidays with friends in the 1980s to rather unusual destinations such as Albania under Enver Hoxha and Ceausescu's Romania, a far cry from Inverness. Indeed, in Albania one of Ewing's friends was knocked down in a car accident: a real achievement in a country which had hardly any cars.

KILMARNOCK AND LOUDOUN

Predecessor Constituencies: Kilmarnock (1945–79).

1999

Electorate: 61,454
Turnout: 39,349 (64.03%)

Candidate	Party	Votes	Votes%	Change%
Margaret Jamieson	Labour	17,345	44.08	−5.70
Alex Neil	SNP	14,585	37.07	+2.55
Lyndsay McIntosh	Conservative	4,589	11.66	+0.85
John Stewart	Liberal Democrat	2,830	7.19	+3.20

Labour majority: 2,760 (7.01%)
Swing: 4.14% Labour to SNP

1997

Electorate: 61,376
Turnout: 47,409 (77.24%)

Candidate	Party	Votes	Votes%	Change%
Desmond Browne	Labour	23,621	49.82	+5.04
Alex Neil	SNP	16,365	34.52	+3.81
Douglas Taylor	Conservative	5,125	10.81	−8.22
John Stewart	Liberal Democrat	1,891	3.99	−1.50
William Sneddon	Referendum	284	0.60	—
William Gilmour	NLP	123	0.26	—

Labour majority: 7,256 (15.3%)
Swing: 0.62% SNP to Labour

1945–92

	Lab%	Con%	SNP%	Lib%	Other%	Turnout%
1992	44.8	19.0	30.7	5.5	—	80.0
1987	48.5	19.6	18.2	13.7	—	78.0
1983	43.6	24.7	9.0	22.7	—	75.6
1979	52.6	29.1	18.3	—	—	81.1
1974O	45.7	18.9	30.2	5.2	—	80.4
1974F	47.2	27.7	15.3	9.8	—	83.2

	Lab%	Con%	SNP%	Lib%	Other%	Turnout%
1970	59.3	27.8	6.9	6.0	–	79.2
1966	68.5	31.5	–	–	–	79.0
1964	62.3	26.7	–	11.0	–	82.8
1959	62.7	37.3	–	–	–	82.4
1955	60.9	39.1	–	–	–	81.1
1951	60.7	39.3	–	–	–	86.7
1950	56.6	35.8	–	5.4	2.2	86.2
1946B	59.7	32.5	7.8	–	–	68.4
1945	59.4	40.6	–	–	–	76.1

Kilmarnock and Loudoun involves Kilmarnock and smaller towns such as Darvel and Stewarton. It is an urban constituency also containing rural areas around Kilmarnock. It features traditional industries in decline, such as textiles, as well as still prosperous whisky and manufacturing industries. The constituency was safely Labour until the rise of the SNP in the 1970s. It was the seat held by former Secretary of State for Scotland Willie Ross from 1946 until his retirement in advance of the 1979 general election. After Ross, Labour's Willie McKelvey was elected in 1979 until his retirement in 1997. McKelvey's late decision to retire allowed a rapid selection process to replace him and the selection of favourite son Des Browne as his successor. The time factor in 1997 neatly side-stepped the necessity for an all-woman short-list in the constituency, and aided Browne's selection.

The SNP initially gained prominence in Kilmarnock at the 1974 general elections, when it received 14,655 votes at the October election. This performance pushed it into second place, but it was still 7,529 votes behind Labour: a result almost identical to that of 1997. Support for the SNP dissipated after 1974, but began to increase again in the 1980s and 1990s. The party adopted a high-profile candidate, Alex Neil, at UK and Scottish elections, who was able to benefit from an old Labour appeal and made the seat ever more marginal in three different contests from 1992 until 1999. However, he was never able to win the seat and was still 2,760 votes adrift at the Scottish election of 1999.

The SNP organisation in the seat was extremely effective from the mid-1980s onwards as the party began to win council wards, at district and regional level, and then repeat these successes following local government reorganisation. At one time, the SNP controlled Kilmarnock and Loudoun District Council, and it is very close behind Labour on the current East Ayrshire Council. For example, at the last council elections in 1999, Labour won 17 seats with 45.75 per cent of the vote compared to the SNP's 14 seats and 40.83 per cent: the SNP thus outperforming its Scottish election result of the same day.

SNP support is therefore entrenched rather than transient. This situation presents a considerable challenge to Labour, though the party will be confident of success given the 1997 and 1999 results. Labour won comfortably in 1997 and less so in 1999 due in part to turnout. Both Labour and SNP votes in 1999 were numerically lower compared to 1997, even though the SNP's share of the vote increased. However, any Labour complacency will give the SNP a considerable opportunity for success. The SNP will require a new candidate to replace MSP Alex Neil, but had not selected at the time of writing. This perennial SNP-Labour contest will likely remain of interest for some time but is unlikely to become a marginal at Westminster elections unless there is a considerable improvement in SNP fortunes.

MP Des Browne was born in 1952 in Stevenson and was educated at St Michael's Academy, Kilwinning and studied in law at Glasgow University. He practised as a solicitor from 1976 until becoming an advocate in 1993. This career proved short-lived as he was elected to Westminster in 1997 after a last-minute selection following the retiral of the former sitting MP, Willie McKelvey. At Westminster, Browne served on the Northern Ireland Affairs Committee in 1997–8 before getting his feet on the ladder of ministerial promotion with his appointment as a Parliamentary Private Secretary to Donald Dewar at the former Scottish Office from 1998 to 1999. He then returned to the back benches and sits on the Select Committee on Public Administration.

MSP Margaret Jamieson was born in Kilmarnock in 1953 and educated at Grange Academy, Kilmarnock and at Ayr College. She worked in public sector catering as a cook with Arran Health Board and then Strathclyde Regional Council from 1969 onwards before becoming an official for the National Union of Public Employees in 1979, a union which subsequently became Unison. She held this position until her election in 1999. She was also a former Chair of Scottish Labour's Women's Committee. She sits on the Audit and Health and Community Care Committees of the Scottish Parliament and is a member of the Cross Party Groups for Children, Citizenship, Income, Economy and Society, Drug Misuse and Women.

KIRKCALDY

Predecessor Constituencies: Kirkcaldy Burghs (1945–70) and Kirkcaldy (1974–79).

1999

Electorate: 51,640
Turnout: 28,342 (54.88%)

Candidate	Party	Votes	Votes%	Change%
Marilyn Livingstone	Labour	13,645	48.14	-5.42
Stewart Hosie	SNP	9,170	32.35	+9.42
Michael Scott-Hayward	Conservative	2,907	10.26	-3.40
John Mainland	Liberal Democrat	2,620	9.24	+0.57

Majority: 4,475 (15.79%)
Swing: 7.42% Labour to SNP

1997

Electorate: 52,186
Turnout 34,973 (67.02%)

Candidate	Party	Votes	Votes%	Change%
Lewis Moonie	Labour	18,730	53.56	+7.98
Stewart Hosie	SNP	8,020	22.93	+0.31
Charlotte Black	Conservative	4,779	13.66	-8.44
John Mainland	Liberal Democrat	3,031	8.67	-1.03
Victor Baxter	Referendum	413	1.18	—

Majority: 10,710 (30.63%)
Swing: 3.84% SNP to Labour

1945-92

	Lab%	Con%	SNP%	Lib%	Other%	Turnout%
1992	46.0	21.8	22.5	9.6	—	75.1
1987	49.6	21.3	11.7	17.4	—	76.5
1983	40.3	26.3	9.0	24.3	—	71.9
1979	53.9	26.2	19.9	—	—	77.4
1974O	45.4	16.5	32.0	6.1	—	75.0
1974F	47.0	27.3	25.7	—	—	79.3
1970	56.1	32.1	11.8	—	—	74.5

	Lab%	Con%	SNP%	Lib%	Other%	Turnout%
1966	59.6	27.0	13.4	–	–	75.4
1964	60.0	29.1	10.9	–	–	77.2
1959	58.3	32.5	–	9.2	–	80.5
1955	59.3	40.7	–	–	–	75.2
1951	60.6	39.4	–	–	–	84.6
1950	60.0	40.0	–	–	–	84.8
1945	45.0	29.5	17.0	–	8.5	76.2

This constituency contains the main town of Kirkcaldy, Adam Smith's birth-place, and the surrounding coastal towns of Buckhaven, Burntisland and Kinghorn. This is a traditional Labour seat, due to the coal-mining background of the constituency, though the Conservatives also gained a decent vote by today's standards up until 1992 due to the presence of middle-class areas in the seat. Indeed, 51.8 per cent of the housing was owner-occupied in the seat in 1991, a proportion that has probably increased since then. Labour has won this seat at every election since 1924, barring the exceptional and solitary Tory victory of 1931.

Though Labour's majority in recent years in Kirkcaldy has varied from 5,000 to 10,000, it has seldom faced a direct challenge from any of its competitors. Labour has tended to benefit from a split vote amongst a divided opposition, and, when challenged, has held on comfortably. For example, in its best general election performance in Kirkcaldy in October 1974, the SNP only got within 6,101 votes of Labour. This result was bested at the Scottish election of 1999, with Labour's majority narrowed to 4,475, but this change was largely due to a low turnout amongst Labour voters rather than a dramatic SNP surge.

Certainly, in recent years it is the SNP which has emerged to challenge Labour, even though it has had very limited success in the constituency over the years. It made slight but steady increases in its support from 1992 to 1999, to put it in firm second place to Labour. However, the gap is a substantial one and it is unlikely that SNP activists will ever be dancing in the streets of Raith following a UK or Scottish election. The party's candidate in the seat from 1992 to 1999, Stewart Hosie, was selected to fight Dundee East at the next Westminster elections and the SNP has selected a parliamentary researcher, Shirley-Anne Sommerville, to fight Kirkcaldy. Labour, meantime, can look at a relatively safe seat which it will retain if it avoids complacency at future elections.

The strength of Labour in the Kirkcaldy wards on Fife Council is such that it should look to the general election with confidence. Greater turnout, especially amongst core supporters, will ensure this seat remains Labour for some time, though the level of male claimant unemployment of 10.1 per cent, the ninth highest in Scotland, is not a statistic Labour will like. Aside from the Nationalists, the other parties are weak performers in the constituency. This has been the case historically with the Liberals, and has also become the case more recently with the Conservatives, who have seen their position in the constituency eroded over the years and then decimated in 1997 and 1999.

MP Lewis Moonie was born in 1947 in Dundee. First elected MP for Kirkcaldy in 1987, he was educated at Nicolson Institute, Stornoway and Grove Academy, Dundee, before studying medicine at St Andrews and Edinburgh Universities. He was briefly at university, a Conservative supporter and then joined the Communist Party in 1971. He trained as a GP and worked as a hospital doctor before becoming a clinical pharmacologist and medical adviser with a range of pharmaceutical companies in the UK and Europe. He then worked for Fife Health Board in the area of community medicine through the 1980s. He was a regional councillor in Fife from 1982 to 1986. At Westminster he was a member of the Social Services Committee from 1987-88 and the Treasury Select Committee from 1989-90. He became Opposition front-bench Spokesman on Technology from 1990-92, Science and Technology from 1992-94, Industry 1994-95 and was National Heritage Spokesman on Broadcasting from 1995 to 1997. As an old-fashioned Labour moderate, Moonie seemed to have missed his calling with the creation of New Labour and the transition from opposition to government saw him dropped from the front-bench. Instead, he became Chair of the influential Finance and Services Committee from 1997 onwards, a member of the House of Commons Commission from 1997 and of the Treasury Select Committee from 1998. However, on the resignation of Peter Kilfoyle in January 2000, protesting about the political direction and priorities of New Labour, Moonie made a surprising comeback, being promoted to the post of Under-Secretary for Defence.

MSP Marilyn Livingstone was born in 1953. She was a councillor in Fife and also Head of the Business School at Fife College in Glenrothes before her election in 1999. She was a member of the Equal Opportunities and Enterprise and Lifelong Learning Committees of the Parliament from May 1999 to December 2000, and then became a member of the Enterprise and Life-long Learning Committee. She is also a member of the Cross Party Groups on Children, Strategic Rail Services and Women. In addition, she is Convenor of the Labour group in the Scottish Parliament.

As Convenor of the Scottish Parliamentary Group of MSPs she is a crucial link between the Executive and backbench MSPs and has a vital role in communicating any disquiet MSPs feel about things. She had an important role in the Abolition of Warrant Sales Bill debate in April 2000 alerting ministers to backbench opinion and has quietly earned a reputation as someone who is a hard worker and can be trusted by all sides.

LINLITHGOW

Predecessor Constituencies: Linlithgowshire (1945) and West Lothian (1950–79).

1999

Electorate: 54,262
Turnout: 33,782 (62.26%)

Candidate	Party	Votes	Votes%	Change%
Mary Mulligan	Labour	15,247	45.13	-9.01
Stewart Stevenson	SNP	12,319	36.47	+9.66
Gordon Lindhurst	Conservative	3,158	9.35	-3.17
John Barrett	Liberal Democrat	2,643	7.82	+1.94
Irene Ovenstone	Independent	415	1.23	–

Labour majority: 2,928 (8.66%)
Swing: 9.33% Labour to SNP

1997

Electorate: 53,706
Turnout: 39,654 (73.84%)

Candidate	Party	Votes	Votes%	Change%
Tam Dalyell	Labour	21,469	54.14	+4.94
Kenneth MacAskill	SNP	10,631	26.81	-3.34
Thomas Kerr	Conservative	4,964	12.52	-1.19
Andrew Duncan	Liberal Democrat	2,331	5.88	-1.07
Kenneth Plomer	Referendum	259	0.65	–

Labour majority: 10,838 (27.33%)
Swing: 4.14% SNP to Labour

1945–92

	Lab%	Con%	SNP%	Lib%	Other%	Turnout%
1992	45.0	17.5	30.3	7.2	–	78.7
1987	47.3	14.8	24.9	12.6	0.3	77.5
1983	45.1	19.1	18.4	17.0	0.5	75.2
1979	54.9	19.7	24.8	–	0.6	78.1
1974O	45.3	10.0	40.9	3.4	0.4	78.8
1974F	45.3	19.0	35.0	–	0.7	80.6

	Lab%	Con%	SNP%	Lib%	Other%	Turnout%
1970	52.9	18.1	28.2	–	0.8	76.7
1966	52.4	11.2	35.3	–	1.1	79.6
1964	50.3	18.0	30.4	–	1.2	79.5
1962B	50.9	11.4	23.3	10.8	3.6	71.1
1959	60.3	39.7	–	–	–	77.9
1955	59.7	40.3	–	–	–	75.4
1951	60.5	39.5	–	–	–	84.9
1950	60.6	35.6	–	–	3.8	79.1
1945	64.1	35.9	–	–	–	73.2

Linlithgow is an Edinburgh commuter town with an old-fashioned, quaint High Street, a magnificent palace and loch. The rest of the seat carries with it the traditions and scars of ex-mining areas: Bathgate, Blackburn and Whitburn. Bathgate was the site of a well-known British Motor Corporation plant opened in 1961 to replace the employment of the mines, but it closed in the 1980s and was immortalised in the Proclaimers, *Letter from America* with the lament 'Bathgate no more, Linwood no more'.

West Lothian was first won by Labour's Manny Shinwell in 1922, who lost it in 1931, before George Mathers won it and held it from 1935 until 1951. John Taylor then represented the seat from 1951 to 1962. A 1962 by-election pitted Tam Dalyell against the SNP's William Wolfe for the first of seven contests; this was in many ways the start of the modern SNP as Wolfe polled 23.3 per cent. Slowly over the next six contests Wolfe chiselled away at Labour's majority, reducing it to 2,690 in October 1974; this was as near as he would get and in 1979 in the last Dalyell–Wolfe contest Labour's majority inflated to 20,082.

The seat was renamed Linlithgow in the 1983 redistribution and contests have never been as exciting since. Tam has gone on with majorities of 11,361 in 1983 and 10,373 in 1987; the latter saw a heavyweight contest between Dalyell and Jim Sillars, standing for the first time under the SNP's banner, but he made little impression on Labour's majority.

In 1992, Dalyell's majority fell to 7,026 over the SNP's Kenny MacAskill; in 1997 a rematch between the two saw Dalyell re-elected for the eleventh time with Labour's majority increasing to 10,838 as the SNP slipped again. In 1999, Labour's vote fell by 5,000 while the SNP vote rose by 1,700 to reach its highest vote since October 1974 and reduce Labour's majority to 2,928. Linlithgow has long been an SNP target seat, combining as it does Nationalist history (and folklore) with the local government base of a sizeable SNP group on West Lothian Council, and if the SNP ever break through in Central Scotland, Linlithgow will be high on their list.

MP Tam Dalyell was born in 1932 in Edinburgh and served as MP for West

Lothian from 1962 until 1983 (first winning the seat in a 1962 by-election); he has been MP for Linlithgow from 1983. Educated at Edinburgh Academy, Eton, King's College, Cambridge, and Moray House, Edinburgh, Dalyell was first employed as a teacher in Bo'ness Academy from 1957 to 1961 and as Deputy Director of Studies on the ship-school *Dunera* from 1961 to 1962.

On entering Parliament, Dalyell became a member of the Public Accounts Committee from 1962 to 1966, Parliamentary Private Secretary to R. H. S. Crossman from 1964 to 1970, Vice-Chair of the PLP from 1974 to 1976 and Opposition Spokesman on Science from 1980 to 1982 – Dalyell's only frontbench experience in nearly forty years in the House. He was also for one year from 1985 to 1986 a member of Labour's NEC, elected on the hard left Campaign Group ticket, an unholy alliance that ended in tears. Dalyell's background of Eton and Cambridge and being the tenth baronet of the Binns has given him the confidence to plough a lonely, obsessional course – one of his ancestors is the only person ever to escape from the Tower of London. In the 1974 to 1979 Parliament he doggedly pursued his own government over its devolution plans, giving birth to 'the West Lothian Question' named after his constituency, which was so titled by Enoch Powell. Post-1979, he was a constant thorn in Mrs Thatcher's flesh: over the sinking of the Argentinian cruiser *Belgrano*, the Westland helicopter crisis which saw Heseltine and Leon Brittan resign from Thatcher's Cabinet, and the bombing of Pan Am flight 103 over Lockerbie.

The return of a Labour Government in 1997 seemed to emphasise his other-worldliness and blunt his effectiveness. His criticisms of Labour's proposals on Scottish devolution ('a motorway without exit') lacked the force of two decades previous. His willingness to ally himself with the Conservative front of an anti-devolution campaign angered many in the party, even his own tolerant constituency, and there was talk of trying to deselect him if he could not be persuaded to retire. This came to nothing and Dalyell is standing again. He has in his twilight years been the subject of a recent biography by the historian Russell Galbraith.

MSP Mary Mulligan was born in 1960 in Liverpool and educated at Notre Dame High School, Liverpool, and Manchester University where she gained a BA Hons in Economic and Social Studies. She worked as an Assistant Staff Manager in British Home Stores from 1981 to 1982 and as an Assistant Manager in the Edinburgh Woollen Mill from 1982 until 1986.

Mulligan was elected to Edinburgh District Council from 1986 until 1996 and Edinburgh City Council from 1995 to 1999 and was Chair of the Housing Committee from 1992 until 1997. She was also Vice-Chair of the Women's Committee and a member of the Recreation Committee from 1998 to 1999. In the Scottish Parliament, Mulligan was Convenor of the Education, Culture and Sport Committee and a member of the Cross Party Groups on Children, Epilepsy, Sports and Women. In Henry McLeish's first ministerial reshuffle in October 2000, Mulligan became Parliamentary Private Secretary to the First Minister.

LIVINGSTON

Predecessor Constituencies: created anew from Midlothian and West Lothian in 1983.

1999

Electorate: 62,060
Turnout: 36,570 (58.93%)

Candidate	Party	Votes	Votes%	Change%
Bristow Muldoon	Labour	17,313	47.34	−7.55
Greg McCarra	SNP	13,409	36.67	+9.21
Douglas Younger	Conservative	3,014	8.24	−1.16
Martin Oliver	Liberal Democrat	2,834	7.75	−1.04

Labour majority: 3,904 (10.67%)
Swing: 8.38% Labour to SNP

1997

Electorate: 60,296
Turnout: 42,834 (71.04%)

Candidate	Party	Votes	Votes%	Change%
Robin Cook	Labour	23,510	54.89	+9.04
Peter Johnston	SNP	11,763	27.46	+1.51
Hugh Craigie Halkett	Conservative	4,028	9.40	−8.72
Ewan Hawthorn	Liberal Democrat	2,876	6.71	−2.38
Helen Campbell	Referendum	444	1.04	—
Matthew Culbert	SPGB	213	0.50	—

Labour majority: 11,747 (27.43%)
Swing: 3.77% SNP to Labour

1983–92

	Lab%	Con%	SNP%	Lib%	Other%	Turnout%
1992	44.4	19.4	26.6	8.6	1.0	74.6
1987	45.6	18.7	16.6	19.1	—	74.1
1983	37.3	23.9	13.3	25.4	—	71.6

Livingston is one of Scotland's post-war New Towns which housed Scotland's over-spill from its urban centres in a grand plan of socialist and idealist social engineering.

Livingston was a magnet for families from across the Central Belt, Glasgow and Edinburgh. Around it are the ex-mining villages such as Broxburn and Uphall and communities such as Calder, all with long Labour traditions and memories. Livingston is one of the newest seats in Scotland, only appearing on the electoral map in 1983.

Its creation in 1983 saw Robin Cook, MP for Edinburgh Central, undertake a 'chicken run' – shifting from a marginal seat to the comparative safety of Livingston, as his current seat had been made marginal by boundary changes. Cook's calculations were proved correct as Labour lost Edinburgh Central, while Cook won Livingston with 37.3 per cent, 4,551 ahead of the Liberal–SDP Alliance with 25.4 per cent of the vote and the Conservatives, 23.9 per cent. In 1987, Cook increased this to 11,105, falling back to 8,105 in 1992.

In 1997, Labour's vote rose to 54.9 per cent and its majority to 11,747; in the 1999 elections, Bristow Muldoon presided over Labour's vote falling by 6,000, while the SNP picked up just under 2,000 votes, reducing Labour's majority to 3,904. Livingston, being a new seat, does not have the Labour–SNP history of Linlithgow, but it is very similar, politically and socio-economically. If the SNP achieve the critical mass to challenge Labour seriously in the Central Belt, seats like Livingston are where something has to happen.

MP Robin Cook was born in 1946 in Bellshill and elected MP for Edinburgh Central from 1974 until 1983 and for Livingston since 1983. Educated at Aberdeen Grammar School, Royal High School, Edinburgh, and Edinburgh University with an MA Hons in English Literature and an uncompleted PhD on Charles Dickens, he was briefly a teacher in Bo'ness Academy from 1969 to 1970 and a Tutor-Organiser for the Workers' Educational Association from 1970 to 1974. He was elected to Edinburgh City Council from 1971 to 1974. Cook first contested Edinburgh North in 1970 and won Edinburgh Central by 961 votes on his 28th birthday in February 1974.

Cook is a devolution sceptic, turned champion, having voted against Labour's devolution plans during the 1974 to 1979 government and campaigned energetically for a 'No' vote in the 1979 referendum. He was Treasury and Economic Affairs Spokesman from 1980 to 1983 and then after Labour's defeat in 1983 was Neil Kinnock's campaign manager for the party leadership; he was subsequently elected to the Shadow Cabinet holding frontbench posts from 1983 until 1997, and in 1993 and 1994 finished top of the PLP ballot. He was then European Community Affairs Spokesman from 1983 to 1985, Trade and Industry from 1986 to 1987, Health and Social Security from 1987 to 1989 and Health from 1989 to 1992. In 1992, after Labour's fourth defeat, Cook took the role of John Smith's campaign manager in his bid for the leadership and became Trade and Industry Spokesman from 1992 until 1994 and Shadow Foreign Secretary from 1994 until 1997.

Over Labour's long years in opposition, Cook gained a reputation as a combative debater in the House who was both feared and respected by the Tories. His demolition of Conservative ministers over the 'arms to Iraq' affair and the subsequent Scott Report was a particular high. However, as Foreign Secretary, he is increasingly marginalised from key domestic decisions, and New Labour's rationale has never been one he has found appealing. He has an uneasy relationship with his biggest potential ally, Gordon Brown, the tensions between them mirroring those between Brown and Blair; Cook is the senior of the two, and was eventually outshone by Brown, upon his later arrival in the House in 1987.

The public end to his 29-year marriage with Margaret Cook, after revelations of an affair with his secretary, tarnished his reputation, although her vindictive public attacks on him probably gained him as much sympathy as it did damage. Cook's isolation in the Labour Government made some suggest in the Scottish Parliament's first year and a half that he could have been a likely successor to Donald Dewar as First Minister. Such speculation ended with the death of Donald Dewar and the election of Henry McLeish as First Minister. Westminster now remains the sole focus for Robin Cook's ambitions, both real and fantasy. Cook has been the subject of a biography by the BBC journalist John Kampfner.

MSP Bristow Muldoon was born in 1964 and educated at Cumbernauld High School, Strathclyde University and the Open University. Muldoon worked in a range of InterCity railway posts, starting as a Management Trainee and rising to be a Group Manager, Catering Manager and Team Manager on the West and East Coast lines from 1986 until 1996. He then became a Train Services Manager with Great North Eastern Railways in 1997 and a Business Analyst from 1998 to 1999.

He was elected to Lothian Regional Council from 1994 to 1996 and became Vice-Chair of the Economic Development Committee from 1994 to 1996 and a councillor on West Lothian Council from 1995 to 1999. He was Convenor of Community Services there from 1995 to 1999. Muldoon is a member of the Subordinate Legislation Committee of the Scottish Parliament and was a member of the Local Government Committee from May 1999 to December 2000, and joined the Transport and Environment Committee in January 2001. He is also a member of the Cross Party Groups on Epilepsy, Strategic Rail Services (which he is Secretary of) and Tobacco Control.

MIDLOTHIAN

Predecessor Constituencies: Midlothian and Peeblesshire Northern (1945), Midlothian and Peeblesshire Southern (1945) and Midlothian and Peebles (1950–1).

1999

Electorate: 48,374
Turnout: 29,755 (61.51%)

Candidate	Party	Votes	Votes%	Change%
Rhona Brankin	Labour	14,467	48.62	-4.89
Angus Robertson	SNP	8,942	30.05	+4.54
John Elder	Liberal Democrat	3,184	10.70	+1.52
George Turnbull	Conservative	2,544	8.55	-2.35
Douglas Pryde	Independent	618	2.08	—

Labour majority: 5,525 (18.57%)
Swing: 4.71% Labour to SNP

1997

Electorate: 47,552
Turnout: 35,249 (74.13%)

Candidate	Party	Votes	Votes%	Change%
Eric Clarke	Labour	18,861	53.51	+5.35
Laurence Millar	SNP	8,991	25.51	+2.28
Anne Harper	Conservative	3,842	10.90	-6.66
Richard Pinnock	Liberal Democrat	3,235	9.18	-0.81
Keith Docking	Referendum	320	0.91	—

Labour majority: 9,870 (28.00%)
Swing: 1.54% SNP to Labour

1955–92

	Lab%	Con%	SNP%	Lib%	Other%	Turnout%
1992	43.9	20.1	21.9	13.1	1.0	77.9
1987	48.3	18.2	10.6	22.0	0.9	77.2
1983	42.7	21.9	6.2	29.2	—	75.0
1979	47.8	26.4	16.8	9.0	—	77.8
1974O	41.5	16.0	35.6	6.9	—	77.4

	Lab%	Con%	SNP%	Lib%	Other%	Turnout%
1974F	44.6	28.4	27.0	–	–	81.6
1970	52.9	31.5	15.6	–	–	75.6
1966	56.7	27.0	16.3	–	–	77.5
1964	61.3	38.7	–	–	–	78.9
1959	60.2	39.8	–	–	–	81.3
1955	60.2	39.8	–	–	–	78.1

Midlothian and Peeblesshire, Southern (1945), Midlothian and Peebles (1950–1)

	Lab%	Con%	SNP%	Lib%	Other%	Turnout%
1951	55.3	44.7	–	–	–	83.8
1950	52.8	38.7	–	8.5	–	82.9
1945	55.8	32.4	–	11.8	–	73.5

Midlothian and Peeblesshire, Northern (1945)

	Lab%	Con%	SNP%	Lib%	Other%	Turnout%
1945	45.7	47.9	–	–	6.4	70.1

Midlothian is situated south of Edinburgh and contains a host of small, traditional working-class towns and villages such as Bonnyrigg, Dalkeith, Loanhead and Newtongrange. Prior to the 1983 boundary redistribution, Midlothian had grown to 101,000 voters, unheard of by the normal size of Scottish constituencies and making it one of the largest seats in the UK, let alone Scotland. It was reduced in size by the creation of a new seat of Livingston.

In 1945 when there were two Midlothian and Peebles seats, one was Conservative and one Labour. The Northern Division was held by Lt-Col Lord John Hope with a 1,177 lead, Southern by David Pryde by 6,496. The combined seat returned Labour's Pryde in 1950 with a majority of 7,188 and he held the seat until 1959. James Hill followed from 1959 to 1966 and subsequently Alex Eadie from 1966 to 1992. Labour were never really under threat in any of these years, the nearest thing being October 1974 when Eadie's majority was cut to 4,048 over the SNP.

In 1992, Eric Clarke secured victory with 43.9 per cent, while the SNP moved dramatically into second place adding 5,000 votes to their support and reducing Labour's majority to 10,334. In 1997, Clarke increased Labour's vote by just over 1,000, while the SNP slightly moved their vote up. In 1999, Rhona Brankin standing for Labour saw her vote fall by over 4,000, while the SNP's remained static on a reduced turnout, leaving Labour with a 5,525 majority. Labour still look safe for the foreseeable future in this seat, but the SNP have come on by leaps and bounds in recent years; in 1983 they polled a pathetic 6.2 per cent in the seat, whereas in 1999 they achieved 30 per cent. Whether they can go that extra distance which has proven so problematic in Labour's Central heartlands is another question.

MP Eric Clarke was born in 1933 in Edinburgh and has been MP for Midlothian since 1992. He was educated at St Cuthbert's School, Edinburgh, Holy Cross Academy, Leith, W. M. Ramsey Technical College, Edinburgh, and Esk Valley Technical College, Dalkeith. At the age of 16 years, Clarke became a coalminer and worked in the pits from 1949 to 1977, while also becoming a Midlothian County Councillor from 1962 to 1974 and a Lothian Regional Councillor from 1974 to 1978.

Clarke became General Secretary of the National Union of Mineworkers Scottish Area in 1977 and held the post for twelve years. An open, engaging, self-proclaimed 'democratic Marxist' in the best traditions of the NUM, he was privately critical of Arthur Scargill's vanguardist posturing which led the 1984 to 1985 strike to be such a disaster for the industry and the union. A member of Labour's NEC from 1983 until 1988, he was dropped as the NUM's nominee on Scargill's instructions and in 1989 he was made redundant as General Secretary of the NUM Scotland. Clarke won Midlothian in 1992 and has established a reputation as a combative defender of the coal industry. He is retiring at the next election.

MSP Rhona Brankin was born in 1950 and educated at Jordanhill College School, Glasgow, Aberdeen University, Northern College, Dundee, and Moray House, Edinburgh. She has worked in a variety of teaching and learning support posts, in Dingwall Primary from 1975 to 1977, Invergordon Academy from 1983 to 1984, South Lodge Primary, Invergordon, from 1984 to 1988, Alness Academy from 1988 to 1990 and Inverness High School from 1990 until 1994. She then became a lecturer in special educational needs at Northern College, Dundee, from 1994 until 1999.

Brankin was Chair of the Scottish Labour Party from 1995 to 1996 and has been associated with the Blairite Scottish Labour Forum, which organised a purge of leftish opponents of the leadership in the run-up to the 1997 election, and she has also been a member of the Scottish Constitutional Convention. In the 1999 elections, she was campaign spokesperson on Health, Sports and Arts, and after the elections was given the post of Deputy Minister for Culture and Sport as Deputy to the Minister for Children and Education, which she held until October 2000. In Henry McLeish's first ministerial reshuffle in October 2000, Brankin became Deputy Minister for Rural Development, working as deputy to Ross Finnie.

MORAY

Predecessor Constituencies: Moray and Nairn (1945–79) and Banff (1945–79).

1999

Electorate: 58,388
Turnout: 33,576 (57.85%)

Candidate	Party	Votes	Votes%	Change%
Margaret Ewing	SNP	13,027	38.80	-2.77
Ali Farquharson	Labour	8,898	26.50	+6.67
Andrew Findlay	Conservative	8,595	25.60	-1.97
Patsy Kenton	Liberal Democrat	3,056	9.10	+0.18

SNP majority: 4,129 (12.30%)
Swing: 4.72% SNP to Labour.

1997

Electorate: 58,302
Turnout: 39,766 (68.21%)

Candidate	Party	Votes	Votes%	Change%
Margaret Ewing	SNP	16,529	41.57	-3.05
Andrew Findlay	Conservative	10,963	27.57	-9.97
Lewis Macdonald	Labour	7,886	19.83	+7.95
Debra Storr	Liberal Democrat	3,548	8.92	+2.95
Paddy Mieklejohn	Referendum	840	2.11	—

SNP majority: 5,566 (14.00%)
Swing: 3.46% Conservative to SNP

1983–92

	Lab%	Con%	SNP%	Lib%	Other%	Turnout%
1992	11.9	38.1	44.3	5.7	—	72.5
1987	11.3	35.0	43.2	10.5	—	72.7
1983	7.3	39.2	35.2	18.3	—	71.1

Moray and Nairn (1945–79)

	Lab%	Con%	SNP%	Lib%	Other%	Turnout%
1979	8.7	40.1	38.9	12.3	–	77.5
1974O	9.7	40.0	41.2	9.1	–	74.7
1974F	7.0	43.7	49.3	–	–	79.8
1970	22.8	49.4	27.8	–	–	72.2
1966	34.1	48.1	–	17.8	–	68.0
1964	27.3	50.8	–	21.9	–	69.4
1959	25.0	52.7	–	22.3	–	73.6
1955	39.4	60.6	–	–	–	67.9
1951	39.8	60.2	–	–	–	74.5
1950	40.1	59.9	–	–	–	75.0
1945	38.4	61.6	–	–	–	61.8

Banff (1945–79)

	Lab%	Con%	SNP%	Lib%	Other%	Turnout%
1979	14.2	44.6	41.2	–	–	72.5
1974O	7.3	37.9	45.9	8.9	–	72.5
1974F	6.4	34.5	46.1	13.0	–	75.7
1970	17.4	38.7	22.9	21.0	–	68.9
1966	24.3	41.3	–	34.4	–	65.1
1964	26.6	47.8	–	25.6	–	67.8
1959	29.4	70.6	–	–	–	63.3
1955	30.2	69.8	–	–	–	54.7
1951	29.1	70.9	–	–	–	65.6
1950	26.3	58.1	–	15.6	–	74.1
1945	20.9	49.5	–	29.6	–	66.5

The seat contains the towns of Buckie, Burghead, Elgin, Forres, Lossiemouth and Lhanbryde as well as a large part of Speyside and a considerable number of whisky distilleries. Moray was a traditional Tory seat from 1923 until the emergence of the SNP in the 1970s. The current seat is comprised of parts of the old Moray and Nairn and Banff constituencies, which were both won by the SNP in February and October 1974. The Nationalists did not have particularly deep roots in the constituencies, indeed they only contested them for the first time in 1970. However, since then the SNP has been the main challenger to the Tories and has taken and held the Moray seat from 1987 to the present day. Through all of these elections both the Conservative and SNP votes have remained relatively constant in terms of both numbers and percentages, though Conservative support declined markedly to disturb this pattern in 1997 and 1999.

The seat is strongly SNP, but cannot be seen as safely SNP. For example, the Tory wipeout in 1997 produced large majorities for the Nationalists in Angus and Banff and Buchan, but a relatively disappointing majority in Moray. The party has also never again touched the 49 per cent gained by former MP Winnie Ewing in Moray and Nairn back in February 1974. Therefore this seat is not so safe as it might appear. However, if the SNP is to lose, the question is which party will it lose to? Conservative support and organisation in the seat have declined in the last decade to place the Tories third at the Scottish election of 1999. Labour, meantime, has grown in popularity but could not realistically expect to overturn the SNP.

There are worrying signs for the Nationalists in Moray. At the Scottish election in 1999 the SNP vote actually fell compared to the 1997 general election and it was Labour which gained support to take second place from the Tories. Labour support has edged upwards in recent elections in a manner similar to the Perth seat assessed below. Essentially, Labour has gained and maintained a level of representation on the local authority in the main town of Elgin to give it electoral credibility in the constituency. As the seat has been consistently won by the Nationalists and the Tories have declined, it has been less easy for the SNP to use the anti-Tory card to rally Labour voters to oust the Conservatives. Labour won 6 council seats at the 1999 election, both in Elgin and in Buckie, and the SNP's council representation collapsed. The SNP had controlled the council for the first time from 1995 until 1999, but lost most of its seats to end up with only 2 councillors: a huge embarrassment given that it won the Scottish Parliament seat on the same day. However, it was not the Conservatives who gained from the council election results but a strong group of independents. The independents won 15 council seats to take control of the council, with the Tories only winning one councillor.

The Moray seat is, of course, home to part of the Ewing dynasty within the SNP. It was won by Winnie Ewing in February 1974, by removing the Conservative Secretary of State for Scotland, Gordon Campbell. It was then regained in 1987 by Margaret Ewing, Winnie's daughter-in-law. Margaret Ewing was previously MP for East Dunbartonshire from 1974 to 1979 and married Winnie's eldest son, Fergus, who is now the MSP for Inverness East, Nairn and Lochaber. Margaret Ewing is also the MSP for Moray, following the 1999 election, and will not contest the seat at Westminster. The SNP candidate to replace her is Angus Robertson, a graduate of Aberdeen University, a fluent German-speaker who was previously a journalist with Austrian radio and currently works for the SNP in the Scottish Parliament.

MP/MSP Margaret Ewing was born in Lanark in 1945, was educated at Biggar High School and has degrees from Glasgow and Strathclyde Universities and a teaching diploma from Jordanhill. Before becoming an MP, she was a special needs teacher and also worked as a freelance journalist. She had two spells at Westminster, first, as MP for East Dunbartonshire from 1974 to 1979, part of which became

Strathkelvin and Bearsden, which she contested unsuccessfully in 1983, and then as MP for Moray from 1987 onwards.

At Westminster she was a member of the Select Committee on European Legislation from 1992 to 1998 and was a member of the European Scrutiny Committee. She has held a number of positions within the SNP, including deputy leader from 1983 to 1987, and SNP Parliamentary Group Convenor – in Westminster from 1987 to 1999 and currently in the Scottish Parliament from 1999. She joined the Rural Development Committee in January 2001 and is a member of the Cross Party Groups for Oil and Gas, Palliative Care, Men's Violence Against Women and Strategic Rail Services and is Joint Convenor of the group on Epilepsy.

Ewing, as Margaret Bain, was one of the leading left-wing firebrands of the SNP in the 1970s, but has considerably mellowed with age. She opposed the left-wing '79 Group after the 1979 election accusing them of 'rent a mob' tactics in terms of promoting civil disobedience. After her election as MP for Moray in 1987, she has proved to be a hard-working constituency MP and latterly MSP, supporting local campaigns to retain RAF Lossiemouth and Kinloss, which are in her seat.

She stood against Alex Salmond for the National Convenorship of the SNP in 1990, and despite being the initial favourite, was comprehensively defeated by the margin of 486 to 186 votes. As Parliamentary Leader of the SNP at Westminster, she negotiated a deal with the Conservatives over the European Committee of the Regions in 1993 to gain Scotland extra places which saw the SNP vote with the Tories over Maastricht, which was widely seen as a misjudgment. Her profile and influence in the party has never really recovered since she lost the party leadership to Salmond and despite her undoubted abilities she is not fully utilised by the party leadership.

MOTHERWELL AND WISHAW

Predecessor Constituencies: Motherwell (1945–70), Motherwell and Wishaw (1974–9) and Motherwell South (1983–92).

1999

Electorate: 52,613
Turnout: 30,364 (57.71%)

Candidate	Party	Votes	Votes%	Change%
Jack McConnell	Labour	13,955	45.96	-11.44
James McGugan	SNP	8,879	29.24	+6.77
William Gibson	Conservative	3,694	12.17	+1.18
John Milligan Socialist	Labour	1,941	6.39	+4.21
Roger Spillane	Liberal Democrat	1,895	6.24	-0.13

Labour majority: 5,076 (16.72%)
Swing: 9.10% Labour to SNP

1997

Electorate: 52,252
Turnout: 36,619 (70.08%)

Candidate	Party	Votes	Votes%	Change%
Frank Roy	Labour	21,020	57.40	+0.86
James McGugan	SNP	8,229	22.47	+1.04
Scott Dickson	Conservative	4,024	10.99	-4.62
Alex Mackie	Liberal Democrat	2,331	6.37	+0.31
Christopher Herriot	Socialist Labour	797	2.18	–
Thomas Russell	Referendum	218	0.60	–

Labour majority: 12,791 (34.93%)
Swing: 0.09% Labour to SNP

1945–92

	Lab%	Con%	SNP%	Lib%	Other%	Turnout%
1992	57.1	16.0	20.4	6.2	0.4	76.2
1987	58.3	14.5	15.3	11.3	0.6	75.5
1983	52.4	20.0	9.8	17.8	–	72.9
1979	56.9	28.9	12.3	–	1.9	77.8

	Lab%	Con%	SNP%	Lib%	Other%	Turnout%
1974O	44.6	18.2	31.9	2.9	2.4	75.4
1974F	46.7	30.6	20.0	–	2.7	77.0
1970	53.2	32.2	9.9	–	4.7	73.7
1966	60.8	35.2	–	–	4.0	74.7
1964	58.8	37.3	–	–	3.9	78.9
1959	53.7	43.0	–	–	3.3	81.1
1955	53.9	46.1	–	–	–	76.5
1954B	56.4	39.3	–	–	4.3	70.5
1951	57.3	42.7	–	–	–	84.7
1950	54.3	34.0	9.3	–	2.4	84.5
1945	52.7	20.6	26.7	–	–	72.8
1945B	48.6	–	51.4	–	–	54.0

Motherwell and Wishaw, not surprisingly, contains the towns of Motherwell and Wishaw. It was the successor constituency to Motherwell South. Politically, Motherwell was first won by Labour in 1924. It was very briefly held by the Communist MP J. Walton Newbold from 1922 to 1923, not a tradition Jack McConnell, the sitting MSP, will be trying to revive. Labour lost the seat in 1931 and regained it in 1935, only to sensationally lose it in an April 1945 by-election, at which the SNP leader Robert McIntyre triumphed. It was a wartime by-election and the opponents to the sitting party did not contest such seats. However, the SNP did, forced an election and carried the seat over Labour with a stunning victory winning by a majority of 617. Unfortunately for the SNP, the contest took place just three months before the general election of 1945, which produced a Labour landslide and returned the Motherwell seat to Labour.

That was the first and last SNP victory in this seat, albeit an historic one as it was the SNP's first ever seat. The only other time the Nationalists presented a realistic challenge was in October 1974 and even then, Labour gained 44.6 per cent of the vote and a comfortable majority. The SNP's 31.9 per cent still left them 4,962 votes behind Labour. Indeed, Labour support in the constituency has been consistently high in the post-war period. Its lowest level of support was in October 1974, and it gained well over 50 per cent at successive general elections until the Scottish election of 1999.

The constituency is safely Labour and has a strong working-class tradition allied to the former status of Motherwell as a steel town. It was the home of Ravenscraig steel works until its demise a few years ago and the sitting MP for the area, Frank Roy, is a former steelworker from the Ravenscraig plant. Following the lengthy demise of steel in the constituency, the area has experienced high unemployment and has the thirteenth highest male unemployment with a total of 8.6 per cent male unemployment on the claiment count in June 2000, despite the efforts of the Lanarkshire Development Agency. The seat also had 62.5 per cent of its housing under local authority control in 1991: joint highest in Scotland with Airdrie and Shotts. Electorally, given the recent string of results in the constituency, it is difficult to imagine anything but a thumping victory for Labour at the general election. Due to the fall in turnout amongst Labour voters, the 1999 result somewhat flatters the SNP, which only marginally increased its level of votes compared to 1997.

MP Frank Roy was born in 1958 in Motherwell, was educated at St Joseph's High School, Motherwell and was a steelworker at Ravenscraig from 1977 to 1991 before gaining an HNC in Marketing from Motherwell College and a BA in Consumer and Management Studies from Glasgow Caledonian University. He worked as personal assistant to Helen Liddell in Monklands East from 1994 to 1997 and was Parliamentary Private Secretary to Mrs Liddell at the Scottish Office in 1998 to 1999 and then to John Reid at the Scotland Office from 1999 to 2001. Roy then briefly became Helen Liddell's Parliamentary Private Secretary. He recently came to prominence over the betting scandal surrounding the election of the Speaker, Michael Martin. Roy resigned from his post with Liddell in February 2001, when he advised the Irish Prime Minister, Bertie Ahern, not to visit Carfin Grotto due to the possibility of sectarian troubles. Roy came out of this a damaged and diminished figure but it did not do Liddell or Reid any good either, as well as harming the reputation of Scotland as a modern, tolerant country.

MSP Jack McConnell was born in Irvine in 1960 and grew up and was educated on the Isle of Arran in the Firth of Clyde. He is a graduate of Stirling University where he gained a BSc in Mathematics and a Diploma in Education. He was President of the Students' Association from 1980 to 1982, becoming Vice-President of NUS (Scotland) from 1982 to 1983. He worked as a maths teacher at Lornshill Academy in Alloa from 1983 to 1992 and was elected as a councillor in Stirling District from 1984 to 1993 where he was Chair of the Leisure and Recreation Committee from 1986 to 1987 and the Equal Opportunities Committee from 1986 1990. McConnell served as Council Treasurer from 1988 to 1992 and leader from 1990 to 1992 and also stood in Perth and Kinross in the 1987 election winning 15.9 per cent of the vote and finishing fourth.

As a Stirling councillor and leader of the council he was at the forefront of developing innovative policies on delivering services. McConnell was throughout the 1980s a leading figure in the Labour Co-ordinating Committee (Scotland), the then Bennite group formed to develop a radical policy prospectus in the party. After Labour's election defeat in 1987, he was a founder member of Scottish Labour Action, the pro-home rule nationalist pressure group, where he was instrumental in pushing for greater autonomy for the Scottish party and developing the 'dual mandate' thesis, which argued that Scottish Labour would use a Scottish election victory as a mandate for unilateral action while also fighting to win at a UK level.

He was appointed General Secretary of the Scottish Labour Party after the election defeat of 1992, a move which was seen as dampening down demands for a more autonomous and pro-devolution approach. As General Secretary he had to deal with a host of internal managerial and resource issues and post-1997, address a number of disciplinary problems associated with Labour scandals in the West of Scotland. He worked briefly with the public relations company Beattie Media in the period between his resignation as General Secretary in 1998 and election as an MSP. This caused him trouble and embarrassment when the 'Lobbygate' scandal blew up over access to Scottish Executive ministers in 1999. McConnell was fully cleared of any impropriety by the resulting enquiry, but his reputation was left damaged. He also attempted to serialise his memoirs of his period as General Secretary in *Scotland on Sunday*, a move widely seen as misjudged and which resulted in McConnell having to pull them from the paper after one week. At the same time, he faced a serious challenge to win the Motherwell and Wishaw Labour nomination from Bill Tynan, who later became the MP for Hamilton South. McConnell won the ballot in November 1998 by two votes – 270 to 268 – with five spoilt ballot papers and 20 out of 180 postal ballots (mostly thought to be for Tynan) ruled out.

During the election, McConnell was campaign spokesperson on the Environment, which was seen as a marginal post, but post-election, he became Minister for Finance, responsible for finance and budgets, negotiations with the Treasury, as well as Europe and modernisation of government. This gave McConnell a considerable platform for developing influence across departments and with ministers. He was also seen as part of 'the Big Macs' who urged caution and compromise on Section 28/Clause 2A, along with Tom McCabe and Henry McLeish, and he faced strong local pressure from his CLP critical of the Executive's position.

Dewar's sudden death in October 2000 forced the barely concealed succession battle out into the open. The party leadership would have preferred to have had no contest, instead anointing Henry McLeish, but McConnell resisted the pressure and stood for the leadership. Without the backing of a single ministerial colleague, McConnell fought a carefully focused campaign touching on a number of key themes: worries about interference from the UK party and backbench anger about lack of consultation by the Executive. This nearly paid its reward, as McConnell clearly won a majority of backbench MSPs and lost by the narrow margin of 44:36 to McLeish. McLeish's resulting reshuffle saw McConnell gain the post of Minister for Education, Europe and External Relations with responsibility for pre-school and school education, children and young people, as well as supporting the First Minister and Deputy Minister in external relations, particularly links with Europe.

McConnell's first problem as Minister for Education was to sort out the mess of the Scottish Qualifications Authority inherited from Sam Galbraith and he acted with typical decisiveness within days, sacking the Chief Executive and the entire board, evidence of a more dynamic approach. McConnell's prospects have been undoubtably enhanced by his standing for the Labour leadership, the campaign he fought and the widespread support he gained. He has now stolen a march on his colleagues Wendy Alexander and Susan Deacon, and is the unquestioned leader of Labour's modernisers, a position which will give him a new-found influence at the heart of the administration.

OCHIL

Predecessor Constituencies: Clackmannan (1983–92) and Clackmannan and East Stirlingshire (1945–79).

1999

Electorate: 57,083
Turnout: 36,867 (64.58%)

Candidate	Party	Votes	Votes%	Change%
Richard Simpson	Labour	15,385	41.73	-3.28
George Reid	SNP	14,082	38.20	+3.82
Nick Johnston	Conservative	4,151	11.26	-3.32
Jamie Mar and Kellie	Liberal Democrat	3,249	8.81	+3.64

Labour majority: 1,303 (3.53%)
Swing: 3.55% Labour to SNP

1997

Electorate: 56,572
Turnout: 43,786 (77.4%)

Candidate	Party	Votes	Votes%	Change%
Martin O'Neill	Labour	19,707	45.01	+1.95
George Reid	SNP	15,055	34.38	+8.32
Allan Hogarth	Conservative	6,383	14.58	-9.39
Ann Watters	Liberal Democrat	2,262	5.17	-1.73
Derek White	Referendum	210	0.48	—
Ian McDonald	D Nationalist	104	0.24	—
Mike Sullivan	NLP	65	0.15	—

Labour majority: 4,652 (10.63%)
Swing: 3.19% Labour to SNP

1945–92

	Lab%	Con%	SNP%	Lib%	Other%	Turnout%
1992	49.1	17.3	26.9	6.7	—	78.3
1987	53.7	14.9	20.9	10.5	—	76.7
1983	45.8	18.0	19.0	17.2	—	75.6
1979	41.9	18.0	40.1	—	—	81.7

	Lab%	Con%	SNP%	Lib%	Other%	Turnout%
1974O	36.4	10.4	50.7	2.5	–	81.8
1974F	36.4	19.5	43.5	–	0.6	82.6
1970	50.7	28.2	15.5	5.6	–	75.7
1966	55.3	24.6	20.1	–	–	77.5
1964	57.2	30.6	12.2	–	–	79.8
1959	59.3	40.7	–	–	–	80.7
1955	58.7	41.3	–	–	–	79.8
1951	58.7	41.3	–	–	–	85.7
1950	56.5	33.5	–	10.0	–	83.4
1945	62.9	37.1	–	–	–	71.7

Ochil is a relatively small constituency in geographical terms. Much of it revolves around the area covered by Clackmannanshire Council, with the Hillfoots towns of Menstrie, Alva, Tillicoultry and Dollar running along the Ochil Hills, as well as Alloa, Clackmannan and Tullibody. However, the seat also runs west through the University of Stirling to affluent Bridge of Allan (both upper and lower), meaning a considerable student and middle-class electorate. To the east it runs to Kinross and to the south across the River Forth to take in small towns such as Cowie, Fallin and Plean in East Stirlingshire: this latter fact has great electoral significance as will be explained below. Economically, the Clackmannanshire part of the constituency has suffered serious job losses in recent years, with the further decline of the textile industry, which has made unemployment, economic development and the area's poor transport links key political issues. Scottish Executive intervention in the area's economy, with special support packages and promises to fund improved transport links, will have bolstered Labour's vote in the seat.

Politically, this seat has been an SNP-Labour battleground for three decades, one in which Labour has more frequently emerged triumphant. Though this seat was safely Labour for most of the twentieth century, the Tories actually triumphed when the seat was known as West Stirlingshire in 1918, 1924 and 1931. Labour's Tom Johnston represented the seat from 1922 to 1924, 1929 to 1931 and 1935 to 1945 and became Secretary of State for Scotland in Churchill's wartime coalition from 1941 to 1945. In the 1970s, Clackmannan and East Stirlingshire became a marginal through the SNP's successes in 1974, when George Reid triumphed first, winning the seat in February, then winning it again in October with as much as 25,998 votes and a 7,341 majority over Labour's Dick Douglas (MP from 1970 until February 1974 for the seat and soon to successfully contest Dunfermline West in 1979) at the October election. However, SNP support retreated in the 1980s as the seat became safely Labour. The Nationalists then made a comeback in the 1990s to make Ochil a marginal again.

At the last two elections, the SNP's candidate was George Reid, who had originally won the seat in 1974: doing so with 50.7 per cent of the vote in the October election. However, Labour held on well in 1997 with a 4,652 majority; they won too in 1999, though only marginally by 1,303 votes. What will give the SNP hope at the next Westminster election is the party's performance in council elections in the constituency. The SNP won control of Clackmannanshire Council in 1999, breaking out of its strongholds in the Hillfoots towns to win a number of wards from Labour in Alloa and a subsequent by-election in Tullibody in 2000. It also succeeded in winning the University ward of Logie in 1999 (of which Jack McConnell was a former councillor). However, despite such advances in 1999, Labour still won Ochil at the Scottish election, though the constituency has become highly marginal.

Though the SNP does well in the Clackmannanshire and Kinross parts of the Ochil seat, it does less well on the Stirling side: especially in the small towns to the east of Stirling that Labour dominates. Indeed, it is in towns such as Cowie, Fallin and Plean where Labour's Ochil majority is obtained – especially at the 1999 Scottish election. Unless the SNP manages to eclipse Labour rather than match them in Clackmannanshire, then Labour's advantage in East Stirlingshire will continue to give them control of the constituency. The SNP has selected the Clackmannanshire council leader, Keith Brown, to fight the seat at the next Westminster election. He is a local councillor in Alva and has a very high profile in the local media and will ensure another close contest with Labour. Given the SNP's council success and raised profile in the area through MSP George Reid, this is perhaps the party's best chance of capturing the seat. But, Labour has held this seat at many elections and could do so again. This result may prove too close to call come election night.

MP Martin O'Neill was born in 1945 and educated at Trinity Academy, Edinburgh, Heriot-Watt University and Moray House College of Education. He worked as an insurance clerk from 1963 to 1967 and then as a secondary school teacher in Edinburgh. He was a frontbench Labour spokesperson for Trade and Industry and Defence before Labour was elected to government in 1997, but fell out of favour. O'Neill was Defence Spokesman from 1988 to 1992 in the latter years of the Kinnock leadership as the party moved from unilateralism to multilateralism and abandoned its outright opposition to Trident. O'Neill invited much left criticism because of his soft-left revisionism and was never successful in being elected to the Shadow Cabinet over this period, only retaining his post due to Neil Kinnock's patronage. He has been Chair of the Select Committee on Trade and Industry since 1996, which has given him a media profile over certain issues in Scotland such as the Dounreay inquiry.

MSP Dr Richard Simpson was born in Edinburgh in 1942. He was educated at Perth Academy and Trinity College, Glenalmond and graduated in Medicine from Edinburgh University and was a GP from 1970 onwards as well as a psychiatrist from 1976 onwards until his election in 1999. He was a partner in a GP practice in Bridge of Allan in the Ochil constituency and was active in his local CLP. In the Scottish Parliament he sits on both the Finance and the Health and Community Care Committees. On the Health Committee, he gained a high profile through his investigation into the consultation processes of Greater Glasgow Health Board in relation to the proposed secure unit at Stobhill Hospital. He also sits on the Cross Party Groups for Children, Drug Misuse, Epilepsy, Information, Knowledge and Enlightenment, Older People, Age and Aging, Palliative Care, Strategic Rail Services and Tobacco Control. He is not a natural politician and has appeared uncomfortable with the rough and tumble of political campaigning, but has been a steadying hand on the Labour backbenches on some issues such as Section 28/Clause 2a. His medical experience and involvement in a number of organisations over the years such as Forth Valley Health Board, Strathcarron Hospice and the Scottish Association for Mental Health give him a breadth of experience in medicine. His political inexperience and low profile within Labour will probably limit his career prospects in the Parliament, which will deprive the Executive of a potential future Health Minister.

ORKNEY AND SHETLAND

Predecessor Constituencies: none, but separated for Scottish elections and joined at Westminster.

1999 Orkney

Electorate: 15,658
Turnout: 8,918 (56.95%)

Candidate	Party	Votes	Votes%	Change%
Jim Wallace	Liberal Democrat	6,010	67.39	+15.40
Christopher Zawadzki	Conservative	1,391	15.60	+4.37
John Mowat	SNP	917	10.28	-2.42
Angus MacLeod	Labour	600	6.73	-11.54

Liberal Democrat majority: 4,619 (51.79%)
Swing: 5.52% Conservative to Liberal Democrat

1999 Shetland

Electorate: 16,978
Turnout: 9,978 (58.77%)

Candidate	Party	Votes	Votes%	Change%
Tavish Scott	Liberal Democrat	5,435	54.47	+2.48
Jonathan Wills	Labour	2,241	22.46	+4.19
William Ross	SNP	1,430	14.33	+1.63
Gary Robinson	Conservative	872	8.74	-3.49

Liberal Democrat majority: 3,194 (32.01%)
Swing: 0.86% Liberal Democrat to Labour

1997

Electorate: 32,291
Turnout: 20,665 (64%)

Candidate	Party	Votes	Votes%	Change%
Jim Wallace	Liberal Democrat	10,743	51.99	+5.57
James Paton	Labour	3,775	18.27	-1.57
Willie Ross	SNP	2,624	12.70	+1.54
Hope Anderson	Conservative	2,527	12.23	-9.79
Francis Adamson	Referendum	820	3.97	—

Candidate	Party	Votes	Votes%	Swing %
Christian Wharton	NLP	116	0.56	–
Arthur Robertson	Independent	60	0.29	–

Liberal Democrat majority: 6,968 (33.72%)
Swing: 3.57% Labour to Liberal Democrat

1945–92

	Lab%	Con%	SNP%	Lib%	Other%	Turnout%
1992	19.8	22.0	11.2	46.4	–	65.5
1987	18.7	23.3	–	41.7	16.3	68.7
1983	13.1	25.6	15.4	45.9	–	67.8
1979	17.5	21.3	4.8	56.4	–	67.2
1974O	12.4	14.2	17.2	56.2	–	66.8
1974F	15.4	22.6	–	62.0	–	71.1
1970	21.1	31.9	–	47.0	–	68.0
1966	18.6	22.3	–	59.1	–	65.2
1964	17.4	20.0	–	62.6	–	72.8
1959	17.3	18.5	–	64.2	–	71.3
1955	15.8	20.4	–	63.8	–	66.1
1951	16.3	26.2	–	57.5	–	69.0
1950	21.3	31.9	–	46.8	–	67.7
1945	29.8	36.0	–	34.2	–	55.5

Orkney and Shetland comprise the two island groups to the north of Scotland. Each is distinct in character from Scotland and from each other, due to their geography, political affiliations and Norse past: immortalised in the writing of the late George Mackay Brown of Stromness (Greenvoe). Each has a reliance on ferries for trade and communications and a significant stake in the oil industry, the last being particularly true of Shetland. The islands enjoy a degree of autonomy within Scotland due to their distinctive local authority structures, which enjoy a capacity to gain oil revenues that is unique. Fishing and agriculture are also important parts of the islands' economies, with farming more important on Orkney because of its preponderance of rolling, green fields compared to the treeless, somewhat barren Shetland.

Politically, the islands, separately and together, have been Liberal for as long as most people can remember. The Liberal candidate even beat the National Liberal in 1922, though the Tories won the seat in 1935 and 1945. Former Liberal leader Jo Grimond – who promised to lead his members to the sound of gunfire – held the seat comfortably from 1950 to 1983. His successor, Jim Wallace, won the seat from 1983 onwards before choosing to become the Orkney MSP at the Scottish election in 1999 and retire from Westminster. In order to protect the position of the islands within a devolved Scotland, Orkney and Shetland were afforded separate representation in the Scottish Parliament, though the seat remains unified at Westminster elections.

The Shetland seat was won at the Scottish election by Liberal Democrat Tavish Scott, so that Liberal domination in the constituency has been maintained. Wallace's percentage performance in 1999 was extremely impressive, but then the party also gained well over 50 per cent in Shetland too, so the Westminster seat will be comfortably Liberal Democrat at the next election. Despite such strong Liberal partisanship in historical and recent times, the islands retain a tradition of independent-voting at local elections. Independents hold all 21 council seats in Orkney, indeed all council candidates except one were independents. In Shetland, the Liberal Democrats made some inroads into the non-partisan nature of council politics by winning 8 of the 22 council seats, with the remaining 14 councillors elected as independents.

Challenges to the Liberals/Liberal Democrats in Orkney and Shetland have been few and far between. Traditionally, the Tories came second to the Liberal Democrats in the seat, though this has changed in recent years. The SNP has never performed well in the islands, even with Winnie Ewing's intervention in 1983. The only other challenge came with the formation of the Orkney and Shetland Movements in the 1980s. These autonomy movements sought to enhance the political and economic autonomy of the islands within Scotland and the UK. They combined to win 14.5 per cent of the vote at the 1987 general election but have since faded away. The Shetland Movement had six councillors in Shetland from 1995 until 1999, but contested no seats in 1999. Neither party was around to contest the Scottish election in 1999. The disappearance of the two movements says much about their temporary nature as well as the fact that other parties adopted their aims and objectives. Island autonomy and oil tax powers were maintained by all governments before and after devolution, the island councils were retained after local government reorganisation in 1995 and the fact that each island group received an MSP in the Scottish Parliament provided them with an enhanced status that undermined support for autonomy.

MP/MSP (Orkney) Jim Wallace was born in Annan in 1955. He was educated at Annan Academy, Downing College, Cambridge, and Edinburgh University (LLB) and became a solicitor in 1979. He joined the Liberals in the 1970s at university and was chair of the Edinburgh University Liberal Club from 1976 to 1977 and a member of the party's Scottish Executive Committee from 1976 to 1985. He contested the Dumfries constituency in the 1979 general election, quickly followed by the South of Scotland seat at the European Parliamentary elections of that year. He was selected to replace Jo Grimond in Orkney and Shetland – one of the party's few safe seats – and became MP for that seat in 1983. He has been leader of the Scottish Liberal Democrats since 1992, following on from Malcolm Bruce, and was the Liberal and then Liberal Democrat chief whip at Westminster from 1987 until 1992. He was active in the Constitutional Convention as the Scottish Liberal Democrat leader, and then became a member of the Consultative Steering Group which drew up the draft standing orders and procedures of the Scottish Parliament in 1998. He is Deputy First Minister and Minister for Justice in the Scottish Executive.

He was also Acting First Minister when Donald Dewar underwent heart surgery in the summer of 2000, and in the tragic circumstances of Dewar's death in October 2000, prior to the election of Henry McLeish. Balancing two positions within the Executive has not been easy, but Wallace performed well as Justice Minister and as Acting First Minister, with some strong performances at First Minister's question time. In time, his efforts as Justice Minister will probably establish him as a key reforming member of the first Scottish Executive, with reforms of land ownership and family law, and the institution of key Liberal Democrat policies. Despite his longevity as an MP and as Liberal Democrat leader, he is not a well-known face in Scotland, perhaps down to a lack of charisma and less than inspiring TV appearances. He also suffered from his promise to abolish student tuition fees during the Scottish election campaign when the party joined a coalition with Labour and established an independent committee to consider the issue which eventually saw, to the Liberal Democrats credit, the abolition of tuition fees for students and the institution of a progressive system for funding further and higher education.

MSP Tavish Scott was born in Inverness in 1966 and grew up on Shetland. He was educated at Anderson High School, Lerwick and graduated from Napier University in 1989 with a degree in Business Studies, and worked for Jim Wallace in the House of Commons, followed by a stint as press officer for the Scottish Liberal Democrats in 1990. Since then he ran the family farm in Shetland and became a local councillor in Lerwick from 1994 to 1999, and was vice-chair of Shetland Council's Roads and Transport Committee. He was the Liberal Democrat spokesperson for Transport and the Environment and sat on both the European and Transport and Environment Committees of the Parliament in 1999 to 2000. He was also a member of the Cross Party Groups on Crofting, Oil and Gas, Strategic Rail Services and Sports and was the Convenor of the group on Renewable Energy. Tavish Scott successfully got the first members' bill through the Scottish Parliament – the very unsexy and media unfriendly Sea Fisheries (Shellfish) (Amendment) Bill which amended the Sea Fisheries (Shellfish) Act of 1967: a landmark for both Scott and the Parliament's legislative processes. Scott's Parliamentary performances were rewarded with promotion to become Deputy Minister of Parliament and Liberal Democrat Business Manager with a role on the Parliamentary Bureau.

PAISLEY NORTH

Predecessor Constituencies: none.

1999

Electorate: 49,020
Turnout: 27,750 (56.61%)

Candidate	Party	Votes	Votes%	Change%
Wendy Alexander	Labour	13,492	48.62	-10.84
Ian Mackay	SNP	8,876	31.99	+10.07
Peter Ramsay	Conservative	2,242	8.08	-1.49
Tamsin Mayberry	Liberal Democrat	2,133	7.69	+0.76
Fiona Macdonald	SSP	1,007	3.63	-

Labour majority: 4,616 (16.63%)
Swing: 10.46% Labour to SNP

1997

Electorate: 49,725
Turnout: 34,135 (68.65%)

Candidate	Party	Votes	Votes%	Change%
Irene Adams	Labour	20,295	59.46	+7.59
Ian Mackay	SNP	7,481	21.92	-1.58
Kenneth Brookes	Conservative	3,267	9.57	-6.11
Alan Jeffs	Liberal Democrat	2,365	6.93	-0.77
Robert Graham	Pro-Life	531	1.56	-
Edwin Matthew	Referendum	196	0.57	-

Labour majority: 12,814 (37.54%)
Swing: 4.59% SNP to Labour

1983–92

	Lab%	Con%	SNP%	Lib%	Other%	Turnout%
1992	50.7	16.4	23.3	8.2	1.4	73.4
1990B	44.0	14.8	29.4	8.3	3.6	53.7
1987	55.5	15.8	12.9	15.8	-	73.5
1983	45.6	21.4	8.0	23.7	1.3	68.5

Paisley is situated on the south side of the Clyde between the parliamentary seats of West Renfrewshire (which was to play an important role in Paisley politics in the 1990s) and the Glasgow seats of Govan and Pollok. It is Scotland's fifth largest town, and proud of its independent status. Prior to 1983, Paisley was represented by one seat, and divided into two in the 1983 boundary changes – North being the new seat and South the successor seat.

Paisley North includes parts of Paisley, along with Renfrew and Linwood – a town made famous by the ill-fated Rootes Group car plant to build the Hillman Imp opened in 1963. Paisley has a proud history and sense of its own identity, but parts of North are some of the most deprived areas of the West of Scotland. Ferguslie Park within North is a council estate with endemic unemployment, crime, drugs and poverty, the site of numerous urban regeneration initiatives, of flooding from the Clyde in the late 1990s and allegations about community initiatives and council malpractice. Paisley North is the sixteenth most unhealthy constituency in Scotland, just ahead of South in terms of unhealthiness; 31 per cent of its residents live in poverty and in June 2000 its male unemployment was 8.2 per cent.

North's creation in 1983 witnessed Allen Adams holding the seat with a 7,587 majority for Labour over the Liberal-SDP Alliance, which he doubled to 14,442 in 1987. Paisley politics were then shocked by the deaths within a month of each other of the town's two MPs, Allen Adams and Norman Buchan. The subsequent by-elections held on 29 November 1990 saw Margaret Thatcher resign and John Major become Prime Minister all in the last week of campaigning. Both by-elections returned Labour MPs with sharply reduced majorities; Irene Adams, widow of Allen, being returned in North with a majority of 3,770 over the SNP.

The 1992 election increased Labour's majority to 9,321 over the SNP; boundary changes translated that into a notional majority of 10,414, which Labour widened to 12,814 over the Nationalists in 1997. Irene Adams increased Labour's support by 1,000, while the SNP vote fell by 1,000 and the Conservatives' by 2,500. Paisley politics were then shattered by the suicide of Gordon McMaster, MP for Paisley South. Allegations centred on the neighbouring MP for West Renfrewshire, Tommy Graham, and his role in spreading gossip and innuendo about McMaster's sexuality, as well as his being involved pre-1997 in trying to deselect Irene Adams. A Labour Party investigation subsequently expelled Graham and sent him into political obscurity.

The 1999 Scottish Parliament elections were uncomfortable ones for Labour in Paisley, but in North, Wendy Alexander, sister of Douglas Alexander, MP for South, was returned with a majority of 4,616, seeing her vote fall by nearly 7,000, while the SNP's support increased by 1,400. Paisley North in its short but troubled history has shown the strength of its commitment to Labour and should continue to do so at UK and Scottish elections.

MP Irene Adams was born in 1947 in Paisley and elected for Paisley North in a

November 1990 by-election, succeeding her late husband, Allen Adams, who had been MP for Paisley from 1979 to 1983 and for Paisley North from 1983 until 1990. Educated at Stanley Green High School, Paisley, she was elected to Paisley Town Hall from 1970 to 1974, Renfrew District Council from 1974 to 1978 and Strathclyde Regional Council from 1978 to 1984.

Adams is on the pro-devolutionist left wing of the party and after Labour's unexpected defeat in 1992 was one of the main supporters of the cross-party initiative 'Scotland United', along with Labour MPs George Galloway and John McAllion. After the 1997 election she became involved in a bitter dispute with neighbouring Labour MP Tommy Graham. It was alleged that he had carried out a campaign against Paisley South MP Gordon McMaster which had played a part in his suicide. Graham had also been involved in attempts to undermine Adams and have her deselected. An internal party enquiry led to Graham's expulsion from Labour, facing the prospect of political oblivion, with Adams's position strengthened.

MSP Wendy Alexander was born in 1963 in Glasgow and educated at Park Mains High School, Erskine, Lester B. Pearson College, Vancouver, Glasgow University, Warwick University and INSEAD Business School, France. She was Parliamentary Assistant to George Galloway from 1987 to 1988 and Research Officer to the Scottish Labour Party from 1988 to 1992, a Management Consultant at Booz Allen and Hamilton from 1994 to 1997, before becoming Special Adviser to the Secretary of State for Scotland from 1997 to 1998 where she had special responsibility for the legislation to establish the Scottish Parliament. She was Chair of Glasgow University Club from 1984 to 1985, a member of Scottish Labour Action, the pro-home rule pressure group, and a contributor to a wide range of books and publications, ranging from *The World is Ill-Divided: Women's Work in Scotland*, *The State and the Nations* and *A Different Future: A Modernisers' Guide to Scotland*. In the Scottish Parliament elections, Alexander was campaign spokesperson on the economy, but after the election, rather than get the Enterprise portfolio as everyone thought she would, she became Minister for Communities. As one of several ministers who have never previously held public office, she had to make a fast transition to the world of high politics, more so because she had previously been a backroom adviser. Alexander is universally acknowledged as being incredibly bright and driven, not words usually associated with Scottish Labour politicians, but many observers feel she has not developed her personal skills so well, and has a tendency to be seen as patronising and lecturing in her style.

In her first year as a Minister she was involved in one of the biggest political controversies in Scotland for years after she announced the Executive's intention to abolish Section 28 which banned the 'promotion' of homosexuality in schools. Alexander drew the wrath of the Catholic Church and of Brian Souter, millionaire owner of Stagecoach, who bankrolled a private referendum against the Executive's policy. Section 28 was eventually abolished, but at much cost to the Executive's integrity and to Alexander personally, who had acted honourably, but bore the brunt of much of the tabloid campaigns. In Henry McLeish's first ministerial reshuffle in October 2000, Alexander was given the post she originally wanted, Minister for Enterprise and Lifelong Learning, where she is responsible for a number of areas, including meeting the challenge of the knowledge economy, lifelong learning, further and higher education, digital Scotland, tourism and the quangos, Scottish Enterprise and Highlands and Islands Enterprise. Alexander, in her first few months in the post, has already shown that she is much more comfortable and suited to this post than she was as Minister for Communities. She has already made it a priority to drive ahead with a dynamic pro-enterprise policy and has shaken up complacent public agency the Scottish Tourist Board, which was presiding over declining tourist numbers coming to Scotland.

Alexander was spoken of, while Donald Dewar was First Minister, as a potential successor to him, and seen by many as his preferred candidate. However, her prospects were not aided by the Section 28/Clause 2A debacle, and Dewar's death came too soon for her to put her name forward. Jack McConnell's decision to stand against Henry McLeish and his impressive support means that he has stolen an advance on his colleague in the race to claim the honour of being the leading light of the party's modernisers. Alexander did not stand either for the post of Deputy Leader of the party, for which she was seen as Gordon Brown's preferred candidate, leaving the relatively unknown Cathy Jamieson to take the post.

PAISLEY SOUTH

Predecessor Constituencies: Paisley (1945–79).

1999

Electorate: 53,637
Turnout: 30,656 (57.15%)

Candidate	Party	Votes	Votes%	Change%
Hugh Henry	Labour	13,899	45.34	−12.17
Bill Martin	SNP	9,404	30.68	+7.30
Stuart Callison	Liberal Democrat	2,974	9.70	+0.33
Sheila Laidlaw	Conservative	2,433	7.94	+0.73
Paul Mack	Independent	1,273	4.15	—
Jackie Forrest	SWP	673	2.20	—

Labour majority: 4,495 (14.66%)
Swing: 9.73% Labour to SNP

Westminster By-election 6 November 1997

Electorate: 54,050
Turnout: 23,435 (43.36%)

Candidate	Party	Votes	Votes%	Change%
Douglas Alexander	Labour	10,346	44.15	−13.36
Ian Blackford	SNP	7,615	32.49	+9.11
Eileen McCartin	Liberal Democrat	2,582	11.02	+1.65
Sheila Lawson	Conservative	1,643	7.01	−1.66
John Deighan	Pro-Life	578	2.47	—
Frances Curran	SSA	306	1.31	+0.92
Charles McLauchlan	Socialist Ind Labour	155	0.66	—
Chris Herriot	Socialist Labour	153	0.65	—
Kenneth Blair	NLP	57	0.24	—

Labour majority: 2,731 (11.65%)
Swing: 11.23% Labour to SNP

1997

Electorate: 54,050
Turnout: 37,351 (69.12%)

Candidate	Party	Votes	Votes%	Change%
Gordon McMaster	Labour	21,482	57.51	+6.71
Bill Martin	SNP	8,732	23.38	-1.18
Eileen McCartin	Liberal Democrat	3,500	9.37	+0.48
Robert Reid	Conservative	3,237	8.67	-6.69
James Lardner	Referendum	254	0.68	–
Sean Clerkin	SSA	146	0.39	–

Labour majority: 12,750 (34.13%)
Swing: 3.95% SNP to Labour

1945–92

	Lab%	Con%	SNP%	Lib%	Other%	Turnout%
1992	50.7	15.9	24.1	9.1	0.3	75.0
1990B	46.1	13.4	27.5	9.8	3.1	55.5
1987	56.2	14.7	14.0	15.1	–	75.3
1983	41.4	20.7	13.0	24.1	0.7	72.6
1979	55.8	26.1	15.7	–	–	72.8
1974O	44.8	15.6	33.1	6.5	–	72.2
1974F	48.4	30.3	21.3	–	–	75.2
1970	54.1	32.4	7.3	6.2	–	71.5
1966	60.0	23.2	–	16.8	–	76.5
1964	52.9	13.2	–	33.9	–	79.8
1961B	45.4	13.2	–	41.4	–	68.1
1959	57.3	42.7	–	–	–	78.9
1955	56.4	43.6	–	–	–	76.2
1951	55.3	31.0	–	13.7	–	84.4
1950	56.1	36.5	–	7.4	–	84.0
1948B	56.8	–	–	43.2	–	76.0
1945	55.6	32.7	–	10.0	1.7	73.9

Paisley South comprises the southern part of the town of Paisley along with Johnstone. It is the nineteenth most unhealthy constituency in Scotland, just behind Paisley North; 31 per cent of its residents live in poverty and in June 2000 its male unemployment rate was 7.6 per cent.

In 1948, John MacCormick stood as a National Liberal candidate with Conservative support on a pro-home rule ticket based on the Scottish Convention.

This decision contributed to the Attlee Government becoming more hostile to the Convention and home rule; Labour's Douglas Johnston in a two-horse race saw his majority cut to 6,545. In 1961, Labour's Douglas Robertson again nearly lost Paisley to the Liberals in a by-election, and they polled respectably in the following 1964 general election, before their star waned once more.

John Robertson was elected as Labour MP in October 1974 with a 5,590 lead over the SNP and in 1976 established the Scottish Labour Party with Jim Sillars. However, Robertson chose not to stand again in 1979 and Labour's Allen Adams was elected with a 13,755 lead over the Conservatives. In 1983 the division into Paisley North and South saw Norman Buchan returned in South with a 6,529 majority over the Liberal-SDP Alliance, which he widened to 15,785 in 1987. The death of Buchan in 1990 coinciding with that of Allen Adams, MP for North, produced the unusual situation of two by-elections on the same day in adjoining constituencies. Gordon McMaster held South for Labour with a 5,030 majority over the SNP Iain Lawson, previously a Conservative member; this majority increased to 9,549 over the SNP in 1992.

Boundary changes before 1997 gave Labour a notional 10,469 majority over the SNP. In that year's contest, McMaster increased Labour's vote by 1,000, as the SNP's fell by the same amount, resulting in a 12,750 majority over the SNP. McMaster was a bright, able MP who had been leader of Renfrewshire West council and could have expected office. However, three months after the May election triumph, he committed suicide. McMaster's tragic death turned Paisley politics upside down. It revealed the dark side of local politics, with Paisley named 'a town called malice'. McMaster had believed Tommy Graham, MP for West Renfrewshire, had been carrying out a campaign of rumour and invective to undermine him, and, after a party investigation, Graham was eventually expelled from the Labour Party.

The November 1997 by-election was a difficult contest for Labour, but Douglas Alexander, a promising and committed 'Brownite', held the seat relatively easily. On a 43 per cent turnout, Labour's vote was more than halved, falling by 11,000; the SNP achieved an 11 per cent swing, but saw their own vote fall by 1,000 votes as they reduced Labour's majority to 2,731. The Scottish Parliament elections increased Labour's lead over the SNP to 4,495. Hugh Henry saw Labour's vote fall 7,000 from the May 1997 total on a reduced turnout, as the SNP vote rose by 700. Both the Lib Dems and Conservatives increased their shares and Paul Mack, an ex-Labour councillor, polled respectably as an Independent. Paisley South has been through the wars and back in recent years, and Labour must be hoping for a period of peace and quiet, so they can rebuild their local dominance.

MP Douglas Alexander was born in 1967 in Glasgow and was returned as MP for Paisley South in a November 1997 by-election. Educated at Park Mains High School, Erskine, and Lester B. Pearson College, Vancouver, like his big sister Wendy, he then parted company with her, going to Edinburgh University and Pennsylvania University. Alexander, who was admitted as a solicitor in 1995, was prior to becoming an MP an adviser and close confidant of Gordon Brown. He stood in the 1995 Perth and Kinross by-election in what was a key Tory-SNP seat and tested some of New Labour's emerging themes: trying out the concept of 'Middle Scotland' and running a combative, aggressive anti-SNP campaign that lifted Labour from third to second adding 3,000 to Labour's vote as the SNP won the seat.

After the 1997 election, he developed, with Brown, Scottish Labour's more unionist strategy for the Scottish Parliament elections. This saw Alexander and Brown pen a pamphlet *New Scotland, New Britain*. Alexander ran the party's Scottish Parliament campaign with a hard anti-nationalist line under the banner 'Divorce is an Expensive Business' which shocked many in the party. It clearly worked in that Labour comfortably won the election, and Alexander clearly seemed to believe the potency of his propaganda. Alexander became Labour's General Election Co-ordinator for the 2001 UK election, a role which will see him working closely with his ally and mentor Gordon Brown, and is widely tiped for promotion afterwards.

MSP Hugh Henry was born in Glasgow in 1952 and educated at St Mirin's Academy, Paisley, University of Glasgow and Jordanhill College of Education. He worked as an accountant for IBM from 1973 to 1975 and then became a teacher with Strathclyde Region from 1976 to 1979. Henry switched after this to becoming a Welfare Rights Officer in Social Work from 1979 to 1983 and a Community Care Manager with Community Enterprise in Strathclyde from 1993 to 1996.

He was elected a councillor on Renfrewshire District Council from 1984 to 1996 and West Renfrewshire Council from 1995 to 1999 where he was leader of the council for those four years. He was also COSLA's spokesperson on European and International Affairs from 1996 to 1999. In the Scottish Parliament he became Convenor of the European Committee as well as a member of the Health and Community Care Committee the latter of which he left in December 2000. He is also a member of the Cross Party Groups on Children, Epilepsy and Tobacco Control.

PERTH

Predecessor Constituencies: Perth and East Perthshire (1945–79), Kinross and West Perthshire (1945–79) and Perth and Kinross (1983–95).

1999

Electorate: 61,034
Turnout: 37,396 (61.27%)

Candidate	Party	Votes	Votes%	Change%
Roseanna Cunningham	SNP	13,570	36.29	-0.09
Ian Stevenson	Conservative	11,543	30.87	+1.54
Jillian Richards	Labour	8,725	23.22	-1.44
Chic Brodie	Liberal Democrat	3,558	9.51	+1.47

SNP majority: 2,027 (5.42%)
Swing: 0.82% SNP to Conservative

1997

Electorate: 60,313
Turnout: 44,551 (73.87%)

Candidate	Party	Votes	Votes%	Change%
Roseanna Cunningham	SNP	16,209	36.38	+1.99
John Godfrey	Conservative	13,068	29.33	-11.13
Douglas Alexander	Labour	11,036	24.77	+11.57
Chic Brodie	Liberal Democrat	3,583	8.04	-3.92
Robert MacAuley	Referendum	366	0.82	–
Matthew Henderson	UK Independence	289	0.65	–

SNP majority: 3,141 (7.06%)
Swing: 6.56% Conservative to SNP

Perth and Kinross (1983–95)

	Lab%	Con%	SNP%	Lib%	Other%	Turnout%
1995B	22.9	21.4	40.4	11.8	3.4	62.1
1992	12.5	40.2	36.0	11.4	–	76.9
1987	15.9	39.6	27.6	16.9	–	74.4
1983	9.9	40.2	25.1	24.7	–	72.3

Kinross and West Perthshire (1945–79)

	Lab%	Con%	SNP%	Lib%	Other%	Turnout%
1979	8.5	50.5	29.4	11.6	–	79.6
1974O	7.7	41.7	41.5	9.1	–	75.1
1974F	9.9	52.8	23.1	14.2	–	77.8
1970	15.2	57.3	18.6	8.9	–	74.1
1966	18.7	60.8	20.5	–	–	73.5
1964	18.8	66.6	14.1	–	0.5	75.0
1963B	15.2	57.3	7.3	19.5	0.6	76.1
1959	16.8	68.2	15.0	–	–	71.0
1955	24.8	75.2	–	–	–	70.5
1951	23.8	76.2	–	–	–	73.2
1950	18.6	55.4	–	26.0	–	76.9
1945	32.0	68.0	–	–	–	67.4

Perth and East Perthshire (1945–79)

	Lab%	Con%	SNP%	Lib%	Other%	Turnout%
1979	13.4	41.9	35.5	9.2	–	77.3
1974O	13.6	38.9	40.8	6.7	–	73.8
1974F	15.1	47.3	27.2	10.4	–	78.3
1970	23.8	52.0	17.0	7.2	–	73.6
1966	27.9	56.5	15.6	–	–	72.3
1964	24.7	57.9	17.4	–	–	75.6
1959	18.2	58.2	23.1	–	–	75.6
1955	20.5	56.7	22.8	–	–	73.5
1951	25.7	59.4	14.9	–	–	78.3
1950	26.4	56.1	9.3	8.2	–	81.6
1945	32.6	63.1	4.3	–	–	65.3

This traditionally Conservative seat comprises the city of Perth and the towns of Auchterarder, Crieff and Comrie. The seat no longer contains Kinross, which was transferred to Ochil before the 1997 election, but the Perth seat does contain a significant amount of territory to the west of Perth. The dour image of the area is an outdated one as anyone sipping cappuccino in the piazza to the north of Perth City Hall will realise.

Electorally, the seat was predominantly Conservative from 1945 to 1987, with the exception of the SNP's challenge in October 1974 in the former Kinross and West Perthshire seat. This seat was held by the former Prime Minister, Alec Douglas-Home, from 1963 to February 1974, then held by maverick Tory Nicky Fairbairn until his death in 1995. Fairbairn only held on by 53 votes from the SNP in October 1974, but the drop in SNP support at succeeding elections assisted the Conservatives. The intervention of the Liberal-SDP Alliance also aided the Conservatives in 1983, but the SNP began to recover after that and turned the seat into a Conservative-SNP marginal again.

When Fairbairn died in 1995, the SNP won the subsequent by-election through Roseanna Cunningham. She had initially fought the constituency in 1992 and, following the by-election victory, held it at the 1997 election – the first time the SNP held a by-election gain – and at the 1999 Scottish election. Her decision to retire from Westminster and concentrate on her role as an MSP has brought the need for a new candidate. The SNP selected Annabelle Ewing, previously candidate in Stirling and Hamilton South, to contest the seat.

Though the SNP has done well in Perth at recent elections, the seat remains susceptible to a Conservative recovery as well as a surge in support for Labour which could hand the Tories victory. The SNP's majority in the constituency has been relatively low at recent elections, especially at the Scottish election in 1999 when it won the seat with only 2,027 votes. Indeed, Perth was one of the few constituencies in which the Tories actually increased their vote in 1999, to put them back in second place. The Tory recovery in the council elections and the sharp drop in SNP council representation in 1999 also offer signs of potential change at the next general election. The Conservatives will target this seat and selected Elizabeth Smith as their candidate in January 2000. She is a political advisor to Malcolm Rifkind at Scottish Conservative Central Office in Edinburgh.

Of course, the party that has done best in the constituency in recent years has been Labour. Its performance at the 1995 by-election, in which Douglas Alexander came second to the SNP, has been maintained with good performances in 1997 and 1999. The party is more than holding its own, with good local council results in Perth town itself. If it does well at the next general election, it could gain sufficient votes from the SNP to assist the Tories: as SNP canvassers will be reminding voters. The SNP should hang on in the seat, but this is anything but a safe SNP prospect.

MP/MSP Roseanna Cunningham was born in Glasgow in 1951 but emigrated to Perth, Australia, as an eight-year-old child. She has degrees in politics (from University of Western Australia) and law (from Edinburgh) as well as a Diploma in Legal Practice from Aberdeen. She worked for the SNP as a researcher before becoming a solicitor in first Dumbarton and then Glasgow District councils; she then became an advocate in 1990. Cunningham was a supporter of the left-wing '79 Group set up after the SNP's electoral humiliation in the 1979 election. In 1982, the party leadership proscribed the group, expelling its leading members, then reducing the sentences to suspension. Cunningham was not disciplined, but her brother, Chris Cunningham was one of the seven prominent members of the '79 Group suspended and he never rejoined the Nationalists.

She was elected to Westminster at the Perth by-election in 1995, caused by the death of Nicky Fairbairn. However, she had not been the perfect candidate of the SNP leadership who wished to have Alasdair Morgan, later to be MP and MSP for Galloway and Upper Nithsdale. Winnie Ewing tried to stop her being the SNP candidate in the Perth and Kinross by-election by dragging up old personal animosities over a long-dead affair she had had with the first husband of Margaret Ewing. At that by-election, her republican views generated some controversy, as she styled the monarchy 'the pinnacle of the British class system'. However, Perth and Kinross was not as Royalist as the Tories thought and the 'republican rose' swept into Westminster at that election.

In the Scottish Parliament, she was the Convenor of the Justice and Home Affairs Committee from 1999 to 2000 until the SNP's reshuffle following John Swinney's election as SNP leader in September 2000. However, she remained as the SNP's spokesperson on Justice, Equality and Land Reform. Her leadership of the committee and parliamentary performances, especially the quizzing of ministers, have shown her as a highly effective Parliamentarian. Her popularity within the SNP was also demonstrated by her victory in the SNP deputy leadership election in 2000, when she defeated fellow MSP Kenny McAskill for the post of Senior Vice-Convenor, which will further elevate her political and media profile within Scotland. She is also a reknowned Trekkie with a considerable sci-fi book and video collection.

ROSS, SKYE AND INVERNESS WEST

Predecessor Constituencies: Ross and Cromarty (1945–79) and Ross, Cromarty and Skye (1983–92).

1999

Electorate: 55,845
Turnout: 35,415 (63.42%)

Candidate	Party	Votes	Votes%	Change%
John Farquhar Munro	Liberal Democrat	11,652	32.90	−5.82
Donnie Munro	Labour	10,113	28.56	−0.1
Jim Mather	SNP	7,997	22.58	+3.01
John Scott	Conservative	3,351	9.46	−1.47
Douglas Briggs	Independent	2,302	6.50	−

Liberal Democrat majority: 1,539 (4.34%)
Swing: 2.86% Liberal Democrat to Labour

1997

Electorate: 55,639
Turnout: 39,955 (71.81%)

Candidate	Party	Votes	Votes%	Change%
Charles Kennedy	Liberal Democrat	15,472	38.72	+0.04
Donnie Munro	Labour	11,453	28.66	+9.79
Margaret Paterson	SNP	7,821	19.57	+0.75
Mary McLeod	Conservative	4,368	10.93	−10.93
Les Durance	Referendum	535	1.34	−
Alan Hopkins	Green	306	0.77	−

Liberal Democrat majority: 4,019 (10.08%)
Swing: 4.88% Liberal Democrat to Labour

1945–92

	Lab%	Con%	SNP%	Lib%	Other%	Turnout%
1992	15.3	23.0	18.6	41.6	1.6	73.9
1987	19.1	19.7	11.8	49.4	−	72.7
1983	14.0	33.7	13.8	38.5	−	72.8

	Lab%	Con%	SNP%	Lib%	Other%	Turnout%
1979	20.1	42.4	23.6	13.9	–	76.4
1974O	16.8	38.9	35.7	8.6	–	69.5
1974F	19.8	36.1	23.0	21.1	–	75.1
1970	26.0	33.2	11.7	29.1	–	71.7
1966	30.4	27.6	–	42.0	–	71.2
1964	27.7	32.1	–	40.2	–	69.4
1959	29.1	47.2	–	23.7	–	65.3
1955	37.7	62.3	–	–	–	61.9
1951	35.8	64.2	–	–	–	57.5
1950	37.4	–	–	–	62.6	63.1
1945	37.2	–	–	–	62.8	61.9

This vast rural constituency takes in a geographically large area stretching from the Black Isle across to Fort William and then the Isle of Skye. The constituency is interesting because it has changed over time from being a Conservative-Liberal marginal to a Labour-Liberal Democrat marginal through the rise of Labour at the last two elections. Historically, this seat has had a rich Liberal tradition which it has maintained after the days of National Liberal and Conservative alliance in the 1950s. Captain Jack MacLeod won Ross and Cromarty as an Independent Liberal with a 4,102 majority over Labour in 1945 and retained the seat in 1950. He then stood as a National Liberal and Conservative in a straight fight with Labour and easily held the seat in 1951, holding it until 1964.

When the Liberals began to contest the constituency again in 1959, their popularity was there for all to see and the party re-emerged quickly to win Ross and Cromarty in 1964 and 1966. The Conservatives then regained the seat in 1970 as the Liberal vote fell away. Indeed, the main challenge to the Tories in this period came in the shape of the SNP in October 1974. The Nationalists' 35.7 per cent left them only 663 votes behind the Tories.

Increased support for the Tories and the appearance of the SNP dented Liberal fortunes throughout the 1970s, reaching their nadir in October 1974 when the Liberals could only muster 8.6 per cent of the vote. However, normal service was resumed in the 1980s. Charles Kennedy became the youngest MP at Westminster at the 1983 general election, winning narrowly over Tory Energy Minister Hamish Gray, whilst standing as a candidate for the new SDP increasing the vote of the centre from 14 per cent won by the Liberals to 38.5 per cent for the Liberal-SDP Alliance. Kennedy retained the seat at successive elections, though he received his greatest challenge in 1997 at the hands of Labour's Donnie Munro, the former Runrig singer. That Munro subsequently lost out to John Farquhar Munro at the Scottish election in 1999: an unusual mainland contest between two native Gaelic speakers.

Labour's recent success in the constituency is testament to Donnie Munro's popularity as a candidate, but also to Labour's rural popularity in Scotland. Though Labour's West of Scotland/Central Belt image is enduring, it recorded strong performances in small town and rural Scotland in 1997 to appear as much more of a national party: itself unusual in Scotland's geographically fragmented party system. Labour did well in seats such as Ross, Skye and Inverness West, Inverness East, Nairn and Lochaber, Dumfries, Perth, and Tweeddale, Ettrick and Lauderdale. However, in Ross, Skye and Inverness West, this surge may well be over, especially given popular unrest over agriculture policy and fuel prices. The Westminster incumbent, Charles Kennedy, has always been popular within the constituency and is now leader of the Liberal Democrats. He should retain this seat with a comfortable majority, especially as his party held the seat at the Scottish election, though Labour will target this seat as a possible gain given its strong back-to-back showings in 1997 and 1999.

MP Charles Kennedy was born in Inverness in 1959, went to Lochaber High School, Fort William and was first elected to this seat in 1983, as Westminster's youngest MP. He joined the Labour Party at the age of 15, but at Glasgow University decided to join the Social Democrats, partly after hearing Roy Jenkins speak, but also because the Labour Club, unlike the Social Democrats, did not engage in debating. Kennedy was also President of Glasgow University Union, where he became known as 'Taxi Kennedy', due to his propensity to get numerous taxis across the campus and his large expenses. He won the Observer Mace debating contest in 1982, was a journalist with BBC Highland in Inverness before heading to university in Indiana, and was set to continue his PhD there until his unexpected election in 1983 as an SDP MP.

He has been SDP and Liberal Democrat spokesperson for a range of policy areas. Kennedy was Liberal-SDP Spokesman on Health and Social Services, as well as Scotland from 1983 to 1987, Election Spokesman on Social Security from January to June 1987, Liberal Democrat Interim Joint Spokesman on Social Security in 1988, Trade and Industry Spokesman 1988–9, Health Spokesman 1989–92, Europe Spokesman 1992–7, followed by Agriculture and Rural Affairs Spokesman from 1997 to 1999. He has also been a member of the Select Committee on Social Services from 1985–7, the Select Committee on House of Commons Televising in 1998 and the Standards and Privileges Committee from 1997 to 1999. He was a pro-merger SDP MP and was Liberal Democrat President from 1990 to 1994 and is now the party leader after his election by party members in 1999.

As Liberal Democrat leader, he faces fundamental challenges in relation to the future direction of the party. Whilst Ashdown moved between co-operation and constructive opposition with Labour at Westminster, Kennedy faces a situation in which the Liberal Democrats are in government with Labour in Scotland as well as constructive opponents at Westminster. The party's relationship with Labour and the maintainence of a distinct Liberal Democrat political identity given co-operation with Labour and New Labour's move to the centre ground since the mid-1990s all suggest Kennedy faces a difficult task in improving on the party's 1997 performance.

MSP John Farquhar Munro was born in 1934 and educated in Plockton and at the Sea Training College in Sharpness. He served in the Merchant Navy for ten years before working as a contractor for many years. He also ran a croft from 1971 until 1997. He was formerly a councillor for many years, on the old Inverness-shire County Council from 1966 until 1974, on Skye and Lochalsh District Council from 1974 until 1995, where he was council Convenor from 1984 until 1995, and on Highland Council from 1978 to 1982 and 1995 to 1999, where he served as Liberal Democrat group leader, chair of the Roads and Transport Committee and the Highland Council Rail Network Partnership. In the Scottish Parliament he was a member of the Equal Opportunities and Rural Affairs Committees from May 1999 to December 2000, before joining the Transport and Environment Committee in January 2001. He became the Liberal Democrat Spokesperson on Transport and Gaelic in November 2000. Farquhar Munro is an independent minded Liberal Democrat MSP and was one of only three Liberal Democrat MSPs who voted against going into coalition with Labour in May 1999, the others being Donald Gorrie and Keith Raffan. He is a native Gaelic speaker and has proved an active campaigner for land reform in the Parliament, sponsoring a debate on the sale of the Black Cuillin and being severely critical of the Executive's limited approach to land reform. He sits on the Cross Party Groups for Gaelic, Animal Welfare, Epilepsy and Strategic Rail Services and is Joint Convenor of the group on Crofting.

ROXBURGH AND BERWICKSHIRE

Predecessor Constituencies: created a new in 1983 from Roxburgh, Selkirk and Peebles.

1999

Electorate: 47,639
Turnout: 27,846 (58.52%)

Candidate	Party	Votes	Votes%	Change%
Euan Robson	Liberal Democrat	11,320	40.61	-5.89
Alasdair Hutton	Conservative	7,735	27.75	+3.88
Stuart Crawford	SNP	4,719	16.93	+5.60
Suzanne McLeod	Labour	4,102	14.72	-0.24

Liberal Democrat majority: 3,585 (12.86%)
Swing: 4.88% Liberal Democrat to Conservative

1997

Electorate: 47,259
Turnout: 34,931 (73.91%)

Candidate	Party	Votes	Votes%	Change%
Archy Kirkwood	Liberal Democrat	16,243	46.50	+0.04
Douglas Younger	Conservative	8,337	23.87	-10.28
Helen Eadie	Labour	5,226	14.96	+6.20
Malcolm Balfour	SNP	3,959	11.33	+0.70
John Curtis	Referendum	922	2.64	-
Peter Neilson	UK Independence	202	0.58	-
David Lucas	NLP	42	0.12	-

Liberal Democrat majority: 7,906 (22.63%)
Swing: 5.16% Conservative to Liberal Democrat

1983–92

	Lab%	Con%	SNP%	Lib%	Other%	Turnout%
1992	8.6	34.3	10.2	46.9	-	77.6
1987	8.8	37.2	4.8	49.2	-	76.8
1983	7.4	39.6	2.7	50.3	-	75.0

Roxburgh and Berwickshire was created from the division of David Steel's old seat Roxburgh, Selkirk and Peebles into two seats in the 1983 boundary redistribution. Steel chose to stand in the Tweeddale, Ettrick and Lauderdale seat and Archy Kirkwood in Roxburgh and Berwickshire. The largest town in Roxburgh and Berwickshire is Hawick, with smaller towns including Jedburgh and Kelso. It is a predominantly rural constituency covered in part by the Southern Uplands and much farmland; it is known the world over for its textile industries, tourism, and as the Scottish home of rugby.

Roxburgh's birth saw an intriguing contest in 1983 between Archy Kirkwood, the Liberal-SDP Alliance candidate and the Conservative Iain Sproat, who was MP for Aberdeen South and had assessed the Borders seat was a safer prospect after boundary changes. This was a complete misjudgment as the Conservatives held Aberdeen South, while Kirkwood defeated Sproat by 3,396 votes. Kirkwood then marginally increased his majority to 4,008 in 1987 and 4,257 in 1992 on both occasions over the Conservatives.

In 1997, Archy Kirkwood increased his majority over the Conservatives to 7,906 as the Lib Dem vote rose marginally in numbers and per cent, the Conservatives declined by 3,000 and Labour moved from fourth to third picking up 2,000 in their support. The 1999 elections resulted in the Lib Dems winning the seat with a 3,585 majority over the Conservatives; the Lib Dem vote fell by 5,000, while the Conservatives slipped by 500 and the SNP rose by 1,000 moving into third ahead of Labour. The Lib Dems' victory with 40.6 per cent was the lowest vote they have achieved in five contests in the seat, while the Conservative share in 1999 was the first time their vote rose in percentage terms. The Lib Dems look safe here for the time being, but a serious Conservative revival cannot be entirely ruled out at some point.

MP Archy Kirkwood was born in 1946 in Glasgow and has been MP for Roxburgh and Berwickshire since 1983. Educated at Cranhill School and Heriot-Watt University, he qualified as a solicitor and notary public and then worked as an aide to David Steel MP from 1971 to 1975 and 1977 to 1978, while in between he was youth campaign director of Britain in Europe at the time of the 1975 referendum.

Kirkwood was Liberal Spokesman on Health and Social Sciences from 1985 to 1987, Liberal-SDP Alliance Spokesman on Overseas Development in 1987, Spokesman on Scotland from 1987 to 1988, Liberal Democrat Convenor on Welfare, Health and Education from 1988 to 1989, Deputy Chief Whip and Spokesman on Welfare and Social Security from 1989 to 1992, Chief Whip from 1993 to 1997 and Spokesman on Community Care from 1994 to 1997. He has been Liberal Democrat Social Security Spokesperson from 1997 and Chair of the Social Security Select Committee since 1997. Kirkwood was initially a member of the Labour Party before working for David Steel and has never entirely lost the sentiments that took him into Labour, having been a member of CND and positioned on the radical wing of the Liberal Democrats.

MSP Euan Robson was born in 1954 in Corbridge, Northumberland, and educated at Trinity College, Glenalmond, University of Newcastle-upon-Tyne where he obtained a BA Hons in History, and Strathclyde University, gaining a MSc in Political Science. He worked as a teacher at the King Edward VI School, Morpeth, from 1976 to 1979, was Deputy Secretary, Gas Consumers' Northern Council from 1981 until 1986 and Scottish Manager, Gas Consumers' Council from 1986 to 1999. Robson was also a councillor on Northumberland County Council from 1981 to 1989 and was Secretary to the Liberal-SDP Alliance Group from 1981 to 1987.

He was Liberal Democrat Spokesperson for Rural Affairs and Team Leader on Fisheries from May 1999 to December 2000 when he became Spokesperson on Justice. He served on the Audit Committee of the Scottish Parliament and Justice Committee from May 1999 to December 2000 and now serves on both the Justice I and Justice II Committees. He is also a member of the Cross Party Groups on Borders Rail, Oil and Gas, of which he is Secretary, Rail Services and Agriculture and Horticulture.

STIRLING

Predecessor Constituencies: Stirlingshire West (1945–79), Stirling, Falkirk and Grangemouth (1974–79) and Stirling and Falkirk Burghs (1945–71).

1999

Electorate: 52,904
Turnout: 35,805 (67.68%)

Candidate	Party	Votes	Votes%	Change%
Sylvia Jackson	Labour	13,533	37.80	−9.65
Annabelle Ewing	SNP	9,552	26.68	+13.29
Brian Monteith	Conservative	9,158	25.58	−6.94
Iain McFarlane	Liberal Democrat	3,407	9.52	+3.87
Simon Kilgour	Independent	155	0.43	−

Labour majority: 3,981 (11.12%)
Swing: 11.47% Labour to SNP

1997

Electorate: 52,491
Turnout: 42,958 (81.84%)

Candidate	Party	Votes	Votes%	Change%
Anne McGuire	Labour	20,382	47.45	+8.83
Michael Forsyth	Conservative	13,971	32.52	−6.66
Ewan Dow	SNP	5,752	13.39	−1.11
Alistair Tough	Liberal Democrat	2,675	6.23	−0.50
William McMurdo	UK Independence	154	0.36	−
Elaine Olsen	Value	24	0.06	−

Majority: 6,411 (14.93%)
Swing: 7.75% Conservative to Labour

1983–92

	Lab%	Con%	SNP%	Lib%	Other%	Turnout%
1992	38.5	40.0	13.7	7.0	0.8	82.3
1987	36.5	37.8	10.7	14.9	−	78.1
1983	27.9	40.0	8.2	23.9	−	75.7

Stirling and Falkirk Burghs (1945–71); Stirling, Falkirk and Grangemouth (1974–79)

	Lab%	Con%	SNP%	Lib%	Other%	Turnout%
1979	56.5	26.6	16.9	–	–	78.9
1974O	43.2	14.1	39.8	2.9	–	79.4
1974F	41.9	23.6	34.5	–	–	81.2
1971B	46.5	18.9	34.6	–	–	60.0
1970	50.7	34.8	14.5	–	–	73.1
1966	52.7	31.2	14.4	–	1.7	77.1
1964	52.4	37.6	10.0	–	–	79.9
1959	49.6	43.8	6.6	–	–	81.1
1955	48.2	45.1	6.7	–	–	79.7
1951	52.3	47.7	-	–	–	86.1
1950	49.0	45.5	3.7	–	1.8	84.4
1948B	49.0	42.8	8.2	–	–	72.9
1945	56.1	43.9	–	–	–	71.5

Stirlingshire West (1945–79)

	Lab%	Con%	SNP%	Lib%	Other%	Turnout%
1979	47.7	25.7	18.3	8.3	–	82.0
1974O	39.0	18.4	38.2	4.4	–	80.7
1974F	40.8	29.5	29.7	–	–	82.7
1970	48.9	29.7	21.4	–	–	79.0
1966	48.6	25.4	26.6	–	–	82.4
1964	58.8	41.2	–	–	–	81.2
1959	57.5	42.5	–	–	–	83.6
1955	54.6	45.4	–	–	–	80.4
1951	56.0	44.0	–	–	–	86.7
1950	55.6	44.4	–	–	–	85.7
1945	54.4	45.6	–	–	–	75.0

The Stirling constituency does not just involve the town of Stirling itself, but a broad swathe of towns and villages through to the Trossachs and north-west towards Crianlarich. The constituency contains Aberfoyle, Callander, Doune, Dunblane, Killin, Lochearnhead and a host of smaller settlements such as Gargunnock and Thornhill. It stretches along beautiful countryside and lochs such as Loch Earn, Loch Tay, Loch Lubnaig and Loch Katrine, that cut through the mountains within the constituency. Much of it is picture postcard country with a deserved reputation for tourism and heaps of history: Stirling Castle, the Wallace Monument, Bannockburn and Inchmahone Priory.

Politically, the seat has been a Conservative-Labour marginal since its formation in 1983. The former MP, Michael Forsyth, held the seat for the Conservatives from 1983 to 1997. He was an able and popular local MP with an effective political organisation running out of the Tory office in Stirling. Forsyth was frequently tipped to lose the seat, but clung on in 1987 and 1992 against the odds. In 1987, Forsyth in the second contest with Michael Connarty, then left-wing leader of the local council, held on by 548 votes, and in 1992, he triumphed against Labour's Kate Phillips by 703 votes, as both parties increased their votes by 2,000 votes. His success was due to his assiduous work as a local MP as well as his ability to mobilise support in the rural areas, small towns and the Conservative parts of Stirling. The 1997 Labour landslide was to prove a bridge too far for Forsyth, despite his prominence as Secretary of State for Scotland. Forsyth was one of three senior government ministers to lose their seats in Scotland on 1 May, along with Malcolm Rifkind and Ian Lang.

Whilst Labour had challenged in Stirling on numerous occasions, and indeed had held the seat in its previous incarnations, it proved ineffective in campaigning in the constituency until 1997. In 1996, Labour selected the experienced Anne McGuire as the candidate. She was selected early via an all-women's short-list and was able to devote considerable time to campaigning in the constituency before the election. Labour established an office in Stirling with a full-time organiser, who proceeded to develop the latest New Labour campaign techniques in the constituency in advance of the general election. Telephone canvassing of the constituency began in 1996, beginning with Labour's weakest areas, and Anne McGuire engaged in a tour of the constituency that year which took her around all the towns and villages where the Conservatives were strong. This tour was significant as Stirling is one of those seats in which the local voters like to see and meet the candidates on their own turf. Taking the fight to these areas, rather than just concentrating on Stirling town, was of great benefit to Labour, though given the nature of the landslide this seat would have swung Labour's way regardless: however, that is being wise after the event.

Whilst Labour's ability to turn a highly marginal seat into one with a healthy majority in 1997 is a guide to the future of the seat, two other things are significant. First, the SNP did extraordinarily well in 1999. It gained its best ever result in Stirling with a substantial numerical and percentage increase in its support and pushed the Tories into third place. Second, the Conservatives enjoyed a very mixed showing in 1999. At the Scottish election, a high-profile Conservative, Brian Montieth, managed to come third in a two-horse race. But, on the same day, the Conservatives experienced a strong comeback at the local elections in Stirling – though this was perhaps predictable given the party's local election disaster in 1995. The Tories followed up their good showing in the local elections by taking a seat from the SNP at a council by-election in 2000. However, the circumstances of this contest were quite unique as the former councillor had been removed from office by the SNP and then the council for non-attendance.

Though the Conservatives may recover support in Stirling at the next election, Labour is likely to hold on. The local MP and MSP have good political profiles in the constituency and have worked hard to establish themselves on local issues. The absence of Forsyth does not help. He will not fight the seat again following his elevation to the House of Lords. The Tories selected Geoff Mawdsley as their candidate in February 2000. He is a political advisor to Scottish Tory leader David McLetchie, and comes from Edinburgh. He will have to work hard to establish a profile in the constituency to overtake Anne McGuire at the general election.

MP Anne McGuire was born in 1949 in Glasgow and educated at Our Lady of St Francis, Glasgow, Glasgow University in Politics and History and then Notre Dame College of Education in Glasgow. She worked as a teacher, as Development Officer of Community Service Volunteers from 1984 to 1988, becoming Scottish National Officer from 1988 to 1993, and then Deputy Director of the Scottish Council for Voluntary Organisations from 1993 to 1997. She was briefly a Strathclyde Regional Councillor from 1980–2 and was shortlisted for a number of seats, including the Govan by-election in 1988, only for male candidates to triumph – disastrously in the case of Govan – despite her obvious talent. McGuire was election agent to Norman Hogg in Cumbernauld and Kilsyth in the 1983, 1987 and 1992 elections, became a member of the Scottish Labour Executive in 1984 and was Chair of the party from 1992–3.

She was also one of three candidates for consideration as Labour's Scottish General Secretary after the 1992 election defeat, the others being Johanna Lamont and Jack McConnell, with the latter appointed. There was widespread criticism of the appointment at the time, because two able women had been passed over and Scottish Labour was having severe problems selecting women candidates in winnable seats. When she was finally selected in Stirling it was via the all-women's shortlist. She was identified as one of the leading figures in the 'Network', seen by some on the left of the party as a sinister organisation, but by its supporters, as an attempt to bring Blairite modernisation to the party north of the border. After the 1997 election, this became known as Scottish Labour Forum. At Westminster, she was a member of the European Legislation Committee from 1997 to 1998 and was Parliamentary Private Secretary to Donald Dewar at the Scottish Office from 1997 to 1998. She is currently an assistant whip.

MSP Sylvia Jackson was born in 1946. She is a chemistry and education graduate of Hull University, with a PhD in education from Stirling University. She was a teacher, education researcher and lecturer before her election, lecturing most recently at Moray House. She was formerly chair and secretary of Central Region Labour Party, a member of the Scottish Policy Forum and Chair of Labour's Local Government Committee in Scotland. She has been a member of the Local Government Committee since May 1999 and was a member of the European Committee of the Scottish Parliament from May 1999 to December 2000. She has sponsored a number of member's debates in the Scottish Parliament, including the first piece of member's business on Cornton Vale Prison, and has developed a strong profile in the local media around Stirling.

STRATHKELVIN AND BEARSDEN

Predecessor Constituencies: Dumbarton District of Burghs (1945) and Dunbartonshire East (1950–79).

1999

Electorate: 63,111
Turnout: 42,390 (67.17%)

Candidate	Party	Votes	Votes%	Change%
Sam Galbraith	Labour	21,505	50.73	−2.13
Fiona McLeod	SNP	9,384	22.14	+5.82
Charles Ferguson	Conservative	6,934	16.36	−3.73
Anne Howarth	Liberal Democrat	4,144	9.78	−0.04
Maxi Richards	Anti-Drug	423	1.00	−

Labour majority: 12,121 (28.59%)
Swing: 3.98% Labour to SNP

1997

Electorate: 62,974
Turnout: 49,712 (71.00%)

Candidate	Party	Votes	Votes%	Change%
Sam Galbraith	Labour	26,278	52.86	+6.77
David Sharpe	Conservative	9,986	20.09	−2.47
Graeme McCormick	SNP	8,111	16.32	+3.42
John Morrison	Liberal Democrat	4,843	9.74	+1.46
David Wilson	Referendum	339	0.68	−
Janice Fisher	NLP	155	0.31	−

Labour majority: 16,292 (32.77%)
Swing: 9.62% Conservative to Labour

	Lab%	Con%	SNP%	Lib%	Other%	Turnout%
1992	42.3	36.0	12.5	9.1	0.2	82.3
1987	38.1	33.4	7.1	21.4	–	82.1
1983	25.6	36.4	9.2	28.7	–	79.3
1979	37.8	34.1	20.6	7.5	–	83.
1974O	30.3	31.2	31.2	7.3	–	80.7
1974F	29.6	36.7	22.3	11.4	–	85.0
1970	44.7	37.0	11.3	4.7	2.3	77.8
1966	52.2	36.4	9.0	–	2.4	80.6
1964	55.0	42.0	–	–	3.0	82.5
1959	51.1	44.9	–	–	4.0	84.2
1955	48.7	46.4	–	–	4.9	81.6
1951	51.3	44.6	–	–	4.1	86.6
1950	52.6	43.4	–	4.0	–	86.0
1945	65.2	34.8	–	–	–	73.2

Strathkelvin and Bearsden is situated north of Glasgow, and along with Eastwood to the south of the city sits outside the local authority boundaries of Glasgow and houses the middle-class professionals who work in Glasgow, but choose to live and pay council tax outside. The main towns are Bearsden, Bishopbriggs and Kirkintilloch. Even in the most affluent parts of the seat, at a council level the Liberal Democrats, rather than the Conservatives, enjoy support as the main opposition to Labour.

As Dumbarton, and then Dunbartonshire East, Labour held this seat for the immediate post-war era. In February 1974, in a three-way split between Labour, Conservatives and SNP, the Tory Barry Henderson won the seat on 36.7 per cent from Labour, only to lose it months later in October 1974 to the SNP's Margaret Bain who won 31.2 per cent and a majority of 22 over Henderson, with Labour in third place 400 votes behind. In 1979, Labour's Norman Hogg came from third to win the seat over the Conservatives' Michael Hirst with a 2,324 majority, but in 1983 in the new Strathkelvin and Bearsden, Hirst won with a 3,700 lead over the Liberal-SDP Alliance.

Scottish Labour's year of triumph, 1987, witnessed Sam Galbraith defeating Hirst with a majority of 2,452. This showed the difference between 'Bearsden man' and 'Basildon man', namely, Scottish Labour's ability to win middle-class support. In 1992, Galbraith broke the pattern of recent volatility, holding the seat with an increased majority of 3,162 over the Conservatives. The 1997 boundary changes increased Labour's majority to a notional 6,948, and in the 1997 election

Galbraith was returned with a vastly increased majority of 16,292 over the Conservatives. Labour's vote rose by 2,500, while the Conservatives fell by nearly 7,000.

Galbraith was the Labour candidate in the first Scottish Parliament elections and saw a 5,000 fall in Labour's vote, while the Nationalists moved from third to second as their vote increased by over 1000. Labour's majority over the SNP was an impressive 12,121. Strathkelvin and Bearsden has become in a relatively short time a safe Labour seat; this is still, even for the West of Scotland, unnatural territory for Labour, but the Conservatives who held this seat as recently as 1987 now poll 16 per cent and any serious challenge to Labour's new-found dominance looks unlikely.

MP/MSP Sam Galbraith was born in 1945 and was elected MP for Strathkelvin and Bearsden in 1983 and MSP for the seat from 1999. Educated at Greenock High School and the University of Glasgow, Galbraith became a consultant neurosurgeon with Greater Glasgow Health Board and worked at the Institute of Neurological Sciences, Southern General Hospital, Glasgow, from 1978 until 1987.

He was appointed a Spokesperson on Scotland and Health from 1988 to 1992 and then on Employment from 1992 to 1993. Following serious health problems, surgery and a period of recuperation, Galbraith entered government as Under-Secretary at the Scottish Office responsible for health and arts from 1997 to 1999. In the Scottish Parliament elections he was campaign spokesperson for Health, Sports and Arts. After the elections, he was a member of Labour's five-strong negotiating team with the Liberal Democrats on forming a coalition, and subsequently became Minister for Children and Education. Galbraith was seen as one of the tried and tested safe Westminster hands who would guide and aid those less experienced, but he was involved in two of the biggest controversies of the Parliament. In April 2000, he was involved in producing the Scottish Executive U-turn on Section 28/Clause 2A, introducing statutory guidelines on sex education in schools. Many felt Galbraith should have done the decent thing and resigned. In August 2000, a major crisis exploded on the accuracy and reliability of the Higher Still grades given to students, and several resignations occurred in the Scottish Qualifications Authority. There were this time even more widespread calls for Galbraith to resign but, although he emerged weakened, he had every intention of remaining in post and seeing through the crisis.

The election of Henry McLeish as First Minister provided an ideal opportunity in his ministerial reshuffle to sack Galbraith, but McLeish chose to remain loyal to him. Instead, he was moved from the controversial area of Education, and given the post of Minister for the Environment, which was detached from Sarah Boyack's portfolio (she being the other minister who had been most vulnerable to the sack). Environment has never been an area Galbraith has shown any prior interest or expertise in, but it has been given to him at the moment to save Henry McLeish from the embarrassment of having to sack one of his colleagues.

TAYSIDE NORTH

Predecessor Constituencies: created anew from Perth and East Perthshire (1945–79) and Angus South (1945–79).

1999

Electorate: 61,795
Turnout: 38,055 (61.58%)

Candidate	Party	Votes	Votes%	Change%
John Swinney	SNP	16,786	44.11	−0.74
Murdo Fraser	Conservative	12,594	33.09	−2.63
Marion Dingwall	Labour	5,727	15.05	+3.77
Peter Regent	Liberal Democrat	2,948	7.75	−0.40

Majority: 4,192 (11.02%)
Swing: 0.94% Conservative to SNP

1997

Electorate: 61,398
Turnout: 45,591 (74.25%)

Candidate	Party	Votes	Votes%	Change%
John Swinney	SNP	20,447	44.85	+6.06
Bill Walker	Conservative	16,287	35.72	−10.65
Ian McFatridge	Labour	5,141	11.28	+4.32
Perer Regent	Liberal Democrat	3,716	8.15	+0.26

Majority: 4,160 (9.13%)
Swing: 8.36% Conservative to SNP

1983–92

	Lab%	Con%	SNP%	Lib%	Other%	Turnout%
1992	7.1	46.7	37.5	8.7	—	77.6
1987	8.8	45.4	32.9	12.9	—	74.7
1983	5.4	51.0	24.3	19.2	—	72.6

This constituency stretches in the east to Brechin and Forfar, westwards through Blairgowrie and Coupar Angus, then to the north to Birnam and Dunkeld, Pitlochry and Blair Atholl and to the west along Loch Rannoch. Tayside North was established in 1983, but it has its origins in Perth and East Perthshire (see Perth for results). The seat was formerly safely Conservative from 1924 to 1970, until Douglas Crawford won narrowly by 793 votes for the SNP in October 1974. The Tories regained the seat in 1979 and held it with maverick Conservative Bill Walker, before John Swinney regained the seat for the Nationalists in 1997 and again at the Scottish election in 1999.

Historically this was one of the SNP's earliest contested seats, partly attributable to the fact that the party leader in the 1960s, Arthur Donaldson, lived in Forfar in the constituency. The Nationalists contested Perth and East Perthshire as early as 1945, and Donaldson himself served as Provost of Forfar. The Nationalists therefore had a foothold in this seat for decades which had them coming second to the Tories as far back as 1955 and 1959. The party was organised in the seat for several decades and improvements in campaigning organisation after 1992 helped deliver the seat to the Nationalists in 1997.

However, despite such longevity in this seat, the SNP has not cast aside the Conservative challenge. Though the Tory vote declined between the 1997 and 1999 elections, the party remains strong in Tayside North. If the Tory vote picks up in Scotland at the next Westminster election, then this is one seat they would expect to recover. The SNP itself faces a new situation as the sitting MP John Swinney is standing down from Westminster to concentrate on the Scottish Parliament. He was SNP candidate at successive elections from 1992 to 1999 and has built a political profile in the constituency. He is also now SNP leader and leader of the opposition in the Scottish Parliament. The new SNP candidate for Westminster is Pete Wishart, the Runrig musician who has been an SNP office-bearer in recent years. The SNP, however, is not merely strong at national elections in the constituency, but also at local elections and should win and win well. A large part of the SNP's contingent on Perth and Kinross Council has come from Tayside North over recent years, whilst other parts of the seat elect SNP members to Angus Council. The SNP therefore has strength in depth in this area.

MP/MSP John Swinney was born in Edinburgh in 1964 and educated at Forrester High School, Edinburgh and Edinburgh University, from which he has a degree in Politics. He was employed as a researcher on the Scottish Coal Project at Napier University, as an economic consultant in SNP leadership contender Alex Neil's consultancy company and then as a strategic planner with Scottish Amicable before his election to Westminster in 1997. He contested Tayside North for the first time in 1992 and has been one of the SNP's rising stars for more than a decade, holding a series of key posts within the party such as National Secretary, Vice-Convenor for Publicity and Deputy Leader. Now, of course, he is SNP leader, following his crushing victory over Alex Neil. In the Scottish Parliament, he was Convenor of the Enterprise and Lifelong Learning Committee from 1999 to 2000 and played a key role in the development of co-operative relations between the committee and the then Enterprise Minister, Henry McLeish, in the areas of economic development agencies and tourism. The committee was also notable for establishing links with the business community, through its sponsorship of 'business in the chamber' in 1999, which featured business representatives debating economic development policy within the Scottish Parliament chamber for a day. However, since his convincing election as SNP leader in September 2000, he will serve as leader of the opposition rather than a committee convenor.

How he develops as a party leader and as McLeish's main opponent in the Scottish Parliament chamber remains to be seen. Swinney was the architect of the SNP's 'A Penny for Scotland' policy in the 1999 Scottish Parliament elections, whereby the SNP tried to outflank Labour by promising extra public spending, not by tax increases, but by refusing Gordon Brown's 'tax bribe'. Most voters saw this as a tax increase, and it allowed Labour to pour cold water over the SNP's plans. After the election, the extent to which the SNP engaged in a post-election analysis was minimal, although it was recognised that 'A Penny for Scotland' had been tactically mishandled. In the leadership contest between Swinney and Neil, there was little sense of revisionism by either participant, with Swinney defending 'A Penny for Scotland', which has been compared to the SNP's equivalent of John Smith's 1992 Shadow Budget, while Neil still vainly defended the ill-fated 'Free by '93' campaign of which he had been the architect.

Swinney is already an SNP old hand at 36, despite having only been elected in 1997 to Westminster. He takes over the SNP when it is at a higher plateau than it has been at any point since October 1974. Whether Swinney has the political skills and acumen to take the SNP to the next stage of the political transformation, and shift it from a credible party of opposition which they now undoubtably are, to being a party of government, and ultimately, independence, will be the main challenge of his leadership.

TWEEDDALE, ETTRICK AND LAUDERDALE

Predecessor Constituencies: Roxburghshire and Selkirkshire (1945–51) and Roxburgh, Selkirk and Peebles (1955–79).

1999

Electorate: 51,577
Turnout: 33,715 (65.37%)

Candidate	Party	Votes	Votes%	Change%
Ian Jenkins	Liberal Democrat	12,078	35.82	+4.60
Christine Creech	SNP	7,600	22.54	+5.44
George McGregor	Labour	7,546	22.38	-5.03
John Campbell	Conservative	6,491	19.25	-2.86

Liberal Democrat majority: 4,478 (13.28%)
Swing: 0.42% Liberal Democrat to SNP

1997

Electorate: 50,891
Turnout: 39,001 (76.64%)

Candidate	Party	Votes	Votes%	Change%
Michael Moore	Liberal Democrat	12,178	31.22	-3.82
Keith Geddes	Labour	10,689	27.41	10.99
Alister Jack	Conservative	8,623	22.11	-8.57
Ian Goldie	SNP	6,671	17.10	-0.06
Christopher Mowbray	Referendum	406	1.04	—
John Hein	Liberal	387	0.99	—
Duncan Paterson	NLP	47	0.12	—

Liberal Democrat majority: 1,489 (3.81%)
Swing: 7.41% Liberal Democrat to Labour

1945–92

	Lab%	Con%	SNP%	Lib%	Other%	Turnout%
1992	10.8	31.7	17.0	39.9	0.6	78.1
1987	11.4	29.6	9.1	49.9	—	76.5

	Lab%	Con%	SNP%	Lib%	Other%	Turnout%
1983	7.6	28.9	5.0	58.5	–	77.0
1979	8.5	31.3	7.1	53.1	–	82.0
1974O	8.9	27.4	20.0	43.7	–	79.2
1974F	6.3	33.6	8.0	52.1	–	86.1
1970	9.6	41.1	6.8	42.3	0.2	80.8
1966	13.6	40.8	–	45.6	–	84.9
1965B	11.3	38.6	–	49.2	0.9	82.2
1964	15.8	42.8	2.5	38.9	–	82.2
1959	21.0	50.2	–	28.8	–	80.0
1955	20.2	47.7	–	32.1	–	80.8
1951	20.8	40.6	–	38.6	–	84.9
1950	24.7	36.4	–	39.4	–	82.1
1945	28.9	37.9	–	33.2	–	73.6

Tweeddale can be found in the Scottish Borders between Lothian and the city of Edinburgh to the north and Roxburgh and Berwickshire to the south. Its towns include Galashiels, Peebles and Selkirk, while parts of Midlothian, including Penicuik were added in the last boundary changes. As Roxburghshire and Selkirkshire, and then Roxburgh, Selkirk and Peebles, this seat has long Conservative traditions. In 1945 the Conservative Lt Col Lord William Scott held it with the narrow majority of 1,628 over the Liberals and in 1950 the Tories narrowly lost the seat to the Liberals with a majority of 1,156 – one of two Liberal gains in Scotland that year (the other being Orkney and Shetland which Jo Grimond won). Their hold on Roxburghshire was to be very brief and in 1951 the Conservatives' Charles Donaldson won it back with a slender majority of 829.

The Conservatives held the newly named Roxburgh, Selkirk and Peebles until 1965 when a 26-year-old David Steel won it from the Conservatives; in 1970 after prominently supporting a swathe of sixties liberal legislation and causes (abortion, gay rights, anti-apartheid), Steel's majority was cut to 550 votes. He held on and increased his majority to 7,443 over the Conservatives in October 1974 and became Liberal Party leader in 1976, before seeing his majority rise to 10,690 over the Conservatives in 1979.

Steel held on comfortably in the new Tweeddale, Ettrick and Lauderdale seat in 1983 and 1987 as Liberal Party leader, elections where the potential of third-party breakthrough stretched Steel's skills and stamina to the limit. However, the mould singularly failed to break and in 1987 his majority fell dramatically to 5,942 over the Conservatives. At the following election, Steel got a bigger shock as his majority fell further to 2,520; this was put down by commentators to several years' excessive Lib-Labbery in Scotland in the Scottish Constitutional Convention, with other colleagues such as Malcolm Bruce in Gordon suffering similar fates.

Boundary changes in 1997 cut the Lib Dem lead over the Tories to a notional 1,735 and, with Steel deciding to quit Westminster after thirty years, Lib Dem prospects looked poor. However, they held on with a 1,489 lead over Labour as Keith Geddes moved into second place increasing his vote by 4,000 (11 per cent), while the Conservatives, slipping to third, lost 3,500 votes. The Lib Dems' share of 31.2 per cent was their lowest vote in the seat since 1959 and the lowest vote for any winning candidate in the 1997 election. The Lib Dems after that scare held on easily in 1999, increasing their majority to 4,478 over the SNP and winning 35.8 per cent of the vote. Thus in the last three contests the Lib Dems have faced in second place three different parties – SNP, Labour, Conservatives – and have seen them all off. Tweeddale's second incarnation as a Liberal seat looks set to continue for a while.

MP Michael Moore was born in 1965 and elected MP for Tweeddale, Ettrick and Lauderdale in 1997, taking over the Liberal Democrat mantle in the seat from David Steel who had been MP for 32 years. Educated at Strathallan School, Jedburgh Grammar School and Edinburgh University, with a BA Hons in Politics and Modern History, he worked as a Research Assistant to Archy Kirkwood from 1987 to 1988 and as a Chartered Accountant from 1991 to 1997 becoming a manager in Corporate Finance Practice at Coopers and Lybrand from 1993 to 1997. He was the Liberal Democrats' Scottish Spokesman on Business and Employment from 1995 to 1997, Spokesman on the Economy and Health from 1997 and a member of the Scottish Affairs Select Committee. He was the campaign manager of the Lib Dems for the Scottish Parliament elections, and despite being an MP, headed the Lib Dems' five-strong negotiating team with Labour on agreeing a coalition government. He has been Scottish Spokesman of the Lib Dems from 1999.

MSP Ian Jenkins was born in 1941 in Rothesay and educated at Rothesay Academy and Glasgow University, obtaining a MA Honours in English Language and Literature and a Diploma in Education. He was a teacher of English at Clydebank High School from 1964 until 1970 and Principal Teacher of English, Peebles High School, from 1970 to 1999.

He is Liberal Democrat Spokesman for Education Culture and Sport, is Deputy Convenor of the Subordinate Legislation Committee and the Education, Culture and Sport Committee of the Parliament. Jenkins is also a member of the Cross Party Groups on Borders Rail and Media, both of which he is Vice-Convenor of, Tobacco Control and Sport.

WESTERN ISLES

Predecessor Constituencies: none.

1999

Electorate: 22,412
Turnout: 13,954 (62.26%)

Candidate	Party	Votes	Votes%	Change%
Alasdair Morrison	Labour	7,248	51.94	-3.66
Alasdair Nicholson	SNP	5,155	36.94	+3.54
Jamie McGrigor	Conservative	1,095	7.85	+1.21
John Horne	Liberal Democrat	456	3.27	+0.20

Labour majority: 2,093 (15.00%)
Swing: 3.6% Labour to SNP

1997

Electorate: 22,983
Turnout: 16,106 (70.08%)

Candidate	Party	Votes	Votes%	Change%
Calum MacDonald	Labour	8,955	55.60	+7.79
Anne Lorne Gillies	SNP	5,379	33.40	-3.79
Jamie McGrigor	Conservative	1,071	6.65	-1.85
Neil Mitchison	Liberal Democrat	495	3.07	-0.37
Ralph Lionel	Referendum	206	1.28	—

Labour majority: 3,576 (22.2%)
Swing: 5.79% SNP to Labour

1945–92

	Lab%	Con%	SNP%	Lib%	Other%	Turnout%
1992	47.8	8.5	37.2	3.4	3.2	70.4
1987	42.7	8.1	28.5	20.7	—	70.1
1983	30.1	9.6	54.5	5.8	—	66.5
1979	32.3	10.6	52.5	4.6	—	67.5
1974O	24.7	8.3	61.5	5.5	—	61.5
1974F	19.1	6.9	67.0	—	6.9	67.4
1970	38.4	18.5	43.1	—	—	64.8

	Lab%	Con%	SNP%	Lib%	Other%	Turnout%
1966	61.0	20.2	–	18.8	–	61.5
1964	55.1	14.0	–	30.9	–	66.9
1959	53.6	46.4	–	–	–	64.2
1955	57.3	42.7	–	–	–	59.6
1951	48.7	40.7	5.0	5.6	–	60.5
1950	53.2	–	–	44.1	2.7	55.7
1945	45.7	21.3	–	33.0	–	53.3

The Western Isles seat has existed as a single entity for decades, even when its area was divided between different county councils. The seat stretches from the Butt of Lewis to Barra, incorporating the isles of Lewis, Harris, North Uist, Benbecula, South Uist and a host of smaller isles. Its main towns are Stornoway, Tarbert and Lochmaddy, though Stornoway has the largest share of the population by a long way. The seat is distinctive both in UK and Scottish terms as it is a Gaelic-speaking area with a significant crofting population, a dependency on ferry transport from Caledonian MacBrayne and a religious makeup which has a conservative, sabbatarian aspect to it. Whilst the south of the constituency is Catholic, and Scottish/Highland not Irish Catholic, the north is Free Church of Scotland (the wee frees), which explains the sabbatarian outlook, with Sunday closing still practised and a require-ment for the MP and MSP to recognise such attitudes when dealing with social/moral questions in their respective Parliaments. Because of this situation, one can suppose the local MSP, Alasdair Morrison, did not have a very entertaining time during the Section 28/Clause 2A debate in the Scottish Parliament from 1999 to 2000.

Politically, and despite its moral and social conservatism, the seat has never been anything but Labour or SNP for decades. The SNP's Donald Stewart won the seat in 1970 and held it until his retirement before the 1987 general election, usually winning with more than 50 per cent of the vote. In 1987 the seat reverted to Labour, evidence that previous SNP sucess was due to the impact of Stewart's personality in the seat rather than simply the popularity of the SNP. The current MP, Calum MacDonald, has held the seat comfortably ever since, a feat also achieved by Alasdair Morrison in 1999 at the Scottish election. Indeed, their level of support is compa-rable to that enjoyed by Donald Stewart.

Both MacDonald and Morrison have benefited from their local status, their ability as native Gaelic-speakers and the popularity of Labour. As this is a distinctive constituency with a tradition of Independent council representation, it is also clear that the local MP and MSP attract something of a personal vote attached to their political performance which favours the incumbent. Labour is therefore likely to hold this seat for some time to come, barring an SNP landslide.

MP Calum MacDonald was born in 1956 in Stornoway, the son of a crofter and weaver. He was educated at Bayble School and Nicolson Institute, Stornaway and studied political philosophy at Edinburgh University and the University of California, Los Angeles. He was elected in 1987 and was Parliamentary Private Secretary to Donald Dewar at the Scottish Office in 1997, before becoming Parliamentary Under-Secretary of State in the Scottish Office from 1997 to 1999, with responsibility for Housing, Transport and the EU. He was also a member of the Select Committee on Agriculture from 1987 to 1992. MacDonald was helped in his election in 1987 by Kenneth Macmillan, the son of Malcolm Macmillan, Labour MP for the area from 1935 until 1970. He has been both a crofter, following in his father's footsteps and an academic, having been a teaching fellow in political philosophy at the University of California from 1982–5, as well as working in his brother's local retail business selling kitchen and bathroom fittings from 1986–7. He has an eclectic range of political perspectives which make him difficult to categorise: pro-European (he was one of only five Labour MPs to vote in favour of the Maastricht Treaty in 1993), anti-abortion and embryo experimentation, he is also a committed devolutionist and supporter of the Gaelic language.

MSP Alasdair Morrison was born on North Uist in 1968. He is Deputy Minister for Enterprise in the Highlands and Islands and Gaelic. He became when the new Executive was established the youngest minister in the government, having just turned 30 years of age. First working to Henry McLeish, he now works with Wendy Alexander, where the expectation is of a more pro-active, dynamic environment. Morrison is responsible for a wide array of areas: Highlands and Islands Enterprise, the University of the Highlands and Islands, tourism and Gaelic. He is one of two native Gaelic-speakers in the Parliament and was formerly a BBC journalist in Stornoway and has also been editor of the Gaelic newspaper *An Gaidheal Ur*. His brother John is BBC Scotland's Political Correspondent.

WEST RENFREWSHIRE

Predecessor Constituencies: Renfrewshire West (1945–79) and Renfrew West and Inverclyde (1983–92).

1999

Electorate: 52,452
Turnout: 34,037 (64.89%)

Candidate	Party	Votes	Votes%	Change%
Patricia Godman	Labour	12,708	37.34	-9.22
Colin Campbell	SNP	9,815	28.84	+2.33
Annabel Goldie	Conservative	7,243	21.28	+2.71
Neal Ascherson	Liberal Democrat	2,659	7.81	+0.16
Allan McGraw	Independent	1,136	3.34	—
Patrick Clark	SWP	476	1.40	—

Labour majority: 2,893 (8.50%)
Swing: 5.77% Labour to SNP

1997

Electorate: 52,348
Turnout: 39,786 (76.00%)

Candidate	Party	Votes	Votes%	Change%
Thomas Graham	Labour	18,525	46.56	+3.69
Colin Campbell	SNP	10,546	26.51	+5.90
Charles Cormack	Conservative	7,387	18.57	-9.21
Bruce MacPherson	Liberal Democrat	3,045	7.65	-0.77
Shaw Lindsay	Referendum	283	0.71	—

Labour majority: 7,979 (20.05%)
Swing: 1.11% Labour to SNP

1945–92

	Lab%	Con%	SNP%	Lib%	Other%	Turnout%
1992	36.6	32.9	20.2	10.0	—	80.3
1987	38.7	29.8	10.1	21.4	—	80.5
1983	29.0	32.7	8.7	29.5	—	78.0
1979	44.5	31.0	13.1	11.4	—	81.2

	Lab%	Con%	SNP%	Lib%	Other%	Turnout%
1974O	38.5	26.8	28.6	6.1	–	80.1
1974F	40.3	35.4	15.2	9.1	–	82.9
1970	48.0	43.2	8.8	–	–	79.5
1966	54.3	45.7	–	–	–	81.6
1964	46.1	43.8	–	10.1	–	82.9
1959	46.5	53.5	–	–	–	82.6
1955	44.8	55.2	–	–	–	83.0
1951	46.2	53.8	–	–	–	84.9
1950	46.1	53.9	–	–	–	77.6
1945	48.8	44.9	6.3	–	–	70.2

West Renfrewshire is situated between Greenock and Inverclyde and the two Paisley seats. It includes a variety of small and medium towns such as Port Glasgow, Erskine, Bridge of Weir and Kilmacolm. This is divided social territory containing both areas like Port Glasgow with a history of heavy manufacturing and shipbuilding and commuter towns such as Bridge of Weir with their desirable middle-class dwellings.

Renfrew West was first won by Labour in 1922, lost in 1924, regained in 1929, lost in the debacle of 1931, before Labour won it again in 1945 by a majority of 1,214, losing it once more to the Conservative John Maclay in 1950 with a 3,102 majority. The Conservatives then proceeded to hold the seat until Norman Buchan won it back for Labour in 1964; by 1979 he had built up his majority to 8,572 over the Conservatives. The 1983 boundary redistribution created Renfrew West and Inverclyde which was notionally a marginal seat. Local MP Norman Buchan moved to the safety of Paisley South, and Dickson Mabon, Labour MP for Greenock since 1955, stood in Renfrew West under the Liberal-SDP Alliance banner. The result was a three-way cliffhanger with the Conservatives winning the seat from Labour. Anna McCurley won with a 1,322 majority over Mabon, with Labour in third place 200 votes behind. In 1987 Tommy Graham, hardly an obvious choice in a marginal seat, took Labour from third to first, increasing its vote by 5,000 and beating McCurley by 4,063 votes despite the Conservative tally falling by a mere 100 votes; Mabon stood again and saw his support decline by 2,500.

In 1992 a strong performance by the Conservative Annabel Goldie cut Graham's majority in half to 1,744 as she put nearly 2,000 on the Conservative vote, while the SNP moved from fourth to third putting 5,000 on their support. The 1997 boundary changes made the new West Renfrewshire a more secure seat for Labour with a notional 6,046 majority. In 1997, Graham put an additional 1,000 votes on Labour's vote, while the SNP re-established themselves in second place increasing their vote by 2,000, as the Conservative vote fell by nearly 4,000. There then followed two years of allegations and scandal centred on local Labour politics in the wake of the suicide in July 1997 of Gordon McMaster, Labour MP for Paisley South, in which Tommy Graham was implicated for spreading rumours about McMaster's sexuality; he was immediately suspended from the party, pending the allegations being investigated, and expelled a year later.

The Scottish Parliament elections were awaited by Labour with unease, and came as a relief. Patricia Godman, wife of Norman Godman, MP for Greenock and Inverclyde, presided over a fall in Labour's support of nearly 6,000 votes, while the SNP vote marginally declined and the Conservatives Annabel Goldie managed the feat of holding on to most of her 1997 vote. Allan McGraw, standing as an Independent on a pro-Graham ticket, polled respectably. West Renfrewshire is a fairly safe Labour seat that it managed to hold even in the difficult circumstances of 1999, which bodes well for future elections.

MP Tommy Graham was born in 1943 in Glasgow and elected MP for Renfrew West and Inverclyde from 1987 until 1997 and for West Renfrewshire from 1997. Educated at Crookston Castle Secondary School, Glasgow, and Stow College of Engineering, Glasgow, Graham became a machine tool engineer with Rolls Royce and an office manager in a firm of solicitors.

Elected to Renfrew District Council from 1974 to 1977 and Strathclyde Regional Council from 1978 until 1986, Graham was heading for a life of political obscurity until, after the 1997 election Gordon McMaster, the MP for Paisley South, committed suicide and named Graham in his suicide note as responsible for a campaign of smear and innuendo. Graham was immediately suspended and eventually expelled from the Labour Party. Together with Mohammed Sarwar, his fellow suspended Scots Labour MP in 1997, he suffered the embarassment of having his face used by the Tory backed 'Think Twice' anti-devolution campaign in the referendum, to remind voters of the potential face of Scottish Labour in any Parliament. Graham had been reduced to the unacceptable face of Scottish Labour – one of the Labour Jimmies as they are called – and also one that is facing political extinction after the next election.

MSP Patricia Godman was born in 1939 and educated at St Gerard's and Jordanhill College where she gained her CQSW Social Work qualification. She has worked as a social worker and bank clerk, and was elected to Strathclyde Regional Council and Glasgow City Council where she served as Vice-Convenor of the Social Work Resources Committee.

Godman is married to Norman Godman, MP for Greenock and Inverclyde since 1983. Prior to the 1992 election she stood in the Glasgow Kelvin Labour selection against sitting MP George Galloway, winning 57 per cent of party members, but losing due to the trade union block vote which was stitched up in time-honoured style. In the Scottish Parliament, Godman is Convenor of the Local Government Committee and was a member of the Subordinate Legislation Committee from May 1999 to December 2000. She is also a member of the Cross Party Groups on Children, Epilepsy, and Refugees and Asylum Seekers.

Section Two

REGIONAL SEATS

The Scottish Parliament's electoral system divides the country into 73 First Past The Post seats and eight regions each of which elect seven additional members providing a total of 56 'top up' MSPs. Voters have two votes – one for their FPTP constituency and one for a party list in their regions. The seven regional seats in each area are divided between the parties according to the relative strengths of their regional vote, to give as proportional a result as possible for the whole Parliament.

This means there is a relationship between how many seats a party wins under FPTP and how many it wins via the regional seats. Thus, Labour does relatively well under FPTP and so does not win many 'top up' seats, whereas the Conservatives and SNP who are under-represented via FPTP do well out of the regional seat system. This complex system means that whether a party wins or loses a FPTP seat has consequences for the regional seat allocation, e.g., Labour unexpected success in holding Glasgow Govan meant that Labour did not win one 'top up' seat in Glasgow. This results in a Scottish Parliament which much more accurately reflects the wishes of the Scottish electorate than would have been possible under a purely FPTP system.

CENTRAL SCOTLAND

The Central Scotland regional seat runs from Ayrshire to the River Forth, from Kilmarnock and Loudoun in the west through Lanarkshire to Falkirk East by the Forth. This is solid Labour territory and in 1992 and 1997 Labour won every one of the ten Westminster seats. In the 1997 election, Labour won 59.4 per cent of the vote to the SNP's 23.4 per cent with the Conservatives winning 10.4 per cent and the Liberal Democrats 5.2 per cent.

In the 1999 Scottish Parliament elections, Labour polled in constituency votes 46.6 per cent to the SNP's 29.9 per cent. Dennis Canavan, standing as an independent, broke Labour's hegemony in the area easily holding the Falkirk West seat. He also polled well in the regional list vote, winning significant support outside from his constituency seat – enough to cost Labour an additional member. In the regional vote, Labour won 39.3 per cent to the SNP's 27.8 per cent, with five additional members elected for the SNP, their best performance anywhere in Scotland, one for the Conservatives and one for the Liberal Democrats.

Electorate: 551,733
Turnout: 331,064 (60.00%)

Constituency Members Elected

Constituency	Member	Party
Airdrie and Shotts	Karen Whitefield	Labour
Coatbridge and Chryston	Elaine Smith	Labour
Cumbernauld and Kilsyth	Cathie Craigie	Labour
East Kilbride	Andy Kerr	Labour
Falkirk East	Cathy Peattie	Labour
Falkirk West	Dennis Canavan	MP for Falkirk West
Hamilton North and Bellshill	Michael McMahon	Labour
Hamilton South	Tom McCabe	Labour
Kilmarnock and Loudoun	Margaret Jamieson	Labour
Motherwell and Wishaw	Jack McConnell	Labour

Constituency Party Shares of the Vote

Party	Votes	% Share
Labour	154,095	46.55
SNP	98,858	29.86
Conservative	31,567	9.53
Liberal Democrat	21,911	6.66
MP for Falkirk West	18,511	5.59
Socialist Labour	4,648	1.40
SSP	1,116	0.34
SFPP	358	0.11

Additional Members Elected

Lyndsay McIntosh	Conservative
Donald Gorrie	Liberal Democrat
Linda Fabiani	SNP
Michael Matheson	SNP
Alex Neil	SNP
Gil Paterson	SNP
Andrew Wilson	SNP

Regional List Party Shares of the Vote

Party	Votes	% Share
Labour	129, 822	39.28
SNP	91,802	27.78
Conservative	30,243	9.15
MP for Falkirk West	27,700	8.38
Liberal Democrat	20,505	6.20
Socialist Labour	10,956	3.32
Scottish Green	5,926	1.79
SSP	5,739	1.74
SUP	2,886	0.87
Pro-Life	2,567	0.78
SFPP	1,373	0.42
NLP	719	0.22
Ind Progress	248	0.08

Electorate: 551,733

Turnout: 330,486 (59.90%)

LINDA FABIANI (SNP) was born in Glasgow in 1956. She was educated at Hyndland School, Glasgow and has an HND from Napier University and a Housing diploma from Glasgow University. She was an administrator with Glasgow Housing Association from 1982 to 1985, administration and housing officer with Clydebank Housing Association from 1985 to 1988, then development manager with Bute Housing Association from 1988 to 1994, followed by Director of East Kilbride Housing Association from 1995 until her election in 1999. She contested the East Kilbride constituency in 1999 and came second. She sat on the Transport and Environment Committee in the Scottish Parliament from 1999 to 2000, became a member of the Equal Opportunities Committee in 2000, was the SNP's deputy shadow spokesperson for Transport and the Environment from 1999 to 2000 and then for Social Justice from September 2000 onwards. She sits on the Cross Party Groups for Women, Renewable Energy, and Refugees and Asylum Seekers and is a member of the Holyrood Progress Group.

DONALD GORRIE (Liberal Democrat) was born in India in 1933. He was educated at Hurst Grange, Stirling, Oundle School and Corpus Christi, Oxford and worked as a school teacher and part-time lecturer at university and college. He was a long-standing councillor in Edinburgh, first elected in Corstorphine in 1971. He went on to hold the same ward until the 1997 general election. He was both a district and regional councillor for the area and Liberal/Liberal Democrat group leader on each council. He stood for Parliament in Edinburgh West in 1970, 1974 and 1992, before winning in 1997. However, he was not selected to fight his Westminster seat in the Scottish elections and had to settle for the Central Scotland regional list. He has proved in the Parliament to be a highly independent, principled politician and thus a nightmare for the party managers. He has been a forceful and vocal critic of the coalition negotiations between the Labour Party and Liberal Democrats and was one of three Lib Dem MSPs to vote against coalition, the others being John Farquhar Munro and Keith Raffan. Gorrie has also, along with the SNP's equally single minded Margo McDonald, been the most notable opponent of the escalating costs of the Holyrood Building Project. He will serve for only one term and retire from Westminster at the next election. In the Scottish Parliament he is a member of the Procedures and Finance Committees and previously sat on the Local Government Committee. He also sits on the Cross Party Groups for Drug Misuse, Older People, Age and Aging, Sports, and Refugees and Asylum Seekers. He is convenor of the group on Children.

LYNDSAY McINTOSH (Conservative) was born in 1955 in Glasgow. She was educated at Duncanrig Senior Secondary School, Langside College, Dundee College of Commerce and Dundee College of Technology, and was employed as a legal secretary from 1973 to 1975 before joining the civil service, where she worked from

1975 until 1984. She was also employed as a business consultant before the election in 1999, at which she contested the Kilmarnock and Loudoun constituency. She joined the Conservative Party in 1988 and was a member of its executive from 1989 onwards. She sat on the Justice and Home Affairs Committee in the Parliament from May 1999 to December 2000 and now sits on the Justice II Committee and is the Conservative deputy spokeperson on Home Affairs. She is a member of the Cross Party Groups on Animal Welfare, Children, Drug Misuse, Information, Knowledge and Enlightenment, Media, Women, and Men's Violence Against Women.

MICHAEL MATHESON (SNP) was born in 1970 in Glasgow, educated at John Bosco Secondary School and then gained a BSc in Occupational Therapy from Queen Margaret College in Edinburgh as well as a BA and diploma in Social Sciences from the Open University. He worked as an occupational therapist with Highland Regional Council from 1991 to 1993, then Central Regional Council from 1993 until 1997 and subsequently with Stirling Council from 1997 to 1999. He joined the SNP in 1989 and stood in the Hamilton North and Bellshill constituency at the 1997 election and in Falkirk West in 1999. He is the SNP's Shadow Deputy Minister for Justice and Equality and sat on the Justice and Home Affairs Committee in the Scottish Parliament from May 1999 to December 2000 and is now a member of the Justice I Committee. He is a member of the Cross Party Group on Sports.

ALEX NEIL (SNP) was born in 1951 in Irvine. He was educated at Dalmellington High School, Ayr and is an economics graduate of Dundee University and worked as a researcher for Scottish Labour before joining the breakaway Scottish Labour Party with Jim Sillars in 1976. He was general secretary of the party from 1977 to 1979, amongst other things fighting off the entryist attentions of the International Marxist Group. He ran his own economics consultancy for a number of years before his election in 1999 as well as working as director of the Prince's Scottish Youth Business Trust and Cumnock and Doon Enterprise Trust. He joined the SNP in 1986, is a leading fundamentalist within the party, and fought the Glasgow Central by-election in 1989 followed by the Kilmarnock and Loudoun constituency, all unsuccessfully, in 1992, 1997 and 1999.

In the 1992 general election, he was architect of the 'Free by '93' campaign – widely seen as triumphalist and out of touch with the electorate's sense of priorities. In 1996 he caused controversy when at the SNP conference he compared George Robertson, then Shadow Scottish Secretary, to Lord Haw Haw, the Nazi collaborator. He sat on the Social Inclusion Committee of the Scottish Parliament and was the SNP's social security spokesperson until September 2000. He has sponsored two bills within the Parliament and played an active role in supporting other MSPs' bills, such as Tommy Sheridan's warrant sales bill. He is a member of the Cross Party Groups on Children, Citizenship, Income, Economy and Society,

Epilepsy, Information, Knowledge and Enlightenment, Older People, Age and Aging, Media, and Tobacco Control. He was a member of the Finance Committee from May 1999 to December 2000. He was formerly Vice-Convenor for Policy within the SNP and contested the SNP leadership election following Alex Salmond's departure in 2000 — without success as he and his fundamentalist colleagues were heavily defeated in internal party elections. Following his electoral defeat he decided not to hold any frontbench post within the Scottish Parliament and opted to become Convenor of the Enterprise and Lifelong Learning Committee within the Parliament: the post previously held by John Swinney.

GIL PATERSON (SNP) was born in Glasgow in 1942 and educated at Possilpark Secondary School, Glasgow. He held a number of jobs with Forbes Brothers, Singers and Scottish Gas before in 1973 establishing and running his own garage business in Bishopbriggs, Gil's Motor Factors, until his election in 1999. He was a former councillor on Strathclyde Regional Council and had held a number of Executive posts within the SNP, such as Vice-Convenor for local government and administration. He contested the Glasgow Central by-election back in 1980, Strathkelvin and Bearsden in 1987 and the Airdrie and Shotts constituency at the Scottish election. He sits on the Procedure and Local Government Committees in the Scottish Parliament and did not endear himself within the SNP or amongst his own fundamentalist colleagues by suggesting that new party leader John Swinney would lead the SNP to the right. He is convenor of the Cross Party Group on Men's Violence Against Women in the Scottish Parliament.

ANDREW WILSON (SNP) was born in 1970 in Lanark. He was educated at Coltness High School, Wishaw and studied economics and politics at Strathclyde University and St Andrews University. He was an economist with the Forestry Commission and the Scottish Office before joining the SNP's HQ staff. After the 1997 referendum he joined the economics department of the Royal Bank of Scotland, before the election in 1999 in which he contested the Cumbernauld and Kilsyth constituency as a first-time candidate. He is the SNP's spokesperson on finance in the Parliament and sits on the Finance Committee. He is a member of the Cross Party Group on Information, Knowledge and Enlightenment. A rising star with a head for figures who has a key part to play in presenting the economic arguments for independence, he encountered controversy with his *Sunday Times* lecture at the 1999 SNP conference on the role of British identity in an independent Scotland. This annoyed the sensitivities of the fundamentalists, while he also irritated many voters with his comments about the Union Jack flag being synonymous with reaction and repression. Wilson has spent over a decade at the top of the SNP and has only just turned 30. He seems destined for future things in the party with his greatest obstacle possibly being the suspicion he arouses in some of his own side.

GLASGOW

The Glasgow regional seat contains all ten Glasgow constituencies, one of which (Glasgow Rutherglen) is partly in the South Lanarkshire Council area. In 1992 and 1997 Labour won all ten constituency seats. In both elections the only marginal seat was Glasgow Govan, won back by Labour from the SNP in 1992, and which Labour held on to in 1997 despite a strong SNP challenge. The overall Glasgow result in the 1997 election saw Labour win 60.4 per cent of the vote to the SNP's 19.2 per cent, with the Conservatives winning 8.5 per cent and the Liberal Democrats 7.3 per cent. In the 1999 Scottish Parliament elections, Labour was only threatened again in the Glasgow Govan constituency, but held on narrowly. It thus won all ten of the city's constituencies, one of only two regional seats in Scotland in which Labour won all the FPTP seats, the other being the neighbouring West of Scotland. Labour won 49.4 per cent of the constituency vote to the SNP's 27.9 per cent. In the regional vote, Labour won 43.9 per cent to the SNP's 25.5 per cent. This saw four SNP additional members elected, and one each for the Conservatives, Liberal Democrats and Scottish Socialists. The election of Tommy Sheridan as the first national representative for the Scottish Socialist Party was the result of significant support for the party in the regional member vote right across Glasgow beyond Sheridan's Pollok stronghold.

Constituency Members Elected

Constituency	Member	Party
Glasgow Anniesland	Donald Dewar	Labour
Glasgow Baillieston	Margaret Curran	Labour
Glasgow Cathcart	Michael Watson	Labour
Glasgow Govan	Gordon Jackson	Labour
Glasgow Kelvin	Pauline McNeill	Labour
Glasgow Maryhill	Patricia Ferguson	Labour
Glasgow Pollok	Johann Lamont	Labour
Glasgow Rutherglen	Janis Hughes	Labour
Glasgow Shettleston	Frank McAveety	Labour
Glasgow Springburn	Paul Martin	Labour

Constituency Party Shares of the Vote

Party	Votes	% Share
Labour	126,784	49.35
SNP	71,566	27.86
Liberal Democrat	20,756	8.08
Conservative	19,897	7.74

Party	Votes	% Share
SSP	16,177	6.30
SWP	920	0.36
Socialist Labour	620	0.24
Comm Brit	190	0.07

Electorate: 531,956
Turnout: 256,910 (48.30%)

Additional Members Elected

Bill Aitken	Conservative
Robert Brown	Liberal Democrat
Dorothy-Grace Elder	SNP
Kenneth Gibson	SNP
Nicola Sturgeon	SNP
Sandra White	SNP
Tommy Sheridan	SSP

Regional List Party Shares of the Vote

Party	Votes	% Share
Labour	112,588	43.92
SNP	65,360	25.50
Conservative	20,239	7.90
SSP	18,581	7.25
Liberal Democrat	18,473	7.21
Scottish Green	10,159	3.96
Socialist Labour	4,391	1.71
Pro-Life	2,357	0.92
Scottish Unionist Party	2,283	0.89
British Communist	521	0.20
Humanist	447	0.17
Natural Law	419	0.16
Socialist Party of GB	309	0.12
Choice	221	0.09

Electorate: 531,956
Turnout: 256,348 (48.19%)

BILL AITKEN (Conservative) was born in 1947 in Glasgow and educated at Allan Glen's School, Glasgow, and Glasgow College of Technology. After training with the Association of Chartered Insurance, he worked at Eagle Star and AGF Insurance as an insurance underwriter and most recently a sales developer. Aitken was first elected to Glasgow City Council in 1976 and served for 23 years. In that time he presided over the declining fortunes of the Glasgow Conservatives. In 1977 to 1979 he was Convenor of the City Licensing Committee and Vice-Convenor of the Personnel Committee as the Tories briefly ran the city. He was later leader of the Tory opposition from 1980 to 1984 and 1992 to 1996, with the Conservative group down to five councillors in the latter period. When Aitken stood down in 1999 they were reduced to one.

Aitken contested the Anniesland constituency for the Scottish Parliament and was elected for Glasgow Regional seat. Upon his election, he became Conservative Deputy Business Manager, and a deputy member of the Scottish Parliamentary Bureau. Aitken is Deputy Spokesman on Local Government and Housing, the Conservatives' spokesman on Glasgow, and was a member of the Social Inclusion, Housing and Voluntary Sector Committee and Audit Committees from May 1999 to December 2000 and is now a member of the Social Justice Committee. He is also a member of the Cross Party Groups on Animal Welfare, Information, Knowledge and Enlightenment, Shipbuilding, and Tobacco Control, of which he is Treasurer.

ROBERT BROWN (Liberal Democrat) was born in 1946 in Newcastle-upon-Tyne and educated at Gordons School, Huntly, and Aberdeen University where he gained an LLB. He worked as a Law Assistant at Edmonds & Ledingham from 1969 to 1972, as Deputy Procurator Fiscal, Dumbarton 1972 to 1974, and as Assistant, then Partner, and finally Senior Civil Partner at Ross Harper & Murphy, from 1974 to 1999.

Brown was elected to Glasgow District Council from 1977 until 1992 and was leader of the Lib Dem Group for the same period. He has stood six times for the Glasgow Rutherglen seat – five Westminster elections – October 1974, 1979, 1983, 1987 and 1997, and the Scottish Parliament elections – before getting elected for the Glasgow Region. He is a member of the Scottish Parliamentary Corporate Body, Scottish Lib Dem Spokesman on Communities and Housing, and was a member of the Social Inclusion, Housing and Voluntary Sector Committee from May 1999 to December 2000, and is now a member of the Social Justice Committee. He is also involved in the Cross Party Groups on Children, Citizenship, Income, Equality and Society, Epilepsy, Older People, Rail Services, Shipbuilding, of which he is Vice-Convenor, Tobacco Control, and Refugees and Asylum Seekers.

Brown has also been Convenor of the Scottish Lib Dem Policy Committee from 1996 to 1999 and was responsible for drawing up the Scottish Lib Dem manifestos in 1997 and 1999. He has gained an enviable reputation for local campaigning and advocacy and was Chair of Rutherglen and Cambuslang Citizen's Advice Bureau from 1983 until 1988 and from 1993 until 1998.

DOROTHY-GRACE ELDER (SNP) stood for the SNP in the Glasgow Baillieston seat in the Scottish Parliament elections and achieved the highest swing to the SNP in the entire elections. She was elected for the Glasgow Regional seat through being placed by SNP activists second top of their list. She has been one of Scotland's leading journalists for the last thirty years and has been a reporter with D. C. Thomson, the *Glasgow Herald* and a freelance writer and columnist. Elder has won numerous awards for her journalism including UK Reporter of the Year and the 1995 Oliver Award for services to children. She was until her election, a *Scotland on Sunday* columnist under the heading Rattling the Cage, where she got up the noses of many parts of Scottish public life, and the Scottish Labour establishment in particular.

She is an impassioned, outspoken and slightly unpredictable politician, who brings out as much fear and anxiety in the SNP leadership as she does in her opponents. She is also a trustee of the Yorkhill Children's Fund, Royal Hospital for Sick Children, Glasgow. In the Scottish Parliament, she sits on the Health and Community Care Committee and on the Cross Party Groups on Animal Welfare, Borders Rail, Epilepsy and Men's Violence Against Women and Children.

KENNETH GIBSON (SNP) was born in 1961 and educated at Bellahouston Academy, Glasgow, and Stirling University with a BA in Economics. He worked as a systems development officer with British Steel from 1982 to 1986, at the Glasgow Garden Festival from 1987 to 1988 and as a sales representative and trainer in the pharmaceutical industry from 1988 to 1999. He was elected to Glasgow City Council from 1992 to 1999, before handing over his Mosspark ward, which he won from Labour in 1992, safely to his mother Iris. He was leader of the SNP opposition on the council from 1998 to 1999. Gibson previously stood in Monklands East in 1987 and in the Scottish Parliament elections for the Glasgow Pollok seat where he finished second reducing Labour's majority to 4,642. He is SNP Spokesperson on Local Government and sits on the Local Government Committee.

TOMMY SHERIDAN (SSP) was born in 1964 in Glasgow and educated at Lourdes Secondary School, Glasgow, and Stirling University where he gained a BA Joint Honours in Economics and Politics. Sheridan was a member of the Labour Party in the 1980s, and of the Trotskyite group Militant; he came to public attention as one of the leading organisers against the poll tax and as President of the Anti-Poll Tax Federation. In October 1991 he was involved in a street protest which prevented a warrant sale in Glasgow and was charged and detained at Saughton Prison, Edinburgh.

While in jail, Sheridan stood for the Glasgow Pollok seat in the 1992 election and won 19.2 per cent of the vote under the auspices of Scottish Militant Labour, than a month later was elected to Glasgow City Council to the Pollok ward with 52 per cent – a ward he still represents as councillor. He stood for the Glasgow seat in the 1994 European elections and in Pollok in the 1997 general elections gaining 11.1 per cent of the vote for the Scottish Socialist Alliance in a much altered seat.

Sheridan became the National Convenor of the Scottish Socialist Party prior to the Scottish Parliament elections in May 1999, when he stood in the Pollok seat winning 21.5 per cent, and was elected for the Glasgow Regional seat with 7.3 per cent. In the Scottish Parliament, Sheridan sits on the Equal Opportunities Committee and is a member of the Cross Party Groups on Animal Welfare, Sports, of which he is Vice-Convenor, and Refugees and Asylum Seekers. In his first year, Sheridan has become one of the undoubted stars of the Parliament and pioneered the backbench bill on the Abolition of Warrant Sales which passed its Stage One reading in April 2000 against the wishes of the Labour-Lib Dem Executive. He stood for the Rectorship of St Andrews University in early 2000 and polled respectably, narrowly losing to Andrew Neil, the right-wing free-marketeer. Sheridan is one of the last in the line of the Red Clydeside tradition of articulate, passionate working-class radicals and has one of the worst voting records in the Parliament, balancing the role of campaigner and parliamentarian. He has written an autobiography with the journalist Joan MacAlpine: *A Time to Rage*. He also co-authored with Alan McCombes *Imagine: A Socialist Vision for the 20th Century* published at the end of 2000, which outlines the revolutionary socialist case for Scotland.

Tommy Sheridan spent a second period in jail with a week behind bars immediately before christmas 2000 in Greenock Prison. The reason this time was Sheridan's refusal to pay a £250 fine for breach of the peace after an anti-nuclear protest at Faslane submarine base. Sheridan turned the event, like most things he is involved in into a publicity success and wrote a 'Prison Diary' for the Sunday papers which underlined his celebrity status.

NICOLA STURGEON (SNP) was born in 1970 in Irvine and educated at Greenwood Academy, Irvine, and the University of Glasgow where she gained an LLB (Hons) and a Diploma in Legal Practice. She was a trainee solicitor in Glasgow from 1993 to 1995, a solicitor in Stirling from 1995 to 1997 and a solicitor at Drumchapel Law Centre, Glasgow, from 1997 to 1999.

She first stood at the age of 21 in Glasgow Shettleston in the 1992 election and then in the Labour-SNP marginal of Glasgow Govan in 1997 where she succeeded in nearly halving Labour's majority to 2,914. She stood again in Govan in the Scottish Parliament elections and – though she further reduced Labour's majority to 1,756 – had in fact been everyone's favourite to win after two years of constant Labour scandals. Elected as a Regional member through being top of the SNP's Glasgow list, she was SNP Spokesperson on Children and Education in the first year of the Parliament and is now Spokesperson on Health and Community Care. She was a member of the Education, Culture and Sport Committee from 1999 to 2000 and is now a member of the Health and Community Care Committee and of the Cross Party Groups on Children, Epilepsy, Shipbuilding and Women. Sturgeon joined the SNP in 1986, was Vice-Convenor, Publicity from 1997 to 1999 and a former Spokesperson on Energy and Youth Affairs. She was John Swinney's campaign manager in his successful bid for the party leadership in September 2000, is one of the rising stars of the SNP and has been in the limelight for nearly a decade, while having just turned 30.

SANDRA WHITE (SNP) was born in Govan, Glasgow, in 1951 and educated at Garthamlock Secondary School, Glasgow College and Cardonald College, Glasgow. She was elected to Renfrewshire Council from 1989 until 1999 as a full-time councillor and was Convenor of the Property and Construction Services Committee as well as being Deputy Housing Spokesperson.

White joined the SNP in 1983, contested Glasgow Kelvin in 1987 and Glasgow Hillhead in 1992. In the Scottish Parliament election she stood again in Glasgow Kelvin and was elected for the Glasgow Region. As an MSP she is SNP Deputy Spokesperson on Equality and Race Relations and SNP Deputy Whip. White was a member of the Public Petitions and Social Inclusion, Housing and the Voluntary Sector Committees from May 1999 to December 2000, and then became a member of the Social Justice Committee. She is involved in the Cross Party Groups on Animal Welfare, Epilepsy, Older People, Rail Services, Men's Violence against Women and Children, and Refugees and Asylum Seekers.

HIGHLANDS AND ISLANDS

The Highlands and Islands is Scotland's largest regional seat, running from the Mull of Kintyre in the Firth of Clyde to the northernmost stop of mainland Britain, John O' Groats, and the islands of Orkney and Shetland. The pattern of party competition in the Highlands and Islands varies considerably from the politics of the Scottish Central Belt. There is to some extent a genuine four-party system in the Highlands and Islands, although the Conservatives have been squeezed here of late, as they have elsewhere, and last had representation in 1987 when they lost Moray.

In the 1997 election, a mere two thousand votes separated the Liberal Democrats (27.7 per cent), Labour (27.0 per cent) and SNP (26.7 per cent), with the Conservatives in fourth place (16.2 per cent). The Lib Dems won five seats to Labour's two and the SNP's one, with the only constituency change being Labour winning Inverness East, Nairn and Lochaber from the Lib Dems with the aid of the retirement of Russell Johnston, previously the Lib Dem MP.

In 1999, the three parties were again separated on the constituency vote by two thousand votes, with the SNP this time finishing on top with 28.5 per cent to the Liberal Democrats' 28.3 per cent and Labour's 27.4 per cent. Only one constituency changed hands, the ever volatile Inverness East, Nairn and Lochaber, which was won by the SNP's Fergus Ewing from Labour, leaving the Lib Dems overall with five seats to the SNP's two and Labour's one. On the regional list vote, the SNP finished in the lead with 27.7 per cent ahead of Labour's 25.5 per cent and the Lib Dem's 21.4 per cent. The composition of the additional members was very different in this regional seat, with Labour winning three 'top up' seats, its only ones in the whole of Scotland, and the Conservatives and SNP two each.

Constituency Members Elected

Constituency	Member	Party
Argyll and Bute	George Lyon	Liberal Democrat
Caithness, Sutherland and Easter Ross	Jamie Stone	Liberal Democrat
Inverness East, Nairn and Lochaber	Fergus Ewing	SNP
Moray	Margaret Ewing	SNP
Orkney	Jim Wallace	Liberal Democrat
Ross, Skye and Inverness West	John Farquhar Munro	Liberal Democrat
Shetland	Tavish Scott	Liberal Democrat
Western Isles	Alasdair Morrison	Labour

Constituency Party Shares of the Vote

Party	Vote	% Share
SNP	57,555	28.51
Liberal Democrat	57,034	28.25
Labour	55,254	27.37
Conservative	28,890	14.31
Independent	3,138	1.55

Electorate: 326,553

Turnout: 201,871 (61.82%)

Additional Members Elected

Jamie McGrigor	Conservative
Mary Scanlon	Conservative
Rhoda Grant	Labour
Maureen MacMillan	Labour
Peter Peacock	Labour
Winnie Ewing	SNP
Duncan Hamilton	SNP

Regional List Party Shares of the Vote

Party	Votes	% Share
SNP	55,933	27.73
Labour	51,371	25.47
Liberal Democrat	43,226	21.43
Conservative	30,122	14.94
Scottish Green	7,560	3.75
Ind Noble	3,522	1.75
Socialist Labour	2,808	1.39
Highlands and Islands Alliance	2,607	1.29
SSP	1,770	0.88
Mission	1,151	0.57
Int Independent	712	0.35
Natural Law Party	536	0.27
Independent R	354	0.18

Electorate: 326,553

Turnout: 201,672 (61.76%)

WINNIE EWING (SNP) – Madame Ecosse – was formerly MEP for the Highlands and Islands from 1979 until 1999, though she had been a nominated member of the European Parliament since 1975. She joined the SNP in 1946 has spawned a considerable political family, with her son Fergus and daughter-in-law Margaret both fellow MSPs, and a daughter, Annabelle, seeking election to Westminster too. She is the oldest member of the Scottish Parliament, born in 1929 in Glasgow, and hence was acting Presiding Officer when the Parliament opened in May 1999. She was educated at Queen's Park School, Glasgow, Glasgow University and has been a solicitor since 1952. She has been Secretary and Treasurer of the Glasgow Bar Association and President of the Glasgow Soroptimist Club in 1966.

She was elected to Westminster on two separate occasions: in 1967 at the historic Hamilton by-election, and then for Moray and Nairn from February 1974 to 1979, unseating the Conservative Secretary of State for Scotland. After the 1979 electoral reversal for the SNP, there followed a period of factional infighting between different groups. In 1982, Ewing set up with Robert McIntyre, the Campaign for Nationalism, whose aim was to advance a more traditional nationalism and oppose the left-wing agenda of the '79 Group which involved such 'young turks' as Alex Salmond and Roseanna Cunningham. Once the party leadership acted against the '79 Group, Ewing and company, disbanded their group.

In the European Parliament she was a formidable campaigner for the Highlands, especially in its search for objective 1 status in EU regional funding. In Brussels and Strasbourg, she was chair of the Committee for Youth and Culture from 1984 to 1987, which was a boon for someone representing such a small party. She also sat on the Committee on Economic and Monetary Affairs and Industrial Policy from 1994 to 1999, the Committee on Budgetary control from 1994 to 1997, the Committee on Legal Affairs and Citizens' Rights and was vice-chair of the Committee on Fisheries 1998 to 1999. She was also a substitute member on a number of European Committees. She sat on the European Committee in the Scottish Parliament from 1999 to 2000 and is a member of the Public Petitions Committee. She has been President of the SNP since 1988. She is also joint convenor of the Cross Party Group on Crofting and a member of the group on Animal Welfare.

Winnie Ewing is one of the best known names and faces of post-war Scottish politics. Her famous by-election victory at Hamilton in 1967 fundamentally reshaped Scottish politics in numerous different levels: inventing the modern SNP, bringing the constitutional question to the centre of Scottish politics, and, along with Margo MacDonald's victory in Govan seven years later, shifting forceful, articulate women centre stage in what had previously been very much a man's world. Along with Margo and Jim Sillars, she is a Nationalist icon, someone who has instant recognition and has played a crucial role in the changing shape of the SNP and Scottish politics. She enjoyed a starring moment in the opening day of the Scottish Parliament, on 12 May 1999, when as the oldest member of the house she was temporarily in the Presiding Officer's role and opened it with the words: 'The Scottish Parliament hereby adjourned on 25 March 1707 is hereby reconvened.' These deeply nationalistic sentiments have become one of the defining moments of the Parliament.

RHODA GRANT (Labour) was born in Stornoway in 1963 and educated at Plockton High School, Inverness College and the Open University, where she gained a BSc Honours in Social Sciences. She worked in the public sector before the election, in administrative and clerical positions in Highland Regional Council. She was a clerical assistant, an accounts assistant responsible for the European Social Fund and also a senior administrator within the council, before becoming an administrator with UNISON in 1993. She sits as Labour's parliamentary representative on Labour's Scottish Executive Committee and was a member of the Parliament's Finance and Rural Affairs Committees from May 1999 to December 2000, and is now a member of the Public Petitions and Rural Development Committees. She sits on the Cross Party Groups for Gaelic, Children, Information, Knowledge and Enlightenment, Oil and Gas, Strategic Rail Services, Media, Women, Agriculture, Men's Violence Against Women, and Renewable Energy. She is also joint convenor of the group on Crofting.

DUNCAN HAMILTON (SNP) was born in 1973 in Troon. He was educated at Bearsden Academy, Glasgow University where he gained a MA Hons in History and Edinburgh University obtaining a LLB in Scottish Law. He was also between 1997–98 a Kennedy Scholar at the Kennedy School of Government at Harvard University. He was personal assistant to Alex Salmond before his election in 1999 and contested the Argyll and Bute constituency at the Scottish election. He was the SNP's deputy spokesperson on health and community care from 1999 to 2000, before becoming deputy for Enterprise and Lifelong Learning (Highlands and Islands) in September 2000. He also sat on the Health and Community Care Committee of the Scottish Parliament from 1999 to 2000 before becoming a member of the Enterprise and Lifelong Learning Committee from January 2001. He is a member of the Cross Party Groups on Animal Welfare and Sports. He writes a weekly column for the *Evening Times*, which has not proven popular with certain Labour MSPs. In particular, his *Evening Times* article in June 1999 attacked Labour women MSPs as 'overweight, inarticulate and an embarrassment to their party.' Hamilton was publicly humbled and forced to apologise for such inappropriate and offensive language.

MAUREEN MacMILLAN (Labour) was born in 1943 in Oban and was educated at Oban High School, Edinburgh University and Moray House. She was a community councillor and teacher for many years, as a supply and part-time teacher from 1976 to 1983 then at Millburn in Inverness from 1983 to 1999. She was also involved in the women's movement in the Highlands as a founder member and director of Ross-shire Women's Aid refuge and vice convenor of the Highland Domestic Abuse Forum. She sat on the European and Justice and Home Affairs Committees in the Scottish Parliament from May 1999 to December 2000, before joining the Transport and Environment Committee in January 2001. She is a member of the Cross Party Groups on Gaelic, Epilepsy, Oil and Gas, Palliative Care, Strategic Rail Services, Women, Agriculture and Horticulture, and Renewable Energy.

JAMIE McGRIGOR (Conservative) was born in 1949 in London and educated at Eton and Neuchatel University in Switzerland. He worked in shipbuilding insurance for many years and as a stockbroker for Laurence Trust & Co. before returning to Scotland to run a fish farm as well as his own cattle and sheep farm on Loch Awe. He stood for the Conservatives at the 1997 general election in the Western Isles and contested the same seat in 1999. He sits on the Equal Opportunities Committee of the Scottish Parliament and is the Conservatives' deputy spokesperson on rural affairs. He is a member of the Cross Party Groups on Gaelic, Animal Welfare, Citizenship, Income, Economy and Society, Epilepsy, Tobacco Control, Agriculture and Horticulture, and Men's Violence Again Women. He is convenor of the Cross Party Group on Children and joint convenor of the group on Crofting. He is also a keen fisherman.

PETER PEACOCK (Labour) has born in 1952 in Edinburgh and educated at Hawick High School and Jordanhill College of Education where he obtained a diploma in Youth Work and Community Service. He was a long-serving Independent councillor in Highland Region and then Highland Council from 1982 to 1999 which included a spell as leader of Highland Council from 1995 to 1999 and was also a member of the Committee of the Regions. He only joined the Labour Party one year prior to the Scottish Parliament elections and his placing on the Highlands list in the pole position by the party leadership – thus practically guaranteeing his election, caused widespread local resentment. He worked as a community education worker in Orkney, as Citizens' Advice Scotland Area officer for the Highlands, and as a business and training consultant before his election in 1999. He was appointed as Deputy Minister for Children and Education in the Scottish Executive after the election in 1999 and became Deputy Minister for Finance and Local Government in 2000.

MARY SCANLON (Conservative) was born in 1947 in Dundee. She was educated at Craigo School, Montrose and Dundee University graduating, in economics and politics, and has a postgraduate diploma in personnel management. She worked in further and higher education as a lecturer in business administration and economics before her election in 1999. She lectured at Perth College, Dundee Institute of Technology and then Inverness College. She stood in a number of seats before election as a list MSP, including North East Fife in 1992, and Inverness East, Nairn and Lochaber at the 1997 and 1999 elections. She is Conservative spokesperson on health and social work and sits on the Health and Community Care Committee in the Scottish Parliament. She is a member of the Cross Party Groups on Drug Misuse, Epilepsy, Information, Knowledge and Enlightenment, Palliative Care, and Tobacco Control.

LOTHIANS

The Lothians regional seat includes the six Edinburgh constituencies and the commuter seats of Linlithgow, Livingston and Midlothian in a kind of greater Edinburgh conurbation. In 1992 and 1997, Lothians has reflected Labour's growing dominance in this area, the Conservatives' decline and the SNP's historic weakness in the capital.

In 1997, Labour won 45.9 per cent of the vote to the Conservatives' 19.2 per cent while the SNP won 18.4 per cent and the Liberal Democrats 14.9 per cent. Labour won eight out of the nine seats, gaining Edinburgh Pentlands from the Conservatives, while the Liberal Democrats won Edinburgh West from the Conservatives. In the 1999 Scottish Parliament elections, on constituency votes Labour won 40.2 per cent to the SNP's 26.9 per cent with no seats changing hands, although the SNP polled respectably in both Linlithgow and Livingston. On the regional vote, Labour won 30.2 per cent to the SNP's 25.7 per cent with the additional members distributed three to the SNP, two to the Conservatives, one to the Lib Dems and one to the Scottish Greens, their first ever national elected representative in Scotland.

Constituency Members Elected

Constituency	Member	Party
Edinburgh Central	Sarah Boyack	Labour
Edinburgh East and Musselburgh	Susan Deacon	Labour
Edinburgh North and Leith	Malcolm Chisholm	Labour
Edinburgh Pentlands	Iain Gray	Labour
Edinburgh South	Angus MacKay	Labour
Edinburgh West	Margaret Smith	Liberal Democrat
Linlithgow	Mary Mulligan	Labour
Livingston	Bristow Muldoon	Labour
Midlothian	Rhona Brankin	Labour

Constituency Party Shares of the Vote

Party	Vote	% Share
Labour	133,612	40.19
SNP	89,306	26.86
Conservative	52,778	15.87
Liberal Democrat	52,138	15.68
SSP	2,434	0.73
Independent	1,033	0.31
SWP	482	0.14
Ind Dem	364	0.11
Braveheart	191	0.06
Ind You	134	0.04

Electorate: 539,656

Turnout: 332,472 (61.61%)

Additional Members Elected

James Douglas–Hamilton	Conservative
David McLetchie	Conservative
David Steel	Liberal Democrat
Fiona Hyslop	SNP
Kenny MacAskill	SNP
Margo MacDonald	SNP
Robin Harper	Scottish Green

Regional List Party Shares of the Vote

Party	Votes	% Share
Labour	99,908	30.23
SNP	85,085	25.74
Conservative	52,067	15.75
Liberal Democrat	47,565	14.39
Scottish Green	22,848	6.91
Socialist Labour	10,895	3.30
SSP	5,237	1.58
Liberal	2,056	0.62
Witchery	1,184	0.36
Pro–Life	898	0.27
Rights	806	0.24
NLP	564	0.17
Braveheart	557	0.17

Party	Votes	% Share
Socialist Party of GB	388	0.12
Independent Voice	256	0.08
Independent Ind	145	0.04
Anti-Corr	54	0.02

Electorate: 539,656

Turnout: 330,513 (61.25%)

LORD JAMES DOUGLAS HAMILTON (Conservative) was born in 1942 and elected MP for Edinburgh West from October 1974 until 1997. He stood in the Scottish Parliament elections in Edinburgh West and was elected for the Lothians Regional seat. He was educated at Eton and Balliol College, Oxford where he graduated with an MA in Modern History, and then Edinburgh University where he gained an LLB in Scots Law.

Douglas-Hamilton, or 'Lord James' as he is affectionately known, was President of Oxford University Conservative Association in 1963, while at the same time gaining a Boxing Blue. He was called to the Scottish Bar in 1968 and served as an Advocate and Interim Procurator Fiscal Depute from 1968 to 1972.

As a Westminster MP, he was a Scottish Conservative Whip in Opposition from 1977 to 1979 and a Government Whip and Lord Commissioner of the Treasury 1979 to 1981, Parliamentary Private Secretary to Malcolm Rifkind, first, at the Foreign Office, then as Secretary of State for Scotland, over the period 1983 to 1987. In 1987, with the Scottish Conservative representation cut in half, he became Scottish Office Minister with responsibility for Home Affairs and Environment, then from 1992 to 1995 was Minister for Education and Housing, and from 1995 to 1997, Minister for Health and Home Affairs. In the Scottish Parliament he became Conservative Chief Whip and Business Manager as well as a member of the Scottish Parliamentary Bureau. He is also a member of the Standards Committee and of the Cross Party Groups on Animal Welfare, Children, Epilepsy, Tobacco Control, and Renewable Energy.

Lord James is the second son of the 14th Duke of Hamilton who went down in history when Rudolf Hess flew to meet him on his ill-fated peace mission of May 1941. Douglas-Hamilton has written a book on the subject, *The Truth about Rudolf Hess*, but conspiracy theorists will forever wonder if it tells the whole truth.

ROBIN HARPER (Green) was born in 1940 in Thurso and educated at St Marylebone Grammar School, Elgin Academy, Aberdeen University and Heriot-Watt University. He has been a teacher at Crookston Castle Secondary School, Glasgow, from 1962 to 1963, Braehead School from 1964 to 1968 and Kolanya

School, Kenya from 1968 to 1970. From 1972 to 1999 Harper taught Modern Studies at Boroughmuir High School, Edinburgh. He has also been an actor, musician and guitar teacher for Fife and Edinburgh local authorities and is a former music director of the Edinburgh Children's Theatre Workshop. Harper was also on Lothian Children's Panel from 1985 to 1988 and Lothian Health Board from 1990 to 1995. He is currently Rector of Edinburgh University.

Harper has stood in numerous elections for the Scottish Greens, contesting Edinburgh Central in 1992 and Edinburgh Pentlands in 1997 for Westminster and the 1989 and 1994 European elections as well as the 1998 North East Scotland Euro by-election. He is the first Green representative ever to have been elected to a UK Parliament. He sits on the Transport and Environment Committee of the Scottish Parliament and on the Cross Party Groups on Crofting, Animal Welfare, Citizenship, Income, Economy and Society, Epilepsy, Rail Services, Agriculture and Horticulture, Renewable Energy, and Refugees and Asylum Seekers – all of which he is Vice-Convenor of, and Children, which he is Convenor of.

FIONA HYSLOP (SNP) was born in 1964 in Irvine and educated at Ayr Academy, Glasgow University where she gained an MA Hons in Economics and Sociology, and the Scottish College of Textiles where she got a Diploma in Industrial Administration. She has worked in a variety of posts in sales and marketing for Standard Life Assurance from 1986 to 1999, most recently as a Marketing Manager.

She joined the SNP in 1986 and stood for Westminster in 1992 in Edinburgh Leith, and in 1997 in Edinburgh Central. In the Scottish Parliament, she is SNP Spokesperson on Housing and Social Justice as well as Policy Co-ordinator from September 2000, and was a member of the Social Inclusion, Housing and Voluntary Sector Committee until the end of 2000 and is now on the Social Justice Committee, as well as the Information, Knowledge and Enlightenment Cross Party Group. She has been a member of the SNP National Executive since 1990 and has been seen as a rising star both in the party and the Parliament. In her first year as an MSP, Hyslop, as Deputy Convenor of the Social Inclusion Committee, clashed dramatically with the Convenor, Margaret Curran, over whether Curran had allowed a committee report on housing stock transfers to be amended by the Executive. Neither came out a clear victor, but this was an early indication that Hyslop can effectively combine combative debate with the new politics.

KENNY MacASKILL (SNP) was born in 1958 in Edinburgh and educated at Linlithgow Academy and Edinburgh University where he gained an LLB (Hons). He subsequently became a solicitor, working as a senior partner of an English law firm and as Director of the Legal Services Agency.

MacAskill joined the SNP in 1981 and first came to prominence in the bitter SNP civil war which erupted in the aftermath of the party's 1979 election defeat. He became one of the leading lights in the left-wing '79 Group and was one of its seven prominent members who were expelled as a result of the SNP leadership's proscription of it in 1982; this was commuted to suspension. He then became, after the 1987 election, the SNP Spokesperson on the Poll Tax where his mixture of charm and enthusiasm was interpreted outside and inside the SNP as over-eagerness and a lack of judgement. He has also been a Vice-Convenor of Policy and SNP Treasurer and stood for the post of senior Vice-Convenor in September 2000: the 'de facto' deputy leader, losing to Roseanna Cunningham.

He has previously contested Livingston in the 1983 and 1987 Westminster elections and Linlithgow in 1992 and 1997. In the 1999 election, he stood in Edinburgh East and Musselburgh and was elected for the Lothians Region. In the Parliament, MacAskill was SNP Principal Spokesperson on Transport and Environment and is now Spokesperson on Enterprise and Lifelong Learning. He is Convenor of the Subordinate Legislation Committee. He is also a member of the Cross Party Groups on Borders Rail, Epilepsy, Tobacco Control and Renewable Energy, of which he is Convenor. MacAskill is undoubtedly an SNP MSP to watch; he was once a committed 'fundamentalist', who, since being elected, has signalled the need for the SNP to develop a more serious political strategy for winning independence.

MARGO MacDONALD (SNP) was born in 1944 in Hamilton and was previously MP for Glasgow Govan from November 1973 to February 1974. 'Margo' may have only been a SNP MP then for four months, but the result shook Scottish politics and Labour to the core. Since then MacDonald has become a Nationalist icon alongside Winnie Ewing and Jim Sillars, to whom she was later married.

MacDonald was educated at Hamilton Academy and Dunfermline College and was a teacher from 1963 to 1965, a freelance writer and journalist, Director of Shelter (Scotland) from 1978 to 1981, a Radio Forth broadcaster from 1981 to 1983, Editor of Topical Programmes from 1983 to 1985 and a political and current affairs reporter from 1985 to 1991. As Chief Executive of Network Scotland from 1991 to 1994 she devised a series of helplines offering specialist services: Drugline, Smokeline, National AIDS Helpline and others.

She joined the SNP in 1966, and was President of Edinburgh University Scottish Nationalists. MacDonald first stood in Paisley in the 1970 general election winning 7.3 per cent of the vote, won Govan in November 1973, lost it in the February 1974 election and stood in the Hamilton by-election in 1978 against Labour's George Robertson – the SNP's defeat being one of the significant events in their electoral retreat in the 1970s. MacDonald was one of the leading figures of the left-wing '79 Group which was established after the party's 1979 electoral disaster to appeal to Central Belt Labour voters with a radical, socialist agenda. The establishment of this group made it possible for Jim Sillars, the ex-Labour MP and founder of the mini-sized Scottish Labour Party to join the SNP. In 1982, the SNP hierarchy acted against the '79 Group suspending seven prominent members. MacDonald resigned from the party in disgust and did not rejoin it until a decade later after the 1992 election.

MacDonald contested Edinburgh South in the 1999 elections and was elected for the Lothians Region. She sat in the Parliament on the European Committee and Enterprise and Lifelong Learning Committee from May 1999 to December 2000, before joining the Justice II and Subordinate Legislation Committees in January 2001. She is also a member of the Cross Party Groups on the Media and Palliative Care.

MacDonald, as she would be the first to admit, caused unease in the SNP leadership with her election as an MSP. She is well known for her unique brand of 'off-message' politics and is seen as an opponent of the SNP leadership's gradualist line, preferring a more fundamentalist nationalist approach. She was openly sceptical pre-election of the SNP 'A Penny for Scotland' campaign, but did not overtly rock the boat. Her first year as an MSP has given her an enormous profile and she has proved a tireless and effective critic of the Holyrood Building Project from the outset. She was disciplined by the SNP leadership for breaking party rules by speaking to the media after an SNP group meeting, a move which seemed mistaken given the regard with which she is held in the SNP grass roots.

DAVID McLETCHIE (Conservative) was born in 1952 in Edinburgh and educated at George Heriot's School, Edinburgh, and Edinburgh University where he gained an LLB (Hons). He worked as an apprentice solicitor with Shepherd and Wedderburn from 1974 to 1976, as a solicitor with Tods Murray from 1976 to 1980 and as a partner from 1980 heading the department dealing with tax, estates and trusts.

McLetchie stood in the Edinburgh Central seat in the 1979 general election, losing to Robin Cook, and in Edinburgh Pentlands in the Scottish Parliament elections, gaining election via the Lothians Regional seat. He was President of the Scottish Conservatives from 1994 to 1997 and after the 1997 wipeout served on the Strathclyde Commission which reformed the party's structure and organisation. In September 1998, McLetchie was elected leader of the Scottish Conservatives, defeating Phil Gallie, and was widely seen as the most effective election campaigner of the four main party leaders during the first Scottish Parliament election. In his first year and a half in the Parliament, McLetchie has presided over significant progress with the Tories, giving them a moderate centre-right voice distinct from William Hague's populist agenda. He also sits on the Cross Party Groups on Epilepsy, Older People, and Palliative Care.

DAVID STEEL (elected as Liberal Democrat, now the Presiding Officer) was born in 1938 in Kirkcaldy and was MP for Roxburgh, Selkirk and Peebles from 1965 until 1983 and then Tweeddale, Ettrick and Lauderdale from 1983 until 1997. He was educated at Prince of Wales School, Nairobi, George Watson's College, Edinburgh, and Edinburgh University where he gained an LLB. Before his election as an MP, Steel was briefly an interviewer with BBC Scotland from 1964 to 1965. After his election in 1965, Steel promoted a successful bill to legalise abortion and was President of the Anti-Apartheid Movement of Great Britain from 1966 to 1969 and Chair of Shelter Scotland from 1969 until 1973. In 1976, he became leader of the Liberal Party and negotiated the Lib-Lab pact to maintain Labour in office. He played a leading role in the creation of the Liberal-SDP Alliance in 1981 after the breakaway of Roy Jenkins and the 'Gang of Four' from an unelectable Labour Party. The two parts of the Alliance merged in 1988 into what became the Liberal Democrats and Steel bowed out as leader, after twelve years pursuing realignment and 'breaking the mould' of British politics.

Steel was Joint Chair with Labour's Harry Ewing of the Scottish Constitutional Convention from 1989 until 1995, a founder member of the International Institute for Democracy and Electoral Assistance in 1995 and from 1995 to 1997 was Executive Chairman of the Countryside Movement and Vice-Chair of the Countryside Alliance. Steel's election as Presiding Officer of the Scottish Parliament on 12 May 1999 was the first vote of the new body. He is also a member of the Scottish Parliament Corporate Body and Scottish Parliamentary Bureau. Steel's immense parliamentary experience has been a crucial resource for the Parliament in finding its feet and in the developing relationship between it and the Executive. At points, Steel has seemed to restrict MSPs in ways reminiscent of Westminster, but at other important junctions, he has ruled in favour of the rights of MSPs. He attracted controversy in September 1999 when in a speech to the Church of Scotland Church and Nation Committee, he attacked the media's reporting of the Parliament as 'bitch journalism', a remark he later had to clarify that he was making as an individual, not as Presiding Officer. He is author of a number of books, including *A House Divided* on the Lib-Lab pact of 1977 to 1978 and *Against Goliath* (1989) addressing his ambition of realigning centre-left politics and modernising Britain, its attitudes and constitutional arrangements.

MID-SCOTLAND AND FIFE

Mid-Scotland and Fife runs through from the rural seats of Tayside North and Perth through Stirling and Ochil to the county of Fife. In 1997 Labour won 40.0 per cent of the vote to the SNP's 25.3 per cent while the Conservatives won 21.1 per cent and the Liberal Democrats 12.6 per cent. The Conservatives had at the 1992 election held three seats in this area and lost all three of them in 1997: Tayside North and Perth to the SNP and Stirling to Labour. The SNP also polled well in the Labour seat of Ochil, leaving Labour with six seats to the SNP's two and one for the Lib Dems.

In the 1999 Scottish Parliament elections, Labour won 36.4 per cent of the constituency vote to the SNP's 31.5 per cent. However, despite the SNP running Labour so close no constituency changed hands and the best the Nationalists had to show was their reduction of Labour's majority in Ochil to 1,303 – a disappointment given it was one of their target seats. Labour won 33.4 per cent of the regional vote to the SNP's 28.7 per cent and Conservatives 18.6 per cent, resulting in both the Conservatives and SNP winning three 'top up' seats and the Liberal Democrats one.

Constituency Members Elected

Constituency	Member	Party
Dunfermline East	Helen Eadie	Labour
Dunfermline West	Scott Barrie	Labour
Fife Central	Henry McLeish	Labour
Fife North East	Iain Smith	Liberal Democrat
Kirkcaldy	Marilyn Livingstone	Labour
Ochil	Richard Simpson	Labour
Perth	Roseanna Cunningham	SNP
Stirling	Sylvia Jackson	Labour
Tayside North	John Swinney	SNP

Constituency Party Shares of the Vote

Party	Vote	% Share
Labour	111,154	36.40
SNP	96,102	31.45
Conservative	56,709	18.56
Liberal Democrat	39,191	12.82
Independent	2,432	0.80

Electorate: 509,387

Turnout: 305,588 (59.99%)

Additional Members Elected

Keith Harding	Conservative
Nick Johnston	Conservative
Brian Monteith	Conservative
Keith Raffan	Liberal Democrat
Bruce Crawford	SNP
Tricia Marwick	SNP
George Reid	SNP

Regional List Party Shares of the Vote

Party	Votes	% Share
Labour	101,964	33.36
SNP	87,659	28.68
Conservative	56,719	18.56
Liberal Democrat	38,896	12.73
Scottish Green	11,821	3.87
Socialist Labour	4,266	1.40
SSP	3,044	1.00
Pro-Life	735	0.24
NLP	558	0.18

Electorate: 509,387

Turnout: 305,662 (60.01%)

BRUCE CRAWFORD (SNP) was born in Perth in 1955 and educated at Kinross High School and Perth High School. He worked for the Scottish Office from 1974 until 1999. He was a councillor with Perth and Kinross District and then Perth and Kinross Council from 1988 onwards. He was Convenor of the Environmental Health Committee from 1988 to 1992 and then council leader from 1996 to 1999. He still sits on the council as SNP Group Leader. He is also a board member of Scottish Enterprise Tayside and several other local bodies in the area. In the Scottish Parliament he was SNP chief whip from 1999 to 2000 before becoming Shadow Minister for Transport and Environment following the Swinney reshuffle of September 2000. Within the Scottish Parliament he sat on the European Committee from 1999 to 2000 before joining the Transport and Environment Committee in 2000 and he is a member of the Cross Party Group on Older People, Age and Aging.

KEITH HARDING (Conservative) was born in 1938 and educated at Chipping Norton Grammar School and Oxford College of Further Education. Professionally, he was a banker and newsagent; he has been a councillor on Stirling Council since 1986 and was council leader from 1991 to 1995. He was elected to the new single-tier Stirling Council in 1995 and remains a councillor for Torbrex in Stirling. He was also vice-chair of Forth Valley Health Board. He is Conservative spokesperson for local government and housing and sits on the Parliament's Local Government Committee where he has looked bored and uncomfortable during discussions on local government reform to which the Conservatives are opposed. He is a member of the Cross Party Group on Palliative Care.

NICK JOHNSTON (Conservative) was born in 1948 in Filey and is a Yorkshireman transplanted to Kinross. He was educated at North Kesteven Grammar School and Sandhurst and became an actuary with Mercantile and General Reinsurance Company from 1969 until 1971, before working in marketing for Gillette and the *Scotsman*. Before his election he was managing director of the Eastern Western Motor Group in Scotland. He contested Ochil at the Scottish election in 1999 and is the deputy convenor of the Parliament's Audit Committee as well as a member of the Enterprise and Lifelong Learning Committee. He sits on the Cross Party Groups for Children, Drug Misuse, Information, Knowledge and Enlightenment, Oil and Gas, Palliative Care, and Strategic Rail Services. He is the Conservatives' spokesperson on industry, economy and finance and a fan of Teddy Taylor.

TRICIA MARWICK (SNP), a miner's daughter was born in Cowdenbeath in 1953 and worked as a public affairs officer for Shelter from 1992 until her election in 1999. She contested the Fife Central constituency at the 1992, 1997 and 1999 elections and was the SNP's Deputy Business Manager in the Parliament until September 2000 when she became Business Manager. She has been a member of the Standards Committee from May 1999, was a member of the Justice and Home Affairs Committee from 1999 to 2000, and also had a brief period on the Equal Opportunities Committee. She also now serves as a member of the Parliamentary Bureau. She is a member of the Cross Party Groups for Animal Welfare (as befits the co-sponsor of the anti-fox hunting members bill), Epilepsy, Palliative Care, and Men's Violence Against Women.

BRIAN MONTEITH (Conservative) was born in 1957 and educated at Parsons Green Primary, Portobello High School, Edinburgh and Heriot-Watt University. Before the election he was a public affairs consultant with Dunedin Public Relations, and had also worked as a researcher at the Centre for Policy Studies and for Michael Forsyth Associates. He was a prominent No campaigner at the 1997 Scottish referendum, something he might wish to forget, though his opponents will not. He was a first-time candidate in 1999 contesting the Stirling constituency at the Scottish election where he came a disappointing third to both Labour and the SNP. He is the Tory spokesperson for education, arts, culture and sport and sits on the Education Committee in the Parliament. He is a member of the Cross Party Groups for Sport and Agriculture and Horticulture. He writes a regular diary for the *Herald* and remains a Hibs football supporter. He has had an active and energetic right-wing past and was Chairman of the Scottish Federation of Conservative Students from 1979 to 1981, and was a prominent member of the Federation at a UK level in the mid-1980s at a time when they had such a hard right reputation, they were viewed as an embarrassment to Thatcher and Tebbit. He has also been active in a host of campaigns and was a founder member of Students Against the Devolution Act 1978 and Conservatives Against Apartheid. For someone who has such a consistent anti-devolutionist and uncompromising Unionist past, Monteith has proven remarkably adept at using the Parliament to promote his views, perhaps not that surprising considering his public relations background.

KEITH RAFFAN (Liberal Democrat) was born in 1949 in Aberdeen and educated at Robert Gordon's College, Aberdeen, Trinity College Glenalmond, and then at Corpus Christi College, Cambridge. He was a leftist Tory who was chair of Pressure for Economic and Social Toryism (PEST) the predecessor to the Tory Reform Group, and worked as a journalist on the *Spectator, Daily Express,* and *Sunday Express* from 1974 to 1983. Then, he was elected as Conservative MP for Delyn in North Wales between 1983 and 1992. He sat on the Welsh Affairs Select Committee throughout his tenure at Westminster. He was pro-devolution, hence part of the reason for his departure from the Tories to the Liberal Democrats after 1992, and had previously stood for the Tories in Scotland back in 1974 in East Aberdeenshire.

From 1992 until 1994 he worked as a PR consultant in New York, and from 1994 to 1999 as a presenter and interviewer with HTV in Wales. He stood for the Liberal Democrats at the North East European Parliamentary by-election in November 1998 and then stood as a regional list candidate in Mid-Scotland and Fife in 1999. In the Scottish Parliament, he has the reputation of being a maverick of sorts and was the only member of his party who did not vote for Donald Dewar in May 1999 as First Minister, instead choosing to abstain. He was also one of only three Liberal Democrat MSPs who voted against entering a coalition with Labour, the others being Donald Gorrie and John Farquhar Munro. In the Parliament, he sat on the Finance and Social Inclusion Committees from May 1999 to Decmber 2000 and joined the Audit Committee in January 2001. He was the Liberal Democrat spokesman for Health and Community Care from November 2000 to January 2001. He was a member of the Cross Party Groups for Media and Tobacco Control and is convenor of the group on Drug Misuse. He resigned as Lib Dem spokesman on Health following the Scottish Parliament debate on the Sutherland Commission proposals.

GEORGE REID (SNP) was born in Tullibody in 1939. He was educated at St Andrews University and Union College in the USA. He worked as a journalist and producer before his election to Westminster in 1974, with the *Daily Express* from 1962 to 1964, STV from 1964 to 1966 and Granada from 1966 to 1969. He was then head of News and Current Affairs at STV from 1969 to 1974. He was elected as MP for Clackmannanshire and East Stirling from 1974 to 1979 and contested the successor constituency, Ochil, in 1997 and 1999. In between the 1979 defeat and 1999 election success, he was a TV and radio presenter with the BBC until 1984 and then public affairs director with the International Red Cross in Geneva until 1996, followed by a period as a consultant. He was the vice-convenor of fundraising for the SNP and also their external affairs spokesperson until the 1999 election. He is Deputy Presiding Officer within the Scottish Parliament and chairs the Convenors' Liaison Group within the Parliament. He is likely to replace David Steel as Presiding Officer in the next Scottish Parliament given his effectiveness as deputy and co-operative links with the different parties.

NORTH EAST SCOTLAND

North East Scotland runs along the north-east coast of Scotland and includes the two major cities of this area, Aberdeen and Dundee, and most of their hinterlands. The regional seat, like the neighbouring Highlands and Islands, stands aloof from the political patterns of the Scottish Central Belt, reflecting an often genuine four-party system. In 1997, Labour came out on top winning 30.9 per cent of the vote to the SNP's 26.1 per cent, with the Conservatives on 22.4 per cent and the Liberal Democrats 18.9 per cent. The electoral map, as in elsewhere in Scotland, was shaped by Conservative losses with Aberdeen South a Tory gain in 1992 won back by Labour and Aberdeenshire West and Kincardineshire won by the Lib Dems. Gordon, a 'notional' Conservative seat in 1992, was also 'lost' to the Lib Dems – leaving Labour with five seats to two each for the Lib Dems and SNP.

In November 1998, the SNP convincingly won the North East Scotland Euro by-election with 48.0 per cent of the vote, with Labour pushed into third place, giving the party a good deal of confidence in this area. In the 1999 Scottish Parliament elections, the SNP polled well here, but not well enough to make a break-through: winning 33.1 per cent of the constituency vote to Labour's 26.2 per cent. The SNP's rise in popularity saw it run Labour close in Aberdeen North and Dundee West, but win no extra constituency seats, and the only seat to change hands was the three way marginal Aberdeen South which was won by the Lib Dems from Labour. This resulted in Labour winning four constituencies, Lib Dems three and SNP two. In the regional vote, the SNP won 32.4 per cent to Labour's 25.5 per cent and the Conservatives 18.3 per cent resulting in the 'top up' seats being secured by four SNP and three Conservative members.

Constituency Members Elected

Constituency	Member	Party
Aberdeen Central	Lewis Macdonald	Labour
Aberdeen North	Elaine Thomson	Labour
Aberdeen South	Nicol Stephen	Liberal Democrat
Aberdeenshire West and Kincardine	Mike Rumbles	Liberal Democrat
Angus	Andrew Welsh	SNP
Banff and Buchan	Alex Salmond	SNP
Dundee East	John McAllion	Labour
Dundee West	Kate MacLean	Labour
Gordon	Nora Radcliffe	Liberal Democrat

Constituency Party Shares of the Vote

Party	Vote	% Share
SNP	94,462	33.10
Labour	74,648	26.16
Liberal Democrat	60,540	21.21
Conservative	50,901	17.84
Independent	2,559	0.90
SSP	2,063	0.72
SWP	206	0.07

Electorate: 518,521

Turnout: 285,379 (55.04%)

Additional Members Elected

David Davidson	Conservative
Alex Johnstone	Conservative
Ben Wallace	Conservative
Brian Adam	SNP
Richard Lochhead	SNP
Irene McGugan	SNP
Shona Robison	SNP

Regional List Party Shares of the Vote

Party	Votes	% Share
SNP	92,329	32.35
Labour	72,666	25.46
Conservative	52,149	18.27
Liberal Democrat	49,843	17.46
Scottish Green	8,067	2.83
Socialist Labour	3,557	1.25
SSP	3,016	1.06
Independent Watt	2,303	0.81
Independent SB	770	0.27
NLP	746	0.26

Electorate: 518,521

Turnout: 285,446 (55.05%)

BRIAN ADAM (SNP) was born in 1948 in Newmill and educated at Keith Grammar School and as a biochemist and pharmacologist at Aberdeen University from which he has BSc and MSc degrees. He worked for Glaxo from 1970–3, Aberdeen City Hospital from 1973 to 1988 and then as Senior biochemist at Aberdeen Royal Infirmary from 1988 until his election in 1999. He was a councillor on Aberdeen City Council from 1988 onwards and contested the Aberdeen North constituency, which includes his council ward at the elections of 1997 and 1999. He came very close to taking the seat from Labour in 1999. He sat on the Parliament's Audit Committee and Social Inclusion Committee from May 1999 to December 2000, now sits on the Procedures and Social Justice Committees and is SNP Deputy Whip and became Deputy Business Manager after September 2000. He is a member of the Cross Party Groups on Borders Rail, Drug Misuse, Epilepsy, Oil and Gas, Palliative Care, Media and Tobacco Control.

DAVID DAVIDSON (Conservative) was born in 1943 in Edinburgh and was educated at Trinity Academy, Edinburgh, and went on to study pharmacy at Heriot-Watt University and Business Administration at Manchester Business School. He was a pharmacist and managed a chain of pharmacies before his election, in addition to managing a family farm. He was also a director of Unichem and a founder of the Association of Scottish Community Councils. He was a local councillor in Stirling Council from 1995 to 1999 before standing in the north east and fighting the Banff and Buchan constituency at the Scottish Parliament election. He is deputy spokesperson on Industry and sits on the Finance Committee in the Parliament. He sits on the Cross Party Groups for Information, Knowledge and Enlightenment, Oil and Gas, and Agriculture and Horticulture.

ALEX JOHNSTONE (Conservative) was born in 1963, educated at Mackie Academy, Stonehaven and was a farmer before his election in 1999. He contested the Gordon constituency for the Tories in 1999 and is the party's spokesperson on rural affairs. He was also convenor of the Parliament's Rural Affairs Committee and is now Convenor of the Rural Development Committee. This post puts him at the heart of the rural affairs agenda and, in particular, the debate over the fox-hunting bill produced as a member's bill by Labour MSP Mike Watson, which is likely to dominate the committee's workload for a considerable time. He serves on the Cross Party Groups for Crofting, Animal Welfare, and Agriculture and Horticulture.

RICHARD LOCHHEAD (SNP) was born in Paisley in 1969 and educated at Williamwood High School, Clarkston, Glasgow Central College of Commerce, and Stirling University, where he gained a degree in Politics. He worked with the South of Scotland Electricity Board from 1987 to 1989, before studying at Stirling. After graduating from Stirling he was constituency assistant and then office manager for Alex Salmond in Banff and Buchan and also worked as an economic development officer with Dundee City Council before his election. He stood in Gordon at the general election of 1997 followed by Aberdeen Central in 1999. He is the SNP's deputy spokesperson for rural affairs, with responsibility for fishing, and sat on the Parliament's Rural Affairs Committee and now sits on the Rural Development Committee and was a member from May 1999 to December 2000 of the European Committee. He is a member of the Cross Party Groups on Oil and Gas and the Media.

IRENE McGUGAN (SNP) was born in 1952 in Angus, educated at Forfar Academy and studied social work and child protection at Aberdeen and Dundee Universities. She engaged in voluntary work for a number of years, including with Voluntary Service Overseas in India, was a social worker with Tayside Regional Council from 1985 to 1996 and was a childcare manager in Angus Council's Social Work department before her election. She contested Aberdeen South at the Scottish election in 1999. She sits on the Scottish Parliament's Education Committees and was a member of the Rural Affairs Committee from 1999 to 2000. She has also been an active campaigner for the Scots language within the Parliament. She became Shadow Deputy Minister for Education, Culture and Sport in September 2000. She serves on the Cross Party Groups for Children and Oil and Gas and is also a Kirk elder and so has probably felt at home on the Mound.

SHONA ROBISON (SNP) was born in Alva in 1966 and educated at Alva Academy, Glasgow University (MA in social sciences) and Jordanhill College, where she gained a postgraduate certificate in community education. She worked for Glasgow City Council before her election, as a community worker and home care organiser. She contested the Dundee East constituency at the 1997 and 1999 elections. She was deputy convenor of the Equal Opportunities Committee in the Scottish Parliament and now serves on the Health and Community Care Committee and is the Secretary to the SNP's Parliamentary Group. She became Shadow Deputy Minister for Health and Community Care in September 2000 and is also convenor of the Cross Party Group on Refugees and Asylum Seekers.

BEN WALLACE (Conservative) was born in 1970 in Farnborough, educated at Millfeild School, Somerset and Sandhurst, and was an army officer from 1991 until 1998, serving in Northern Ireland and Central America. He was Conservative candidate in Aberdeenshire West and Kincardine in 1999 and is the deputy spokesperson for Health in the Parliament, where he sits on the European Committee and was a member of the Health and Community Care Committee from May 1999 to December 2000. He is a member of the Cross Party Groups for Epilepsy, Oil and Gas, Agriculture and Horticulture, and Refugees and Asylum

Seekers. However, since his election in 1999 he sought selection as Tory candidate for a number of Westminster seats, so his tenure in the Scottish Parliament may prove a short one.

SOUTH OF SCOTLAND

The South of Scotland regional seat extends across Scotland from the Ayrshire coast along the Firth of Clyde to the Firth of Forth, encompassing along the way the Scottish Borders and Dumfries and Galloway. In 1997 this area voted Labour 43.4 per cent, Conservative 22.6 per cent, SNP 19.1 per cent, Liberal Democrat 13.4 per cent. The Conservatives lost Dumfries to Labour and Galloway and Upper Nithsdale to the SNP, while the already 'notional' Labour seat of Ayr in 1992 shifted even more emphatically to Labour. This gave an overall result of Labour winning six seats, the Lib Dems two and the SNP one. In the 1999 Scottish Parliament elections, Labour won 37.2 per cent of the constituency vote, while the SNP won 25.7 per cent and the Conservatives 23.0 per cent. No constituencies changed hands, with the biggest movement and surprise being the Conservative Phil Gallie's near victory in Ayr reducing Labour's majority to 25 votes. In the regional vote, Labour won 31.0 per cent to the SNP's 25.2 per cent and the Conservatives 21.6 per cent, producing an additional member representation of four Conservative 'top up' members, their highest number in any regional seat, and three SNP members.

Constituency Members Elected

Constituency	Member	Party
Ayr	Ian Welsh	Labour
Carrick, Cumnock and Doon Valley	Cathy Jamieson	Labour
Clydesdale	Karen Gillon	Labour
Cunninghame South	Irene Oldfather	Labour
Dumfries	Elaine Murray	Labour
East Lothian	John Home Robertson	Labour
Galloway and Upper Nithsdale	Alasdair Morgan	SNP
Roxburgh and Berwickshire	Euan Robson	Liberal Democrat
Tweeddale, Ettrick and Lauderdale	Ian Jenkins	Liberal Democrat

Constituency Party Shares of the Vote

Party	Vote	%Share
Labour	117,799	37.19
SNP	81,516	25.74
Conservative	72,690	22.95
Liberal Democrat	44,739	14.12

Electorate: 510,634

Turnout: 316,744 (62.03%)

Additional Members Elected

Phil Gallie	Conservative
David Mundell	Conservative
Murray Tosh	Conservative
Alex Fergusson	Conservative
Michael Russell	SNP
Adam Ingram	SNP
Christine Creech (now Christine Grahame)	SNP

Regional List Party Shares of the Vote

Party	Votes	%Share
Labour	98,836	31.04
SNP	80,059	25.15
Conservative	68,908	21.64
Liberal Democrat	38,157	11.99
Socialist Labour	13,887	4.36
Scottish Green	9,468	2.97
Liberal	3,478	1.09
SSP	3,304	1.04
UK Independence	1,502	0.47
Natural Law Party	775	0.24

Electorate: 510,634

Turnout: 318,370 (62.35%)

ALEXANDER FERGUSSON (Conservative) was born in 1949 in Leswalt, Wigtownshire, and educated at Eton and the West of Scotland Agricultural College gaining an Ordinary National Diploma in Agriculture. He worked as a farm management consultant from 1970 to 1971, and as a farmer from 1971 to 1999 ran a 1,500-acre family farm. He was also a restaurant owner from 1981 to 1986 and President of the Blackface Sheepbreeders' Association until 1999.

Fergusson stood for the Conservatives in the Galloway and Upper Nithsdale constituency in 1999 and was elected for the South of Scotland Regional seat. He is Scottish Conservative Deputy Shadow Spokesman for Rural Affairs with special responsibility for fisheries. He served on the Rural Affairs Committee of the Scottish Parliament and now sits on the Rural Development Committee. He is also a member of the Cross Party Groups on Animal Welfare, Borders Rail, Drug Misuse, Epilepsy, Palliative Care, Tobacco Control, and Agriculture and Horticulture, the last of which he is Joint Convenor of.

PHIL GALLIE (Conservative) was born in 1939 in Portsmouth and educated at Dunfermline High School, Rosyth Dockyard Technical College and Kirkcaldy Technical College. He worked as an apprentice electrical fitter in HM Dockyard, Rosyth, from 1955 to 1960, as an Electrical Engineer in the merchant navy, Ben Line from 1960 to 1964, and in several power stations in Scotland and England from 1964 to 1992.

Gallie was Conservative MP for Ayr from 1992 to 1997, inheriting the seat from George Younger in 1992 and against all expectations holding it that year with a majority of 85 votes. Gallie had previously stood for Westminster, contesting Cunninghame North in 1983 and Dunfermline West in 1987, and as an MP was a member of the Scottish Affairs Select Committee from 1992 to 1997. After losing his Westminster seat in 1997, Gallie contested the leadership of the Scottish Conservatives in September 1998, losing to David McLetchie. He stood in the Ayr seat in the Scottish Parliament, losing to Labour's Ian Welsh by the narrowest of margins: 25 votes. Gallie was subsequently elected as a list MSP for the South of Scotland and is Conservative Spokesperson on Home Affairs, was a member of the Justice and Home Affairs Committee and Public Petitions Committee from May 1999 to December 2000 and is now a member of the Justice I Committee. He is involved in the Cross Party Groups on Animal Welfare – of which he is Convenor – and Agriculture and Horticulture and Renewable Energy.

Gallie is a populist right-wing working-class Tory in the Teddy Taylor mould, increasingly rare in the Scottish and UK party. In the Commons, he was associated with the right-wing Eurosceptic tendency of the party, but did not rebel on any major votes. His mixture of populism and pugnaciousness adds liveliness to the Conservative ranks in the Parliament.

CHRISTINE GRAHAME (SNP, elected as Christine Creech) was born in 1944 in Burton-on-Trent and educated at Boroughmuir School, Edinburgh, Edinburgh University and Moray House College of Education. She worked as a secondary teacher at Woodmill High School in Fife and at Whithorn Secondary School from 1966 to 1982, and as a solicitor, then a partner in Alan Dawson, Simpson and Hampton, moving to J. & R.A. Robertson where she was Senior Litigation Assistant from 1985 to 1998, and then to Dickson, McNiven & Dunn from 1998 to 1999.

Grahame stood for the SNP in Tweeddale, Ettrick and Lauderdale in 1992 and in the South of Scotland seat in the 1994 European elections. In 1999, she stood in Tweeddale again and was elected for the South of Scotland Regional seat. She was SNP Spokesperson for Older People for the first year and is now Spokesperson for Social Security. She was a member of the Public Petitions Committee and the Justice and Home Affairs Committee, from May 1999 to December 2000, and joined the Justice Committee in January 2000. She is also a member of the Cross Party Groups on Animal Welfare, Borders Rail, Drug Misuse, Epilepsy, and Older People.

ADAM INGRAM (SNP) was born in 1951 in Kilmarnock and educated at Kilmarnock Academy and Paisley College where he gained a BA (Hons) in Business Economics. He was a manager in A. H. Ingram and Son, the family bakery firm, from 1971 to 1976, Senior Economic Assistant with the Manpower Services Commission from 1985 to 1986, then a Researcher and Lecturer at Paisley College from 1987 to 1988, before latterly being an economic development consultant from 1989 to 1999.

Ingram stood in the Carrick, Cumnock and Doon Valley constituency for the SNP in 1999 and was elected for the South of Scotland Regional seat. In the Parliament, he became SNP Deputy Finance Spokesperson in 2000, after being Alex Neil's campaign manager for the SNP leadership. He sits on the Finance Committee and was a member of the Standards Committee from May 1999 to December 2000. He is also a member of the Cross Party Groups on Animal Welfare, Borders Rail, Drug Misuse, Older People, Rail Services, Men's Violence Against Women, and Children.

DAVID MUNDELL (Conservative) was born in 1962 in Dumfries and educated at Lockerbie Academy, Edinburgh University and Strathclyde Business School where he gained an MBA. He worked as a corporate lawyer with Biggart, Baillie and Gifford in Glasgow from 1989 to 1991, as Group Legal Adviser with BT Scotland from 1991 until 1998 and as Head of National Affairs from 1998 to 1999.

Mundell was elected to Annandale and Eskdale District Council from 1984 to 1986 and Dumfries and Galloway Council from 1986 to 1987 for the Conservatives. He stood in the Dumfries seat in 1999 and was elected for the South of Scotland Regional seat. He is Scottish Conservative Deputy Shadow Spokesperson for Education. He was a member of the European Committee from May 1999 to December 2000. He is also a member of the Cross Party Groups on Borders Rail, Children, Information, Knowledge and Enlightenment, of which he is Convenor, Rail Services, and the Media. Mundell is a former member of the Management Board of the International Teledemocracy Centre and an accredited Alternative Dispute Resolution Mediator. He shot to prominence in his first year, when he was criticised for retaining a £10,000 per annum BT consultancy after being elected an MSP, which was promptly wound up.

MICHAEL RUSSELL (SNP) was born in Bromley, Kent, in 1953 and educated at Marr College, Troon, and Edinburgh University. He has had a rich and varied array of posts in the cultural industry sector: Creative Producer with the Church of Scotland 1974 to 1977, as Director of Cinema Sgire in the Western Isles from 1977 to 1981, Secretary General of the Association of Film and TV in the Celtic Countries 1983 to 1991, and Director of Eala Bhan from 1991. He was Chief Executive of the Scottish National Party from 1994 to 1999. As well as Chief Executive, Russell has held a range of responsible posts in the SNP. He was Vice-Convenor for Publicity from 1987 to 1991, campaign manager of the Alex Salmond leadership campaign in 1990 and Elections Director from 1994 to 1999. He stood in the Clydesdale seat in 1987 and in Cunninghame South in 1999, being returned as an MSP for the South of Scotland Regional seat.

Russell was a member of the Scottish Parliamentary Bureau, and was SNP Business Manager and Principal Shadow Spokesperson for Culture, Broadcasting and Gaelic from May 1999 to September 2000; he is now Spokesperson for Children and Education. He was a member of the Procedures Committee from May 1999 to December 2000. He is also involved in the Cross Party Groups on Gaelic, of which he is the Vice-Convenor, Borders Rail, Epilepsy, Information, Knowledge and Enlightenment, Media, of which he is Vice-Convenor, and Tobacco Control.

Russell has been a leading force in the modernisation of the SNP in the last ten years, helping to turn it into an effective, efficient and professional party in both organisation and policy. For the last decade, he has worked hand in hand with Alex Salmond on this project, the nearest the SNP could get to a Peter Mandelson figure. The immense progress he has made has aroused suspicion and opposition and put him under intense pressure, which was seen in the Scottish Parliament elections, when there were rumours of a rift in the Salmond-Russell axis. Post-election, Russell conceded that the election campaign, which he had led, had been characterised by several tactical mistakes, notably the way the party presented its 'A Penny for Scotland' campaign. Russell is one of the central players in the SNP and will have a crucial role in the party's progress under devolution. He is a widely published author and has written *A Poem of Remote Lives*, *The Enigma of Werner Hissling* and *In Waiting: Travels in the Shadow of Edwin Muir*.

MURRAY TOSH (Conservative) was born in 1950 in Ayr and educated at Kilmarnock Academy, Glasgow University and Jordanhill College of Education. He worked as a history teacher at Ravenspark Academy, Irvine, in 1975, as Principal Teacher of History, Kilwinning Academy, from 1977 to 1984 and at Belmont Academy, Ayr, from 1984 to 1989.

Tosh first stood for national office in Ayr in the October 1974 election for the Liberals, and first stood with the Conservatives in Glasgow Hillhead in 1983. He was elected to Kyle and Carrick District Council from 1987 to 1996 and was Deputy Leader of the Conservative Group from 1992 to 1996, Convenor of the Housing Committee and Vice-Convenor of the Planning and Development Committee.

In the 1999 elections, Tosh stood in the Cunninghame South seat and was returned for the South of Scotland. He is Scottish Conservative Principal Shadow Spokesman for Transport and Environment, Convenor of the Procedures Committee and a member of the Transport and Environment Committee. He is also a member of the Borders Rail Cross Party Group, of which he is the vice-convenor, and the

Renewable Energy Group, of which he is the Convenor. As befits someone who came late in life to the Conservatives, Tosh has gained a reputation for being an open-minded, pragmatic politician interested in getting things done.

WEST OF SCOTLAND

The West of Scotland seat includes nine constituencies all to the west of Glasgow on both the north and south banks of the Clyde. Many of these seats have nothing in common bar their commuter status to the neighbouring city of Glasgow. In 1997, this area voted Labour 51.3 per cent to SNP 19.9 per cent, Conservative 18.2 per cent and Liberal Democrats 9.2 per cent. Labour won all nine constituency seats, gaining Eastwood from the Conservatives.

In the 1999 Scottish Parliament elections, Labour won 43.5 per cent of the constituency vote to the SNP's 26.9 per cent and Labour retained all nine of the seats it was defending. West of Scotland was one of only two regional seats where Labour won all the FPTP seats, the other being Glasgow. In the regional vote, Labour won 38.6 per cent of the vote to the SNP's 25.9 per cent and Conservatives 15.7 per cent. This produced an additional member representation of four SNP 'top up' members to two for the Conservatives and one for the Lib Dems.

Constituency Members Elected

Constituency	Member	Party
Clydesdale and Milngavie	Des McNulty	Labour
Cunninghame North	Allan Wilson	Labour
Dumbarton	Jackie Baillie	Labour
Eastwood	Ken MacIntosh	Labour
Greenock and Inverclyde	Duncan McNeil	Labour
Paisley North	Wendy Alexander	Labour
Paisley South	Hugh Henry	Labour
Strathkelvin and Bearsden	Sam Galbraith	Labour
West Renfrewshire	Patricia Godman	Labour

Constituency Party Shares of the Vote

Party	Vote	%Share
Labour	135,046	43.51
SNP	83,392	26.87
Conservative	50,793	16.36
Liberal Democrat	34,970	11.27
Independent	2,758	0.89
SSP	1,864	0.60
SWP	1,149	0.37
Anti-Drug	423	0.14

Electorate: 498,466

Turnout: 310,395 (62.27%)

Additional Members Elected

Annabel Goldie	Conservative
John Young	Conservative
Ross Finnie	Liberal Democrat
Lloyd Quinan	SNP
Fiona McLeod	SNP
Kay Ullrich	SNP
Colin Campbell	SNP

Regional List Party Shares of the Vote

Party	Votes	%Share
Labour	119,663	38.55
SNP	80,417	25.91
Conservative	48,666	15.68
Liberal Democrat	34,095	10.98
Scottish Green	8,175	2.63
SSP	5,944	1.91
Socialist Labour	4,472	1.44
Pro-Life	3,227	1.04
Individual	2,761	0.89
SUP	1,840	0.59
NLP	589	0.19
Ind Water	565	0.18

Electorate: 498,466

Turnout: 310,414 (62.27%)

COLIN CAMPBELL (SNP) was born in 1938 in Ralston, Paisley, and was educated at Paisley Grammar School, at Glasgow University leaving with an MA Hons in History, and at Jordanhill College of Education. He worked as a history teacher in Hillhead High School from 1961 to 1963, at Paisley Grammar School from 1963 to 1967, as Principal Teacher of Greenock Academy from 1967 to 1973, Deputy Head of Merksworth High from 1973 to 1977, Deputy Head Teacher of Westwood Secondary from 1977 until 1989 and as a part-time tutor with the Senior Studies Institute at Strathclyde University from 1995 to 1998.

Campbell was a councillor on Renfrewshire Council from 1995 until 1999 and is a Church of Scotland Elder. He has stood several times for the SNP in national elections, contesting the West Renfrewshire and Inverclyde seat in 1987 and 1992 and West Renfrewshire in 1997 and 1999, and was elected to the West of Scotland Regional seat. He also stood in Strathclyde West in the 1989 and 1994 European elections. Campbell has been SNP Defence Spokesperson since 1995 and in the Scottish Parliament is Shadow Spokesman on Defence. He sat on the Local Government Committee from May 1999 to December 2000, before joining the European Committe in January 2001. He is also involved in the Cross Party Groups on Children, Epilepsy, and Tobacco Control.

ROSS FINNIE (Liberal Democrat) was born in 1947 in Greenock and educated at Greenock Academy. He worked as an Audit Assistant with Arthur Anderson and Company from 1970 to 1973, as Manager of Corporate Finance, British Bank of Commerce from 1973 to 1974, Manager of Corporate Finance, James Findlay Bank from 1974 until 1986, Director of Glasgow Corporate Finance, Singer and Friedlander from 1986 to 1991, and set up his own chartered accountancy practice, Ross Finnie, and Company from 1991.

He served on Inverclyde District Council from 1977 until 1996 and Inverclyde Council from 1995 to 1999 and was Convenor of Planning on the former from 1977 to 1980, group leader of the Lib Dems from 1988 until 1996 and leader of the Opposition from 1995 to 1999. Finnie was Chair of the Scottish Liberal Party from 1982 to 1986, Chair of their General Election Committee from 1995 to 1997 and Chair of the Scottish Candidates Vetting Panel from 1997 to 1999. He stood in West Renfrewshire in the 1979 general election and in Stirling in 1983. In the 1999 elections he stood in Greenock and Inverclyde where he polled respectably – putting 12 per cent on the Lib Dem vote and cutting Labour's majority to 4,313.

Finnie was one of the five-strong Lib Dem negotiating team with Labour after the election which led to the formation of the Labour-Lib Dem partnership administration. Finnie became, along with Jim Wallace, one of two Lib Dem Executive ministers as Minister for Rural Affairs. Initially seen in the press as a 'Captain Mainwaring' figure out of time and place, Finnie has grown in office and is now generally seen as a safe pair of hands. So much so that when his first major crisis arrived in May 2000, when he was not notified by his Westminster counterpart, Nick Brown, of genetically modified seeds being used in Scotland, he came through it relatively unscathed. Finnie has made a promising start and has in the first year and a half been one of Jim Wallace's closest confidants.

ANNABEL GOLDIE (Conservative) was born in Glasgow in 1950 and educated at Greenock Academy and Strathclyde University where she gained an LLB. She has been self-employed as a partner in law firms since 1978 and was a partner in the Glasgow firm Donaldson, Alexander, Russell and Haddow. She is a member of the Royal Faculty of Procurators in Glasgow, the Law Society and the Scottish Law Agents Society. Goldie has a long record of involvement in voluntary organisations and has been a Director of the Prince's Scottish Youth Trust, a member of the West of Scotland Advisory Board of the Salvation Army and is a Church of Scotland Elder.

She has held a number of posts in the Scottish Conservatives:Vice-Chair in 1992, Deputy Chairman 1995 to 1997 and 1997 to 1998, Chair in 1997 and became Deputy Leader in 1998. Goldie previously stood in West Renfrewshire and Inverclyde in 1992 and in West Renfrewshire in 1999. In the Scottish Parliament, Goldie is Spokesperson on the Economy, Industry and Finance and is a member of the Enterprise and Lifelong Learning Committee, of which she is Deputy Convenor. She was a member of the Audit Committee from May 1999 to December 2000. She has quickly established a reputation as an effective and often, humorous debater, skilled in out-manoeuvring ministers and opponents; in one debate she challenged Wendy Alexander, then Minister for Communities, and many years her junior, with the words 'as one spinster to another'. The McLetchie-Goldie leadership has given the Scottish Conservatives as good a first year and a half in the Scottish Parliament as they have the right to imagine, given their years of opposition to it.

FIONA McLEOD (SNP) was born in 1957 in Glasgow and educated at Bearsden Academy, Edinburgh University, Glasgow University obtaining an MA Hons in Medieval and Modern History, and Strathclyde University gaining a Postgraduate Diploma in Librarianship. She worked as a school librarian in Balfron High School from 1983 to 1987, as a college librarian in Glasgow North College of Nursing from 1987 to 1989 and at Huntershill Marie Curie Library Centre from 1995 to 1998.

McLeod joined the SNP in 1974 and contested Strathkelvin and Bearsden in the Scottish Parliament elections, being returned for the West of Scotland Regional seat. In Parliament, she was SNP Deputy Spokesperson for Children and Sport and is now Deputy Spokesperson for Transport and Environment. She was also a member of the Education, Culture and Sport Committee from 1999 to 2000 and now sits on the Transport and Environment and Subordinate Legislation Committees and the Cross Party Groups on Children, Drug Misuse, Epilepsy, Information, Knowledge and Enlightenment, of which she is Honorary Secretary, Palliative Care, Women, and Sports.

LLOYD QUINAN (SNP) was born in 1957 in Edinburgh and educated at Holy Cross Academy, St Augustine's High School, Edinburgh, Leith Academy, Edinburgh, Queen Margaret College, Edinburgh, where he obtained a Diploma in Drama and Spoken Word and Rochester University, New York. Quinan worked as an actor from 1978 to 1983 and as a theatre director from 1982 to 1989, before becoming a freelance TV presenter, producer and director from 1988 until 1999. He is most widely known for presenting STV's nightly Weather Reports and a late night discussion programme called *Trial By Night*.

Quinan joined the SNP in 1974 and first stood in the Scottish Parliament elections contesting Dumbarton and being returned for the West of Scotland Regional seat. He was SNP Deputy Shadow Spokesperson for Social Inclusion, Trade Unions and the Voluntary Sector for the first year of the Parliament, resigning over the SNP leadership's decision to discipline Margo MacDonald. He was also a member of the Social Inclusion, Housing and Voluntary Sector Committee from 1999 to 2000 and now sits on the Audit and European Committees and the Cross Party Groups on Citizenship, Income, Economy and Society, and the Media.

KAY ULLRICH (SNP) was born in 1943 in Prestwick and educated at Ayr Academy and Queen's College, Glasgow, where she gained a CQSW in Social Work. Ullrich worked as a Butlins Redcoat from 1961 to 1964, a swimming instructor with North Ayrshire Council from 1973 to 1981, a school social worker at Westwood Secondary from 1984 to 1986, a hospital social worker at Crosshouse Hospital from 1986 to 1988, becoming a child care social worker in Ardrossan, Saltcoats and Stevenson from 1988 to 1992, and a senior social worker with Criminal Justice Services, Kilmarnock, from 1992 to 1997.

Ullrich stood several times for the SNP in national polls, contesting Cunninghame South in the 1983 and 1987 elections, Motherwell South in 1992, Monklands East in the 1994 by-election, and Cunninghame North in the 1999 elections, being elected for the West of Scotland Regional seat. Ullrich just failed to win Monklands East in a bitterly fought by-election with Labour in June 1994, reducing Labour's majority from 15,712 to just 1,640 after John Smith's death, but some felt that given Labour's problems over local council corruption and malpractice which became known as 'Monklandsgate', she had missed a golden opportunity and was in some way at fault.

Ullrich was SNP Spokesperson on Health and Social Policy from 1995 and in the Parliament Principal Shadow Spokesperson for Health and Community Care from 1999 to 2000, before becoming Chief Whip. She was a member of the Health and Community Care Committee and is now a member of the Equal Opportunities and Standard Committees and of the Cross Party Groups on Animal Welfare, Epilepsy, Oil and Gas, and Palliative Care.

JOHN YOUNG (Conservative) was born in Glasgow in 1930 and educated at Hillhead High School, Glasgow and the Scottish College of Commerce. He has worked in a range of jobs and occupations from a stint in the RAF from 1949 to 1951 to working as an export sales administrative manager, contracts manager and a PR consultant. Young served on Glasgow Council for a staggering 35 near-continuous years: Glasgow Corporation from 1964 to 1973, Glasgow District Council from 1974 to 1996 and Glasgow City Council from 1995 to 1999. He was leader of the minority Tory administration from 1977 to 1979 when the Tories elected 25 councillors across the city, whereas today they have a solitary representative; he was also leader of the opposition from 1979 to 1980, 1988 to 1992 and 1996 to 1998.

He first stood for national office in Rutherglen in 1966, then in Glasgow Cathcart in 1992 and Eastwood in 1999, gaining election to the West of Scotland seat. He is Deputy Spokesperson on Transport and Environment and a member of the Scottish Parliament Corporate Body and is also a member of the Cross Party Groups on Animal Welfare, Epilepsy, and Older People. Young has been Secretary of the Scottish-South African Society from 1986 to 1988 during the years of apartheid, and has been Vice-Chairman of the Scottish Pakistani Association. He was also a member of the Rifkind Commission devising a policy prospectus for the Scottish Conservatives for the Parliament and is author of *A History of Cathcart Conservative Association 1918–93*.

Section Three

SAFE AND MARGINAL SEATS

1999 Scottish Parliament Elections

Labour top ten votes

1	Coatbridge and Chryston	59.35
2	Glasgow Anniesland	58.81
3	Glasgow Springburn	58.56
4	Fife Central	57.31
5	Dunfermline East	55.89
6	Airdrie and Shotts	55.21
7	Hamilton South	54.39
8	East Lothian	54.02
9	Glasgow Shettleston	53.95
10	Cunninghame South	52.82

Labour lowest ten votes

1	Orkney	6.73
2	Gordon	11.75
3	Aberdeenshire West and Kincardine	13.01
4	Banff and Buchan	13.62
5	Fife North East	14.40
6	Roxburgh and Berwickshire	14.72
7	Tayside North	15.05
8	Falkirk West	18.77
9	Angus	20.02
10	Argyll and Bute	20.11

SNP top ten votes

1	Banff and Buchan	52.61
2	Angus	46.49
3	Tayside North	44.11
4	Galloway and Upper Nithsdale	39.28
5	Moray	38.80
6	Ochil	38.20
7	Dundee West	37.15
8	Western Isles	36.94
9	Livingston	36.67
10	Glasgow Govan	36.65

SNP lowest ten votes

1	Orkney	10.28
2	Shetland	14.33
3	Edinburgh West	16.80
4	Roxburgh and Berwickshire	16.93
5	Fife North East	17.73
6	Aberdeen South	19.17
7	Eastwood	19.30
8	Ayr	19.47
9	Dumfries	19.81
10	Glasgow Anniesland	20.21

Conservative top ten votes

1	Ayr	38.01
2	Tayside North	33.09
3	Eastwood	32.70
4	Perth	30.87
5	Galloway and Upper Nithsdale	30.22
6	Aberdeenshire West and Kincardine	29.52
7	Edinburgh Pentlands	28.93
8	Roxburgh and Berwickshire	27.75
9	Dumfries	27.15
10	Moray	25.60

Conservative lowest ten votes

1	Cumbernauld and Kilsyth	4.45
2	Glasgow Maryhill	5.19
3	Glasgow Pollok	5.25
4	Glasgow Springburn	5.31
5	Falkirk West	5.63
6	Fife Central	5.84
7	Greenock and Inverclyde	5.93
8	Glasgow Shettleston	6.14
9	Glasgow Baillieston	6.44
10	Western Isles	7.85

Liberal Democrat top ten votes

1	Orkney	67.39
2	Shetland	54.47
3	Roxburgh and Berwickshire	40.61
4	Fife North East	37.81
5	Gordon	36.74
6	Edinburgh West	36.46
7	Aberdeenshire West and Kincardine	35.92
8	Tweeddale, Ettrick and Lauderdale	35.82
9	Argyll and Bute	34.89
10	Ross, Skye and Inverness West	32.90

Liberal Democrat lowest ten votes

1	Falkirk West	2.83
2	Western Isles	3.27
3	Glasgow Baillieston	3.43
4	Glasgow Pollok	3.57
5	Ayr	4.44
6	Glasgow Shettleston	4.59
7	Glasgow Govan	5.61
8=	Carrick, Cumnock and Doon Valley	5.94
8=	Fife Central	5.94
10	East Lothian	6.03

1997 UK General Election

Labour top ten votes

1	Glasgow Shettleston	73.16
2	Glasgow Springburn	71.36
3	Coatbridge and Chryston	68.32
4	Dunfermline East	66.81
5	Glasgow Baillieston	65.69
6	Hamilton South	65.50
7	Glasgow Maryhill	64.94
8	Hamilton North and Bellshill	64.01
9	Cunninghame South	62.73
10	Glasgow Anniesland	61.84

Labour lowest ten votes

1	Aberdeenshire West and Kincardine	9.08
2	Fife North East	10.28
3	Gordon	10.30
4	Tayside North	11.28
5	Banff and Buchan	11.81
6	Roxburgh and Berwickshire	14.96
7	Angus	15.63
8	Argyll and Bute	15.67
9	Galloway and Upper Nithsdale	16.33
10	Orkney and Shetland	18.27

SNP top ten votes

1	Banff and Buchan	55.77
2	Angus	48.27
3	Tayside North	44.85
4	Galloway and Upper Nithsdale	43.91
5	Moray	41.57
6	Perth	36.38
7	Glasgow Govan	35.05
8	Kilmarnock and Loudoun	34.52
9	Ochil	34.38
10	Western Isles	33.40

SNP lowest ten votes

1	Edinburgh West	8.84
2	Aberdeen South	9.76
3	Fife North East	10.86
4	Roxburgh and Berwickshire	11.33
5	Dumfries	12.07
6	Ayr	12.57
7	Orkney and Shetland	12.70
8	Edinburgh South	12.92
9	Edinburgh Pentlands	13.01
10	Aberdeenshire West and Kincardine	13.06

Conservative top ten votes

1	Tayside North	35.72
2	Aberdeenshire West and Kincardine	34.92
3	Ayr	33.82
4	Eastwood	33.56
5	Stirling	32.52
6	Edinburgh Pentlands	32.38
7	Galloway and Upper Nithsdale	30.52
8	Perth	29.33
9	Dumfries	28.04
10	Edinburgh West	27.98

Conservative lowest ten votes

1	Glasgow Shettleston	5.53
2	Glasgow Maryhill	5.88
3	Glasgow Springburn	5.99
4	Glasgow Pollok	6.03
5	Western Isles	6.65
6	Cumbernauld and Kilsyth	7.68
7	Glasgow Baillieston	7.75
8	Coatbridge and Chryston	8.55
9	Hamilton South	8.64
10	Paisley South	8.67

Liberal Democrat top ten votes

1	Orkney and Shetland	51.99
2	Fife North East	51.22
3	Roxburgh and Berwickshire	46.50
4	Edinburgh West	43.20
5	Gordon	42.61
6	Aberdeenshire West and Kincardine	41.08
7	Argyll and Bute	40.20
8	Ross, Skye and Inverness West	38.72
9	Caithness, Sutherland and Easter Ross	35.59
10	Tweeddale, Ettrick and Lauderdale	31.22

Liberal Democrat lowest ten votes

1	Western Isles	3.07
2	Glasgow Pollok	3.47
3	Cumbernauld and Kilsyth	3.80
4	Glasgow Baillieston	3.82
5	Glasgow Shettleston	3.96
6	Kilmarnock and Loudoun	3.99
7	Dundee East	4.14
8	Airdrie and Shotts	4.17
9	Glasgow Springburn	4.27
10	Cunninghame South	4.53

1999 Scottish Parliament Elections

Top Ten Largest Labour Majorities

1	Glasgow Anniesland	38.60
2	Coatbridge and Chryston	34.45
3	Glasgow Springburn	32.40
4	East Lothian	30.77
5	Dunfermline East	29.33
6	Strathkelvin and Bearsden	28.59
7	Hamilton South	27.68
8	Airdrie and Shotts	27.05
9	Glasgow Shettleston	26.62
10	Fife Central	26.40

Top Ten Smallest Labour Majorities

1	Ayr	0.07
2	Dundee West	0.42
3	Aberdeen North	1.43
4	Ochil	3.53
5	Eastwood	5.08
6	Glasgow Govan	6.65
7	Kilmarnock and Loudoun	7.01
8	Edinburgh Pentlands	7.29
9	West Renfrewshire	8.50
10	Linlithgow	8.66

1997 UK General Election

Top Ten Largest Labour Majorities

1	Glasgow Shettleston	59.18
2	Glasgow Springburn	54.87
3	Coatbridge and Chryston	51.30
4	Dunfermline East	51.26
5	Maryhill	47.99
6	Hamilton South	47.98
7	Glasgow Baillieston	46.59
8	Hamilton North and Bellshill	44.92
9	Glasgow Anniesland	44.73
10	Carrick, Cumnock and Doon Valley	42.84

Top Ten Smallest Labour Majorities

1	Inverness East, Nairn and Lochaber	4.90
2	Eastwood	6.19
3	Aberdeen South	7.64
4	Glasgow Govan	9.04
5=	Ochil	10.63
5=	Edinburgh Pentlands	10.63
7	Ayr	14.63
8	Stirling	14.93
9	Kilmarnock and Loudoun	15.30
10	Dumfries	19.47

1999 Scottish Parliament Elections

Liberal Democrat Majorities

1	Orkney	51.79
2	Shetland	32.01
3	Caithness, Sutherland and Easter Ross	16.87
4	Fife North East	14.09
5	Tweeddale, Ettrick and Lauderdale	13.28
6	Roxburgh and Berwickshire	12.86
7	Gordon	12.48
8	Edinburgh West	11.02
9	Aberdeenshire West and Kincardine	6.40
10	Argyll and Bute	6.39
11	Aberdeen South	5.07
12	Ross, Skye and Inverness West	4.34

SNP Majorities

1	Banff and Buchan	35.58
2	Angus	25.78
3	Moray	12.30
4	Tayside North	11.02
5	Galloway and Upper Nithsdale	9.06
6	Perth	5.42
7	Inverness East, Nairn and Lochaber	1.06

1997 UK General Election

Liberal Democrat Majorities

1	Orkney and Shetland	33.72
2	Fife North East	24.75
3	Roxburgh and Berwickshire	22.63
4	Argyll and Bute	17.03
5	Gordon	16.57
6	Edinburgh West	15.22
7	Ross, Skye and Inverness West	10.06
8	Caithness, Sutherland and Easter Ross	7.75
9	Aberdeenshire West and Kincardine	6.16
10	Tweeddale, Ettrick and Lauderdale	3.81

SNP Majorities

1	Banff and Buchan	31.97
2	Angus	23.66
3	Moray	14.00
4	Galloway and Upper Nithsdale	13.39
5	Tayside North	9.13
6	Perth	7.05

Section Four

SOCIO-ECONOMIC CHARACTERISTICS OF CONSTITUENCIES

Male Claimant Unemployment Figures: June 2000

	Constituency	%
1	Glasgow Springburn	13.4
2	Glasgow Pollok	13.1
3	Glasgow Maryhill	11.9
4	Glasgow Anniesland	11.8
5	Glasgow Baillieston	11.5
6	Dundee East	11.2
7	Cunninghame South	10.8
8	Glasgow Shettleston	10.6
9	Kirkcaldy	10.1
10	Glasgow Govan	9.9
11	Dundee West	9.3
12	Fife Central	8.6
13	Motherwell and Wishaw	8.6
14	Kilmarnock and Loudoun	8.5
15	Western Isles	8.5
16	Dumbarton	8.2
17	Paisley North	8.2
18	Glasgow Cathcart	8.1
19	Airdrie and Shotts	8.0
20	Clydebank and Milngavie	7.9
21	Glasgow Kelvin	7.8
22	Caithness, Sutherland and Easter Ross	7.8
23	Carrick, Cumnock and Doon Valley	7.8
24	Falkirk West	7.7
25	Paisley South	7.6
26	Ayr	7.5
27	Cunninghame North	7.6
28	Hamilton South	7.4
29	Hamilton North and Bellshill	7.3
30	Greenock and Inverclyde	7.2

	Constituency	%
31	Angus	7.1
32	Coatbridge and Chryston	7.1
33	Galloway and Upper Nithsdale	6.7
34	Edinburgh North and Leith	6.3
35	Dumfries	6.1
36	Glasgow Rutherglen	6.1
37	Argyll and Bute	6.0
38	Dunfermline West	6.0
39	Aberdeen Central	5.8
40	Dunfermline East	5.7
41	Ross, Skye and Inverness West	5.6
42	Linlithgow	5.6
43	Ochil	5.6
44	Clydesdale	5.4
45	Falkirk East	5.4
46	West Renfrewshire	5.2
47	Stirling	5.1
48	Moray	5.1
49	Cumbernauld and Kilsyth	4.9
50	Livingston	4.8
51	Edinburgh Central	4.5
52	Edinburgh East and Musselburgh	4.4
53	Roxburgh and Berwickshire	4.4
54	Inverness East, Nairn and Lochaber	4.4
55	East Kilbride	4.4
56	Aberdeen North	4.3
57	Edinburgh South	4.2
58	Shetland	4.1
59	Banff and Buchan	4.1
60	Strathkelvin and Bearsden	3.9
61	Edinburgh Pentlands	3.9
62	Perth	3.7
63	North Tayside	3.5
64	Edinburgh West	3.5
65	Eastwood	3.5
66	Aberdeen South	3.4
67	North East Fife	3.4
68	East Lothian	3.3
69	Midlothian	3.3
70	Tweeddale, Ettrick and Lauderdale	3.1

	Constituency	%
71	Orkney	2.8
72	Gordon	2.5
73	Aberdeenshire West and Kincardineshire	2.3

Source: Scottish Parliament Information Services

Council Housing as a Percentage of all Households

	Constituency	%
1=	Airdrie and Shotts	62.5
1=	Motherwell and Wishaw	62.5
3	Glasgow Baillieston	61.4
4	Glasgow Springburn	59.3
5	Glasgow Maryhill	58.9
6	Glasgow Pollok	57.1
7	Coatbridge and Chryston	56.0
8	Glasgow Shettleston	55.4
9	Cunninghame South	55.3
10	Glasgow Anniesland	54.9
11	Hamilton North and Bellshill	53.4
12	Linlithgow	52.8
13	Hamilton South	51.3
14	Paisley South	50.4
15	Falkirk West	49.2
16=	Aberdeen North	49.0
16=	Dundee West	49.0
18	Carrick, Cumnock and Doon Valley	47.6
19	Dunfermline East	47.3
20	Greenock and Inverclyde	47.0
21	Kilmarnock and Loudoun	46.8
22	Falkirk East	46.3
23	Paisley North	46.2
24	Clydebank and Milngavie	45.5
25	Glasgow Rutherglen	44.1
26	Livingston	43.5
27	Kirkcaldy	43.4
28	Fife Central	43.0
29	Ochil	42.9
30	Clydesdale	42.7
31	Aberdeen Central	42.5
32	Dundee West	42.0

	Constituency	%
33	Midlothian	41.5
34	Glasgow Cathcart	40.6
35	East Lothian	39.0
36	Cumbernauld and Kilsyth	38.8
37	Dumbarton	36.7
38	Cunninghame North	34.8
39	East Kilbride	34.7
40=	Banff and Buchan	34.3
40=	West Renfrewshire	34.3
42	Caithness, Sutherland and Easter Ross	33.7
43	Roxburgh and Berwickshire	32.6
44	Ross, Skye and Inverness West	32.0
45	Ayr	31.5
46	Stirling	31.4
47=	Edinburgh East and Musselburgh	30.6
47=	Glasgow Govan	30.6
49=	Dumfries	29.7
49=	Dunfermline West	29.7
51	Galloway and Upper Nithsdale	29.2
52	Moray	28.4
53	Aberdeen South	28.1
54	Angus	28.1
55	Perth	27.7
56	Argyll and Bute	27.6
57	Tayside North	27.5
58	Tweeddale, Ettrick and Lauderdale	26.7
59	Inverness East, Nairn and Lochaber	26.1
60	Orkney and Shetland	24.5
61	Edinburgh Pentlands	24.0
62	Glasgow Kelvin	23.6
63	Gordon	22.5
64	Strathkelvin and Bearsden	21.5
65	Western Isles	20.8
66	Fife North East	20.7
67	Edinburgh South	20.3
68	Edinburgh West	18.6
69	Aberdeenshire West and Kincardine	18.3
70	Eastwood	17.2
71	Edinburgh North and Leith	15.8
72	Edinburgh Central	12.9

Source: 1991 Census

Owner Occupation as a Percentage of all Households

	Constituency	%
1	Eastwood	79.5
2	Strathkelvin and Bearsden	75.1
3	Edinburgh West	73.6
4	Western Isles	68.9
5	Edinburgh Pentlands	67.9
6	Edinburgh South	67.1
7	Aberdeenshire West and Kincardine	65.3
8	Gordon	65.0
9	Fife North East	64.6
10	Edinburgh Central	64.2
11	Edinburgh North and Leith	63.9
12	Ayr	62.9
13	East Kilbride	62.8
14	Dunfermline West	62.7
15	Edinburgh East and Musselburgh	62.0
16	Aberdeen South	61.2
17	West Renfrewshire	61.1
18	Orkney and Shetland	60.7
19=	Angus	60.0
19=	Inverness East, Nairn and Lochaber	60.0
21	Tweeddale, Ettrick and Lauderdale	59.9
22	Stirling	59.3
23	Cunninghame North	58.9
24	Dumfries	58.6
25	Perth	58.2
26	Cumbernauld and Kilsyth	58.0
27	Banff and Buchan	56.6
28	Ross, Skye and Inverness West	56.4
29	Moray	55.3
30	Tayside North	54.5
31	Galloway and Upper Nithsdale	54.2
32	Dumbarton	54.1
33	Livingston	52.5
34=	Argyll and Bute	52.4
34=	East Lothian	52.4
36=	Clydesdale	51.8
36=	Kirkcaldy	51.8
38=	Fife Central	51.6

	Constituency	%
38=	Ochil	51.6
40	Caithness, Sutherland and Easter Ross	50.5
41	Falkirk East	49.8
42	Roxburgh and Berwickshire	49.5
43	Midlothian	49.4
44	Glasgow Cathcart	48.6
45	Dunfermline East	48.5
46	Kilmarnock and Loudoun	48.3
47=	Glasgow Govan	48.2
47=	Glasgow Rutherglen	48.2
49	Clydebank and Milngavie	47.7
50	Glasgow Kelvin	47.5
51	Aberdeen North	46.6
52=	Carrick, Cumnock and Doon Valley	46.1
52=	Paisley North	46.1
54=	Dundee East	45.4
54=	Hamilton South	45.4
56	Falkirk West	45.2
57	Greenock and Inverclyde	44.6
58	Paisley South	44.1
59	Linlithgow	43.4
60	Aberdeen Central	43.2
61	Hamilton North and Bellshill	42.5
62	Cunninghame South	41.6
63	Coatbridge and Chryston	40.7
64	Dundee West	38.7
65	Glasgow Anniesland	36.9
66	Glasgow Pollok	36.2
67	Airdrie and Shotts	33.6
68	Motherwell and Wishaw	32.9
69	Glasgow Baillieston	32.0
70	Glasgow Springburn	27.1
71	Glasgow Shettleston	25.1
72	Glasgow Maryhill	24.0

Section Five

SCOTTISH BY-ELECTIONS SINCE 1945

1945

Scottish Universities

	Lab%	Con%	SNP%	Lib%	Others%	Turnout%
1935	–	30.4	14.2	27.8	–	51.2
		27.6		(Nat Lib)		
9–13.4.45	–	71.2	–	28.8	–	44.6
		(Ind)		(Nat Lib)		
1945	8.7	48.8	–	5.7	–	51.6
		(Nat)				
		32.6				
		(Ind)				
		4.2				

Three members elected under STV. Seat abolished before 1950.

Motherwell

	Lab%	Con%	SNP%	Lib%	Others%	Turnout%
1935	50.7	49.3	–	–	–	75.9
12.4.45	48.6	–	51.4	–	–	54.0
1945	52.7	20.6	26.7	–	–	72.8

Robert McIntyre becomes the first SNP MP due to no Conservative standing because of the wartime coalition truce; Labour win seat back at general election three months later.

1945–50

Edinburgh East

	Lab%	Con%	SNP%	Lib%	Others%	Turnout%
1945	56.4	37.3	6.3	–	–	69.4
3.10.45	61.6	38.4	–	–	–	51.0

See 27.1.47

South Ayrshire

	Lab%	Con%	SNP%	Lib%	Others%	Turnout%
1945	61.3	38.7	–	–	–	75.0
7.2.46	63.6	36.4	–	–	–	69.0
1950	60.2	39.8	–	–	–	85.4

Glasgow Cathcart

	Lab%	Con%	SNP%	Lib%	Others%	Turnout%
1945	41.2	58.8	–	–	–	67.6
12.2.46	37.1	52.5	10.4	–	–	55.6
1950	27.3	64.8	–	7.9	–	83.8

Glasgow Bridgeton

	Lab%	Con%	SNP%	Lib%	Others%	Turnout%
1945	–	33.6	–	–	66.4 ILP	58.2
29.8.46	28.0	21.6	13.9	–	34.3 ILP, 2.2 Ind	53.3
1950	59.4	32.3	–	–	8.3	76.9

Wendy Wood stands as Independent Scottish Nationalist.

Scottish Universities

	Lab%	Con%	SNP%	Lib%	Others%	Turnout%
1945	8.7	48.8 (Nat) 32.6 (Ind) 4.2	–	5.7	–	51.6
22–27.11.46	11.5	68.2	–	8.0	12.3	50.7

Seat abolished prior to 1950 election.

Aberdeen South

	Lab%	Con%	SNP%	Lib%	Others%	Turnout%
1945	42.3	46.8	–	10.9	–	71.9
26.11.46	45.2	54.8	–	–	–	65.6
1950	35.5	53.7	–	10.8	–	84.9

Kilmarnock

	Lab%	Con%	SNP%	Lib%	Others%	Turnout%
1945	59.4	40.6	–	–	–	76.1
5.12.46	59.7	32.5	7.8	–	–	68.4
1950	56.6	35.8	–	5.4	2.2	86.2

Willie Ross enters the House of Commons.

Edinburgh East

	Lab%	Con%	SNP%	Lib%	Others%	Turnout%
1945	56.4	37.3	6.3	–	–	69.4
27.1.47	50.6	34.3	5.0	10.1	–	63.0
1950	53.2	38.8	–	8.0	–	83.2

Glasgow Camlachie

	Lab%	Con%	SNP%	Lib%	Others%	Turnout%
1945	–	42.3	–	–	57.7 ILP	65.0
28.1.48	42.1	43.7	–	1.2	6.4 ILP, 6.6 Others	56.8
1950	51.5	48.5	–	–	–	80.7

Conservatives C. S. MacFarlane narrowly wins Camlachie, a Glasgow East End seat, from ILP due to both Labour and ILP standing; Labour win back at the following election.

Paisley

	Lab%	Con%	SNP%	Lib%	Others%	Turnout%
1945	55.6	32.7	–	10.0	1.7	73.9
18.2.48	56.8	–	–	43.2	–	76.0
1950	56.1	36.5	–	7.4	–	84.0

John MacCormick stands with the support of the Conservatives and Liberals on a pro-Home Rule ticket.

Glasgow Gorbals

	Lab%	Con%	SNP%	Lib%	Others%	Turnout%
1945	80.0	20.0	–	–	–	56.8
30.9.48	54.5	28.6	–	–	16.9 Com	50.0
1950	58.0	31.4	–	–	5.8 Com, 4.7	77.3

Best post-war performance by the Communists in a UK by-election.

Stirling and Falkirk

	Lab%	Con%	SNP%	Lib%	Others%	Turnout%
1945	56.1	43.9	–	–	–	71.5
7.10.48	49.0	42.8	8.2	–	–	72.9
1950	49.0	45.5	3.7	–	1.8	84.4

Glasgow Hillhead

	Lab%	Con%	SNP%	Lib%	Others%	Turnout%
1945	33.6	58.5	—	7.9	—	65.8
25.11.48	31.6	68.4	—	—	—	56.7
1950	33.8	60.8	—	5.4	—	82.2

1950–51

Dunbartonshire West

	Lab%	Con%	SNP%	Lib%	Others%	Turnout%
1950	49.3	47.8	—	—	2.9	85.5
25.4.50	50.4	49.6	—	—	—	83.4
1951	51.3	45.4	—	3.3	—	86.6

Glasgow Scotstoun

	Lab%	Con%	SNP%	Lib%	Others%	Turnout%
1950	46.0	46.5	—	4.9	2.6	84.6
25.10.50	47.3	50.8	—	—	1.9	73.7
1951	49.3	50.7	—	—	—	85.1

1951–55

Dundee East

	Lab%	Con%	SNP%	Lib%	Others%	Turnout%
1951	53.8	46.2	—	—	—	87.2
7.7.52	56.3	35.6	7.4	—	0.7	71.5
1955	54.3	45.7	—	—	—	82.3

Edinburgh East

	Lab%	Con%	SNP%	Lib%	Others%	Turnout%
1951	54.1	45.9	—	—	—	83.8
8.4.54	57.6	42.4	—	—	—	61.8
1955	52.5	47.5	—	—	—	75.4

Motherwell

	Lab%	Con%	SNP%	Lib%	Others%	Turnout%
1951	57.3	42.7	—	—	—	84.7
14.4.54	56.4	39.3	—	—	4.3 Com	70
1955	53.9	46.1	—	—	—	76.5

Inverness

	Lab%	Con%	SNP%	Lib%	Others%	Turnout%
1951	35.5	64.5	—	—	—	69.3
21.12.54	22.6	41.4	—	36.0	—	49.2
1955	19.9	41.4	—	38.7	—	67.6

Neil McLean narrowly holds the seat for the Conservatives in both the by-election and general election against a Liberal surge.

Edinburgh North

	Lab%	Con%	SNP%	Lib%	Others%	Turnout%
1951	41.2	58.8	—	—	—	80.0
27.1.55	40.6	59.4	—	—	—	46.4
1955	38.3	61.7	—	—	—	72.0

1955–59

Greenock

	Lab%	Con%	SNP%	Lib%	Others%	Turnout%
1955	51.4	48.6	—	—	—	77.9
8.12.55	53.7	46.3	—	—	—	75.3
1959	50.6	22.6	—	26.8	—	78.9

Edinburgh South

	Lab%	Con%	SNP%	Lib%	Others%	Turnout%
1955	32.5	67.5	—	—	—	77.2
29.5.57	30.9	45.6	—	23.5	—	65.8
1959	28.5	57.6	—	13.9	—	81.2

Glasgow Kelvingrove

	Lab%	Con%	SNP%	Lib%	Others%	Turnout%
1955	44.6	55.4	–	–	–	67.6
13.3.58	48.0	41.6	–	7.6	2.8 ILP	60.5
1959	46.2	50.8	–	–	3.0 ILP	70.9

Labour gain from Conservatives; Conservatives win back at the general election.

Argyll

	Lab%	Con%	SNP%	Lib%	Others%	Turnout%
1955	32.4	67.6	–	–	–	66.6
12.6.58	25.7	46.8	–	27.5	–	67.1
1959	25.9	58.4	–	15.7	–	71.0

Michael Noble holds Argyll for the Conservatives despite post-Torrington Liberal surge.

Aberdeenshire East

	Lab%	Con%	SNP%	Lib%	Others%	Turnout%
1955	31.5	68.5	–	–	–	59.8
20.11.58	27.1	48.6	–	24.3	–	65.9
1959	36.6	63.4	–	–	–	67.1

Galloway

	Lab%	Con%	SNP%	Lib%	Others%	Turnout%
1955	33.1	66.9	–	–	–	69.1
9.4.59	23.9	50.4	–	25.7	–	72.7
1959	20.4	56.2	–	23.4	–	75.6

1959–64

Edinburgh North

	Lab%	Con%	SNP%	Lib%	Others%	Turnout%
1959	36.0	64.0	–	–	–	73.9
19.5.60	30.3	54.2	–	15.5	–	53.8
1964	41.8	58.2	–	–	–	73.6

Paisley

	Lab%	Con%	SNP%	Lib%	Others%	Turnout%
1959	57.3	42.7	–	–	–	78.9
20.4.61	45.4	13.2	–	41.4	–	68.1
1964	52.9	13.2	–	33.9	–	79.8

Fife East

	Lab%	Con%	SNP%	Lib%	Others%	Turnout%
1959	30.1	69.9	–	–	–	75.2
8.11.61	26.4	47.5	–	26.1	–	67.3
1964	25.2	54.2	6.8	13.1	0.7	77.8

John Gilmour returned for the Conservatives. The Labour candidate was a young John Smith, supported by Donald Dewar and others from Glasgow University Labour Club.

Glasgow Bridgeton

	Lab%	Con%	SNP%	Lib%	Others%	Turnout%
1959	63.4	36.6	–	–	–	68.5
10.11.61	57.5	20.7	18.7	–	3.1 ILP	41.9
1964	71.6	28.4	–	–	–	63.6

Best result for the SNP so far in post-war times as their young, energetic candidate Ian McDonald wins plaudits and votes.

West Lothian

	Lab%	Con%	SNP%	Lib%	Others%	Turnout%
1959	60.3	39.7	–	–	–	77.9
14.6.62	50.9	11.4	23.3	10.8	3.6 Com	71.1
1964	50.3	18.0	30.5	–	1.2 Com	79.5

SNP advance continues under William Wolfe; Tam Dalyell returned to the House of Commons; this is the first of seven Dalyell-Wolfe contests in a seat the SNP never manage to win; Conservatives lose their deposit for the first time in post-war politics.

Glasgow Woodside

	Lab%	Con%	SNP%	Lib%	Others%	Turnout%
1959	43.1	49.2	–	7.7	–	75.2
22.11.62	36.1	30.1	11.1	21.7	1.0	54.7
1964	45.6	40.4	5.4	8.3	0.3	74.0

Neil Carmichael gains Woodside for Labour from the Conservatives due to increased Liberal vote.

Kinross and West Perthshire

	Lab%	Con%	SNP%	Lib%	Others%	Turnout%
1959	16.8	68.2	15.0	–	–	71.0
7.11.63	15.2	57.3	7.3	19.5	0.6	76.1
1964	18.8	66.6	14.1	–	0.5 Com	75.0

Election of Sir Alec Douglas-Home to the House of Commons as Prime Minister; subsequent general election sees C. M. Grieve, aka Hugh McDiarmid, stand under the Communist banner.

Dundee West

	Lab%	Con%	SNP%	Lib%	Others%	Turnout%
1959	49.6	48.3	–	–	2.1 Com	82.9
21.11.63	50.6	39.4	7.4	–	2.6 Com	71.6
1964	53.4	44.2	–	–	2.4 Com	81.5

Dumfriesshire

	Lab%	Con%	SNP%	Lib%	Others%	Turnout%
1959	41.6	58.4	–	–	–	77.4
12.12.63	38.5	40.9	9.7	10.9	–	71.6
1964	39.1	48.7	12.2	–	–	81.6

Rutherglen

	Lab%	Con%	SNP%	Lib%	Others%	Turnout%
1959	47.9	52.1	–	–	–	85.8
14.5.64	55.5	44.5	–	–	–	82.0
1964	52.6	42.8	4.6	–	–	86.0

1964–66

Roxburgh, Selkirk and Peebles

	Lab%	Con%	SNP%	Lib%	Others%	Turnout%
1964	15.8	42.8	2.5	38.9	–	82.2
24.3.65	11.3	38.6	–	49.2	0.9	82.2
1966	13.6	40.8	–	45.6	–	84.9

Election of David Steel to the House of Commons.

1966–70

Glasgow Pollok

	Lab%	Con%	SNP%	Lib%	Others%	Turnout%
1966	52.4	47.6	–	–	–	79.0
9.3.67	31.2	36.9	28.2	1.9	1.8 Com	75.7
1970	46.3	44.8	8.9	–	–	72.6

SNP surge allows the Conservatives to take the seat from Labour; last Conservative by-election gain in Scotland for 33 years.

Hamilton

	Lab%	Con%	SNP%	Lib%	Others%	Turnout%
1966	71.2	28.8	–	–	–	73.3
2.11.67	41.5	12.5	46.0	–	–	73.7
1970	52.9	11.4	35.1	–	0.6	80.0

Winnie Ewing sensationally wins Hamilton, previously one of Labour's safest Scottish seats; Labour's Alex Wilson wins it back in 1970, but Scottish politics are never the same again.

Glasgow Gorbals

	Lab%	Con%	SNP%	Lib%	Others%	Turnout%
1966	73.1	22.8	–	–	4.1 Com	61.7
30.10.69	53.4	18.6	25.0	–	2.5 Com, 0.5	58.5
1970	69.3	20.8	7.4	–	2.5 Com	59.8

South Ayrshire

	Lab%	Con%	SNP%	Lib%	Others%	Turnout%
1966	67.2	32.8	–	–	–	75.1
19.3.70	54.0	25.6	20.4	–	–	76.3
1970	61.8	30.2	8.0	–	–	76.9

Jim Sillars enters the House of Commons for the first time standing on an anti-Nationalist Labour platform.

1970–74

Stirling and Falkirk

	Lab%	Con%	SNP%	Lib%	Others%	Turnout%
1970	50.7	34.8	14.5	–	–	73.1
16.9.71	46.5	18.9	34.6	–	–	60.0
1974 (Feb.)	41.9	23.6	34.5	–	–	81.2

Dundee East

	Lab%	Con%	SNP%	Lib%	Others%	Turnout%
1970	48.3	42.4	8.9	–	0.4	76.1
1.3.73	32.7	25.2	30.2	8.3	3.6	70.0
1974 (Feb.)	33.7	26.4	39.5	–	0.4	81.1

Gordon Wilson standing for the SNP just misses winning Dundee East which he goes on to win in the subsequent February 1974 general election and hold until 1987.

Edinburgh North

	Lab%	Con%	SNP%	Lib%	Others%	Turnout%
1970	37.1	52.8	–	10.1	–	70.1
8.11.73	24.0	38.7	18.9	18.4	–	54.4
1974 (Feb.)	26.2	45.8	12.7	15.3	–	76.4

Glasgow Govan

	Lab%	Con%	SNP%	Lib%	Others%	Turnout%
1970	60.0	28.2	10.3	–	1.5 Com	63.3
8.11.73	38.2	11.7	41.9	8.2	–	51.7
1974 (Feb.)	43.2	12.7	40.9	3.2	–	74.9

Margo MacDonald wins Glasgow Govan briefly for the SNP, narrowly failing to hold the seat after dramatic boundary changes in the February 1974 election.

February–October 1974

No by-elections.

1974–79

Glasgow Garscadden

	Lab%	Con%	SNP%	Lib%	Others%	Turnout%
1974 Oct	50.9	12.9	31.2	5.0	–	70.8
13.4.78	45.4	18.5	32.9	–	3.2	69.1
1979	61.5	21.8	15.7	–	1.0	73.2

Donald Dewar holds Glasgow Garscadden against the SNP's Keith Bovey who comes under widespread criticism for his pro-abortion, pro-CND views, particularly from the Conservative candidate, Iain Lawson, who later defected to the SNP.

Hamilton

	Lab%	Con%	SNP%	Lib%	Others%	Turnout%
1974 Oct	47.5	9.5	39.0	4.0	–	77.2
31.5.78	51.0	13.0	33.4	2.6	–	72.1
1979	59.6	23.8	16.6	–	–	79.6

George Robertson holds Hamilton against the SNP's Margo MacDonald and puts the SNP 1970s bandwagon into reverse.

Berwick and East Lothian

	Lab%	Con%	SNP%	Lib%	Others%	Turnout%
1974 Oct	43.3	37.6	13.2	5.9	–	83.0
26.10.78	47.4	40.2	8.8	3.6	–	71.2
1979	43.5	40.2	6.5	9.8	–	82.9

1979–83

Glasgow Central

	Lab%	Con%	SNP%	Lib%	Others%	Turnout%
1979	72.5	16.4	11.1	–	–	59.5
9.4.80	60.4	8.8	26.3	–	4.1	42.8
1983	53.0	19.0	10.3	16.7	1.1	62.9

Glasgow Hillhead

	Lab%	Con%	SNP%	Lib%	Others%	Turnout%
1979	34.4	41.1	10.1	14.4	–	75.7
25.3.82	25.9	26.6	11.3	33.4	2.8	76.4
1983	33.3	23.6	5.4	36.2	2.1	71.9

Roy Jenkins returned to the House of Commons for the SDP; Conservatives lose their last parliamentary seat in Glasgow.

Coatbridge and Airdrie

	Lab%	Con%	SNP%	Lib%	Others%	Turnout%
1979	60.9	27.5	11.6	–	–	75.3
24.6.82	55.1	26.2	10.5	8.2	–	56.3

Redistribution

Glasgow Queen's Park

	Lab%	Con%	SNP%	Lib%	Others%	Turnout%
1979	64.4	24.0	9.4	–	–	68.4
2.12.82	56.0	12.0	20.0	9.4	–	47.0

Redistribution

1983–87

No by-elections

1987–92

Glasgow Govan

	Lab%	Con%	SNP%	Lib%	Others%	Turnout%
1987	64.8	11.9	10.4	12.3	0.6	73.4
10.11.88	37.0	7.3	48.8	4.1	2.8	60.4
1992	48.9	9.9	37.1	3.5	0.5	76.0

Jim Sillars' return to the House of Commons as he wins the previously safe Labour seat of Glasgow Govan; Labour's Ian Davidson wins back the seat in the 1992 general election.

Glasgow Central

	Lab%	Con%	SNP%	Lib%	Others%	Turnout%
1987	64.5	13.0	9.9	10.5	2.0	65.6
15.6.89	54.6	7.6	30.2	1.5	6.0	52.8
1992	57.2	13.9	20.8	6.3	1.8	63.1

Mike Watson wins Glasgow Central against the SNP's Alex Neil, stopping the SNP post-Govan surge.

Paisley North

	Lab%	Con%	SNP%	Lib%	Others%	Turnout%
1987	55.5	15.8	12.9	15.8	–	73.4
29.11.90	44.0	14.8	29.4	8.3	3.6	53.7
1992	50.7	16.4	23.3	8.2	1.4	73.4

Paisley South

	Lab%	Con%	SNP%	Lib%	Others%	Turnout%
1987	56.2	14.7	14.0	15.1	–	75.3
29.11.90	46.1	13.4	27.5	9.8	3.1	55.5
1992	50.7	15.9	24.1	9.1	0.3	75.0

Kincardine and Deeside

	Lab%	Con%	SNP%	Lib%	Others%	Turnout%
1987	15.9	40.6	6.4	36.3	0.6	75.3
7.11.91	7.7	30.6	11.1	49.0	1.6	67.0
1992	9.1	43.7	11.3	35.1	0.7	78.8

Alick Buchanan-Smith's death results in Conservative loss to Lib Dems, Nicol Stephen; Conservatives' George Kynoch wins back at the 1992 election.

1992–97

Monklands East

	Lab%	Con%	SNP%	Lib%	Others%	Turnout%
1992	61.3	16.0	18.0	4.6	0.1	75.0
30.6.94	49.8	2.3	44.9	2.6	0.4	70.0
1997	61.8	8.9	24.4	4.2	0.7	71.4

By-election caused by death of John Smith sees Labour's Helen Liddell hold on narrowly against the SNP's Kay Ullrich.

Perth and Kinross

	Lab%	Con%	SNP%	Lib%	Others%	Turnout%
1992	12.5	40.2	36.0	11.4	–	76.9
25.5.95	22.9	21.4	40.4	11.8	3.5	62.1
1997	24.8	29.3	37.0	8.0	1.5	73.9

Roseanna Cunningham wins Perth and Kinross from the Conservatives; she subsequently holds it at the general election: the first time the SNP had held onto a by-election gain.

1997–

Paisley South

	Lab%	Con%	SNP%	Lib%	Others%	Turnout%
1997	57.5	8.7	23.3	9.4	1.1	69.5
6.11.97	44.1	7.0	32.5	11.0	5.3	43.4

Hamilton South

	Lab%	Con%	SNP%	Lib%	Others%	Turnout%
1997	65.6	8.6	17.6	5.1	3.0	71.1
23.9.99	36.9	7.2	34.0	3.3	9.5 SSP, 9.1	41.6

Labour's Bill Tynan narrowly holds Hamilton South against the SNP's Annabelle Ewing.

Glasgow Anniesland

	Lab%	Con %	SNP%	Lib%	Others%	Turnout%
1997	61.8	11.5	17.1	7.2	2.4	64.0
23.11.00	52.1	10.8	20.8	8.1	7.1 SSP, 1.1	38.4

Falkirk West

	Lab%	Con%	SNP%	Lib%	Others%	Turnout%
1997	59.4	12.1	23.4	5.1	–	72.6
21.12.00	43.5	8.3	39.9	3.2	5.1 SSP	36.6

Labour narrowly hold Falkirk West after Dennis Canavan finally resigns his Westminster seat. Result means UK Labour have held all ten Labour seats in the Parliament – the first time a government has done so in a full Parliament since Churchill in 1951–55.

Scottish Parliament By-elections

Ayr

	Lab%	Con%	SNP%	Lib%	Other%s	Turnout%
1999	38.1	38.0	19.5	4.4	–	66.5
16.3.00	22.1	39.4	29.0	2.5	4.2 SSP, 2.8	56.3

John Scott wins Ayr for the Conservatives from Labour; the first by-election gain for the Conservatives in Scotland since Glasgow Pollok in 1967.

Glasgow Anniesland

	Lab%	Con%	SNP%	Lib%	Others%	Turnout%
1999	58.8	10.7	20.2	6.3	3.5 SSP, 0.5	52.4
23.11.00	48.7	10.6	22.1	6.8	7.1 SSP, 4.7	38.3

Labour hold on comfortably to Glasgow Anniesland seats in simultaneous by-elections for Westminster and Holyrood; the SNP performances in the two contests are its worst in a seat where it is the main challenger to Labour since Hamilton in 1978.

Section Six

SCOTTISH PARLIAMENT ELECTION RESULTS 1999

Constituency Voting Figures

Party	Votes	Votes%	FPTP MSPs
Labour	908,394	38.79	53
SNP	672,758	28.72	7
Conservativ	364,225	15.55	–
Liberal Democrat	333,279	14.23	12
SSP	23,654	1.01	–
MP for Falkirk West	18,511	0.79	1
Socialist Labour	5,268	0.22	–
SWP	2,757	0.12	–
Independent	12,418	0.53	–
Other	804	0.03	–

Regional List Voting Figures

Party	Votes	Votes%	List MSPs	Total MSPs
Labour	786,818	33.64	3	56
SNP	638,644	27.31	28	35
Conservative	359,109	15.35	18	18
Liberal Democrat	290,760	12.43	5	17
Scottish Green	84,024	3.59	1	1
Socialist Labour	55,232	2.36	–	–
SSP	46,635	1.99	1	1
MP for Falkirk West	27,700	1.18	–	1
Pro-Life	9,784	0.42	–	–
Scottish Unionist	7,009	0.30	–	–
Liberal	5,534	0.24	–	–
Natural Law	4,906	0.21	–	–
Independent	7,137	0.31	–	–
Other	15,619	0.67	–	–

Section Seven

UK ELECTION RESULTS IN SCOTLAND 1945–97

1945

	Votes	%	MPs
Conservative	964,143	41.1	27
Labour	1,144,310	47.6	37
Liberal	132,849	5.0	0
ILP	40,725	1.8	3
Communist	33,265	1.4	1
SNP	30,595	1.2	0
Others	44,005	1.9	3*

* J. Mackie, independent Conservative; M. Macdonald, independent Liberal; and J. MacLeod, independent Liberal.

1950

	Votes	%	MPs
Conservative	1,222,010	44.8	31
Labour	1,259,410	46.2	37
Liberal	180,270	6.6	2
Communist	27,559	1.0	0
SNP	9,708	0.4	0
Others	27,727	1.0	1*

* J. Macleod, independent Liberal

1951

	Votes	%	MPs
Conservative	1,349,298	48.6	35
Labour	1,330,244	47.9	35
Liberal	76,291	2.7	1
Communist	10,947	0.4	0
SNP	7,299	0.3	0
Others	3,758	0.1	0

1955

	Votes	%	MPs
Conservative	1,273,942	50.1	36
Labour	1,188,058	46.7	34
Liberal	47,273	1.9	1
Communist	13,195	0.5	0
SNP	12,112	0.5	0
Others	8,674	0.3	0

1959

	Votes	%	MPs
Conservative	1,260,287	47.2	31
Labour	1,245,255	46.7	38
Liberal	108,963	4.1	1
Communist	12,150	0.5	0
SNP	21,738	0.8	0
Others	19,120	0.7	1*

*D. Robertson, independent Conservative

1964

	Votes	%	MPs
Conservative	1,069,695	40.6	24
Labour	1,283,667	48.7	43
Liberal	200,063	7.6	4
Communist	12,241	0.5	0
SNP	64,044	2.4	0
Others	4,829	0.2	0

1966

	Votes	%	MPs
Conservative	960,675	37.7	20
Labour	1,273,916	49.9	46
Liberal	172,447	6.8	5
Communist	16,230	0.6	0
SNP	128,474	5.0	0
Others	638	0.0	0

1970

	Votes	%	MPs
Conservative	1,020,674	38.0	23
Labour	1,197,068	44.5	44
Liberal	147,667	5.5	3
Communist	11,408	0.4	0
SNP	306,802	11.4	1
Others	4,616	0.2	0

1974 (February)

	Votes	%	MPs
Conservative	950,668	32.9	21
Labour	1,057,601	36.6	40
Liberal	229,162	8.0	3
Communist	15,071	0.5	0
SNP	633,180	21.9	7
Others	1,393	0.1	0

1974 (October)

	Votes	%	MPs
Conservative	681,327	24.7	16
Labour	1,000,581	36.3	41
Liberal	228,855	8.3	3
Communist	7,453	0.3	0
SNP	839,617	30.4	11
Others	268	0.0	0

1979

	Votes	%	MPs
Conservative	916,155	31.4	22
Labour	1,211,445	41.5	44
Liberal	262,224	9.0	3
Communist	5,926	0.2	0
SNP	504,259	17.3	2
SLP	13,737	0.5	0
Others	2,891	0.1	0

1983

	Votes	%	MPs
Conservative	801,312	28.4	21
Labour	990,644	35.1	41
SDP/Liberal Alliance	692,367	24.5	8
SNP	331,975	11.8	2
Others	7,820	0.3	0

1987

	Votes	%	MPs
Conservative	713,499	24.0	10
Labour	1,258,177	42.4	50
SDP/Liberal Alliance	570,043	19.2	9
SNP	416,873	14.0	3
Others	10,069	0.3	0

1992

	Votes	%	MPs
Conservative	751,950	25.6	11
Labour	1,142,911	39.0	49
Liberal Democrat	383,856	13.1	9
SNP	629,564	21.5	3
Others	23,417	0.8	0

1997

	Votes	%	MPs
Conservative	493,059	17.5	0
Labour	1,283,353	45.6	56
Liberal Democrat	365,359	13.0	10
SNP	622,260	22.1	6
Others	53,408	1.9	0

Section Eight

EUROPEAN PARLIAMENT ELECTION RESULTS

Share of Vote

	1979	1984	1989	1994	1999
Labour	33.0	40.7	41.9	42.5	28.7
SNP	19.4	17.8	25.6	32.6	27.2
Conservative	33.7	25.7	20.9	14.5	19.8
Liberal Democrat	14.0	15.6	4.3	7.2	9.8
Green	–	0.2	7.2	1.6	5.8
SSP	–	–	–	0.8	4.0
Other	–	–	–	1.7	4.9
Turnout	33.6	33.1	40.8	38.2	24.8

Number of Votes

	1979	1984	1989	1994	1999
Labour	421,968	526,056	666,263	635,955	283,490
SNP	247,926	230,590	406,686	487,237	268,528
Conservative	430,762	332,771	331,495	216,669	195,296
Liberal D'crat	178,433	201,822	68,086	107,811	96,971
Green	–	2,560	115,028	23,314	57,142
SSP	–	–	–	12,113	39,720
Other	–	–	–	12,798	31,163

Seats

	1979	1984	1989	1994	1999
Labour	2	5	7	6	3
SNP	1	1	1	2	2
Conservative	5	2	0	0	2
Liberal Democrat	0	0	0	0	1

1999: Those Elected from the Scotland-wide List

Elspeth Attwooll	Liberal Democrat
Ian Hudghton	SNP
Neil MacCormick	SNP
David Martin	Labour
Bill Miller	Labour
Catherine Stihler	Labour
John Purvis	Conservative
Struan Stevenson	Conservative

ELSPETH ATTWOOLL (Liberal Democrat) was born in Chislehurst in 1943 and elected a Liberal Democrat MEP in 1999. She was educated at St Andrews University where she gained an MA in Politics and Philosophy and an LLB. She is President of the Scottish Women Liberal Democrats, a member of the party's Executive in Scotland and has stood previously five times in the Glasgow Maryhill constituency – 1974, 1979, 1983, 1987 and 1997 – and in the European elections in Glasgow in 1979. Linguistically, she has fluent French and respectable German. Within the European Parliament, she is a member of the Committees on Fisheries, Regional Policy, Transport and Tourism; and the Environment, Public Health and Consumer Policy. She is also a substitute member on the Committee on Employment and Social Affairs and the Delegation for relations with Canada.

IAN HUDGHTON (SNP) was elected to the European Parliament as the SNP Member for North East Scotland at the by-election of November 1998 following the death of Allan Macartney. Ian Hudghton was a councillor on Angus District from 1985 until 1995 and served as Housing Convenor, and was then a member of Angus Council, where he became leader in 1996. He was also a member of Tayside Regional Council, where he was Property Convenor from 1994 to 1996. Whilst a councillor, he became one of Scotland's members of the Committee of the Regions. He was re-elected to the European Parliament in 1999 and sits in the Green-European Free Alliance Group in the Parliament. He is a member of the Employment and Social Affairs, Fisheries, and Economic and Monetary Affairs Committees.

NEIL MacCORMICK (SNP) is a graduate of Glasgow, Oxford and Edinburgh Universities, and has been an SNP MEP since 1999. He is the son of John MacCormick, one of the founders of the National Party of Scotland, and brother of Iain MacCormick, SNP MP for Argyll from February 1974 until 1979. He has been a consistent SNP pro-devolutionist and was a member of the Constitutional Steering

Committee under the Chairmanship of Sir Robert Grieve which produced *A Claim of Right for Scotland* in 1988 which led to the establishment of the cross-party Scottish Constitutional Convention. He has been a law professor at Edinburgh University since 1972, where he was also briefly Dean of the Faculty of Law. He had a distinguished career as an academic, and an international reputation in jurisprudence and philosophy. He contested the Argyll and Bute constituency at the 1997 general election and has been a prominent member of the SNP for as long as the party has been a serious electoral force. In the European Parliament he is a member of the Committee of Legal Affairs and the Internal Market and also serves on the Constitutional Affairs Committee.

DAVID MARTIN (Labour) was born in Edinburgh in 1954 and was elected a Labour MEP for the Lothians seat from 1984 until 1999 and for Scotland from 1999. He was educated at Liberton High School, Heriot-Watt University, where he gained a BA (Hons) in Economics, and Leicester University gaining a MA in European Law and Employment Law. Martin worked as a stockbrocker's assistant and was the Vice-President of Mobile Projects with the St Andrew Animal Fund, an animal rights agency. He was on Lothian Regional Council from 1982 to 1984, and in the European Parliament has been a Rapporteur on Inter-governmental conferences. He has been Vice-President of the European Parliament since 1989 and is now Senior Vice-President with special responsibility for relations with national parliaments. He is a member of the Committee on Budgets, a substitute member of the Committee on Development and Cooperation, and a European Parliament representative to the Joint Assembly of the Agreement between the African, Caribbean and Pacific States and the European Union (ACP-EU). Martin is author of a number of publications and pamphlets on the European Union.

BILL MILLER (Labour) was born in 1954 in Gartocharn and elected Labour MEP for Glasgow from 1994 to 1999 and for Scotland from 1999. He was educated at Paisley Technical College and Kingston Polytechnic and was a Strathclyde Regional Councillor from 1986 to 1994. In the European Parliament he is a member of the Committee on Legal Affairs and the Internal Market and a substitute member of the Committee on Economic and Monetary Affairs.

JOHN PURVIS (Conservative) was born in St Andrews in 1938 and has been a Conservative MEP from 1999. Educated at Glenalmond and St Andrews University, he has been an international banker, and also managed his own finance business. He was previously the MEP for Mid-Scotland and Fife from 1979 to 1984. Within the European Parliament he is a member of the European People's Party and serves on the Industry, External Trade, Research and Energy Committee and the Economic and Monetary Affairs Committee. He is the Conservative spokesperson on Research and Energy.

STRUAN STEVENSON (Conservative) was born in Ballantrae in 1948 and elected a Conservative MEP in 1999. He was educated at Strathallan School and the West of Scotland Agriculture College and worked in the family farming business for a number of years before becoming involved in local government. He was a member of Girvan Council from 1970 to 1974, then elected to Kyle and Carrick District Council from 1974 until 1992, in which he was leader from 1986 to 1988. He stood unsuccessfully for Westminster on three occasions: Carrick, Cumnock and Doon Valley in 1987, Edinburgh South in 1992 and the formerly safe seat of Dumfries in 1997, just as Labour won it in that year's landslide. He was the Conservative candidate at the North East Scotland European Parliamentary by-election in November 1998. Before his election in 1999, he was Director of Saferworld, a defence think tank, from 1992 to 1994, then a Director of PS Communications, a PR and lobbying agency, until 1999. In the European Parliament he is a member of the European People's Party group. He sits on the Agriculture and Rural Development Committee and is a substitute member of the Fisheries Committee and Conservative spokesperson on fisheries.

CATHERINE STIHLER (Labour) was born in 1973 in Bellshill and elected to the European Parliament in 1999 as Catherine Taylor. Educated at Coltness High School, Wishaw and St Andrews University, she has worked as a researcher to Anne Begg MP from 1997 to 1999. She was on the Scottish Labour Executive from 1993 to 1995 and 1997 to 1999 and the NEC from 1995 to 1997. In the European Parliament, she is President of the Public Health Working Group and is a member of the Environment, Public Health and Consumer Policy Committee.

Previous European Election Constituency Results 1979–94

Glasgow

1994

Electorate: 463,364
Turnout: 159,666 (34.5%)

	Party	Votes	Votes%	Change%
B. Miller	Labour	83,953	52.6	−2.8
T. Chalmers	SNP	40,795	25.6	+0.6
T. Sheridan	Scot Militant Lab	12,113	7.6	–
R. Wilkinson	Conservative	10,888	6.8	−3.9
J. Money	Liberal Democrat	7,291	4.6	+2.6
P. O'Brien	Green	2,252	1.4	−4.9
J. Fleming	Socialist	1,125	0.7	–
M. Wilkinson	NLP	868	0.5	–
C. Marsden	ICP	381	0.2	–

1989

Electorate: 491,905
Turnout: 194, 638 (39.6%)

	Party	Votes	Votes%	Change%
J. Buchan	Labour	107,818	55.4	−3.8
A. Brophy	SNP	48,586	25.0	+14.3
A. Bates	Conservative	20,761	10.7	−5.8
D. Spaven	Green	12,229	6.3	–
J. Morrison	Democrat	3,887	2.0	−11.6
D. Chalmers	Communist	1,164	0.6	+0.6
J. Simons	Int Com	193	0.1	+0.1

1984

Electorate: 518,178
Turnout: 153,620 (29.6%)

	Party	Votes	Votes%	Change%
J. Buchan	Labour	91,015	59.2	+10.2
S. Chadd	Conservative	25,282	16.5	-10.8
C. Mason	Liberal/SDP	20,867	10.7	+6.3
N. MacLeod	SNP	16,456	13.6	-5.7

1979

Electorate: 534,414
Turnout: 151,139 (28.3%)

	Party	Votes	Votes%	Change%
J. Buchan	Labour	73,846	49.0	-9.2
B. Vaughan	Conservative	41,144	27.3	+1.4
G. Leslie	SNP	24,776	16.4	+4.9
E. Attwooll	Liberal	11,073	7.3	+3.3

Highlands and Islands

1994

Electorate: 328,104
Turnout: 128,272 (39.1%)

	Party	Votes	Votes%	Change%
W. Ewing	SNP	74,872	58.4	+6.8
M. Macmillan	Labour	19,956	15.6	+1.7
M. Tennant	Conservative	15,767	12.3	-4.5
H. Morrison	Liberal Democrat	12,919	10.1	+1.8
E. Scott	Green	3,140	2.5	- 7.0
M. Carr	Independent	1,096	0.9	—
M. Gimour	NLP	522	0.4	—

1989

Electorate: 317,129
Turnout: 128,590 (40.5%)

	Party	Votes	Votes%	Change%
W. Ewing	SNP	66,297	51.6	+9.7
A. McQuarrie	Conservative	21,602	16.8	+0.8
N. MacAskill	Labour	17,848	13.9	-0.2
M. Gregson	Green	12,199	9.5	–
N. Mitchison	Democrat	10,644	8.3	-19.8

1984

Electorate: 307,265
Turnout: 118,034 (38.4%)

	Party	Votes	Votes%	Change%
W. Ewing	SNP	49,410	41.9	+7.9
R. Johnston	Liberal/SDP	33,133	28.1	-2.6
D. Webster	Conservative	18,847	16.0	-10.1
J. McArthur	Labour	16,644	14.1	-5.9

1979
Electorate: 298,802
Turnout: 118,214 (39.6%)

	Party	Votes	Votes%	Change%
W. Ewing	SNP	39,991	34.0	+4.7
R. Johnston	Liberal	36,601	30.7	+12.5
M. Joughlin	Conservative	30,776	26.1	-6.4
J. Watson	Labour	10,846	9.2	-10.8

Lothians

1994

Electorate: 522,363
Turnout: 200,413 (38.4%)

	Party	Votes	Votes%	Change%
D. Martin	Labour	90,531	44.9	+3.6
K. Brown	SNP	53,324	26.5	+6.1
P. McNally	Conservative	33,526	16.6	-7.0
H. Campbell	Liberal Democrat	17,883	8.9	+4.7
R. Harper	Green	5,149	2.6	-7.8

1989

Electorate: 527,785
Turnout: 219,994 (41.7%)

	Party	Votes	Votes%	Change%
D. Martin	Labour	90,840	41.3	+0.9
C. Blight	Conservative	52,014	23.6	-2.8
J. Smith	SNP	44,935	20.4	+8.4
R. Harper	Green	22,983	10.4	+9.0
K.Leadbetter	Democrat	9,222	4.2	-15.5

1984

Electorate: 526,068
Turnout: 185,581 (35.3%)

	Party	Votes	Votes%	Change%
D. W. Martin	Labour	74,989	40.4	+7.8
I. Henderson	Conservative	49,065	26.4	-9.2
J. D. Mabon	Liberal/SDP	36,636	19.7	+3.9
D. Stevenson	SNP	22,331	12.0	-4.0
L. Hendry	Ecology	2,560	1.4	–

1979

Electorate: 537,420

Turnout: 187,334 (34.9%)

	Party	Votes	Votes%	Change%
I. Dalziel	Conservative	66,761	35.6	+2.7
A. Mackie	Labour	61,180	32.6	-10.7
D. Stevenson	SNP	29,935	16.0	+2.2
R. Smith	Liberal	29,518	15.8	+6.2

North East Scotland

Euro by-election: 26 November 1998

Electorate: 584,061

Turnout: 119,605 (20.5%)

	Party	Votes	Votes%	Change%
I. Hudghton	SNP	57,445	48.0	+5.2
S. Stevenson	Conservative	23,744	19.9	+1.3
K. Walker–Shaw	Labour	22,086	18.5	-9.9
K. Raffan	Liberal Democrat	11,753	9.8	+1.5
H. Duke	SSA	2,510	2.1	–
R. Harper	Green	2,067	1.7	+0.5

1994

Electorate: 573,799

Turnout: 217,148 (37.8%)

	Party	Votes	Votes%	Change%
A. Macartney	SNP	92,890	42.8	+13.4
H. McCubbin	Labour	61,665	28.4	-2.3
R. Harris	Conservative	40,372	18.6	-8.1
S. Horner	Liberal Democrat	18,008	8.3	+2.3
K. Farnsworth	Green	2,569	1.2	-6.1
M. Ward	CPGB	689	0.3	–
L. Mair	NEEPS	584	0.3	–
D. Paterson	NLP	371	0.2	–

1989

Electorate: 559,275
Turnout: 213,206 (38.1%)

	Party	Votes	Votes%	Change%
H. McCubbin	Labour	65,348	30.7	+2.3
A. Macartney	SNP	62,735	29.4	+8.1
J. Provan	Conservative	56,835	26.7	-7.5
M. Hill	Green	15,584	7.3	–
S. Horner	Democrat	12,704	6.0	-10.2

1984

Electorate: 548,711
Turnout: 157,381 (28.7%)

	Party	Votes	Votes%	Change%
J. Provan	Conservative	53,809	34.2	+1.2
F. Doran	Labour	44,638	28.4	+4.2
D. Hood	SNP	33,444	21.3	+3.0
I. Philip	Liberal/SDP	25,490	16.2	-8.3

1979

Electorate: 481,680
Turnout: 157,471 (32.7%)

	Party	Votes	Votes%	Change%
J. Provan	Conservative	51,930	33.0	-1.7
Lord Mackie	Liberal	38,516	24.5	+15.3
D. Clyne	Labour	38,139	24.2	-6.9
C. Bell	SNP	28,886	18.3	-6.6

Scotland Mid and Fife

1994

Electorate: 546,060
Turnout: 208,620 (38.2%)

	Party	Votes	Votes%	Change%
A. Falconer	Labour	95,667	45.8	– 0.3
D. Douglas	SNP	64,254	30.8	+8.2
P. Page	Conservative	28,192	13.5	–7.5
H. Lyall	Liberal Democrat	17,192	8.2	+4.2
M. Johnston	Green	3,015	1.4	–5.0

1989

Electorate: 539,276
Turnout: 221,862 (41.1%)

	Party	Votes	Votes%	Change%
A. Falconer	Labour	102,246	46.1	+3.4
K. MacAskill	SNP	50,089	22.6	+6.3
A. Christie	Conservative	46,505	21.0	–7.2
G. Morton	Green	14,165	6.4	–
M. Black	Democrat	8,857	4.0	–8.9

1984

Electorate: 528,529
Turnout: 187,641 (35.5%)

	Party	Votes	Votes%	Change%
A. Falconer	Labour	80,038	42.7	+11.5
J. Purvis	Conservative	52,872	28.2	–6.9
J. Jones	SNP	30,511	16.3	–7.8
A. Wedderburn	Liberal/SDP	24,220	12.9	+3.3

1979

Electorate: 538,483
Turnout: 188,561 (35.0%)

	Party	Votes	Votes%	Change%
J. Purvis	Conservative	66,255	35.1	+4.8
M. Panko	Labour	58,768	31.2	-8.5
R. McIntyre	SNP	45,426	24.1	+1.1
J. Calder	Liberal	18,112	9.6	+2.9

Scotland South

1994

Electorate: 500,643
Turnout: 200,957 (40.1%)

	Party	Votes	Votes%	Change%
A. Smith	Labour	90,750	45.2	+5.4
A. Hutton	Conservative	45,595	22.7	-9.5
C. Creech	SNP	45,032	22.4	+5.2
D. Millar	Liberal Democrat	13,363	6.7	+1.6
J. Hein	Liberal	3,249	1.6	–
L. Hendry	Green	2,429	1.2	-4.5
G. Gay	NLP	539	0.3	–

1989

Electorate: 497,108
Turnout: 204,220 (41.1%)

	Party	Votes	Votes%	Change%
A. Smith	Labour	81,366	39.8	+4.7
A. Hutton	Conservative	65,673	32.2	-4.8
M. Brown	SNP	35,155	17.2	+3.7
J. Button	Green	11,658	5.7	–
J. McKerchar	Democrat	10,368	5.1	-9.3

1984

Electorate: 484,760
Turnout: 164,389 (33.9%)

	Party	Votes	Votes%	Change%
A. Hutton	Conservative	60,843	37.0	-6.0
R. Stewart	Labour	57,706	35.1	+7.4
E. Buchanan	Liberal/SDP	23,598	14.4	+3.6
I. Goldie	SNP	22,242	13.5	-5.0

1979

Electorate: 450,761
Turnout: 155,480 (34.5%)

	Party	Votes	Votes%	Change%
A. Hutton	Conservative	66,816	43.0	+6.8
P. Foy	Labour	43,145	27.7	-8.5
I. MacGibbon	SNP	28,694	18.5	+5.7
J. Wallace	Liberal	16,825	10.8	-3.9

Strathclyde East

1994

Electorate: 492,618
Turnout: 183,571 (37.3%)

	Party	Votes	Votes%	Change%
K. Collins	Labour	106,476	58.0	+1.8
I. Hamilton	SNP	54,136	29.5	+4.4
B. Cooklin	Conservative	13,915	7.6	-3.8
B. Stewart	Liberal Democrat	6,383	3.5	+1.3
A. Whitelaw	Green	1,874	1.0	-4.0
D. Gilmour	NLP	787	0.4	—

1989

Electorate: 499,616

Turnout: 194,281 (38.9%)

	Party	Votes	Votes%	Change%
K. Collins	Labour	109,170	56.2	-2.4
G. Leslie	SNP	48,853	25.1	+7.5
M. Dutt	Conservative	22,233	11.4	-4.7
A. Whitelaw	Green	9,749	5.0	—
G. Lait	Democrat	4,276	2.2	-5.5

1984

Electorate: 498,458

Turnout: 154,832 (31.1%)

	Party	Votes	Votes%	Change%
K. Collins	Labour	90,792	58.6	+8.8
G. Leslie	SNP	27,330	17.6	+3.1
R. Leckie	Conservative	24,857	16.1	-12.5
P de Seume	Liberal/SDP	11,883	7.7	+0.6

1979

Electorate: 463,656

Turnout: 145,083 (31.3%)

	Party	Votes	Votes%	Change%
K. Collins	Labour	72,263	49.8	-5.3
M. Carse	Conservative	41,482	28.6	+1.0
G. Murray	SNP	21,013	14.5	+1.0
D. Watt	Liberal	10,325	7.1	+3.7

Strathclyde West

1994

Electorate: 489,129
Turnout: 195,881 (40.0%)

	Party	Votes	Votes%	Change%
H. McMahon	Labour	86,957	44.4	+1.7
C. Campbell	SNP	61,934	31.6	+7.8
J. Godfrey	Conservative	28,414	14.5	-7.3
D. Herbison	Lib Dem	14,772	7.5	+3.7
K. Allan	Green	2,886	1.5	-6.3
S. Gilmour	NLP	918	0.5	–

1989

Electorate: 500,935
Turnout: 210,094 (41.9%)

	Party	Votes	Votes%	Change%
H. McMahon	Labour	89,627	42.7	+1.9
C. Campbell	SNP	50,036	23.8	+6.2
S. Robin	Conservative	45,872	21.8	-5.6
G. Campbell	Green	16,461	7.8	–
D. Herbison	Democrat	8,098	3.8	-11.3

1984

Electorate: 499,162
Turnout: 172,291 (34.5%)

	Party	Votes	Votes%	Change%
H. McMahon	Labour	70,234	40.8	+4.7
J. Lair	Conservative	47,196	27.4	-9.8
J. Herriot	SNP	28,866	16.8	+0.3
D. Herbison	Liberal/SDP	25,995	15.1	+4.9

1979

Electorate: 495,799

Turnout: 176,459 (35.6%)

	Party	Votes	Votes%	Change%
A. Fergusson	Conservative	65,608	37.2	+5.3
V. Friel	Labour	63,781	36.1	−7.3
M. Slesser	SNP	29,115	16.5	+ 2.4
T. Fraser	Liberal	17,955	10.2	+ 0.1

Section Nine

LOCAL GOVERNMENT ELECTION RESULTS

Scottish Local Election Results 1974–99

		Lab		Con		SNP		Lib/LibDem		Independent	
	Votes%	Seats	Votes%	Seats	Votes%	Seats	Votes%	Seats	Votes%	Seats
Regional 1974	38.5	172	28.6	112	12.6	18	5.1	11	12.4	114
District 1974	38.4	428	26.8	241	12.4	62	5.0	17	14.1	345
District 1977	31.6	299	27.2	277	24.2	170	4.0	31	9.8	318
Regional 1978	39.6	177	30.3	136	20.9	18	2.3	6	4.9	89
District 1980	45.4	494	24.1	229	15.5	54	6.2	40	6.7	289
Regional 1982	37.6	186	25.1	119	13.4	23	18.1	25	5.1	87
District 1984	45.7	545	21.4	189	11.7	59	12.8	78	6.8	267
Regional 1986	43.9	223	16.9	65	18.2	36	15.1	40	4.8	79
District 1988	42.6	553	19.4	162	21.3	113	8.4	84	6.4	231
Regional 1990	42.7	233	19.6	52	21.8	42	8.7	40	4.5	73
District 1992	34.1	468	23.2	204	24.3	150	9.5	94	7.4	228
Regional 1994	41.8	220	13.7	31	26.8	73	12.0	60	4.2	65
Unitary 1995	43.6	613	11.5	82	26.1	181	9.8	121	7.7	155
Unitary 1999	36.6	545	13.7	108	28.9	201	13.6	148	11.8	135

1999 Local Election Results By Local Authority

		Lab		Con		SNP		Lib Dem		Independent	
	Votes%	Seats	Votes%	Seats	Votes%	Seats	Votes%	Seats	Votes%	Seats
Aberdeen	32.62	21	18.66	7	24.95	4	23.59	11	0.18	0
Aberdeenshire	5.03	0	18.56	8	29.26	23	32.75	27	14.32	10
Angus	18.30	1	17.97	2	46.58	21	8.90	2	8.25	3
Argyll and Bute	10.33	4	9.83	1	20.36	5	15.73	6	43.13	20
Clackm'shire	44.54	8	8.66	1	44.55	9	1.65	0	0.60	0
D'fries & G'way	17.49	8	25.92	14	20.25	5	9.92	6	24.74	13
Dundee	36.64	14	18.51	4	36.99	10	5.73	0	0.00	0
E Ayrshire	45.75	17	9.27	1	40.83	14	1.93	0	2.22	0
E D'shire	45.39	17	17.75	5	24.12	1	12.75	0	0.00	0

	Lab		Con		SNP		LibDem		Independent	
	Votes%	Seats	Votes%	Seats	Votes%	Seats	Votes%	Seats	Votes%	Seats
E Lothian	45.39	17	17.75	5	24.12	1	12.75	0	0.00	0
E Renfrewshire	31.85	9	32.51	8	18.23	0	13.63	2	3.78	1
Edinburgh	31.94	31	23.48	14	20.64	1	23.90	12	0.40	0
Falkirk	42.51	15	6.10	2	34.55	9	3.66	0	11.93	5
Fife	39.38	42	7.00	1	25.98	9	22.29	21	2.21	2
Glasgow	53.55	74	8.01	1	32.03	2	6.13	1	0.00	0
Highland	15.40	10	3.29	0	12.32	7	10.62	12	55.25	48
Inverclyde	37.51	10	5.20	1	22.03	0	34.55	9	0.71	0
Midlothian	45.81	17	7.55	0	30.65	0	15.63	1	0.36	0
Moray	20.92	6	3.84	1	30.04	2	8.33	2	33.41	13
N Ayrshire	47.73	25	18.56	2	31.74	2	0.00	0	1.97	1
N Lanarkshire	55.23	56	4.30	0	35.91	12	1.78	0	2.78	2
Orkney	0.00	0	0.00	0	0.00	0	0.00	0	99.71	21
P'shire & K'ross	16.08	6	29.09	11	34.80	16	16.82	2	3.22	2
Renfrewshire	42.07	21	10.75	1	37.77	15	7.97	3	1.44	0
Scottish Borders	5.35	1	17.39	1	18.08	4	27.99	14	31.19	14
Shetland	0.00	0	0.00	0	0.00	0	25.58	8	71.06	13
S Ayrshire	41.07	17	35.39	13	23.34	0	0.00	0	0.20	0
S Lanarkshire	50.02	54	10.30	2	33.18	10	5.68	1	0.29	0
Stirling	37.97	11	27.16	9	24.83	2	8.96	0	1.08	0
W D'shire	52.17	14	0.18	0	45.42	7	0.00	0	2.24	1
W Lothian	44.86	20	9.04	1	41.38	11	4.50	0	0.22	0
Western Isles	13.94	6	0.00	0	11.99	3	0.00	0	74.07	22

Section Ten

REFERENDUM RESULTS IN SCOTLAND

European Community Membership, 5 June 1975

Result

	%	Votes
Yes	58.4	1,332,186
No	41.6	948,039
Yes Majority:	16.8	384,147

Turnout: 61.4%

Result By Region/Island

	Yes%	No%	Turnout
Borders	72.3	27.7	63.2
Central	59.7	40.3	64.1
Dumfries and Galloway	68.2	31.8	61.5
Fife	56.3	43.7	63.3
Grampian	58.2	41.8	57.4
Highland	54.6	45.4	58.7
Lothian	59.5	40.5	63.6
Strathclyde	57.7	42.3	61.7
Tayside	58.6	41.4	63.8
Orkney	61.8	38.2	48.2
Shetland	43.7	56.3	47.1
Western Isles	29.5	70.5	50.1
Total	58.4	41.6	61.4

Scottish Assembly 1 March 1979

Do You Want the Provisions of The Scotland Act 1978 Put Into Effect?

Result

	%	Votes
Yes	51.6	1,230,937
No	48.4	1,153,502
Yes Majority	3.2	77,435

Turnout: 63.6

Result By Region

	Yes %	Yes Votes	No %	No Votes	Turnout%
Borders	40.3	20,746	59.7	30,780	67.3
Central	54.7	71,296	45.3	59,105	66.7
Dumfries and Galloway	40.3	27,162	59.7	40,239	64.9
Fife	53.7	86,252	46.3	74,436	66.1
Grampian	48.3	94,944	51.7	101,485	57.9
Highland	51.0	44,973	49.0	43,274	65.4
Lothian	50.1	187,221	49.9	186,421	66.6
Strathclyde	54.0	596,519	46.0	508,599	63.2
Tayside	49.5	91,482	50.5	93,325	63.8
Orkney	27.9	2,104	72.1	5,439	54.8
Shetland	27.1	2,020	72.9	5,466	51.0
Western Isles	55.8	6,218	44.2	4,933	50.5
Total	51.6	1,230,937	48.4	1,153,502	63.6

Scottish Parliament 11 September 1997

Result

	Devolution		Tax powers	
	%	Votes	%	Votes
Yes	74.3	1,775,045	63.5	1,512,889
No	25.7	614,400	36.5	870,263
Turnout	60.4		60.4	

Results by Region/Island

	Devolution%	Tax Powers%
Borders	62.8	50.7
Central	76.1	65.6
Dumfries and Galloway	60.7	48.8
Fife	76.1	64.7
Grampian	67.6	55.1
Highland	72.6	62.1
Lothian	76.4	64.9
Strathclyde	75.7	65.0
Tayside	67.4	56.7
Orkney	57.3	47.4
Shetland	62.4	51.6
Western Isles	79.4	68.4
Total	74.3	63.5

By Local Authority: Scottish Parliament

	Yes %	Yes votes	No %	No votes
Aberdeen	71.8	65,035	28.2	25,580
Aberdeenshire	63.9	61,621	36.1	34,878
Angus	64.7	33,571	35.3	18,350
Argyll and Bute	67.3	30,452	32.7	14,796
Clackmannanshire	80.0	18,790	20.0	4,706
Dumfries and Galloway	60.7	44,619	39.3	28,863
Dundee	76.0	49,252	24.0	15,553
East Ayrshire	81.1	49,131	18.9	11,426
East Dunbartonshire	69.8	40,917	30.2	17,725
East Lothian	74.2	33,525	25.8	11,665
East Renfrewshire	61.7	28,253	38.3	17,573
Edinburgh	71.9	155,900	28.1	60,832
Falkirk	80.0	55,642	20.0	13,953
Fife	76.1	125,668	23.9	39,517
Glasgow	83.6	204,269	16.4	40,106
Highland	72.6	72,551	27.4	27,431
Inverclyde	78.0	31,680	22.0	8,945
Midlothian	79.9	31,681	20.1	7,979
Moray	67.2	24,822	32.8	12,122
North Ayrshire	76.3	51,304	23.7	15,931

	Yes %	Yes votes	No %	No votes
North Lanarkshire	82.6	123,063	17.4	26,010
Orkney	57.3	4,749	42.7	3,541
Perthshire and Kinross	61.7	40,344	38.3	24,998
Renfrewshire	79.0	68,711	21.0	18,213
Scottish Borders	62.8	33,855	37.2	20,060
Shetland	62.4	5,430	37.6	3,275
South Ayrshire	66.9	40,161	33.1	19,909
South Lanarkshire	77.8	114,908	22.2	32,762
Stirling	68.5	29,190	31.5	13,440
West Dunbartonshire	84.7	39,051	15.3	7,058
West Lothian	79.6	56,923	20.4	14,614
Western Isles	79.4	9,977	20.6	2,589
Scotland	74.3	1,775,045	25.7	614,400

By Local Authority: Tax-Varying Powers

	Yes %	Yes votes	No %	No votes
Aberdeen	60.3	54,320	39.7	35,709
Aberdeenshire	52.3	50,295	47.7	45,929
Angus	53.4	27,641	46.6	24,089
Argyll and Bute	57.0	25,746	43.0	19,429
Clackmannanshire	68.7	16,112	31.3	7,355
Dumfries and Galloway	48.8	35,737	51.2	37,499
Dundee	65.5	42,304	34.5	22,280
East Ayrshire	70.5	42,559	29.5	17,824
East Dunbartonshire	59.1	34,576	40.9	23,914
East Lothian	62.7	28,152	37.3	16,765
East Renfrewshire	51.6	23,580	48.4	22,153
Edinburgh	62.0	133,843	38.0	82,188
Falkirk	69.2	48,064	30.8	21,403
Fife	64.7	108,021	35.3	58,987
Glasgow	75.0	182,589	25.0	60,842
Highland	62.1	61,359	37.9	37,525
Inverclyde	67.2	27,194	32.8	13,277
Midlothian	67.7	26,776	32.3	12,762
Moray	52.7	19,326	47.3	17,344
North Ayrshire	65.7	43,990	34.3	22,991
North Lanarkshire	72.2	107,288	27.8	41,372
Orkney	47.4	3,917	52.6	4,344

	Yes %	Yes votes	No %	No votes
Perthshire and Kinross	51.3	33,398	48.7	31,709
Renfrewshire	63.6	55,075	36.4	31,537
Scottish Borders	50.7	27,284	49.3	26,497
Shetland	51.6	4,478	48.4	4,198
South Ayrshire	56.2	33,679	43.8	26,217
South Lanarkshire	67.6	99,587	32.4	47,708
Stirling	58.9	25,044	41.1	17,487
West Dunbartonshire	74.7	34,408	25.3	11,628
West Lothian	67.3	47,990	32.7	23,354
Western Isles	68.4	8,557	31.6	3,947
Scotland	63.5	1,512,889	36.5	870,263

Section Eleven

SCOTTISH VOTING INTENTIONS BY OPINION POLLS

Opinion polling in Scotland has often been a fragmented activity. This fact is ably demonstrated below. Whilst we have sought to provide a long-term aspect to polling, evident most clearly in the unbroken run of System 3 polls at Westminster elections and the Scottish Parliament polls, often the available data are very limited and do not run for every year. This is evident in the case of constitutional options where data are very fragmented and occasionally subject to changes in questions that make data comparison difficult.

Westminster Opinion Polls

MORI opinion polls

	Lab	SNP	Con	Lib Dem	Others
Election May 1979	41.5	17.3	31.4	9	0.3
February 1981	40	19	19	18	1
May 1981	42	15	23	20	1
September 1981	44	13	20	22	—
November 1981	35	13	17	34	—
February 1982	39	14	18	29	—
April 1982	34	17	23	25	—
September 1982	38	13	27	21	—
November 1982	43	11	27	19	—
Feb/March 1983	39	10	26	24	—
1 May 1983	35	9	32	23	—
11 May 1983	40	7	34	7	—
June 1983	41	11	27	20	1
Election June 1983	35.1	11.8	28.4	24.5	0.3
March 1984	49	10	28	13	—
April 1984	47	12	27	13	—
September 1984	46	14	26	14	—
November 1984	46	13	28	12	1
April 1985	47	13	22	18	—
September 1985	42	13	21	24	—

	Lab	SNP	Con	Lib Dem	Others	
November 1985	42	11	24	23	—	
February 1986	41	13	22	24	—	
April 1986	45	14	21	19	1	
September 1986	51	15	19	15	—	
November 1986	45	13	26	16	—	
March 1987	47	12	19	21	1	
8–10 May,1987	43	14	25	18	—	
22–23May, 1987	44	12	27	17	—	
Election June 1987	42.4	14.0	24.0	19.2	0.3	
March 1988	50	14	26	10	—	

	Lab	SNP	Con	SDP	Lib Dem	Others	Green
April 1988	50	18	23	2	6	—	1
September 1988	49	17	25	3	6	—	—
December 1988	43	31	19	2	6	—	—
February 1989	45	24	21	4	6	—	—
April 1989	44	25	22	5	3	1	—
June 1989	47	23	22	2	4	—	1
September 1989	49	19	22	3	4	0	3
February 1990	53	17	23	1	3	0	3
April 1990	52	18	22	2	4	—	2
May 1990	56	18	20	—	5	—	1

	Lab	SNP	Con	Lib Dem	Others	Green
June 1990	55	18	21	4	—	2
July 1990	55	18	19	6	—	2
August 1990	51	22	22	4	—	1
September 1990	51	19	21	7	—	2
October 1990	52	19	19	9	—	1
November 1990	49	18	25	7	—	1
December 1990	49	19	24	6	—	2
January 1991	48	20	25	6	—	1
February 1991	51	17	25	6	—	1
March 1991	48	16	26	9	—	1
April 1991	50	15	25	9	—	1
May 1991	49	15	25	10	—	1
June 1991	51	16	24	8	—	1
July 1991	53	15	23	8	—	1
August 1991	50	17	24	8	—	1
September 1991	41	25	23	11	—	—

	Lab	SNP	Con	Lib Dem	Others	Green
October 1991	46	23	22	8	—	1
November 1991	45	22	21	11	—	1
December 1991	44	21	25	10	—	—
16–20 Jan, 1992	45	23	22	10	—	—
20–24 Feb, 1992	42	25	22	—	—	1
12 March, 1992	42	24	23	11	—	—
19 March, 1992	43	27	20	9	—	1
26 March, 1992	42	27	20	10	—	1
2 April, 1992	44	23	21	12	—	—
Election April 1992	39	21	26	13	—	—
23–7 April, 1992	40	21	27	12	—	—
21–5 May, 1992	42	23	25	8	1	1
18–22 June, 1992	42	21	27	9	—	1
23–7 July, 1992	48	19	23	8	—	1
27–31 August, 1992	50	20	21	9	—	1
22–26 September, 1992	46	24	21	8	—	1
22–6 October, 1992	52	21	19	8	—	1
26–30 November, 1992	51	21	20	7	—	1
10–14 December, 1992	49	23	21	7	—	1
21–5 January, 1993	49	22	21	7	—	—

System 3 Opinion Polls

	Lab	SNP	Con	Lib Dem	SLP
Election October 1974	36	30	25	8	—
October 1974	47	33	16	4	—
November 1974	40	32	22	6	—
January 1975	40	31	23	6	—
January 1975	40	29	24	6	—
February 1975	40	29	28	3	—
March 1975	40	24	29	6	—
April 1975	37	27	31	5	—
May 1975	40	26	28	5	—
July 1975	39	24	24	5	—
July 1975	42	22	39	5	—
August 1975	38	24	32	5	—
September 1975	35	27	34	4	—
October 1975	39	26	30	4	—
November 1975	42	26	26	5	—

	Lab	SNP	Con	Lib Dem	SLP
January 1976	30	36	28	5	—
January 1976	33	36	27	3	—
February 1976	24	33	28	6	8
March 1976	34	29	28	4	5
April 1976	31	30	28	5	5
May 1976	35	25	32	4	3
June 1976	34	27	32	4	3
July 1976	33	27	31	5	3
August 1976	30	30	30	4	4
September 1976	30	28	30	9	1
October 1976	31	31	31	3	3
November 1976	24	32	35	7	2
January 1977	28	33	29	6	4
January 1977	33	30	28	6	2
February 1977	29	31	32	5	3
March 1977	27	36	27	5	3
April 1977	28	31	31	6	2
May 1977	33	35	26	4	1
June 1977	28	32	31	6	2
July 1977	32	33	26	5	3
August 1977	29	32	30	5	4
September 1977	31	28	32	6	2
October 1977	36	26	30	6	2
November 1977	35	30	27	5	3
January 1978	34	29	28	6	3
January 1978	38	27	28	5	2
March 1978	35	27	30	5	2
March 1978	38	27	29	4	2
April 1978	47	24	24	3	2
May 1978	47	20	27	4	1
June 1978	47	22	26	4	1
July 1978	48	18	30	4	—
August 1978	52	18	24	3	3
September 1978	48	19	27	4	1
October 1978	53	21	23	3	2
November 1978	48	21	25	4	2
January 1979	45	20	31	2	2
January 1979	40	23	31	4	1
February 1979	40	18	37	4	1
March 1979	45	19	29	6	2

	Lab	SNP	Con	Lib Dem	SLP
April 1979	42	17	30	11	–
Election, May 1979	42	17	31	9	1
June 1979	53	17	21	7	2
July 1979	47	12	29	8	3
August 1979	54	16	23	6	1
September 1979	51	13	25	9	1
October 1979	42	17	31	9	1
November 1979	53	15	22	8	2
January 1980	51	17	24	8	1
January 1980	51	11	24	8	–
February 1980	49	14	27	10	–
March 1980	46	14	29	10	–
April 1980	53	16	24	7	–
May 1980	53	15	23	8	–
June 1980	52	15	22	9	–
July 1980	53	17	21	8	–
August 1980	57	14	20	9	–
September 1980	59	15	19	7	–
October 1980	54	15	21	10	–
November 1980	56	16	18	9	–
January 1981	47	18	19	13	–
February 1981	54	17	16	9	–
March 1981	46	22	17	10	–
April 1981	51	19	15	11	–
May 1981	51	18	18	11	–
June 1981	55	18	15	9	–
July 1981	51	18	18	9	–
August 1981	51	19	17	9	–
September 1981★	52	17	15	16	–
October 1981	42	21	14	22	–
November 1981	40	17	15	27	–
January 1982	38	19	18	25	–
January 1982	40	14	20	25	–
February 1982	46	18	17	18	–
March 1982	39	19	19	2	–
April 1982	42	15	23	20	–
May 1982	46	15	25	14	–
June 1982	43	14	27	16	–
July 1982	44	16	22	17	–
August 1982	42	18	24	16	–

	Lab	SNP	Con	Lib Dem
September 1982	48	14	20	18
October 1982	46	16	26	12
November 1982	45	11	28	14
January 1983	45	15	30	11
January 1983	47	12	30	11
February 1983	47	13	22	18
March 1983	49	13	25	14
April 1983	48	10	25	15
May 1983	44	12	32	12
May 1983	40	12	32	16
June 1983	40	11	26	23
Election, June 1983	35	12	28	25
June 1983	40	11	25	24
July 1983	40	13	27	18
August 1983	40	11	27	22
September 1983	42	10	25	23
October 1983	47	11	27	15
November 1983	48	11	25	14
January 1984	49	11	23	16
January 1984	48	11	24	17
February 1984	51	12	23	13
March 1984	58	10	19	12
April 1984	53	12	22	14
May 1984	52	12	22	14
June 1984	49	12	21	17
July 1984	54	14	19	13
August 1984	50	12	23	14
September 1984	44	15	22	18
October 1984	47	11	26	15
November 1984	46	13	26	15
January 1985	46	14	24	16
January 1985	44	14	26	16
February 1985	47	14	19	20
March 1985	45	14	20	21
April 1985	50	14	17	18
May 1985	50	12	17	22
June 1985	52	13	15	19
July 1985	47	12	17	24
August 1985	47	15	15	24
September 1985	41	13	18	28

	Lab	SNP	Con	Lib Dem
October 1985	45	12	22	21
November 1985	42	15	19	22
January 1986	46	16	15	23
January 1986	46	17	14	22
February 1986	44	16	16	24
March 1986	47	16	14	23
April 1986	45	15	20	20
May 1986	49	14	17	20
June 1986	44	17	19	19
July 1986	44	15	21	21
August 1986	47	15	15	22
September 1986	50	18	16	16
October 1986	52	13	22	13
November 1986	49	18	19	14
January 1987	50	15	19	16
January 1987	48	13	19	21
February 1987	50	11	19	20
March 1987	42	14	18	25
April 1987	42	13	21	23
May 1987	45	17	19	19
Election, June 1987	42	14	24	19
June 1987	49	15	21	15
July 1987	53	14	19	14
August 1987	48	12	24	15
September 1987	50	14	23	12
October 1987	50	12	22	15
November 1987	45	16	23	16
January 1988	49	15	23	12
January 1988	48	16	22	13
February 1988	51	18	18	13

	Lab	SNP	Con	SLD	SDP
March 1988	48	18	23	8	2
April 1988	49	21	22	6	2
May 1988	46	22	22	6	3
June 1988	40	23	25	8	3
July 1988	44	22	25	6	1
August 1988	49	21	23	2	3
September 1988	47	19	23	6	4
October 1988	45	20	23	8	3

	Lab	SNP	Con	SLD	SDP	Green
November 1988	39	30	21	7	2	–
January 1989	36	32	20	7	3	–
January 1989	41	28	20	8	2	–
February 1989	41	27	20	8	3	–
March 1989	41	27	20	7	3	–
April 1989	42	27	19	8	3	–
May 1989	47	25	21	5	1	–
June 1989	46	24	19	5	1	–
July 1989	45	22	21	6	2	4
August 1989	48	22	16	5	2	7
September 1989	48	18	19	7	2	6
October 1989	55	17	18	5	1	3
November 1989	49	20	21	5	2	4
January 1990	50	21	16	6	1	5
January 1990	48	18	21	6	2	3
February 1990	52	17	21	5	1	3
March 1990	54	20	15	7	–	4
April 1990	49	20	19	8	1	3
May 1990	49	23	17	5	2	3

	Lab	SNP	Con	Lib Dem	Green
June 1990	48	23	19	6	4
July 1990	52	20	19	4	4
August 1990	49	20	22	5	3
September 1990	42	24	19	10	3
October 1990	48	24	16	9	3
November 1990	43	23	24	7	3
January 1991	45	23	21	9	2
January 1991	44	18	30	7	2
February 1991	46	22	23	6	3
March 1991	42	22	23	10	2
April 1991	42	18	27	11	2
May 1991	44	20	23	11	2
June 1991	46	16	25	9	3
July 1991	46	20	24	8	2
August 1991	45	19	25	8	2
September 1991	43	23	24	9	1
October 1991	41	24	23	10	2
November 1991	44	23	18	13	2
January 1992	47	21	21	11	1

	Lab	SNP	Con	Lib Dem	Green
January 1992	38	26	23	11	2
February 1992	38	28	22	10	1
March 1992	44	26	22	7	1
April 1992	41	24	21	13	1
Election April 1992	39	21	26	13	1
May 1992	36	25	27	12	1
June 1992	39	23	26	10	2
July 1992	44	22	24	8	1
August 1992	44	22	25	8	1
September 1992	46	20	23	10	1
October 1992	42	27	20	10	1
November 1992	47	23	20	9	1
December 1992	48	22	18	10	1
January 1993	44	23	23	8	1
February 1993	43	26	18	11	1
March 1993	49	22	17	11	1
April 1993	47	21	21	9	1
May 1993	44	22	16	17	1
June 1993	45	23	16	16	1
July 1993	46	25	16	12	1
August 1993	45	24	17	13	1
September 1993	45	24	15	16	1
October 1993	43	24	17	15	1
November 1993	48	25	14	12	1
December 1993	47	23	15	14	1
January 1994	47	23	15	14	1
February 1994	47	22	16	14	1
March 1994	47	25	13	14	1
April 1994	46	26	13	14	1
May 1994	44	27	14	14	1
June 1994	53	24	10	12	1
July 1994	46	30	12	11	1
August 1994	51	27	12	9	1
September 1994	55	24	12	8	−
October 1994	51	29	11	9	3
November 1994	47	27	13	10	−
December 1994	55	25	12	8	1
January 1995	57	22	11	9	1
February 1995	54	23	12	10	−
March 1995	52	25	11	10	1

	Lab	SNP	Con	Lib Dem	Green
April 1995	53	25	11	9	1
May 1995	52	22	13	12	1
June 1995	53	27	11	9	1
July 1995	57	23	11	8	—
August 1995	54	22	12	11	1
September 1995	52	26	12	8	1
October 1995	46	30	13	11	1
November 1995	52	23	13	10	1
December 1995	57	21	13	8	1
January 1996	53	23	11	11	1
February 1996	52	23	12	10	1
March 1996	53	23	12	9	—
April 1996	54	23	13	10	1
May 1996	53	23	13	9	1
June 1996	54	24	12	8	—
July 1996	51	25	15	9	1
August 1996	51	23	15	10	1
September 1996	48	29	15	7	1
October 1996	49	24	13	12	1
November 1996	55	23	11	8	1
December 1996	53	24	12	10	1

	Lab	SNP	Con	Lib Dem	Other
January 1997	50	22	16	10	—
February 1997	52	25	15	8	1
4 March 1997	46	26	16	10	1
26 March 1997	52	20	17	9	—
2 April 1997	53	26	12	9	—
9 April 1997	51	23	14	10	—
16 April 1997	52	24	13	9	—
23 April 1997	47	24	15	12	—
30 April 1997	50	26	14	9	—
Election May 1997	46	22	18	13	1
May 1997	57	23	9	10	1
June 1997	54	23	12	10	1
July 1997	54	24	10	9	1
August 1997	50	25	14	11	1
September 1997	55	23	13	9	1
October 1997	55	22	14	8	1
November 1997	51	24	12	12	1

	Lab	SNP	Con	Lib Dem	Other
December 1997	50	27	12	10	1
January 1998	50	25	11	12	1
February 1998	46	28	14	11	2
March 1998	48	28	12	9	2
April 1998	44	30	14	11	1
May 1998	46	29	14	10	1
June 1998	43	33	14	9	1
Julyt 1998	48	28	13	8	2
August 1998	46	31	13	8	1
September 1998	45	31	13	10	1
October 1998	43	29	14	12	1
November 1998	42	31	13	13	2
December 1998	46	28	13	11	2
January 1999	45	32	11	10	1
February 1999	44	29	14	11	2
March 1999	50	24	13	13	2
April 1999	51	24	13	11	1
May 1999	47	22	13	14	3
June 1999	49	24	13	10	4
July 1999	49	24	13	11	2
August 1999	46	24	16	12	3
September 1999	42	29	14	13	3
October 1999	45	27	12	12	3
November 1999	50	24	12	11	2
January 2000	50	27	12	9	2
January 2000	49	24	14	11	2
February 2000	45	27	15	11	3
March 2000	40	29	16	11	3
April 2000	44	26	17	9	3
May 2000	48	24	14	10	4
June 2000	39	31	17	11	3
July 2000	46	26	15	9	4
August 2000	45	28	15	9	3
October 2000	33	33	15	17	2
November 2000	48	27	13	10	2

* formation of Liberal/SDP Alliance

Scottish Parlaiment Opinion Polls

System 3 Scottish Parliament Opinion Polls

	Lab	SNP	Con	Lib Dem	Other
November 1997	48	29	13	9	1
February 1998	44	33	9	13	1
March 1998	39	38	12	10	1
April 1998	40	40	8	10	1
May 1998	36	41	11	10	1
June 1998	35	44	10	10	1
July 1998					
Constituency	37	45	9	8	–
Regional	32	43	11	12	–
August 1998					
Constituency	40	41	10	9	–
Regional	36	41	9	12	–
September 1998					
Constituency	41	38	11	8	–
Regional	39	40	10	10	–
November 1998					
Constituency	39	37	12	12	–
Regional	37	35	11	14	–
January 1999					
Constituency	39	40	11	10	–
Regional	36	39	11	13	–
January 1999					
Constituency	38	38	11	11	–
Regional	37	38	11	12	–
February 1999					
Constituency	41	39	10	9	1
Regional	38	38	10	13	1
March 1999					
Constituency	39	38	11	11	1
Regional	40	36	10	12	1
2nd April 1999					
Constituency	45	32	10	12	1
Regional	40	32	11	15	1

	Lab	SNP	Con	Lib Dem	Other
22nd April 1999					
Constituency	46	26	11	13	2
Regional	40	27	12	14	4
29th April 1999					
Constituency	44	33	10	10	3
Regional	37	34	10	13	6
May 1999					
Constituency	44	33	10	10	2
Regional	37	34	10	13	5
Election Result 6 May 1999					
Constituency	38.79	28.72	15.55	14.23	–
Regional	33.64	27.31	15.35	12.43	–
June 1999					
Constituency	44	28	10	13	5
Regional	36	30	10	17	8
July 1999					
Constituency	43	28	11	12	6
Regional	34	31	10	13	11
August 1999					
Constituency	41	30	12	12	5
Regional	34	31	10	14	11
September 1999					
Constituency	40	31	12	11	6
Regional	29	29	11	17	12
October 1999					
Constituency	35	35	11	12	7
Regional	32	32	8	15	12
November 1999					
Constituency	39	35	10	10	6
Regional	36	31	9	13	11
December 1999					
Constituency	44	30	9	11	6
Regional	33	30	10	14	13

	Lab	SNP	Con	Lib Dem	Other
January 2000					
Constituency	43	34	8	9	6
Regional	37	33	9	12	10
February 2000					
Constituency	42	31	11	10	6
Regional	34	31	9	14	12
March 2000					
Constituency	37	36	12	9	6
Regional	32	33	11	13	11
April 2000					
Constituency	33	37	14	11	6
Regional	29	34	11	15	11
May 2000					
Constituency	34	35	14	10	8
Regional	30	31	13	14	13
June 2000					
Constituency	40	30	13	10	8
Regional	31	33	13	13	13
July 2000					
Constituency	33	36	12	12	6
Regional	27	35	11	16	12
August 2000					
Constituency	37	35	11	10	6
Regional	33	30	11	12	14
September 2000					
Constituency	34	36	13	9	8
Regional	29	32	13	12	13
October 2000					
Constituency	28	42	10	14	6
Regional	25	38	11	15	10
November 2000					
Constituency	39	35	10	11	5
Regional	30	31	10	17	11

System 3 Opinion Poll Allocation of Seats to the Scottish Parliament (Total = Constituency MSPs + Additional Members)

	Lab	SNP	Con	Lib Dem	Others
Gen Election 1997	63 (56+7)	28 (6+22)	22 (0+22)	16 (11+5)	—
February 1998	68	36	8	17	—
March 1998	55 (49+6)	49 (16+33)	13 (0+13)	12 (7+5)	—
April 1998	59 (49+10)	53 (17+36)	7 (0+7)	10 (6+4)	—
May 1998	53 (42+11)	52 (23+29)	12 (0+12)	12 (8+4)	—
June 1998	52 (32+20)	58 (23+25)	9 (0+9)	10 (7+3)	—
July 1998	46 (35+11	)56 (32+24)	12 (0+12)	15 (6+9)	—
August 1998	55	52	7 (0+7)	15 (6+9)	—
September 1998	59 (52+7)	53 (14+39)	7 (0+7)	10 (7+3)	—
November 1998	55 (51+4)	42	14	18	—
January 1999	55	50	10	14	—
January 1999	56 (50+6)	46 (16+30)	12 (0+12)	15 (7+8)	—
February 1999	57 (51+6)	46 (15+31)	9 (0+9)	17 (7+10)	—
March 1999	59	47 (16+31)	8	15	—
April 1999	60	39	12	18	—
Scottish Election	56 (53+3)	35 (7+28)	18 (0+18)	17 (12+5)	3
October 1999	51 (42+9)	47	7 (1+6)	20	4
November 1999	56	43	9	18	3
December 1999	57 (55 +2)	38 (6 + 32)	12	19	3
January 2000	56	44	9	16	4
February 2000	56	41	9	19	4
March 2000	53 (46+7)	44 (15+29)	11 (0+11)	17 (11+6)	4
April 2000	42	49	14	19	5
May 2000	49	40	16	19	5
June 2000	55	42	10	18	4
July 2000	43 (37+6)	48 (23+25)	12 (1+11)	21 (11+10)	5
August 2000	54	40	13	16	6
September 2000	47	43	16	18	5
October 2000	32	59	13	20	5
November 2000	55	40	10	20	4

MORI Scottish Parliament Opinion Polls

	Lab	SNP	Cons	Lib Dems	Other	
May 1998						
Constituency	42	36	12	8	—	
Region	36	39	11	11	—	
June 1998						
Constituency	40	35	14	11	—	
Region	35	38	13	14	—	
July 1998						
Constituency	40	40	11	8	—	
Region	39	39	10	11	—	
August 1998						
Constituency	36	39	—	—	—	★
Region	36	36	—	—	—	★
September 1998						
Constituency	44	36	12	7	—	
Region	45	34	12	8	—	
January 1999						
Constituency	38	36	15	10	—	
Region	38	34	15	12	—	
February 1999						
Constituency	43	38	9	9	2	
Region	39	37	10	12	2	
March 1999						
Constituency	48	33	—	—	—	★
Region	—	—	—	—	—	★
April 1999						
Constituency	48	34	9	9	—	
Region	44	34	—	—	—	★

★ Incomplete data, polls never published.

MORI Opinion Poll Allocation of Seats to the Scottish Parliament (Total = Constituency MSPs + Additional Members)

	Lab	SNP	Cons	Lib Dems
April 1998	55 (52+3)	52 (13+39)	10 (0+10)	12 (8+4)
June 1998	53 (52+1)	47	13	16
July 1998	56	51	9	13
November 1998	61	45	14	9
January 1999	55	43	17	14
February 1999	56 (52+4)	49 (14+37)	9 (0+9)	15 (7+8)
March 1999	63	47 (8+39)	10 (0+10)	–
April 1999	62	43	9	–

Section Twelve

SCOTTISH CONSTITUTIONAL OPTIONS

MORI

	Independent of UK and EU	Independence in EU	Devolved assembly	No change
December 1988	10	24	46	16
February 1989	11	24	42	20
June 1989	12	22	49	15
September 1989	9	27	44	18
February 1990	10	24	44	19
May 1990	8	29	45	16
June 1990	10	28	43	17
July 1990	10	27	44	19
August 1990	7	31	44	16
September 1990	9	28	44	17
October 1990	9	30	44	15
November 1990	9	28	45	17
December 1990	7	25	49	17
January 1991	7	28	42	21
February 1991	10	23	45	20
March 1991	8	27	42	21
April 1991	9	28	42	19
May 1991	7	26	45	19
June 1991	8	26	47	17
July 1991	8	28	43	18
August 1991	9	26	47	17
September 1991	9	26	45	17
October 1991	9	28	46	15
November 1991	8	26	47	16
December 1991	9	31	40	17
January 1992	9	31	42	15
February 1992	7	29	37	23
12 March 1992	8	26	42	20

	Independent of UK and EU	Independence in EU	Devolved assembly	No change
19 March 1992	8	26	42	23
26 March 1992	7	27	44	20
2 April 1992	6	22	45	23
April 1992	5	22	47	25
May 1992	5	23	48	21
June 1992	5	29	40	23
July 1992	7	28	41	21
August 1992	8	27	41	21
September 1992	9	25	43	20
October 1992	9	28	44	17
November 1992	10	25	42	20
January 1993	8	28	42	18

MORI Scotland: March 1998

Vote for Independence in a Referendum:

Yes 47%

No 40%

25% of Scots believed Scotland would be an independent state within five years.

62% of Scots believed Scotland would be an independent state within 15 years

75% of Scots believed Scotland would be an independent state within 50 years

ICM

	Devolution	Independence	No Change
September 1993	47	34	17
March 1994	44	38	16
June 1994	46	35	15

System 3

	Independence In or out of EU	Independence in EU	Devolution	No Change
May 1993	16	18	49	15
May 1994	10	19	52	16
January 1995	29	47	20	3

ICM

Q: In a referendum, would you vote for independence for Scotland?

	Yes	No	Don't know
5 June 1998	52%	41%	7%
1 July 1998	56%	35%	9%
31 July 1998	49%	44%	7%
5 September 1998	51%	38%	10%
25 September 1998	48%	37%	15%
25 November 1998	49%	43%	8%
12 January 1999	49%	42%	9%
4 February 1999	44%	47%	9%
18 March 1999	42%	47%	11%
4 April 1999	47%	44%	9%
30 January 2000	47%	43%	–

System 3

Support for Independence

	Independence	Devolution	Don't Know
May 1998	34%	58%	8%
December 1998	34%	61%	5%

MORI, Sunday Herald *June 1999: 'Which government institution makes the most difference to your life?'*

Institution	%
Westminster	44
Scottish Parliament	38
European Parliament	11

The Economist 6 November 1999: 'Which institution will have most impact upon you in the future?'

Institution	%
Westminster	8
Scottish Parliament	46
EU	31

ICM, Scotland On Sunday, *30 January 2000: 'Which Parliament will be most important in deciding Scotland's future?'*

Institution	%
Westminster	31
Scottish Parliament	51
European Parlaiment	13

Section Thirteen

SECRETARIES OF STATE FOR SCOTLAND*

The Duke of Richmond and Gordon (Conservative)	1885
Sir George Trevelyan (Liberal)	1886
The Earl of Dalhousie (Liberal)	1886
Arthur Balfour (Conservative)	1886–7
The Marquess of Lothian (Conservative)	1887–92
Sir George Trevelyan (Liberal)	1892–5
Lord Balfour of Burleigh (Conservative)	1895–1903
Andrew Graham Murray (Conservative)	1903–5
The Marquess of Linlithgow (Conservative)	1905
John Sinclair (Liberal)	1905–12
Thomas MacKinnon Wood (Liberal)	1912–16
Harold John Tennant (Coalition)	1916
Robert Munro (Coalition)	1916–22
Viscount Novar (Conservative)	1922–4
William Adamson (Labour)	1924
Sir John Gilmour (Conservative)	1924–9
William Adamson (Labour)	1929–31
Sir Archibald Sinclair (National Government)	1931–2
Sir Godfrey Collins (National Government)	1932–6
Walter Elliot (National Government)	1936–8
John Colville (National Government)	1938–40
Ernest Brown (Coalition)	1940–1
Thomas Johnston (Coalition)	1941–5
Earl of Rosebery (Caretaker)	1945
Joseph Westwood (Labour)	1945–7
Arthur Woodburn (Labour)	1947–50
Hector McNeil (Labour)	1950–1

James Stuart (Conservative)	1951–7
John Maclay (Conservative)	1957–62
Michael Noble (Conservative)	1962–4
William Ross (Labour)	1964–70
Gordon Campbell (Conservative)	1970–4
William Ross (Labour)	1974–6
Bruce Millan (Labour)	1976–9
George Younger (Conservative)	1979–86
Malcolm Rifkind (Conservative)	1986–90
Ian Lang (Conservative)	1990–5
Michael Forsyth (Conservative)	1995–7
Donald Dewar (Labour)	1997–9
John Reid (Labour)	1999–2001
Helen Liddell (Labour)	2001–

*The post was known as the Scottish Secretary from 1885 to 1926, upon which it became known as the Secretary of State for Scotland.

Section Fourteen

SCOTTISH EXECUTIVE MINISTERS SINCE 1999

Scottish Executive Cabinet appointed 29 October 2000

First Minister: Henry McLeish

Deputy First Minister and Minister for Justice: Jim Wallace

Minister for Finance and Local Government: Angus MacKay

Minister for Health and Community Care: Susan Deacon

Minister for Social Justice: Jackie Baillie

Minister for Transport: Sarah Boyack

Minister for Enterprise and Life-long Learning: Wendy Alexander

Minister for Rural Affairs: Ross Finnie

Minister for Education, Europe and External Affairs: Jack McConnell

Minister for Parliament: Tom McCabe

Minister for the Environment: Sam Galbraith

Lord Advocate: Lord Boyd

Deputy Ministers

Deputy Minister for Justice: Iain Gray

Deputy Minister for Health and Community Care: Malcolm Chisholm

Deputys Minister for Enterprise and Life-long Learning, and Gaelic: Alasdair Morrison

Deputy Minister for Social Justice: Margaret Curran

Deputy Minister for Rural Development: Rhona Brankin

Deputy Minister for Education, Europe and External Affairs: Nicol Stephen

Deputy Minister for Sport and Culture: Allan Wilson

Deputy Minister for Finance and Local Government: Peter Peacock

Deputy Minister for Parliament: Tavish Scott

Deputy to Lord Advocate: Iain Davidson

Scottish Executive: appointed May 16th 1999

First Minister: Donald Dewar

Deputy First Minister and Minister for Justice: Jim Wallace

Finance Minister: Jack McConnell

Minister for Health and Community Care: Susan Deacon

Minister for Communities (Local Government, Housing and Social Inclusion): Wendy Alexander

Minister for Transport and the Environment: Sarah Boyack

Minister for Enterprise and Life-long Learning: Henry McLeish

Minister for Rural Affairs: Ross Finnie

Minister for Children and Education (Culture, Arts and Sports): Sam Galbraith

Business Manager and Chief Whip: Tom McCabe

Lord Advocate: Lord Hardie until February 2000, Lord Boyd from February 2000

Deputy Ministers

Deputy Minister for Justice: Angus MacKay

Deputy Minister for Health and Community Care: Iain Gray

Deputy Minister for Enterprise and Life-long Learning: Nicol Stephen

Deputy Minister for Enterprise and Life-long Learning in the Highlands and Islands and Gaelic: Alasdair Morrison

Deputy Minister for Communities (Local Government): Frank McAveety

Deputy Minister for Communities (Social Inclusion, Equality and the Voluntary Sector): Jackie Baillie

Deputy Minister for Rural Affairs (Fisheries): John Home Robertson

Deputy Minister for Children and Education: Peter Peacock

Deputy Minister for Children and Education (Culture, Arts and Sports): Rhona Brankin

Deputy Business Manager: Iain Smith

Deputy to Lord Advocate: Colin Boyd QC (Solicitor General) until February 2000, Iain Davidson from February 2000

Section Fifteen

BIOGRAPHIES OF PROMINENT SCOTTISH POLITICIANS

No biographies of current Scottish politicians such as Alex Salmond or David Steel are carried in this section. For details of these and others, see listings under current constituencies. We have defined Scottish politicians in the broadest sense to include anyone who has contributed significantly to Scottish politics by standing for a Scottish constituency or representing one. Thus, we have included several non-Scottish politicians by birth, such as Winston Churchill and Roy Jenkins, who in long and successful careers, played a part in Scottish politics.

Herbert Henry Asquith 1852–1928

Liberal MP for East Fife 1886–1918, Paisley 1920–24. Home Secretary 1892–95, Chancellor of the Exchequer 1905–08, Prime Minister 1908–16, Leader of the Liberal Party 1908–26. Prime Minister of radical Liberal Government which introduced Lloyd George's 'people's budget' and faced a constitutional crisis with the Lords.

Andrew Bonar Law 1858–1923

Conservative MP for Glasgow Blackfriars 1900–06, Dulwich 1906–10, Bootle 1911–18, Glasgow Central 1918–23. Prime Minister 1922–23, Leader of the Conservative Party 1911–23. Born in New Brunswick, Canada, he came to Glasgow at the age of 11. Briefly Prime Minister, he was leader of the Conservatives for over a decade, in opposition and in government, supporting the Lloyd George coalition.

Robert Boothby 1900–1986

Conservative MP for East Aberdeenshire and Kincardineshire 1924–50, East Aberdeenshire 1950–58. Briefly Minister for Food 1940. Critic of appeasement in the 1930s and ally of Churchill. Well known for the independence of his opinions including opposition to the Suez War and support for European unity and homosexual law reform.

John Buchan 1875–1940

Conservative MP for the Scottish Universities 1927–35. President of the Scottish History Society 1929–32, Governor-General of Canada 1935–40, Chancellor of Edinburgh University 1937. A celebrated writer, Buchan wrote over fifty books in his life, including the spy thrillers featuring Richard Hannay of which the most famous is *The Thirty-Nine Steps*.

Gordon Campbell 1921–

Conservative MP for Moray and Nairn 1959–February 1974. Secretary of State for Scotland in the Heath Government 1970–74. First post-war Secretary of State who was from the minority Scottish party. Defeated by Winnie Ewing in the February 1974 general election.

Henry Campbell-Bannerman 1839–1908

Liberal MP for Stirling Burghs 1868–1908. Prime Minister 1905–08, Leader of the Liberal Party in the Commons 1899–1908. Presided over the Liberal landslide of 1906. His government included such talents as Asquith, Churchill and Lloyd George. He died two weeks after resigning through ill-health.

Winston Churchill 1874–1965

Liberal MP for Dundee 1908–22. Also Conservative MP for Oldham 1900–04, Liberal MP for Oldham 1904–06, for Manchester North West 1906–08, Conservative for Epping 1924–45, for Woodford 1945–64. British Prime Minister 1940–45 and 1951–55, previously in Liberal Government as President of the Board of Trade, Home Secretary and First Lord of the Admiralty. As a Liberal, Churchill was defeated in Dundee by Edwin Scrymgeour, before rejoining the Conservatives and becoming a critic of appeasement in the 1930s.

Donald Dewar 1937–2000

Labour MP for Aberdeen South 1966–70, Glasgow Garscadden 1978–97, Glasgow Anniesland 1997–2000, MSP for Glasgow Anniesland 1999–2000. Shadow Secretary of State for Scotland 1983–92, Shadow Social Security Spokesman 1992–95, Shadow Chief Whip 1995–97, Secretary of State for Scotland 1997–99, First Minister 1999–2000. Dewar was one of Scottish Labour's leading spokespeople in the last two decades in opposition and office. In office, post-1997, he oversaw the successful referendum campaign and the passing of the Scotland Act 1998. He subsequently became the first First Minister of Scotland, forming a Labour-Liberal Democrat administration, and tragically died in office in October 2000.

Alec Douglas Home 1903–1995

Conservative MP for Lanark 1931–45 and 1950–1, Perthshire 1963–October 1974. Minister of State at the Scottish Office 1951–55, Commonwealth Relations Secretary 1955–60, Leader of the House of Lords 1957–60, Foreign Secretary 1960–63. Made 14th Earl Home 1951, renounced peerage 1963, Prime Minister 1963–64, Leader of the Conservatives 1963–65, Foreign Secretary 1970–74. Started political career in the 1930s as Chamberlain's Private Parliamentary Secretary, succeeded Macmillan as Prime Minister and lost 1964 election to Wilson by narrow margin.

Walter Elliot 1888–1958

Conservative, Lanark 1918–23, Glasgow Kelvingrove 1924–45, Scottish Universities 1946-50, Glasgow Kelvingrove 1950–58. Leading Scottish Tory politician, Secretary of State for Scotland 1936–38 and author of 'Toryism and the Twentieth Century' published in 1927. A moderate, thoughtful Conservative, he presided as Secretary of State over the development of administrative devolution and the shift of the Scottish Office to Edinburgh from London.

Nicholas Fairbairn 1933–1995

Conservative MP, Kinross and West Perthshire, October 1974–83, Perth and Kinross 1983–95. Flamboyant Conservative MP and character. Solicitor General for Scotland 1979–82 who was forced to resign after making remarks on a Glasgow rape trial. The first volume of his autobiography was called *A Life is Too Short* was published in 1987.

Michael Forsyth 1954–

Conservative MP for Stirling 1983–97 and Secretary of State for Scotland 1995–97. Tory right-winger and one time ally of Margaret Thatcher. Westminster City Councillor 1978–83, Chairman of the Scottish Tories 1989–90, (where he famously fell out with Malcolm Rifkind and had to be moved by Mrs. Thatcher), Minister of State at the Scottish Office 1990–92, Employment Minister 1992–94, Home Office Minister 1994–95. A supporter of privatisation and the poll tax, he invented the term 'tartan tax' to describe Labour's plans for a Scottish Parliament with tax powers.

Willie Gallacher 1881–1965

Communist MP for West Fife 1935–50. Leader of 'Red Clydeside' shop stewards movement during the First World War. Helped establish Communist Party of Great Britain and as MP for East Fife was the longest serving Communist MP in UK politics. President of the Communist Party from 1956–63. The author of numerous books, pamphlets and publications, his *Revolt on the Clyde*, first published in 1936, significantly contributed to the myth of 'Red Clydeside'.

Andrew Dewar Gibb 1888–1974

One of the founders of the Scottish Party in 1932, a right-wing pressure group which stressed that Scottish home rule could strengthen the Union and Empire. It combined with the National Party of Scotland to lead to the establishment of the SNP in 1934. An expert on Scots law and Professor at Glasgow University, he was Chair of the SNP from 1936–40 and was subsequently heavily involved in the Scottish Convention. He was Chair of the Saltire Society from 1955–7.

Jo Grimond 1913–93

Liberal MP for Orkney and Shetland 1950–83. Leader of the Liberal Party 1956–67, Grimond saved the Liberal Party from near political extinction in the 1950s. Attempted to position them as the non-socialist radical alternative to the Conservatives.

Keir Hardie 1856–1915

Independent Labour MP for West Ham South 1892–5, Labour for Merthyr Tydfil 1900–15. First Scottish Labour candidate who stood in the 1888 Mid-Lanark by-election, founder and Chair of the Independent Labour Party 1893–1900 and 1913–14. A supporter of independent Labour representation, he lost his seat due to his opposition to the Boer War. He was Chair of the International Socialist Bureau in 1914 when the idealism of socialist internationalism was broken by the power of nationalist patriotism; the events of 1914 clearly broke Hardie and he died the following year.

Roy Jenkins 1918–

Social Democratic MP for Glasgow Hillhead 1982–7. Also Labour MP for Central Southwark 1948–50, Birmingham Stechford 1950–76. Minister in 1964–70 and 1974–6 Labour Governments, President of European Commission 1977–81, Leader of the Social Democratic Party 1982–3, leader of Liberal Democrat Peers 1987–97. A major figure of the centre-left in the 20th century, who attempted by creating the SDP to 'break the mould' of British politics, an objective he continued to pursue with his chairmanship of the Jenkins Commission on electoral reform in 1998.

Tom Johnston 1881–1965

Labour MP for West Stirling 1922–24, 1929–31, 1935–45, Dundee 1924–29. Secretary of State for Scotland 1941–45 in Churchill's wartime coalition. He is noted for building economic and social consensus amongst the key institutions and players. He was a member of the Independent Labour Party and editor of Forward, the socialist journal from 1906–33. In 1945, he became Chair of the North of Scotland Hydro-Electric Board. His publications include *Our Scottish Noble Families*, published in 1909, which was a savage critique of the Scots aristocracy and noblery, *The History of the Working Classes in Scotland*, published in 1923, and his autobiography *Memories* which came out in 1952.

David Kirkwood 1872–1955

Labour MP for Dumbarton Burghs, 1922–50, East Dunbartonshire 1950–51. One of the leading 'Red Clydesiders', prominent in the Clyde Workers Committee in 1915–16, and elected to Glasgow Town Council and Westminster in 1922. He quickly moderated his views upon election to Westminster, became Baron Kirkwood in 1951 and his autobiography *My Life of Revolt* published in 1935 contained an introduction by Winston Churchill.

Ian Lang 1940–

Conservative MP for Galloway 1979–83, Galloway and Upper Nithsdale 1983–97. Lloyds insurance underwriter before entering Parliament. Minister of State for Scotland 1987–90, Secretary of State for Scotland 1990–95, Trade Secretary 1995–97. Lang, a moderate Tory, was Secretary of State in John Major's administration and after the 1992 election attempted to introduce a more sensitive unionism to resist devolution.

Jennie Lee 1904–88

Labour MP for North Lanarkshire 1929–31, Cannock 1945–70. Minister for the Arts 1965–70. Well known socialist and womens rights campaigner, she was married to Nye Bevan, leader of the Labour left in the 1940s and 1950s. As Arts Minister she presided over increased arts spending and the establishment of the Open University. She wrote her autobiography *My Life with Nye* which was published in 1980.

John MacCormick 1904–61

One of the founders of the National Party of Scotland in 1928 which became the

SNP in 1934. Party Secretary of the SNP 1934–42, Chairman of the Scottish Convention and National Assembly, which he left the SNP to establish. He stood in the Paisley by-election in 1948 on a pro–home rule ticket with National Liberal and Tory support, nearly defeating Labour and organised the Scottish Covenant in 1949. His autobiography on the home rule movement, *The Flag in the Wind* was published in 1955.

Ramsay MacDonald 1866–1937

Labour MP for Leicester 1906–18, Aberavon 1922–29, Seaham 1929–31, National Labour, Seaham 1931–35, Scottish Universities 1936–37. Born in Lossiemouth, Labour Prime Minister 1924 and 1929–31, head of the National Government 1931–35, Leader of the Labour Party 1922–31. MacDonald was the first Labour Prime Minister in 1924. In his second administration, he reacted to the financial crisis of 1931 by forming a National Government and leaving Labour. He was never forgiven for what was seen in many Labour circles as an act of treachery.

Robert McIntyre 1913–98

McIntyre became the first ever SNP MP when he won Motherwell in a by-election in April 1945 and held it for three months. One of the pivotal figures of the post-war SNP developing them organisationally and politically into a modern credible party. Chairman of the SNP 1946–56 when he wrote the party's new policy document in 1948. President of the SNP 1956–80 and Provost of Stirling 1967–75.

John P. Mackintosh 1929–78

Labour MP for Berwick and Lothian 1966–February 1974, October 1974–8. Academic at Glasgow and Strathclyde Universities before election as an MP. Leading Labour right-wing thinker on social democracy, modernising government and devolution. Author of numerous books on British politics and government including *The British Cabinet* (1962), *The Devolution of Power* (1968) and the posthumous *Mackintosh on Scotland* (1982). His premature death in 1978 was a major loss to Labour.

John Maclean 1879–1923

A member of the British Socialist Party before the First World War, he became Soviet Consul on the Clyde after 1917. Refused to join the Communist Party and set up the Scottish Workers' Party which combined communism and nationalism. Contested Glasgow Gorbals in 1918 and 1922 unsuccessfully. He died in 1923 while campaigning on the hustings in the Gorbals.

John Maxton 1885–1946

Labour MP for Glasgow Bridgeton 1922–32, Independent Labour, Glasgow Bridgeton 1932–46. One of the most inspiring leaders of the 'Red Clydesiders' and recognised across the political divide as one of the talents on Labour's benches. Churchill called him 'the greatest gentleman', he was Chair of the Independent Labour Party from 1926–31 and 1934–9, drew up the Cook/Maxton manifesto in 1928 to win Labour to radical policies and led the ILP split in 1932. His biography was written by Gordon Brown.

Bruce Millan 1927–

Labour MP for Glasgow Craigton 1959–83, Glasgow Govan 1983–8, Secretary of State for Scotland 1976–9 helped steer the Scotland Act 1978 onto the statute books. Appointed European Commissioner in 1988. After Willie Ross, he articulated a more sensitive and convincing devolution policy and was also Shadow Secretary of State for Scotland from 1979–83.

Jimmy Reid 1932–

AEU trade unionist who led the Upper Clyde Shipworkers work-in in 1971, Rector of Glasgow University 1971–4. Reid contested East Dunbartonshire for the Communists in the 1974 elections, and stood in Dundee East for Labour in the 1979 election losing to the SNP. He is now a celebrated journalist and sworn critic of everything to do with the New Labour project. His autobiography, *Reflections of a Clyde-built Man* was published in 1976.

Malcolm Rifkind 1946–

Conservative MP for Edinburgh Pentlands February 1974–97. Opposition front-bench spokesman on Scotland who resigned with Alick Buchanan-Smith in 1976 over Thatcher's u-turn on devolution. Scottish Office minister 1979–82, Foreign Office minister 1982–6, Secretary of State for Scotland 1986–90, Secretary of State for Transport 1990–2, Secretary of State for Defence 1992–5, Foreign Secretary 1995–7. Rifkind, a Conservative moderate, presided over a dramatic decline in Tory electoral fortunes in 1987 and oversaw the implementation of the much despised poll tax.

George Robertson 1947–

Labour MP for Hamilton 1978–97, Hamilton South 1997–9. Shadow Spokesman on

Foreign Affairs 1981–93, Shadow Scottish Secretary 1993–7, Defence Secretary 1997–9, Secretary General of Nato 1999–. As Shadow Scottish Secretary he oversaw Blair's u-turn on a referendum on devolution and was shifted to defence upon Labour's return to power in 1997.

Willie Ross 1911–88

Labour MP for Kilmarnock 1946–79. Secretary of State for Scotland 1964–70 and 1974–6. Ross was a passionate anti-devolutionist and known as 'the hammer of the Nats'. In office, he presided over Labour's minimal conversion to devolution in the 1970s, and was responsible for setting up the Highlands and Islands Development Board and the Scottish Development Agency.

Edwin Scrymgeour 1866–1947

Independent MP for Dundee 1922–31. Prohibitionist and independent socialist, founder of Scottish Prohibition Party in 1904, elected Dundee Town Council 1905, defeated Winston Churchill in 1922 and was elected until 1931 without Labour support.

Manny Shinwell 1884–1986

Labour MP for Linlithgowshire 1922–4, 1928–31, Seaham 1935–50, Easington 1950–70. Minister of Mines 1924, Minister of Fuel and Power 1946–7, Secretary of State for War 1947–50, Minister for Defence 1950–1. A leading 'Red Clydesider' and Minister in the first Labour Government, he defeating Ramsay MacDonald in the 1935 election. He was Chair of Labour's Policy Committee which drafted the 1945 manifesto and wrote three volumes of autobiographies, the last of which was *Lead with the Left*, published in 1981.

Jim Sillars 1937–

Labour MP, South Ayrshire 1970–76, Scottish Labour Party MP, South Ayrshire 1976–9, SNP MP, Glasgow Govan 1988–92. Once widely thought of as a potential future of Scottish Labour, in 1976 Sillars broke away and formed his own Scottish Labour Party over Labour's lukewarm attitude to devolution. He lost his seat in 1979 and joined the SNP in 1980, shaping their 'independence in Europe' policy before sensationally winning Govan in 1988, which he lost in 1992.

John Smith 1938–94

Labour MP for North Lanarkshire 1970–83, Monklands East 1983–94. Leader of the Labour Party 1992–4. Energy Minister 1974–5, Minister of State for Energy 1975–6, Minister for the Privy Council Office 1976–8, Secretary of State for Trade 1978–9. Widely respected Labour leader who combined conviction and determination with a quiet, unassuming manner. A Labour right-winger, he remained in the party after the SDP split in 1981, and as Labour leader after the 1992 election, achieved a massive Labour lead over the Conservatives following 'Black Wednesday'. A passionate supporter of devolution, he once famously described it as 'unfinished business'.

Donald Stewart 1920–92

SNP MP for the Western Isles 1970–87. The first SNP victory at a general election, Stewart was parliamentary leader of the SNP at their high point of 1974–79. He had the difficult task of holding together a disparate political group and in 1979 tabled the no confidence motion which brought down the Labour Government after the inconclusive referendum result.

John Strachey 1901-63

Labour MP for Dundee 1945–50, Dundee West 1950–63, previously Birmingham Aston 1929–31. Minister for Food 1946–50, Minister for War 1950–1. Leading Labour thinker who was a radical, Marxist voice in the 1930s and author of such texts as *The Coming Struggle for Power* written in 1932. In the 1950s, he shifted dramatically and wrote 'Contemporary Capitalism' in 1956, a book which influenced the Croslandite-Gaitskellite social democratic revisionism of the party leadership.

John Wheatley 1869–1930

Labour MP, Glasgow Shettleston 1922–30. Leading figure of the 'Red Clydesiders'. Health MInister in the first Labour Government and responsible for passing the Housing (Financial Provisions) Act 1924 which aided the building of council houses. When Labour was returned in 1929 as a minority government, he felt they should not take office and was not offered any post by MacDonald.

Gordon Wilson 1938–

SNP MP for Dundee East February 1974–87. National Secretary of the SNP 1963–71, National Convenor of the SNP 1979–90. As Secretary, he spearheaded the organisational modernisation of the party in the 1960s, and was at the forefront of developing the 'It's Scotland's Oil' campaign in the early seventies. As Convenor of the party from 1979, Wilson resisted the rise of the left-wing '79 Group and emphasised a more conservative nationalist perspective.

Arthur Woodburn 1890–1978

Labour MP, Clackmannanshire and East Stirlingshire 1959–70. Parliamentary Private Secretary to Tom Johnston 1941–5, Secretary of State for Scotland 1947–50, Shadow Secretary of State 1951–9. As Attlee's longest serving Secretary of State, Woodburn had to counter the rise of the home rule movement at a time when Labour was growing increasingly sceptical. His 1948 White Paper on Scottish Affairs proposed only minor tinkering in Scotland's government.

George Younger 1931–

Conservative MP for Ayr 1964–92. Chairman of the Scottish Conservatives 1964–5, Secretary of State for Scotland 1979–86, Defence Secretary 1986–9. Withdrew in 1963 West Perthshire by-election as Tory candidate to allow Alec Douglas Home to stand. As Mrs. Thatcher's first and longest Secretary of State, Younger had an unenviable task reconciling two opposites, but presided over the continuation of a distinctive Scottish policy tradition.

Section Sixteen

A CHRONOLOGY OF POST-WAR SCOTTISH POLITICS

April 12 1945

Robert McIntyre wins Motherwell by-election for the SNP from Labour with 51.4 per cent to Labour's 48.6 per cent. He is the first SNP MP.

June 1945

Labour manifesto makes no commitment on devolution, but it is mentioned in Speakers Notes and by most Scottish Labour candidates.

July 5 1945

At the UK General Election Labour is returned with a majority of 146. Scottish Labour wins 47.6 per cent of the vote and 37 seats, to the Conservatives 41.1 per cent and 27 seats.

October 1945

Scottish Labour conference passes a Scottish Executive statement calling for an examination of home rule.

January 20 1946

Scottish Council (Development and Industry) established.

October 1946

Scottish Labour conference shows concern at the failure of the Anderson Committee – appointed 1945 – to make progress on home rule.

March 22 1947

The Scottish National Assembly is created by Scottish Convention. The cross-party

Assembly is addressed by Willie Gallacher and John Gollan of the Communists, David Gibson of the ILP and Thomas Scollan, Labour MP. A committee is elected to draw up a detailed home rule plan within one year.

January 29 1948

The Labour Government publishes a White Paper on Scottish Affairs calling for non-controversial bills to be dealt with by the Standing Committee on Scottish Bills and for the establishment of a Scottish Economic Conference.

February 18 1948

John MacCormick stands in Paisley as a National candidate with Conservative and Liberal support; Labour win 56.8 per cent to the National 43.2 per cent.

March 21 1948

The Scottish National Assembly endorses a Blue Print for Scotland calling for a Parliament.

October 1948

The Scottish Labour conference sees critical resolutions withdrawn, after it is agreed that an inquiry into devolution will be included in the next election manifesto.

October 29 1948

Scottish National Assembly launches the National Covenant – a mass petition calling for a Scottish Parliament.

October 1949

The Scottish Labour conference passes 'Forward Scotland' – a statement on the Government's record and Scottish policy. It welcomes the recent White Paper as 'the maximum amount of Scottish control, consistent with full membership of the British Parliament'.

November 3 1949

Scottish Unionists issue *Scottish Control of Scottish Affairs* which criticises the Labour Government's centralisation and proposes a Royal Commission on Scotland.

February 14 1950

Winston Churchill with just over a week to voting declared in an Usher Hall speech in Edinburgh that he would 'never adopt the view that Scotland should be forced into the serfdom of socialism as a result of a vote in the House of Commons.' This is seen as the Conservatives playing 'the Scottish card' against Labour centralisation.

February 23 1950

A Labour Government is returned with a sharply reduced majority of 5. In Scotland, Labour win 46.2 per cent of the vote and 37 seats, to the Conservatives 44.8 per cent and 31 seats.

April 1950

STUC General Council statement 'The Future of Scotland' passed emphasising the territorial unity of the United Kingdom. An amendment from the NUM supporting a Scottish Parliament is defeated by 243 votes to 78.

December 25 1950

The removal of the Stone of Destiny from Westminster Abbey by Scottish nationalists.

October 1951

The Scottish Labour conference calls for a Royal Commission on Home Rule.

October 25 1951

Conservatives returned with an overall majority of 17 despite Labour across the UK winning more votes. In Scotland, the Conservatives win 48.6 per cent of the vote to Labour's 47.9 per cent with both returning 35 MPs.

July 23 1952

The Catto Report, on economic links between Scotland and the UK is published and suggests that Scotland obtains more expenditure than it contributes income.

July 24 1954

The Royal Commission on Scottish Affairs is published, which proposes extra powers for the Scottish Office, and committee changes on Scottish law reform.

May 26 1955

Conservatives returned with an overall majority of 60 under Anthony Eden. In Scotland, the Conservatives win 50.1 per cent – the only time in post-war Scottish politics a party would win a majority of the popular vote – to Labour's 46.7 per cent. The Conservatives win 36 seats to Labour's 34.

March 1956

Gaitskell tells the Scottish Labour conference that Labour no longer supports devolution, while a resolution is passed instructing the Executive to examine issues relating to setting up a Scottish Parliament.

July 26 1956

Nasser, the Egyptian leader, announces the nationalisation of the Suez Canal.

October 31 1956

The Royal Air Force and French Air Force bomb the Suez Canal two days after Israel has attacked Egypt. Hugh Gaitskell condemns the action as the United Kingdom and France face widespread international condemnation.

January 19 1957

The Scottish Labour Executive opposes home rule on 'compelling economic grounds'.

March 25 1957

The European Economic Community (EEC) or 'Common Market' is formed by the Treaty of Rome. Six nations become members: France, West Germany, Italy, Belgium, Netherlands and Luxembourg. The United Kingdom refuses to join.

September 13/14 1958

A Scottish Labour special conference is held. An Executive report 'Scottish Government' says that Scottish problems are only solvable by British-wide solutions.

October 8 1959

Conservatives under Harold Macmillan returned for a third successive term with a majority of 100. Scotland swings to Labour, as the Conservatives win 47.2 per cent of the vote to Labour's 46.7 per cent, while Labour finish ahead in seats by 38 to 31.

November 10 1961

Labour win Glasgow Bridgeton with 54.6 per cent, to the Conservatives 20.7 per cent and SNP's 18.6 per cent.

November 21 1961

Publication of Scottish Council (Development and Industry) Toothill report on the Scottish economy.

June 14 1962

Tam Dalyell wins West Lothian for Labour with 50.8 per cent, while the SNP's William Wolfe achieves 23.3 per cent.

October 15 1964

Harold Wilson is returned with an overall majority of 4. Labour win 48.7 per cent of the vote to the Conservatives 40.6 per cent, and 43 seats to 24.

1965

The Highlands and Islands Development Board set up.

December 9 1965

The National Plan for Scotland published.

March 31 1966

Wilson is returned with an overall majority of 97. Scottish Labour win 49.9 per cent of the vote, its highest ever vote, and return 46 MPs to the Conservatives 20.

March 9 1967

Conservatives win Glasgow Pollok from Labour due to the rise in the SNP vote –

Conservatives 36.9 per cent, Labour 31.2 per cent, SNP 28.2 per cent.

November 2 1967

Winnie Ewing wins Hamilton for the SNP with 46.0 per cent of the vote to Labour's 41.5 per cent.

November 18 1967

Callaghan devalues the pound from $2.80 to $2.40. The next day in a TV broadcast Harold Wilson says 'this does not mean the pound in your pocket has been devalued' to general anger and ridicule.

April 1968

The STUC at its Annual Congress sees Mick McGahey of the NUM move a motion supporting a Scottish Parliament declaring: 'The best nationalists in Scotland are represented in the STUC and the Scottish Labour movement'. The motion is remitted, while an anti-devolution motion is heavily defeated. General Council agree a compromise of a committee of inquiry to report back the following year.

May 18 1968

Ted Heath's 'Declaration of Perth' at the Scottish Conservative conference when he announces the setting up a committee under Sir Alec Douglas Home to look at devolution.

April 15 1969

Wilson sets up the Crowther Royal Commission to examine devolution.

April 1969

The STUC at its Annual Congress supports an interim report which outlines the case for a Scottish Parliament with legislative powers.

October 30 1969

The Glasgow Gorbals by-election is held by Labour with 53.4 per cent to the SNP's 25.0 per cent and Conservatives 18.6 per cent.

March 1970

The Scottish Labour document 'Scottish Government (Mark II)' opposes 'Eire style separatism' and 'Northern Irish style home rule'.

March 19 1970

At the South Ayrshire by-election, Labour's Jim Sillars is returned with 54.0 per cent to the Conservatives 25.6 per cent and SNP's 20.4 per cent.

March 20 1970

The Conservatives Scottish Constitutional Committee chaired by Alec Douglas Home publishes its report 'Scotland's Government' which recommends a directly elected Scottish Convention of 125 members.

May 1970

Scottish Labour's submission to Kilbrandon restates its 1958 decision and opposition to a Scottish Parliament.

June 18 1970

Ted Heath returned in general election with a majority of 30. In Scotland, Labour win 44.5 per cent of the vote and 44 MPs to the Conservatives 38.0 per cent and 23 MPs. The SNP win 11.4 per cent of the vote, winning the Western Isles, but fail to hold Hamilton.

July 30 1971

Upper Clyde Shipworkers occupation and work-in begins led by the AEU shop stewards Jimmy Reid and Jimmy Airlie.

August 16 1971

STUC hold a Special Recall Congress in support of the Upper Clyde Shipworkers work-in.

September 16 1971

Robert McIntyre wins 34.6 per cent of the vote for the SNP in the Stirling and Falkirk by-election.

September 1972

Launch of SNP 'It's Scotland's Oil' campaign.

January 1 1973

The United Kingdom along with the Republic of Ireland and Denmark joins the European Economic Community (EEC).

March 1st 1973

Labour hold Dundee East with 32.7 per cent to the SNP's 30.1 per cent. Gordon Wilson campaigns effectively on the SNP slogan 'It's Scotland's Oil' and subsequently wins the seat in February 1974.

October 6-24 1973

The Arab-Israeli war leads to a quadrupling of oil prices by the Organisation of Petroleum Exporting Countries (OPEC).

October 30 1973

The Scottish Council of the Labour Party publishes *Scotland and the UK* which rejects devolution.

October 31 1973

The Kilbrandon Commission publishes its report outlining the case for devolution.

November 8 1973

Margo MacDonald wins Glasgow Govan for the SNP, with 41.9 per cent of the vote, compared to Labour's 38.2 per cent.

February 28 1974

At the General Election, a Labour minority government is returned. Labour in Scotland win 36.6 per cent of the vote and 40 MPs, the Conservatives 32.9 per cent and 21 MPs, and the SNP 21.9 per cent and 7 MPs.

March 12 1974

Labour Government's Queen's Speech declares : 'My ministers and I will initiate discussions in Scotland . . . and bring forward proposals for consideration'. Harold Wilson, in reply to a question from Winnie Ewing states, 'we will publish a White Paper and a Bill'.

June 3 1974

The Green Paper, *Devolution within the UK: Some Alternatives for Discussion* is published, outlining five devolution proposals based on Kilbrandon.

June 22 1974

The Scottish Executive of the Labour Party votes against all the proposals in 'Devolution within the UK' by 6:5, and by the same majority that 'constitutional tinkering does not make a meaningful contribution towards achieving socialist goals'.

July 24 1974

Labour's NEC supports legislative devolution and the call for a special conference of Scottish Labour.

August 17 1974

The Scottish Labour special conferences supports devolution 'within the context of the political and economic unity of the UK'.

September 7 1974

A White Paper proposes directly elected assemblies for Scotland and Wales.

October 10 1974

At the General Election, the first-ever Scottish Labour manifesto, *Powerhouse Scotland,* is delivered to every home, outlining Scottish Labour's proposals for an Assembly. Labour returned with an overall majority of 3. In Scotland, Labour win 36.3 per cent of the vote and 41 MPs, the SNP 30.4 per cent and 11 MPs, and the Conservatives 24.7 per cent and 16 MPs.

February 11 1975

Margaret Thatcher is elected leader of the Conservative Party.

March 21 1975

The Scottish Labour conference votes 353,000 to 341,000 against substantial economic powers for an Assembly.

June 5 1975

The United Kingdom votes by 67.2 per cent to 32.8 per cent to remain a member of the European Economic Community. Scotland votes 'Yes' by the narrower margin of 58.4 per cent to 41.6 per cent. Shetland and the Western Isles are the only areas of Scotland to vote 'No'. The SNP, along with large parts of a split Labour Party campaign for a 'No' vote.

July 8 1975

The Scottish Development Agency (SDA) is set up.

November 22 1975

A White Paper, *Our Changing Democracy*, proposes a legislative assembly for Scotland, and an executive assembly for Wales.

January 18 1976

The Scottish Labour Party is launched by Jim Sillars and John Robertson.

August 1 1976

Devolution to Scotland and Wales: Supplementary Statement published giving more powers to the Assembly.

November 28 1976

The Scotland and Wales Bill is published.

December 1 1976

Alick Buchanan-Smith, Shadow Secretary of State for Scotland and Malcolm

Rifkind, Scottish spokesman resign over the Shadow Cabinet's decision to oppose Labour's devolution proposals.

December 16 1976

The Scotland and Wales Bill is given a second reading, by 292 to 247 votes, after the government concedes the principle of referendums.

February 19 1977

The Government is defeated on a guillotine motion on the devolution bill by 312 to 283, with 22 Labour MPs voting against and 15 abstaining. The Bill cannot become law due to lack of time.

March 23 1977

Labour survive a no confidence motion by 322 to 298, after agreeing the Lib-Lab pact.

May 1977

SNP make substantial gains in council elections across Scotland, winning 27 per cent of the vote. Labour is left controlling five district councils.

May 4 1977

The Scottish Conservative conference agrees to oppose a directly elected Scottish Assembly.

November 14 1977

The Scotland Bill is given a second reading by 307 votes to 263.

November 16 1977

A guillotine motion on separate Scotland and Wales Bills is carried by 313 to 287.

January 25 1978

The 40 per cent amendment – which became known as 'the Cunningham amendment' because its main advocate was George Cunningham, Labour MP for

Islington South and Finsbury – is passed against the Government's wishes by 168 votes to 142; five Scottish Labour MPs vote for it – Cook, Dalyell, Doig, Hamilton and Hughes.

January 27 1978

Helen Liddell issues a Scottish Labour circular stating that Labour will not become involved in any umbrella devolution organisation. At a subsequent press conference, Liddell states: 'We will not be soiling our hands by joining any umbrella Yes group.'

January 1978

Labour Vote No formed.

February 22 1978

The Scotland Bill is given a third reading by 297 votes to 257.

April 13 1978

Donald Dewar wins the Glasgow Garscadden by-election, with 45.4 per cent of the vote, to the SNP's 32.9 per cent.

May 1978

The SNP do worse than expected in regional elections, with Labour winning 39.6 per cent, the Conservatives 30.3 per cent and SNP 20.9 per cent.

May 31 1978

George Robertson wins the Hamilton by-election with 51.0 per cent to the SNP's 33.4 per cent.

July 30 1978

John Mackintosh, the Labour MP and advocate of devolution, dies.

July 31 1978

The Scotland and Wales Bills are enacted.

October 26 1978

Labour hold Berwick and East Lothian with 47.7 per cent to the Conservatives 40.2 per cent and SNP's 8.8 per cent.

November 1 1978

James Callaghan announces that both the Scottish and Welsh referendums will be held on March 1 1979.

January 3 1979

The 'winter of discontent' begins. Lorry drivers begin a national strike starting a month of national strike action by ambulance drivers, water and sewage workers, dustmen and grave-diggers against the Labour Government's pay policy.

February 1979

Labour Movement Yes formed.

February 13 1979

Lord Home states that a 'No' vote in the referendum is not necessarily a vote against devolution, but Labour's current proposals and the Conservatives will produce a more powerful Assembly.

March 1 1979

In the Scottish devolution referendum, Scotland votes 32.9 per cent yes, 30.8 per cent no, with 36.3 per cent not voting, thus, failing by a substantial margin the 40 per cent threshold of the electorate. A majority of those who voted supported the Labour Government's proposals: 51.6 per cent to 48.4 per cent. The SNP had campaigned energetically for the proposals, and post-referendum analysis shows that SNP voters were the most heavily pro-devolution. On the same day, the Welsh devolution proposals are defeated by a margin of four to one, with 11.9 per cent in favour, 46.9 per cent against and 41.2 per cent not voting.

March 3 1979

The Scottish Labour Executive reaffirms its commitment to devolution, but stops short of calling for implementation of the Scotland Act, asking that the Government 'in reaching the decisions on how to proceed would do so on the basis of a continuing commitment to devolution'.

March 11 1979

At the Scottish Labour conference all emergency resolutions on devolution are withdrawn, leaving the Executive statement that devolution 'will remain at the forefront of the programme', and urging for implementation of the Scotland Act. The Chair, Janey Buchan, refuses to call any pro-devolution MPs in the debate.

March 22 1979

Callaghan declines to set a date for a vote in order to repeal the Scotland Act, and asks for all-party talks as a delaying tactic. A motion of no confidence is tabled by the SNP.

March 28 1979

The Government is defeated on a motion of no confidence, by 311 votes to 310.

May 3 1979

Conservatives returned with a majority of 44. Scotland votes 41.5 per cent Labour, 31.4 per cent Conservative, as the SNP is reduced to 17.3 per cent of the vote, with two MPs.

June 7 1979

The Euro-elections see the Scottish Conservatives win 33.7 per cent and five Euro-seats, Labour 33.0 per cent and two Euro-seats, and the SNP with 19.4 per cent and one seat, as Winnie Ewing is returned for the Highlands and Islands.

June 20 1979

The Repeal of the Scotland Act is passed by 301 to 206, with six Scottish Labour MPs abstaining – Cook, Craigen, Dalyell, Hart, McMahon and Miller.

August 18 1979

The SNP left-wing pressure group, the '79 Group is established with the aim of 'independence, socialism and a Scottish Republic'.

March 1 1980

The Campaign for a Scottish Assembly is set up, aiming to establish a cross-party Convention. It is chaired by Jack Brand, and supported by five Scottish Labour MPs. James Milne, STUC General Secretary, and George Bolton, Vice-President of the NUM, speak at its launch.

March 1980

The Scottish Labour conference supports calls for a Scottish Assembly 'with meaningful powers over the economy of Scotland'.

April 9 1980

Labour hold Glasgow Central, with 60.8 per cent of the vote, to the SNP's 26.3 per cent.

1980

The Labour Co-ordinating Committee is set up to win more left-wing influence in Scottish Labour, with one aim being a higher commitment to a Scottish Parliament.

September 1980

Labour Campaign for a Scottish Assembly is formed, with George Foulkes as Chair, and the support of 15 Scottish Labour MPs.

February 11 1981

Peugeot-Citreon announce the closure of the Linwood car plant. Two days later the STUC launches an unsuccessful campaign to keep the plant open involving politicians, local authorities and business.

May 28 1981

The SNP annual conference supports civil disobedience against the Conservative

Government. Jim Sillars, a leading exponent of what becomes known as 'the Scottish Resistance' is elected Vice-chairman for policy.

October 16 1981

Jim Sillars and five other SNP members break into and occupy Royal High School in Edinburgh, the proposed site of the Scottish Assembly, to protest against unemployment and Tory rule of Scotland.

February 15 1982

Scottish Grand Committee meets in the Royal High School, Edinburgh for the first time.

March 25 1982

The Social Democrats win Glasgow Hillhead from the Conservatives - 33.4 per cent to the Social Democrats, 26.6 per cent to the Conservatives, 25.9 per cent to Labour and 11.3 per cent to the SNP.

April 2 1982

Argentinian armed forces seize the Falkland Islands. The House of Commons sitting the next day in emergency session agrees to send a naval task force.

June 3–5 1982

SNP annual conference. Campaign for Nationalism set up by Winnie Ewing and others to assert a more traditionalist nationalism and oppose the '79 Group. Gordon Wilson proposes the proscribing of all internal party groups in a leadership attempt to take on the '79 Group.

June 24 1982

Tom Clarke wins Coatbridge and Airdrie for Labour with 55.1 per cent to the Conservatives 26.2 per cent and SNP's 10.5 per cent.

August 26 1982

SNP national council votes to expel seven leading '79 Group members.

December 2 1982

Helen McElhone wins Glasgow Queen's Park for Labour with 56.0 per cent to the SNP's 20.0 per cent.

March 1983

Scottish Labour Conference proposes a Scottish Parliament with tax raising and economic powers as part of the Alternative Economic Strategy. Helen Liddell tells the party they cannot affiliate to the Campaign for a Scottish Assembly.

June 9 1983

Conservatives returned for a second term at a UK level. Scotland sees Labour win 35.1 per cent and 41 seats to the Conservatives 28.4 per cent and 21 seats.

February 1984

Scottish Labour Executive agrees to allow party organisations to affiliate to the Campaign for a Scottish Assembly.

June 14 1984

Euro-elections in Scotland see Labour win 40.7 per cent of the vote to the Conservatives 25.7 per cent and SNP's 17.8 per cent. Labour win five of Scotland's eight Euro seats, making three gains from the Tories.

June 6 1987

Conservative third term. Labour wins 42.4 per cent in Scotland and 50 MPs to the Conservatives 24.0 per cent and 10 MPs.

August 1987

Labour Co-ordinating Committee (Scotland) conference on post-election strategies and the need for cross-party co-operation.

September 13 1987

STUC Festival for Scottish Democracy boycotted by SNP and Liberals.

November 1987

Scottish Labour special conference. Labour Executive proposes parliamentary representation of Labour's White Paper on an Assembly.

November 1987

Jim Ross suggests the Campaign for a Scottish Assembly invite a Constitutional Steering Committee to report on establishing a Constitutional Convention.

February 1988

Scottish Labour Action launched.

March 1988

Labour launches Stop It campaign on poll tax of delaying registration.

March 1988

Scottish Labour conference sees Neil Kinnock address conference without mentioning devolution. Kinnock later comments he had not mentioned many issues including 'environmental conditions in the Himalayas'.

July 13 1998

Steering Committee present *A Claim of Right for Scotland*.

August 1988

Scottish Labour Executive votes to undertake an internal consultation exercise on *A Claim of Right* and rejects non-payment of the poll tax.

September 1988

Labour special conference rejects poll tax non-payment.

September 1988

SNP annual conference agrees to support poll tax non-payment and unveils its new 'independence in Europe' policy.

November 10 1988

Jim Sillars wins Glasgow Govan for the SNP with 48.8 per cent to Labour's 37.0 per cent.

November 12 1988

Scottish Labour Executive receives 25 out of 27 responses supporting involvement in the Scottish Constitutional Convention.

January 27 1989

SNP refuse to join Scottish Constitutional Convention.

March 1989

Donald Dewar, just before the Scottish Labour conference, talks of devolution as 'independence in the UK'.

March 1989

Scottish Labour conference sees debates on Scottish Labour Action 'dual mandate' and greater autonomy for the Scottish party referred back.

March 30 1989

First meeting of Scottish Constitutional Convention. Scottish Labour and Liberal Democrat MPs sign *A Claim of Right*.

April 1 1989

Poll Tax introduced in Scotland one year ahead of England and Wales.

June 15 1989

Euro elections see Labour in Scotland win 41.9 per cent to the SNP's 25.6 per cent and Conservatives 20.9 per cent as Labour win seven of the eight Euro seats and the SNP one. Labour hold Glasgow Central with 54.6 per cent to the SNP's 34.6 per cent.

July 1989

Scottish Enterprise and Highlands and Islands Enterprise established.

March 10 1990

Scottish Labour conference agrees to support an alternative electoral system to first past the post for the Scottish Parliament.

September 22 1990

Alex Salmond elected national convener of the SNP defeating Margaret Ewing winning 486 votes to her 186 votes.

October 4 1990

Dick Douglas, MP for Dunfermline West joins the SNP.

November 22 1990

Margaret Thatcher resigns as Prime Minister.

November 27 1990

John Major becomes leader of the Conservatives and Prime Minister.

November 29 1990

Labour win Paisley North and South. In North, Labour wins 44.0 per cent to the SNP's 29.4 per cent, in South, 50.7 per cent to 23.3 per cent.

November 30 1990

Scottish Constitutional Convention publish *Towards Scotland's Parliament*.

March 1991

Scottish Labour conference votes by nearly two to one against a Labour Campaign for Electoral Success motion defending First-Past-the-Post for the Scottish Parliament.

March 21 1991

Abolition of poll tax announced.

November 7 1991

Liberal Democrats win Kincardine and Deeside from the Conservatives with 49.0 per cent to their 30.6 per cent. Conservatives reduced to 9 MPs and third party status in Scottish parliamentary representation.

January 8 1992

British Steel announce the closure of the Ravenscraig steel plant.

January 29 1992

Scotsman poll puts support for independence at historic high of 50 per cent.

April 9 1992

Conservatives returned for a fourth term. Labour in Scotland win 39.0 per cent and 49 MPs to the Conservatives 25.6 per cent and 11 MPs.

April 10/11 1992

Formation of Scotland United, a cross–party pressure group supporting a multi-option referendum.

September 16 1992

'Black Wednesday'. Britain is forced out of the Exchange Rate Mechanism after Norman Lamont pushes interest rates up to 15 per cent and spends billions propping up the pound.

December 12 1992

Democracy Demonstration in Edinburgh at the same time as John Major hosts a European Union summit. Largest ever home rule rally.

March 9 1993

Ian Lang publishes *Scotland in the Union: A Partnership for Good*, a result of the 'taking stock' exercise.

1994

Scottish Council of the Labour Party changes its name to the Scottish Labour Party.

May 12 1994

John Smith, leader of the Labour Party, dies.

June 9 1994

Euro-elections see Labour win 42.5 per cent to the SNP's 32.6 per cent with the SNP winning North East Scotland from Labour.

June 30 1994

Helen Liddell holds Monklands East against the SNP with 49.8 per cent to the SNP's 45.0 per cent.

July 21 1994

Tony Blair elected leader of the Labour Party and John Prescott, deputy leader.

May 25 1995

Roseanna Cunningham wins Perth and Kinross for the SNP from the Conservatives with 40.4 per cent to Labour's 22.9 per cent and the Conservatives 21.4 per cent.

October 1995

Labour and Liberal Democrats agree electoral system for Scottish Parliament of 129 seats based on a broadly proportional system.

November 30 1995

Scottish Constitutional Convention proposals, *Scotland's Parliament, Scotland's Right* published. Michael Forsyth unveils proposals for Scottish Grand Committee.

June 26 1996

Tony Blair announces a two question referendum on Scottish devolution.

August 31 1996

The Scottish Labour Executive support two referendums on a Scottish Parliament as a compromise, the first, the original two vote question and a second ballot, before the tax powers are ever used.

September 6 1996

George Robertson, Shadow Scottish Secretary overrules the Scottish Executive's two referendum policy and returns party policy to a two question referendum.

March 7 1997

Five prominent Labour left-wingers defeated in elections to the Scottish Labour Executive by the Blairite 'Network'.

April 4 1997

Tony Blair on the day of the launch of the Scottish Labour manifesto, in an interview compares the Scottish Parliament's proposed tax varying powers with that of an English 'parish council'. Asked about the West Lothian Question he comments: 'Sovereignty resides with me as an English MP, and that's the way it will stay'.

May 1 1997

Tony Blair returned as Prime Minister with an overall majority of 179. Scottish Labour win 45.6 per cent of the vote and 56 seats, the SNP 22.1 per cent and 6 seats and the Lib Dems 13.0 per cent and 10 seats. The Conservatives lose their last remaining ten seats in Scotland despite winning 17.5 per cent of the vote.

May 15 1997

Referendums (Scotland and Wales) Bill published.

July 24 1997

Scotland's Parliament White Paper published.

July 31 1997

Referendums (Scotland and Wales) Act receives Royal Assent.

September 11 1997

Scottish referendum gives emphatic endorsement of Labour's devolution proposals. A Scottish Parliament is supported by 74.3 per cent to 25.7 per cent and tax-varying powers by 63.5 per cent to 36.5 per cent on a 60.4 per cent turnout.

September 18 1997

Welsh referendum gives narrow majority to devolution proposals by 50.3 per cent to 49.7 per cent on a 50.1 per cent turnout.

November 6 1997

Paisley North by-election sees Labour's Douglas Alexander hold the seat with 44.1 per cent to the SNP's 32.5 per cent.

December 11 1997

Scotland Bill published.

January 13 1998

Consultative Steering Group set up.

May 22 1998

Good Friday Agreement endorsed in Northern Ireland referendum.

June 13 1998

Labour chooses its panel of 166 potential candidates for the Scottish Parliament. Three MPs, Dennis Canavan, Michael Connarty and Ian Davidson are excluded.

September 19 1998

Donald Dewar elected leader of the Scottish Labour Party with 99.8 per cent of the vote at a special conference.

November 19 1998

Scotland Act receives Royal Assent.

January 15 1999

Shaping Scotland's Parliament Consultative Steering Group report published.

February 5 1999

Tony Blair unveils Labour's 'Divorce is an Expensive Business' campaign.

March 12 1999

SNP launch 'A Penny for Scotland' campaign after Gordon Brown's Budget proposes to cut income tax.

May 6 1999

First Scottish Parliament elections. Labour win 38.8 per cent of the first vote to the SNP's 28.7 per cent, Conservatives 15.5 per cent and Liberal Democrats 14.2 per cent. Labour gain 56 seats, to the SNP's 35, Conservatives 18, Liberal Democrats 17, Others 3.

May 12 1999

David Steel elected Presiding Officer.

May 13 1999

Donald Dewar elected First Minister with 71 votes to Alex Salmond's 35, David McLetchie's 18 and Dennis Canavan's 3.

May 14 1999

'Labour–Lib Dem Partnership' for Scotland signed.

May 17 1999

Labour–Lib Dem Executive announced of 11 ministers, 9 Labour, 2 Lib Dems. John Reid succeeds Donald Dewar as Secretary of State for Scotland.

May 18 1999

11 junior ministers announced.

June 10 1999

Euro elections on Scottish regional list system. Labour win 28.7 per cent, SNP 27.2 per cent, Conservatives 19.8 per cent and Liberal Democrats 9.8 per cent. Labour win three seats, the Conservatives and SNP two apiece and the Liberal Democrats one.

June 16 1999

Donald Dewar presents the government's first legislative programme of eight bills.

June 17 1999

Scottish Parliament approves Holyrood Building by 66–57 votes.

July 1 1999

Scottish Parliament officially opened by the Queen.

July 2 1999

Parliament votes to set up an Independent Committee on Tuition Fees by 70–48 votes.

September 23 1999

Labour's Bill Tynan holds Hamilton South in a Westminster by-election with 36.9 per cent to the SNP's 34.0 per cent. Labour's majority is cut from 15,878 to 556.

September 26 1999

'Lobbygate' publication in the *Observer* about Beattie Media, Kevin Reid, John Reid's son and Jack McConnell, Finance Minister.

October 29 1999

Wendy Alexander, Minister for Communities announces the abolition of Section 28/Clause 2A which bans the 'promotion' of homosexuality in schools.

December 21 1999

Cubie Committee Report on Tuition Fees published.

January 27 2000

Scottish Executive proposals on abolishing tuition fees agreed 68–53.

March 16 2000

Conservative John Scott wins the first ever Scottish Parliament by-election from Labour. The Conservatives win 39.4 per cent, SNP 28.9 per cent and Labour 22.1 per cent.

March 28 2000

Brian Souter, owner of Stagecoach announces his intention to fund an unofficial referendum on the Scottish Executive's plans to abolish Section 28/Clause 2A.

April 5 2000

Parliament approves amended Holyrood Building plans of £195 million by 67-58 votes.

April 27 2000

Tommy Sheridan's Abolition of Poindings and Warrant Sales Bill passed 79 to 15. General principle of Ethical Standards in Public Life etc (Scotland) Bill including abolition of Section 28/Clause 2A passed by 103 to 16.

May 30 2000

Unofficial referendum on Section 28/Clause 2A produces 86.8 per cent opposition to repeal on a 34.5 per cent turnout.

July 17 2000

Alex Salmond announces his intention to stand down as national convenor of the SNP.

September 23 2000

John Swinney elected national convener of the SNP defeating Alex Neil, winning 547 votes to Neil's 268 votes. Roseanna Cunningham defeats Kenny MacAskill for the post of deputy convenor.

October 11 2000

Donald Dewar, First Minister dies.

October 21 2000

Henry McLeish elected 'interim' leader of the Scottish Labour Party defeating Jack McConnell by 44 to 36 votes in a mini-electoral college.

October 26 2000

Henry McLeish elected First Minister winning 68 votes to John Swinney's 33, David McLetchie's 19 and Dennis Canavan's 3.

October 29 2000

McLeish engages in the first Scottish Executive reshuffle bringing Jackie Baillie and Angus MacKay into the Cabinet and demoting Sarah Boyack and Sam Galbraith.

November 20 2000

Dennis Canavan withdraws his application to rejoin the Labour Party citing 'additional information' about his exclusion from the Scottish Parliament candidate panel and resigns his Westminster seat.

November 23 2000

Labour holds Glasgow Anniesland in Holyrood and Westminster by-elections. Bill Butler wins the Holyrood contest for Labour with 48.7 per cent to the SNP's 22.1 per cent, while John Robertson wins the Westminster seat with 52.1 per cent for Labour to the SNP's 20.8 per cent.

December 9 2000

Henry McLeish elected leader of the Labour Party and Cathy Jamieson, deputy leader with 99.2 per cent of a mini-electoral college.

December 21 2000

Labour's Eric Joyce narrowly holds Falkirk West in a Westminster by-election. Labour win 43.5 per cent of the vote to the SNP's 39.9 per cent as its majority is slashed from 13,783 to 705.

January 14 2001

Alex Salmond announces that he is standing again for the SNP in Banff and Buchan at the forthcoming Westminster election.

January 24 2001

John Reid becomes Secretary of State for Northern Ireland following Peter Mandleson's departure from the Government. Helen Liddell becomes Secretary of State for Scotland.

January 25 2001

Scottish Parliament agrees to support Sutherland Commission proposals for free care for the elderly after Liberal Democrat backbenchers indicate their unwillingness to support the Scottish Executive's position.

INDEX OF NAMES

Brown, Ronald 102–3
Brown, Russell 65–7
Brown, Stuart 189
Bruce, Adam 128
Bruce, Malcolm 176–8, 226
Buchan, Alan 31
Buchan, Gordon 73
Buchan, Janey 357
Buchan, John 403
Buchan, Norman 218, 229
Buchanan, Carol 119
Buchanan, Elspeth 151, 365
Buchanan-Smith, Alick 15, 345
Burgess, Margaret 59
Burns, Monica 188
Butler, William (Bill) 134
Button, J. 364
Byrne, Jim 166

Calder, J. 364
Callison, Stuart 232
Campbell, Colin 265, 312, 312–3, 367–8
Campbell, Gordon 214, 367, 398, 403
Campbell, Helen 206
Campbell, Hilary 102, 360
Campbell, James 35
Campbell, John 259
Campbell, Menzies (Ming) 128–30
Campbell-Bannerman, Henry 403
Canavan, Dennis 119–22, 346
Carlin-Kulwicki, Gillian 176
Carmichael, Neil 338
Carr, Martin 35, 358
Carse, M. 366
Cashley, Calum 72
Chadd, S. 358
Chalmers, D. 357
Chalmers, Tom 134, 357
Chapman, Douglas 81
Chisholm, Malcolm 102, 288, 399
Christie, A. 363

Churchill, Winston 63, 403, 414
Clark, Katy 131
Clark, Linda 105–7
Clark, Patrick 265
Clarke, Eric 209–11
Clarke, Laurence 166
Clarke, Tom 49–51
Clerkin, Sean 233–34
Clyne, D. 362
Coleshill, Paul 62
Collins, Sir Godfrey 397
Collins, K. 365–6
Colville, John 397
Conn, Ray 183
Cook, Margaret 208
Cook, Pamela 52
Cook, Robin 206–208
Cooklin, B. 365
Coombes, Paul 112
Corbett, Gavin 27
Cormack, Charles 46, 265
Corrie, John 51
Corrie, Robert 166
Craigie, Cathie 52, 54
Crawford, Bruce 296, 296
Crawford, Stuart 244
Creech, Christine see Grahame, Christine
Culbert, Matthew 206
Cullen, Paul 90, 92
Cumbers, Andrew 3
Cunningham, Roseanna 236
Curran, Frances 232
Curran, Margaret 139, 276, 399
Curtis, John 244

Dalhousie, The Earl of 397
Daly, Morag 49
Dalyell, Tam 203–5, 338, 416
Dalziel, J. 361
Dana, Anne 102
Darling, Alistair 94, 96